Ethics for Life

An Interdisciplinary and Multicultural Introduction

JUDITH A. BOSS
Center for the Study of Human Development,
Brown University

Mayfield Publishing Company

Mountain View, California

London • Toronto

To My Students

Library of Congress Cataloging-in-Publication Data
Boss, Judith A.
    Ethics for life / Judith A. Boss
       p. cm.
    Includes bibliographical references and index.
    ISBN 1-55934-575-6
    1. Ethics. I. Title
BJ1012.B595 1997
170-dc21   97-25256
                          CIP

Manufactured in the United States of America
10 9 8 7 6 5 4 3 2 1

Sponsoring editor, Ken King; production editor, Melissa Kreischer; manuscript editor, Jan deProsse; text and cover designer, Donna Davis; design manager, Jean Mailander; photo researcher, Heather Collins; illustrator, Joan Carol; manufacturing manager, Randy Hurst. Cover art, © Zita Asbaghi. The text was set in 10.5/12.5 Berkeley Book by G&S Typesetters, Inc. and printed on acid-free 45# PennTech Penn Plus by R. R. Donnelley & Sons Company.

Photo Credits   **pp. 7, 18, 31,** The Bettmann Archive; **p. 63,** Courtesy of Alexandra Milgram and Yale University; **p. 89,** Giraudon/Art Resource, New York; **p. 96,** The Bettmann Archive; **p. 91** © ORION.1991/MPTV; **p. 94,** The Granger Collection, New York; **pp. 107, 116, 137,** The Bettmann Archive; **p. 150,** From The Dore Bible Illustrations, Dover Publications, 1974; **pp. 155, 161, 163, 172,** The Bettmann Archive; **p. 190,** From Damasio H, Grabowski T, Frank R, Galaburda AM, Damasio AR: The return of Phineas Gage: Clues about the brain from a famous patient. *Science,* 264: 1102–1105, 1994. Department of Neurology and Image Analysis Facility, University of Iowa; **pp. 192, 201,** The Bettmann Archive; **p. 209, p. 216,** Courtesy of Harvard University; **pp. 240, 241,** The Bettmann Archive; **p. 243,** Courtesy of Dan Stock and *The Narragansett Times,* photo by Patrick Feeley; **p. 245,** The Bettmann Archive; **p. 274,** Photography and Illustration Centre/ University College, London; **p. 281,** The Bettmann Archive; **p. 289,** Courtesy of People for the Ethical Treatment of Animals; **pp. 303, 307,** The Bettmann Archive; **pp. 321, 334,** Photo Courtesy of Harvard University; **pp. 343, 344,** The Library of Congress; **pp. 349, 355,** The Bettmann Archive; **p. 358,** Courtesy of Maryknoll Photo Library, New York; **p. 400,** The Granger Collection; **p. 402,** Courtesy of Providence College; **p. 405,** Courtesy of Nel Noddings, Stanford University. **Text** **p. 5,** From *Webster's Encyclopedic Unabridged Dictionary of the English Language,* Random House, Inc., 1989. Reprinted with permission of the publisher.

This book is printed on recycled paper.

Preface

Aristotle wrote that "the ultimate purpose in studying ethics is not as it is in other inquiries, the attainment of theoretical knowledge; we are not conducting this inquiry in order to know what virtue is, but in order to become good, else there would be no advantage in studying it." *Ethics for Life* is a multicultural and interdisciplinary introductory ethics text that provides students with an ethics curriculum which has been shown to significantly improve students' ability to make real-life moral decisions.[1]

One of the frustrations in teaching ethics is getting students to integrate moral theory into their lives. Developing a meaningful philosophy of life, at one time the number one value among entering college freshmen, has declined rapidly in the past twenty years as a motive for attending college. Increased selfish behavior among young people and a decline in altruistic behavior during the college years has become a source of concern and even alarm.[2] Not surprisingly, the level of moral reasoning of as many as 20% of college students is equivalent to that of a junior high student or adult criminal. Racism and hate crimes have become a major problem on many campuses. Criminal activities such as murder, drug dealing, and sexual assaults, to name only a few, have all increased sharply on college campuses over the past few years.[3]

How can we as ethics teachers provide our students with the skills necessary to make better moral decisions in their lives? Traditional ethics courses, which restrict the study of ethics to the purely theoretical realm and avoid any attempts to make students "better" people, have been found to have little or no impact on students' ability to engage in moral reasoning outside of the classroom.[4] While students are able to memorize theories and lines of reasoning long enough to pass the final exam, there is little true understanding and carryover into their moral reasoning outside the classroom. When confronted with real-life moral issues, most students simply revert back to their earlier forms of reasoning based on cultural norms or self-interest.

In the 1970s and early 1980s some professors who were dissatisfied with the traditional theory-laden ethics course replaced it with the values clarification or value-neutral approach. This approach involves "nonjudgmental" and "nondirective" discussions of popular moral issues where students were encouraged to express their own opinions without fear of criticism or judgment. Unfortunately, the values clarification approach has been found to have no positive effect on students' moral development and, in fact, may even inhibit moral growth by sending the message that morality is all relative and hence anything goes as long as it feels good.

These findings have prompted researchers and instructors to look for new ways of approaching ethics education. *Ethics for Life* provides a curriculum that combines traditional ethics theory with a pedagogy based on the latest research on how to enhance moral development in college students. This approach has been found to be effective in improving students' moral judgment, moral behavior, and their self-esteem.[5]

Objective   The primary objective of *Ethics for Life* is to provide a text that is solidly based in the latest research on moral development in college students while at the same time providing students with a broad overview of the major world moral philosophies.

Interdisciplinary and Multicultural Approach   One of the main obstacles students face in taking an ethics course is its perceived lack of relevance to their own lives. Most ethics students are not philosophy majors. Ethics courses also tend to attract a widely diverse group of students, many of whom do not personally relate to the traditional European approach to moral philosophy. *Ethics for Life* includes coverage of, to name only a few, Buddhist ethics, Native American philosophy, ecofeminism, Confucianism, the utilitarian philosophy of Mo Tzu, feminist care ethics, liberation ethics, and the ethics of African philosopher Ibn Khaldun. The inclusion of moral philosophies from all over the world from both women and men not only gives the text a greater appeal to nontraditional students but also helps students to move beyond the implicit cultural relativism in most ethics texts that privileges traditional Western male approaches to ethics.

Moral theory does not occur in isolation, nor is morality practiced within a social vacuum. While the primary focus of this text is philosophical ethics, *Ethics for Life* adopts a more holistic approach. The text is presented in a historical and interdisciplinary context and includes extensive material from anthropology and sociology, political science, religion, psychology, and literature.

Because many students taking an ethics course are weak in critical thinking skills, there is a chapter on moral reasoning that includes sections on constructing moral arguments, resolving moral dilemmas, avoiding logical fallacies, and the relation between moral analysis and practice.

A Developmental Pedagogy   There is a saying that if students cannot learn the way we teach them, we have to teach them the way they learn. In creating ethics curriculums that promote moral development, one of the approaches that has held out the most promise is the use of a cognitive-developmental approach to ethics education combined with experiential education, generally in the form of community service and the discussion of real-life moral dilemmas.

Ethics for Life is organized using a developmental or progressive approach. This approach to the teaching of ethics has been shown to have a higher success rate than the more traditional or values-clarification approaches to ethics, in terms of helping students move beyond ethical relativism and become principled moral reasoners.

Most ethics texts focus only briefly on ethical relativism. However, more than 90 percent of college students are ethical relativists. Rather than talk over students' heads, *Ethics for Life* starts at their level by including a whole section on ethical relativism. The chapters in this book are arranged in the same order that these stages appear in a person's actual moral development. Only later are the students introduced to in-depth discussions of more advanced theories such as deontology, rights ethics, and virtue ethics.

Rather than lecturing from a higher stage of development (the traditional moral-indoctrination approach) or ignoring differences (the values-clarification approach), this approach first entails building a bridge to the students and then guiding them across that bridge toward a higher stage of moral development and "respectfully engaging" them by challenging them to question their own assumptions. This process is also known as a "cognitive apprenticeship" whereby the teacher or mentor (the "expert") teaches the student (the "novice") a new skill by collaborating with them on a task—in this case, dialogue around moral dilemmas and the application of moral theory to hypothetical and real-life issues.[6] Respectful engagement also requires that the teacher take an active role in the dialogue, including challenging students rather than creating an atmosphere of passive indifference and superficial tolerance.

In order to avoid reinforcing students' belief that morality is all a matter of personal opinion and the mistaken impression that most moral decisions involve moral dilemmas, the case studies used in the first part of the book present situations where what is morally right and wrong seems clear-cut. This helps students sort out the relevant moral principles so that they later have a solid foundation for solving more difficult moral dilemmas.

The text makes extensive use of exercises throughout each chapter. The purpose of the exercises is to encourage students to relate the theories in the text to real-life events and issues as well as to their own moral development. In addition to case studies that relate to students' own experience, case studies and personal reflection exercises are chosen with an eye to expanding their concept of moral community. This is accomplished through the use of readings, case studies, and reflective exercises that focus on multicultural issues and problems of racism, sexism, classism, and nationalism.

Also important for moral development is the integration of students' experiences by means of readings in developmental psychology and discussions of the personal meaning and relevance of these experiences to their own personality development. Chapter 6 provides an in-depth discussion of the latest research on moral development. Students are also encouraged throughout the text to relate the material in the text to their own experience and their own moral growth.

Ethics for Life is also set up so it can be used with or without a community service component. John Dewey often reminded us that we learn by doing. Studies show that participation in community service as part of an ethics class has a positive effect on a person's self-esteem and level of empathy as well as their ability to engage in moral reasoning. Community service gives students an opportunity to integrate what they are learning in class into real-life situations. To assist in this goal, exercises are provided in each chapter to help students relate classroom theory to their community service. These exercises are marked with asterisks.

Acknowledgments My deepest gratitude goes to my students, who, through their interest and feedback, provided invaluable guidance in putting this book together. I would also like to thank the reviewers: Cathryn Bailey, Mankato State University; Linda Bomstad, California Polytechnic State University, San Luis Obispo; William R. Brown, Southwest Missouri State University; Karen Hanson, Indiana University; Marshall Missner, University of Wisconsin-Oshkosh; Jon Moran, Southwest Missouri State University; William F. Nietmann, Northern Arizona University; Anita Silvers, San Francisco State University; Doran Smolkin, Kansas State University, H. Peter Steeves, California State University, Chico; Julie C. Van Camp, California State University, Long Beach; and Becky Cox White, California State University, Chico, for their critical comments and encouragement. Thanks to my daughter Katherine Wurtz for proofreading the first drafts of the manuscript and for offering many helpful suggestions. My daughter and colleague Alyssa Boss also provided invaluable feedback and encouragement. In addition, I would like to express my appreciation to the library staffs and other faculty at the University of Rhode Island and Roger Williams University Law School for assisting me with my research and for providing a supportive work space. Last, but certainly not least, my deepest appreciation and admiration goes out to editors Ken King and Jim Bull for their unflagging enthusiasm, encouragement, and patience as well as to Melissa Kreischer, who thoughtfully led the manuscript through production.

1. Judith A. Boss, "Adopting an Aristotelian Approach to Teaching College Ethics," *Philosophy and Community Service Learning* (Washington, DC: Association for the Advancement of Higher Education, 1997); and Judith A. Boss, "The Effect of Community Service Work on the Moral Development of College Ethics Students," *Journal of Moral Education*, 1994, vol. 23, 183–198.
2. Alexander W. Astin, *What Matters in College?* (San Francisco: Jossey-Bass, 1993).
3. Kit Lively, "Campuses Are Hit by Steep Increases for Third Straight Year," *The Chronicle of Higher Education*, April 26, 1996, A37–A49.
4. James Rest, "Why Does College Promote Development in Moral Judgment?" *Journal of Moral Education*, 1988, vol. 17(3), 183–194.
5. Boss, "The Effect of Community Service Work on the Moral Development of College Ethics Students."
6. See William Damon, *Greater Expectations* (New York: The Free Press, 1995), Chapter 7, for a discussion of this method of moral education.

Contents

Section III Morality as Universal 233

SECTION I

The Study of Ethics

Many college ethics students want to skip ethical theory and immediately begin with discussions of compelling moral issues. However, productive discussion of issues requires first establishing a solid foundation in the nuances of ethical theory and moral reasoning.

As a philosophical discipline, ethics is the study of the values and guidelines by which we live as well as the justification of these values and guidelines. The first chapter, "Ethics: An Overview," begins with an introduction to ethics and a brief discussion of different types of ethical theories. It also addresses some of the fundamental philosophical questions that underlie ethics, including questions about human nature, free will versus determinism, moral knowledge, and the nature of philosophical inquiry.

The second chapter, "Moral Reasoning," provides the reader with the skills necessary to analyze and evaluate different moral theories and lines of reasoning. Developing critical thinking skills enables students to make better moral judgments and makes them less likely to be taken in by faulty reasoning.

Ethics education is making a comeback. As such, speculations about what morality is are bombarding us from all sides. This is exciting: We are challenged to be on our toes and to sharpen our analytical skills in order to discern which theories are workable and which ones we need to discard. By figuring out what doesn't work, we can learn a lot. We may not have come up with the perfect theory by the end of this course, but we will have a much better sense of how to make satisfactory moral decisions.

CHAPTER 1

Ethics

An Overview

The ultimate purpose in studying ethics is not as it is in other inquiries, the attainment of theoretical knowledge; we are not conducting this inquiry in order to know what virtue is, but in order to become good, else there would be no advantage in studying it.

—ARISTOTLE, *Nicomachean Ethics*, Bk. 2, Ch. 2

It's the beginning of a new semester. Tomorrow morning is your first ethics class. You only signed up for the class because it was required. "What a waste of time," you grumble as you climb into bed. "What's the point in studying ethics? It doesn't have anything to do with real life. I wish there was no such thing as ethics or morality."

The next morning you wake up and wearily grope your way to the bathroom. As you open the door, you find to your dismay that your roommate has left the bathroom in a total mess. Dirty clothes—your roommate's clothes—are soaking in cold slimy water in the sink and bathtub, and the toilet is caked with grime. Annoyed, you return to your room and shake your roommate's shoulder: "Come on, get up. You promised to clean the bathroom yesterday."

"So what?" your roommate replies. "I don't have to keep my promises if I don't feel like it." And with that, your roommate rolls over and, looking quite peaceful, goes back to sleep.

You are now feeling very annoyed, but you manage to get ready for class, although not in time to have breakfast. You arrive at class right on time; however, the teacher hasn't turned up. You take a seat next to another student who lives in your dormitory. But instead of returning your greeting, he grabs your book bag and heads toward the door. "Stop!" you protest. "That's mine. You can't take that."

He looks at you like you're nuts. "Why not?"

"Because it doesn't belong to you," you reply indignantly. "It's stealing!"

At which he laughs, "You're not making any sense."

"You have no right . . . ," you add.

(CALVIN AND HOBBES © Watterson. Distributed by Universal Press Syndicate, Inc. Reprinted with permission. All rights reserved.)

The thief rolls his eyes: "Didn't you hear the latest news? Ethics, morality—they no longer exist. Isn't that great news! Now we can do whatever we like! And no one can pass judgment on anything we do, including you!"

You wait another twenty minutes for the teacher to show up; then you decide to head over to the cafeteria to get some breakfast. However, the dining staff didn't bother to report to work either. The back door has been smashed open, and trays of donuts and fruit have been taken out onto the quad where a group of administrators and faculty members, including your ethics teacher, are squabbling over the booty. You step up onto a chair that has been tossed out on the curb, to get a better look, when someone comes rushing up from behind and knocks you down.

As you fall, you hear a sickening snap and feel a stabbing pain in your knee. You cry out in agony. Then you recognize the person who knocked you over. It's the dean of your college. You plead for her to call for help. But she only pushes you out of her way and hurries on toward the skirmish on the quad. Off in the distance you hear another cry for help as two men drag a terrified woman into the bushes. No one tries to stop them. A few people stop and peer at you out of curiosity before moving on. Most just stare blankly at you as they walk past. No one offers to help. And why should they? Sympathy and compassion no longer exist. The duty not to cause harm to others or to help those in need no longer exists. No one has any rights that we have to respect anymore. No more stupid obligations, such as sharing with others or keeping our commitments, to prevent us from doing what we enjoy.

As you begin to lose consciousness, you start having second thoughts about the importance of ethics and morality in your life. At that moment, your alarm clock goes off. You get out of bed and wearily grope your way to the bathroom. As you open the door, you realize that your roommate has left the bathroom in a total mess. Annoyed, you return to your room and shake your roommate's shoulder: "Come on, get up. You promised to clean the bathroom yesterday."

"Oh, no," your roommate groans. "I'm sorry, I forgot all about it." After a short pause, your roommate rolls out of bed, complaining under her breath, "I can't think of anything else I'd less rather do." You breathe a sigh of relief and go to the kitchenette to make yourself some breakfast while your roommate begrudgingly cleans the bathroom.

What Is Ethics?

Ethics is a lot like air: It is pretty much invisible. In fact, for many centuries, people did not realize that such a substance as air even existed. So too we often fail to recognize the existence of ethics or morality until someone fails to heed it.

ethics   1. A system of moral principles: *the ethics of a culture*.   2. the rules of conduct recognized in respect to a particular class of human actions or a particular group, culture, etc.: *medical ethics; Christian ethics*.   3. moral principles, as of an individual: *His ethics forbade betrayal of a confidence*.   4. that branch of philosophy dealing with values related to human conduct, with respect to the rightness and wrongness of the motives and ends of such actions.

—*Webster's Encyclopedic Unabridged Dictionary of the English Language*

(New York: Random House, 1989)

The term **ethics** has several meanings. It is often used to refer to a set of standards of right and wrong established by a particular group and imposed on members of that group as a means of regulating and setting limits on their behavior. This use of the word "ethics" reflects its etymology. The etymology of the word "ethics" goes all the way back to the Greek word *ethos*, meaning "cultural custom or habit." The word "moral" is derived from the Latin word *moralis*, which also means "custom." Although some philosophers distinguish between the terms "ethical" and "moral," others, including the author of this text, use the two terms interchangeably.

The identification of ethics and morality with cultural norms or customs reflects the fact that most adults tend to identify morality with cultural customs. Philosophical ethics, also known as *moral philosophy,* goes beyond this limited concept of right and wrong. Ethics, as a philosophical discipline, includes the study of the values and guidelines by which we live and the *justification* for these values and guidelines. Rather than simply accepting the customs or guidelines used by one particular group or culture, philosophical ethics analyzes and evaluates these guidelines in light of accepted universal principles and concerns.

More importantly, ethics is a way of life. In this sense, ethics involves active engagement in the pursuit of the good life—a life consistent with a coherent set of moral values. According to Aristotle, one of the leading Western moral philosophers, the pursuit of the good life is our most important activity as humans. Indeed, studies have found that even criminals believe morality is important—at least for others. Although criminals may not always act on their moral beliefs, they still expect others to do so. Almost all criminals, when asked, state that they do not want their children to engage in immoral behavior and would get angry if one of their children committed a crime.[1]

Aristotle believed that "the moral activities are human *par excellence.*"[2] Because morality is the most fundamental expression of our human nature, it is through being moral that we are the happiest. According to Aristotle, through the repeated performance of good actions, we become moral (and more happy) people. He referred to the repeated practice of moral actions as **habituation.** The idea that practicing good actions is more important for ethics education than merely studying theory is also found in other philosophies, such as Buddhism.

> [A] man becomes just by the performance of the just . . . actions; nor is there the smallest likelihood of a man's becoming good by any other course of conduct. It is not, however, a popular line to take, most men preferring theory to practice under the impression that arguing about morals proves them to be philosophers, and that in this way they will turn out to be fine characters.
>
> —ARISTOTLE, *Nicomachean Ethics,* Bk. 2, Ch. 4

At the age of seventeen, Aristotle became a student at Plato's Academy in Athens, where he remained until Plato's death twenty years later. The Academy was founded by Plato in 388 B.C.E. and lasted over nine hundred years; it is reputed to be Europe's first university.[3] Plato's famous Academy was not like universities today, with organized classes, degrees, and specialized faculty.

The philosopher Plato (c. 427–347 B.C.E.) with his disciple Aristotle (384–322 B.C.E.) at the Academy in Athens, by Renaissance painter Raphael. Founded by Plato in 388 B.C.E., the Academy is reputed to be Europe's first university.

Instead, it was more of a fellowship of intellectuals interested in Athenian culture and the opportunity to listen to and exchange ideas with the great philosopher Plato.

Aristotle later opened his own school, the Lyceum, in Athens. Because Aristotle was a renowned philosopher, scholar, and scientist, his new school attracted many distinguished pupils. The Lyceum contained a garden known as "the walk," where Aristotle supposedly had the habit of walking while teaching his students. In 323 B.C.E., Aristotle was accused of impiety for teaching his students, in their quest for the good life, to continually question the accepted ideas and norms of the time. In 399 B.C.E., the Athenians had sentenced Plato's teacher, Socrates, to death on similar charges. Aristotle fled to Euboea rather than take a chance that "the Attentions should sin a second time against philosophy." He died in Babylon a year later.

Exercises

1. What do you mean (what criteria do you use) when you say that something is morally right or morally wrong? Do all actions have a moral dimension to them? If not, why do some actions involve moral judgments but others are morally neutral?

2. One way to define what we mean by "moral" is to look at the lives of those whom we regard to be good people. These people—be they parents, friends, sports figures, political leaders, reformers, or even fictional beings—serve as our role models and heroes. Heroes used to be important in most people's

lives, but a recent survey found that seventy percent of Americans now-adays have no one they consider a hero. Some people would say that this is a reflection of the moral malaise of our times. Do you agree? Do you have a hero? If so, who is your hero? Explain why.

3. Alexander Astin, one of the foremost researchers on the college experience, reports an increase in hedonistic or self-indulgent behavior and a decline in altruistic behavior among college students in recent years.[4] Why do you think this is happening? Discuss your answer in light of your own college experience. What might be done to reverse this trend?

4. Do you agree with Aristotle that practicing moral virtues and behavior is more important for ethics education than the study of moral theory? How might his approach be integrated into a college ethics course? Can you think of any objections or difficulties that might result from trying to integrate an Aristotelian approach into such a course?

The Role of *Is* and *Ought* Statements in Ethics

Descriptive Statements

Unlike science, which is descriptive, ethics is primarily *prescriptive* with descriptive statements playing a supportive role. **Descriptive statements** tell us what *is*. As Detective Joe Friday, of the television series *Dragnet,* used to say, "Just the facts, Ma'am." Here are some examples of a descriptive statement:

I saw two faculty members pulling a screaming woman into the bushes outside the Classroom Building at 8:54 a.m.

At 11:17 p.m. last night, my roommate said to me, "I promise to clean the bathroom before I go to bed."

This morning I saw Gloria coming out of John's room.

Prescriptive Statements

Prescriptive statements, on the other hand, deal with values. They tell us what *ought to be:*

We *ought* to tell the truth to Detective Friday about what happened on campus this morning.

It is wrong (i.e., we *ought* not to) hurt other people for our own amusement.

People *ought* to keep their promises.

Moral values are only one of many types of values. Nonmoral values include good health; aesthetic values; social values such as power, fame, and popularity; economic values; and political values such as national integrity and solidarity. Only moral values carry the force of the "ought." Although it would be awfully nice to be healthy, wealthy, popular, and a straight A student, moral values, by their very nature, demand that we give them precedence over nonmoral values.

When making moral decisions, we use descriptive statements about the world and about human nature, along with prescriptive statements about moral values. It is important for making an informed moral decision that we first get our facts straight. The social sciences are important to ethics because they systematically test ideas about moral development, human nature, and society. Concepts about human nature are useless, and may even be harmful, if they are not grounded in reality. For example, many moral philosophers, including such great philosophers as Aristotle, have operated on the assumption that women are not as capable of rationality as are men. Domination of women by men has been morally justified on the grounds that women needed the guidance and protection of men.

Good intentions alone are insufficient to guide our moral decision-making. Decisions that are not based on a correct perception of the world can actually have the opposite effect of what was intended. Men may have kept women out of the dog-eat-dog job market out of consideration for their well-being, but the effect was harmful to women.

> The road to Hell is paved with good intentions.
>
> —old English proverb

To use another example, until relatively recently, many physicians lied to patients who were dying. However, the belief that it was better to lie to patients regarding a terminal condition such as cancer was not based on actual observations of the effect of truth-telling on cancer patients. Physicians justified the practice by making hasty generalizations[5] from their limited experience with a few distressed patients. In most cases, this lying harmed the patients and increased their distress, although this was not the intention of the physicians. When properly controlled studies were later carried out regarding the effects of knowing the truth, it was discovered that people with terminal cancer actually did better and lived longer if they knew the truth about their condition.[6]

Ethics goes beyond science and observation, however. We cannot go directly from a descriptive statement about how things are to a statement about how things ought to be. For example, most patients with terminal cancer do better if they know they are dying, but this does not mean that we ought to tell Juan, who is depressed and suicidal, that he has cancer. Similarly, if we see Gloria leaving John's room, this does not necessarily entail that we have a moral obligation to tell Detective Friday or anyone else what we saw. And social scientists have found that a person is more likely to help those who are most like them, but we cannot decide, based on this description alone, that Professor Smith, who is blond and blue-eyed, *ought* to offer tutoring only to her blond and blue-eyed students. Instead, moral judgments and values—such as "do not lie," "be fair," and "do no harm"—need to be brought into the picture when we are making a decision about the right course of action.

Exercises

1. Looking back at the scenario on page 3, construct an imaginary dialogue between yourself and the student who took your book bag. You are trying to convince the student to return your book bag. Which statements in the conversation are descriptive and which are prescriptive? How do the two types of statements support each other? Repeat the dialogue, using only the descriptive statements. Is it as convincing as the dialogue with both types of statements?

2. Do you think that it is morally acceptable for Professor Smith to give preferential treatment to her blond, blue-eyed students? Why or why not? Would it make any difference if she believed it was right? What if her intentions were "good"? For example, suppose that she genuinely believed that only blue-eyed people had intellectual potential and that it was unfair to give non-blue-eyed people the hope (by providing tutoring) that they might be able to succeed in college. Would this excuse her behavior?

3. Make a list of general guidelines that you use in making moral decisions, including your discussion regarding the morality of the actions of Professor Smith in the previous exercise. Where did you get these guidelines? Compare your list with those of other students in the class. To what extent do the lists correspond to each other?

   Is there a general theme or themes underlying your list of guidelines? If so, what are these themes?

4. Some people claim that knowing what is right is harder than *doing* what is right. Others say just the opposite: that doing what you know to be right is harder. Which do you find hardest? Explain why.

   Discuss a time when you put, or were tempted to put, nonmoral values over moral values. How did you resolve the conflict? Were you satisfied with how you resolved the conflict? Explain.

Normative and Theoretical Ethics

. . . a complete moral philosophy would tell us how and why we should act and feel toward others in relationships of shifting and varying power asymmetry and shifting and varying intimacy.   —ANNETTE BAIER, *Ethics* (1986), p. 252

There are two traditional subdivisions of ethics: (1) normative ethics and (2) theoretical ethics. **Theoretical ethics** is concerned with appraising the logical foundations and internal consistencies of ethical systems. Theoretical ethics is also known as **metaethics**; the prefix *meta* comes from the Greek word meaning "about" or "above." **Normative ethics,** on the other hand, gives us hands-on practical guidelines or norms, such as "do not lie" or "do no harm," regarding which actions are right and which are wrong. In other words, theoretical ethics, or metaethics, studies *why* we should act and feel a certain way; normative ethics tells us *how* we should act in particular situations.

Normative Ethics

Normative ethics affects our lives at all levels: personal, interpersonal, social (both locally and globally), and environmental. Each of these levels builds on the previous level. Normative ethics gives us practical guidelines or norms that we can apply to real-life situations. Because of this, it is sometimes referred to as applied ethics. A professional code of ethics is an example of a set of practical moral guidelines.

Moral guidelines are not simply a list of dos and don'ts that others impose upon us, however. As adults, it is not enough just to do as we are told. We expect to be given reasons for acting certain ways or taking certain positions on moral issues. We want a system of values that will offer us guidance in our quest for the good life—lives of happiness for both ourselves and others. In this sense, metaethics and normative ethics are continually drawing from and reinforcing each other. Ethics and lifestyle are intertwined. In this age of rapid communication and global markets, what we do or fail to do often affects not only us and those close to us but people all over the world.

Personal Ethics   At the most basic level, ethics is concerned with us as individuals—our own growth as virtuous people and our search for the good life. Almost all ethicists stress the importance of cultivating a virtuous character and developing proper self-esteem. According to psychologists such as Erik Erikson, one of the first tasks of the young child is the development of self-respect or proper self-esteem. Without developing respect for ourselves, we cannot truly respect and care for others.

Interpersonal Ethics   In our day-to-day relationships with other people, ethics deals with issues such as the rightness or wrongness of particular actions, the nature of our obligations toward others, and their obligations toward us. What rules and codes should guide our behavior? What do we do when there is a conflict between moral principles and no answer is completely satisfactory?

Social Ethics   As we mature, our awareness of and definition of our moral community expands from our immediate family to our peers to humanity in general. The **moral community** is composed of all those beings that have moral worth or value in themselves. Because members of the moral community have moral value, they deserve the protection of the community, and they deserve to be treated with respect and dignity. As adults, we start thinking more about issues of social ethics and social policy that affect the wider community. What is the most just way to distribute scarce resources, such as health care technology? How do my career choices affect society? What is our obligation toward the less-privileged people in our society? What is our obligation as a rich nation toward the poorer nations of the world? What is the best way to solve international disputes?

Environmental Ethics   Environmental ethics expands our moral concerns beyond the human community. There are two distinct approaches to environmental ethics. Most Western philosophers and theologians maintain that only humans can be members of the moral community. According to this point of view, our only obligation to the environment and to other animals is to preserve it for the benefit of humans. Others—such as the Buddhists, Jainists, and many Native American philosophers—argue that the environment itself has moral worth. According to these people, the integrity of the environment ought to be preserved for its own sake.

Whichever view we take, the destruction of the environment has reached a point where it is compromising not only the health of human beings, but all life on this planet. Because of this, our moral obligation toward the environment is becoming an increasingly important moral issue.

Theoretical Ethics

Theoretical ethics (also called theoretical morality or metaethical theories) operates at a more fundamental level than normative ethics. Theoretical ethics takes as its starting point the most basic insights regarding morality. Immanuel Kant, who is widely regarded as one of the greatest moral philosophers, argued that most people already *know* what is right and what is wrong. For example, virtually everyone agrees that, under most circumstances, we ought to keep our promises, refrain from stealing, and help those in distress. Kant used everyday moral insights like these as the starting point for his moral theory.

From here, theoretical ethicists attempt to systematize and explain these basic moral convictions about what is right and what is wrong. Some theories are better at doing this; others contain internal contradictions and have implications that most people would find quite unacceptable. Sometimes what first appears to be a moral insight, such as "white supremacy," may turn out to be the result of cultural conditioning that is in conflict with other more funda-

TABLE 1.1 Metaethical Theories

NONCOGNITIVE	COGNITIVE		
Emotivism	**Relativist Theories**	**Universalist Theories**	
	Ethical Subjectivism	Ethical Egoism	Deontology
	Cultural Relativism	Natural Law Ethics	Virtue Ethics
		Utilitarianism	Rights Ethics

mental moral insights, such as justice and respect for the rights of others. This is why philosophers such as Kant, in their search for a consistent moral theory, made only a tentative presumption regarding the legitimacy of these everyday insights.

Metaethical theories can be divided into cognitive and noncognitive theories. **Noncognitive theories,** such as emotivism, claim that there are no moral truths and that moral statements are neither true nor false but simply expressions or outbursts of feelings. If moral statements are neither true nor false, there is no such thing as objective moral truths. **Cognitive theories,** on the other hand, maintain that moral statements can be either true or false. Cognitive theories can be further subdivided into relativist and universalist theories (see Table 1.1).

The following is a brief introduction to these theories. They will be discussed in much greater depth in subsequent chapters.

Relativist theories state that morality is different for different people. In contrast, **universalist theories** maintain that objective moral truths exist that are true for all humans, regardless of their personal beliefs or cultural norms.

Relativist Theories According to the *relativist theories,* there are no independent moral values. Instead, morality is *created* by humans. Because morality is invented or created by humans, it can vary from time to time and from person to person. **Ethical subjectivism,** the first type of relativist theory, maintains that moral right or wrong is relative to the individual person and that moral truth is a matter of individual opinion or feeling. Unlike reason, **opinion** is based only on feeling rather than analysis or facts. In ethical subjectivism, there can be as many systems of morality as there are people in the world.

Moral values are not absolute but relative to the emotions they express.

—EDWARD WESTERMARCK (sociologist)

Cultural relativists, on the other hand, argue that morality is created collectively by groups of humans and that it differs from society to society. Each society has its own moral norms, which are binding on the people who belong to that society. Each society also defines who is and who is not a member of the moral community. With cultural relativism, each circle or moral system represents a different culture.

We recognize that morality differs in every society, and is a convenient term for socially approved habits.

—RUTH BENEDICT (anthropologist)

Ethical subjectivism and cultural relativism are mutually exclusive theories. When two theories are mutually exclusive, a person cannot consistently hold both theories to be true at the same time. Either morality is created by the *individual* and the opinion of the individual always takes precedence over that of the collective, or else morality is relative to one's *culture* and the moral rule of the culture always take precedence over that of the individual.

Universalist Theories   *Universalist theories,* the second group of cognitive theories, maintain that there are universal moral values that apply to *all* humans and, in some cases, extend beyond the human community. Morality is *discovered,* rather than created, by humans. In other words, the basic standards of right and wrong are derived from principles that exist independently of an individual's or societal opinion.

Unlike relativist theories, most universalist theories include all humans in their moral community rather than just those living in their society, as often

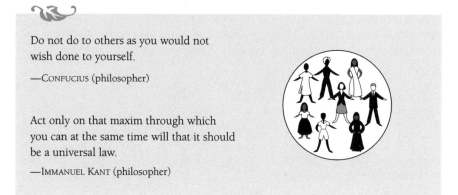

Do not do to others as you would not wish done to yourself.

—CONFUCIUS (philosopher)

Act only on that maxim through which you can at the same time will that it should be a universal law.

—IMMANUEL KANT (philosopher)

happens in cultural relativist theories. Because the basic moral principles are universal, universalist theories can be represented by one circle that includes individuals from all cultures.

There is a great deal of overlap between the different universalist theories. Instead of being mutually exclusive, like ethical subjectivism and cultural relativism, universalist theories, for the most part, emphasize one particular aspect of morality rather than providing a comprehensive picture. Almost all ethicists include aspects of more than one of these theories in their moral philosophy.

Ethics, as a branch of philosophy, however, begins in wonder—not theory. Theories, by their very nature, oversimplify. A theory is merely a convenient tool for expressing an idea. Some theories are better than others for explaining certain phenomena and providing solutions to both old and new problems. When studying the different moral philosophers, we must be careful not to try to pigeonhole their ideas into rigid theoretical boundaries.

Theories are like telescopes. They zoom in on certain key points, rather than elucidate the total extent of thinking about ethics. Because we cannot see and measure morality in the same sense that we can see objects in the physical world, to arrive at moral truths we must rely on other faculties, such as intuition, reason, and sentiment—if, in fact, we will ever be able to discern the nature of moral truth. This puts us in a similar position to the blind men trying to describe the elephant. The Buddha told the following story when he heard that some holy men were quarreling over their beliefs:

> Once a king invited all the blind men to his palace. Then he asked his servant to bring an elephant. The servant did so and said, "An elephant is like this," and told each blind man to feel a different part of the animal. Then the king came and asked the blind men what an elephant was like.
>
> Those who had felt the head said, "Sire, the elephant is like a jar." Those who had felt the ear said, "It is like a winnowing basket." The tusk was likened to a post, the trunk to a plow's pole, the body to a granary, the foot to the base of a column, the rump to a mortar, the tail to a pestle, and the tuft of the tail to a broom. Then they started to quarrel. "I'm right. You are wrong." And this led to fighting.
>
> The Buddha said that those who insist that what they believe is right and everyone else is wrong are like the blind men who thought that a part of the elephant was the whole.[7]

Each of the blind men correctly described a part of the elephant, but they mistook the part for the whole. In a similar manner, because morality covers such a broad scope of issues, different philosophers tend to focus on different aspects of morality. Problems arise when they claim that their insight is the whole picture—that morality is merely consequences, or merely duty, or merely having good intentions. Morality is not a simple concept that can be captured in a nice tidy theory; it is a multifaceted phenomenon.

Exercises

*1. Choose a moral issue from your life as a college student. Discuss how this issue affects decisions in your life at each of the four levels of normative ethics. If you are doing community service, relate your answer to your service learning.

 2. Which of the ethical theories is most like the one you used to make your decision regarding the morality of Professor Smith's behavior in Exercise 2, in the previous section? For example, did you conclude that she ought to give preferential treatment to blond, blue-eyed students, as long as she felt it was right for her to do so? Are her actions moral or immoral only within our particular society? Or is giving preferential treatment to people who look like oneself wrong no matter what the culture?

Metaphysics and the Study of Human Nature

> *In every writer on philosophy there is a concealed metaphysic, usually unconscious; even if his subject is metaphysics, he is almost certain to have an uncritically believed system which underlies his specific arguments.*
>
> —BERTRAND RUSSELL, *The Philosophy of John Dewey*

Ethical theories do not stand on their own but are grounded in other philosophical presumptions about such matters as the role of humans in the universe, the existence of free will, and the nature of knowledge. **Metaphysics** is the branch of philosophy concerned with the study of the nature of reality, including what it means to be human.

Our concept of human nature has a profound influence on our concept of how we ought to live. Are humans basically selfish? Or are we basically altruistic? What is the relationship between humans and the rest of nature? Do humans have a soul? Or are we purely physical beings governed by our instincts and urges? Do we have free will? Or is all of our behavior subject to causal laws?

Metaphysical assumptions about the nature of reality are not simply abstract theories; they can have a profound effect on both ethical theory and normative ethics. Metaphysical assumptions play a pivotal role, for better or for worse, in structuring relations among humans and between humans and the rest of the world.

Metaphysical Dualism

According to **metaphysical dualists**, reality is made up of two distinct and separate substances, the material or physical body and the nonmaterial mind, which is also referred to as the soul or spirit. The body, being material, is subject to causal laws. The mind, in contrast, has free will because it is nonmaterial and rational. Some philosophers believe that only humans have a mind and, hence, only humans have moral value. The belief that adult humans are the central or most significant reality of the universe is known as **anthropocentrism.**

According to most dualists, humans express their nature or essence through reason, which is the activity of the nonmaterial mind. Only through reason can we understand moral truth and achieve the good life. Dualistic philosophies tend to support a hierarchical world view and a morality based on the exclusion of some beings from the moral community—particularly nonhuman animals and humans who are regarded as not fully rational.

> For living is apparently shared with plants, but what we are looking for is the special function of a human being: hence we should set aside the life of nutrition and growth. The life next in order is some sort of life of sense-perception; but this too is apparently shared, with horses, oxen and every animal. The remaining possibility, then, is some sort of life of action on the part of the soul that has reason.
>
> . . . the human function is the soul's activity that expresses reason . . . the human function to be a certain kind of life, and we take this life to be the soul's activity and actions that express reason. The excellent man's function is to do this finely and well. Each function is completed well when its completion expresses the proper virtue. Therefore, the human good turns out to be the soul's proper function.
>
> —ARISTOTLE, *Nicomachean Ethics,* Bk. 1, Ch. 1

Ecofeminist Karen Warren (b. 1947) argues that the domination of women and the domination of nature that typifies Western dualism are inexorably connected.[8] Both, she claims, are based on a hierarchical and dualistic metaphysics and a "logic of domination" that assumes that certain beings (whether human or nonhuman) are morally superior and that those who are superior have a right to dominate those who are subordinate. Warren maintains that one of the goals of feminism is the liberation of nature *and* of women by eliminating oppressive metaphysical categories based on superiority and privilege and by "the creation of a world in which difference does not breed domination."[9]

Mohandas Gandhi (1869–1948), also known as Mahatma ("great soul"), nationalist leader of India, 1931 (right; talking to Jawaharlal Nehru). Gandhi's use of non-violent resistance as a strategy for political and social reform has had a tremendous influence on later civil rights movements, including the 1960s civil rights movement in the United States.

> Without a logic of domination a description of similarities and differences would be just that—a description of similarities and differences . . . Even if humans are "better" than plants and rocks with respect to the conscious ability of humans to radically transform community one does not thereby get any morally relevant distinction between humans and nonhumans, or an argument for the domination of plants and rocks by humans.

Hindu metaethics, like Western dualism, also supports a hierarchical view of reality.[10] In Hindu philosophy, this hierarchy manifests itself primarily within the caste system that is believed to reflect the natural order of the universe. In India, the Hindu caste system and the hierarchical metaphysics upon which it was based was challenged by Hindu statesman-philosopher Mohandas Gandhi (1869–1948). He denounced the caste system as "evil" and "an ineffaceable blot that Hinduism today carries with it."[11] Gandhi's demand for change was strongly influenced by the teachings of another Indian philosopher, Siddhartha Guatama (563 B.C.E.–c. 483 B.C.E.), better known as Buddha or "The Enlightened One."

Of created beings the most excellent are said to be those which are animated; of the animated, those which subsist by intelligence; of the intelligent, mankind; and of men, the Brahmans.

—The Hindu Laws of Manu

Buddhism

Buddha, like Socrates, did not leave behind any writings. What we know of his philosophy comes from the writings of his disciples. At the age of twenty-nine, Buddha left his family and fortune on a quest for Truth. After six years of wandering, meditating, and fasting he received enlightenment while sitting under a Bodhi tree. Leading a moral or right lifestyle is central to Buddha's philosophy. Buddha rejected metaphysical dualism, emphasizing the unity of all reality rather than differences.

According to Buddha, the natural order is not rigidly hierarchical; rather, it is a dynamic web of interactions that condition or influence, instead of determining, our actions. Mind and body are not separate substances but are a manifestation of one substance that is referred to in the Buddhist philosophy as the "One." Because all reality is interconnected, Buddhism opposes the taking of life and encourages a simple lifestyle that is in harmony with and respectful of other humans and of nature in general.

Like the Buddhists, the Lele, a Bantu-speaking tribe living in Zaire, also believe that the world is a single system of interrelationships between humans, animals, and spirits. Avoiding behavior such as sorcery that disrupts this delicate balance of interrelationships is key to the moral life.[12] Some Native American philosophies also stress the interrelatedness of all beings; they do not divide the world into animate and inanimate objects, but rather see everything, including the Earth itself, as having a self-conscious life.[13] This metaphysical view of reality is reflected in a moral philosophy based on respect for all beings and on not taking more than one needs.

One-Substance Theories

Not all Western worldviews are based on metaphysical dualism or the claim that humans have a privileged position in the natural order. There are many variations of nondualistic or one-substance theories. One of the more popular one-substance theories among Western philosophers is **metaphysical materialism.** In this worldview, physical matter is the only substance. Because metaphysical materialists reject, or consider irrelevant, abstract concepts such as mind or soul, morality must be explained in terms of physical matter.

Sociobiology is based on the assumption of metaphysical materialism.

As a branch of biology, sociobiology applies evolutionary theory to the social sciences—including questions of moral behavior. Sociobiologist Edward O. Wilson claims that morality is based on biological requirements and drives.[14] Humans are governed by the same innate rules as other animals. Just as other animals defend their territories and raise families based on certain biological instincts, the behavior and thought of humans is likewise guided by innate **epigenetic rules.**

According to sociobiologists, human social behavior, like that of other social animals, is primarily oriented toward the propagation of the species. This goal is achieved through inborn cooperative behavior that sociobiologists call **biological altruism.** Altruistic feelings are expressed according to epigenetic rules and act to counter our biological tendencies to behave selfishly. Biological altruism accounts for the great sacrifices we are willing to make to help those who *share our genes;* however, sociobiologists do not equate natural with moral. Wilson writes that we as humans "must consciously choose among the alternative emotional guides we have inherited."[15]

One of the problems with an ethics based upon metaphysical materialism is that its reference to biology gives us no guidance in a situation where two epigenetic rules, such as egoism and altruism, are in conflict. For this and other reasons, the majority of philosophers, without denying that biology is important, reject biology as the *basis* for morality.

Determinism Versus Free Will

One of the important questions raised by metaphysics is whether humans have free will or whether all our behavior is causally determined. The creation of the social sciences as a discipline separate from philosophy, Darwin's theory of evolution, and the growing emphasis on the scientific method as the source of truth all contributed to the growing trend in the West to describe human behavior in purely scientific terms. The theory of **determinism** states that all events are governed by causal laws: There is no free will. Humans are governed by causal laws just as all other physical objects and beings are. In other words, according to strict determinism, if we had complete knowledge, we could predict future events with one hundred percent certainty.

Psychoanalyst Sigmund Freud (1856–1939) claimed that humans are governed by powerful unconscious forces and that even our most noble accomplishments are the result of prior events and instincts. Behavioral psychologists such as John Watson (1878–1958) and B. F. Skinner (1904–90) also believed that human behavior is determined by past events in our lives. However, they argued that, rather than the unconscious controlling our actions, so-called mental states are really just a function of the physical body. Rather than being free, autonomous agents, we are simply the products of past conditioning, elaborately programmed computers—according to Watson, an assembled organic machine ready to run.

Existentialist philosophers go to the opposite extreme. According to the existentialists, we are defined only by our freedom. Existentialist Jean-Paul Sartre (1905–80) argues that "there is no human nature, since there is no God to conceive it . . . Man [therefore] is condemned to be free."[16] He argues that, as radically free beings, we each have the responsibility to create our own essence, including choosing the moral principles upon which we act. Because we are free and not restricted by a fixed essence, when we make a moral choice, we can thus be held completely accountable for our actions and choices.

> I do not at all believe in human freedom in the philosophical sense. Everybody acts not only under external compulsion but also in accordance with inner necessity.
>
> —ALBERT EINSTEIN

Buddhist philosophers also disagree with determinism, although they do acknowledge that we are influenced by outside circumstances beyond our control. However, Buddhists also teach that we can rise above the circumstances by practicing detachment. Unlike existentialism, which attempts to ground human freedom in the assertion of the individual self, Buddhists teach that self (*atman*) is illusion; it does not exist. True freedom therefore entails letting go of the illusion of self. This is very different from the Western notion of freedom as independence from others. Only by giving up our attachment to the notion of a permanent self and the concern about being in control of our choices can we achieve freedom and with it *Nirvana* and true wisdom.[17]

Determinism and Excuses

The determinism versus free will debate has important implications for ethics. In particular, this debate has raised serious questions about to what extent we can hold people morally responsible for their actions. Making excuses for our actions is as old as humankind: Adam excused his behavior by blaming Eve for the apple incident. Eve in turn blamed the serpent.

To what extent can we hold people morally responsible for their actions? The scientific trend toward seeing forces outside our control as responsible for our actions has recently been extended to relabeling behavior such as alcoholism and pedophilia as illnesses or "disabilities" rather than moral weaknesses. The belief that human behavior is determined has also influenced how we treat people who commit crimes. In his book *The Abuse Excuse,* criminal defense attorney Alan Dershowitz examined dozens of excuses that lawyers have used successfully in court to enable people to "get away with murder."[18]

Excuses such as "battered woman syndrome," "Super Bowl Sunday syndrome," "adopted child syndrome," "black rage syndrome," "the Twinkies defense," and "'pornography made me do it' syndrome" have all been used in court cases. More and more people, Dershowitz writes, are saying, "I couldn't help myself," to avoid taking responsibility for their actions.

[The term "mental illness" is] being put to work to obscure certain difficulties that at present may be inherent . . . in the social intercourses of people. If this is true, the concept functions as a disguise: instead of calling attention to conflicting human needs, aspirations, and values, the concept of mental illness provides an amoral and impersonal "thing"—an "illness"—as an explanation for problems in living . . . The belief in mental illness, as something other than man's trouble in getting along with his fellow man, is the proper heir to the belief in demonology and witchcraft . . .

—Thomas Szasz, "The Myth of Mental Illness" (1961)

So, when, if ever, are we responsible for our actions? At one extreme, the existentialists claim that we are completely responsible and that there are no excuses. At the other extreme are those, such as the behaviorists, who say that free will is an illusion. Most philosophers accept a position somewhere in the middle, arguing that although we are the products of our biology and our culture, we are also creators of our culture and our destiny.

Exercises

*1. Discuss how your concept of human nature has influenced the way you think about morality. Do people get what they "deserve"? Are some people naturally inferior? Do you think that certain people deserve to have more material goods and a higher social status than others? Should one's degree of rationality correspond to one's status or moral value in society? If you are doing community service work, relate your answer to your service.

2. Do you agree with Karen Warren's theory that sexism and "naturalism" are linked? What is the relationship of sexism and naturalism to an anthropocentric metaphysics? How does this affect how you define your moral community? How might Aristotle have responded to Warren's theory?

3. Warren talks about the importance of using the first-person narrative to raise philosophical questions that more abstract methods of philosophy might overlook.

a. Find a comfortable spot outside or by a window. Have a pad and pencil ready. Putting on the mantle of a metaphysical dualist, look at others, including humans of a different ethnic background or gender, nonhuman animals, plants, and inanimate objects. After five minutes, or however long you need, write down your thoughts and feelings regarding the different beings you see and their moral worth.

b. Now, repeat this exercise, putting on the mantle of a nondualist, such as Buddha or Warren.

c. Again, repeat the exercise, now looking at the world through the eyes of a metaphysical materialist such as B. F. Skinner.

When you have finished the exercise, compare and contrast your experiences. Discuss how adopting the different metaphysical viewpoints affected how you see others and how you view your place in the world.

4. In Alan Dershowitz's book *The Abuse Excuse,* he argues that the current vogue of making excuses for violent actions threatens the ideal of democracy and individual freedom. What do you think he means by this? Do you agree with him? Or do you believe that we are simply the products of our environment and, as such, unable to overcome our past? Support your answers.

5. Victor Salva, director of the 1995 Walt Disney movie *Powder,* was sentenced to jail in 1987 for having oral sex with a twelve-year-old boy who was an actor in a movie he was directing. Salva served fifteen months in prison for his crime. Salva's victim, Nathan Winter, is outraged that Salva is now back directing movies and urges people to boycott his latest film. "He should not be allowed to live his life as if nothing happened," Winter told a journalist. Other people who object to Salva point out that, according to a 1988 Justice Department study, sexual abusers of children are rarely "cured." About one-half of those who are released are later arrested again for the same crime.

Salva, on the other hand, claims that he now regrets his past actions and has "paid for [his] mistakes dearly." Roger Birnbaum of Caravan Pictures, which made the film *Powder* for Disney, supports Salva, arguing that "what happened eight years ago has nothing to do with this movie."

To what extent can people overcome their past? To what extent is their present behavior determined by their past? How can we really know, in a case such as Salva's, if the person *has* changed?

6. Because medical resources are limited for such things as organ transplants and expensive cancer treatments, we must decide how they should be allocated. If a person knowingly engages in behavior that could jeopardize their health, should this be taken into consideration when allocating scarce resources? For example, baseball superstar Mickey Mantle received a liver transplant, even though the damage to his liver was mainly the result of his years of heavy drinking. Mantle died shortly after receiving the transplant. Was it right to give him the liver? Or should someone else who needed a new liver because of an inherited liver disease have been given priority over

Mantle? How does your position in the determinism versus free will debate influence your answers to these questions?

*7. Discuss how our current government policies toward vulnerable populations such as the homeless, children, prisoners, and families living in poverty are influenced by a philosophical view of human behavior as free or determined. If you are doing community service work, illustrate your answer using examples from your service.

Epistemology and Moral Knowledge

Opinion is that exercise of the human will which helps us to make a decision without information. —JOHN ERSKINE, *The Complete Life* (1943)

In the movie *Terminator 2*, the "terminator," an android played by actor Arnold Schwarzenegger, is about to kill two unarmed men who are harassing his friend John Connor. Connor jumps in, just in the nick of time, and pushes the terminator's gun aside.

Connor: You were going to kill that guy!

Terminator: Of course. I'm a terminator.

Connor: Listen to me very carefully. You're not a terminator anymore. You just can't go around killing people.

Terminator: Why?

Connor: What do you mean "why"!? 'Cause you can't!

Terminator: Why?

Connor: Because you just can't.

In this passage, John Connor is making two important points. First, morality transcends our nature. We cannot use the excuse "but it's my nature" to justify our hurtful actions. Morality, including the principle of **non-maleficence** or "do no harm," is binding on everyone. The terminator *is* by nature a killer, but this does not mean that he *ought* to kill. Morality creates in us obligations to carry out or refrain from carrying out certain actions, in a way that our nature or natural tendencies do not. Secondly, basic moral knowledge, according to Connor, is self-evident. We may need to justify our behavior, but we do not have to justify the general moral principles that inform our moral decisions.

Of course, not everyone would agree with John Connor that the principle of non-maleficence entails that it is always morally wrong to kill unarmed people. Disagreement or uncertainty, however, does not negate the existence of moral knowledge. We also disagree about empirical facts, such as the age of our planet, the cause of Alzheimer's disease, whether people in comas can feel pain, and whether it is going to rain on the weekend. When we disagree about an important moral issue, however, we don't generally shrug off the disagreement as a matter of personal opinion. Instead, we try to come up with good reasons for accepting a particular position or course of action. We also expect others to be able to back up their positions or explain their actions. In other words, most people believe that moral knowledge is possible and that it can help us in making decisions about moral issues.

Epistemology

The branch of philosophy that is concerned with the study of knowledge—including moral knowledge—is known as epistemology. **Epistemology** deals with questions about the nature and limits of knowledge and how knowledge can be validated. There are many ways of knowing: Intuition, reason, feeling, and experience are all potential sources of knowledge.

Many Western philosophers believe that reason is the primary source of moral knowledge. **Reason** can be defined as "the power of understanding the connection between the general and the particular."[19] **Rationalism** is the theory that most human knowledge comes through reason rather than through the physical senses.

Other Western philosophers and many non-Western philosophers have challenged the dependence on reason that characterizes much of Western philosophy. They suggest that we discover moral truths primarily through intuition rather than reason. **Intuition** is immediate or self-evident knowledge, as opposed to knowledge inferred from other truths. Intuitive truths do not need any proof. Utilitarians, for example, claim that we intuitively know that pain is a moral evil. Confucians maintain that we intuitively know that benevolence is good. Rights ethicists claim that we intuitively know that all people are created equal. Even the most egoistic people generally accept a sort of **moral minimalism.** That is, they believe that there are certain minimal morality requirements that include, for example, refraining from torturing and murdering innocent, helpless people. The one exception to this are psychopaths, whom we'll be examining later, in the chapter on moral development, Chapter 6.

Cognitive-developmental psychologist Lawrence Kohlberg believes that certain morally relevant concepts, such as altruism and cooperation, are built into us (or at least *almost* all of us). According to Kohlberg, these intuitive notions are part of humans' fundamental structure for interpreting the social world and, as such, they may not be fully articulated.[20] In other words, we may *know* what is right but not be able to explain why it is right.

The difficulty with using intuition as a source of moral knowledge is that these so-called intuitive truths are not self-evident to everyone. White supremacists, for example, do not agree that all people are created equal. On the other hand, some people do not accept certain moral intuitions, but this does not make these moral intuitions false or nonexistent any more than the deafness of some people means that Beethoven's symphonies do not exist.

The Role of Experience

Experience is also a source of moral knowledge. Aristotle emphasized reason as the most important source of moral knowledge, yet he taught that ethics education needs an experiential component to lead to genuine knowledge. Some philosophers carry the experiential component of moral knowledge even further. **Empiricists** claim that all, or at least most, human knowledge comes through the five senses.

Positivism, which was popular in the first half of the twentieth century, represented an attempt to justify the study of philosophy by aligning it with science. The foundation of positivism, also known as "logical empiricism," was the tenet that all knowledge is based on scientific observation of the physical world.

The positivist theory that moral judgments are simply expressions of individuals' emotions is known as **emotivism.** Because statements of moral judgment don't seem to convey any information about the physical world, positivists such as Alfred J. Ayer (1910–89) concluded that these moral judgments are merely subjective expressions of feeling or commands to arouse feelings and stimulate action and, as such, are devoid of any truth value.

. . . the fundamental ethical concepts are unanalyzable, inasmuch as there is no criterion by which one can test the validity of the judgments in which they occur . . . The presence of an ethical symbol in a proposition adds nothing to its factual content. Thus if I say to someone, "you acted wrongly in stealing that money," I am not stating anything more than if I had simply said, "you stole that money." In adding that this action is wrong I am not making any further statement about it. I am simply evincing my moral disapproval. It is as if I had said, "you stole that money" in a particular tone of horror, or written it with the addition of some special exclamation marks. The tone, or the exclamation marks, adds nothing to the meaning of the sentence . . .

We can see why it is impossible to find a criterion for determining the validity of ethical judgments. It is not because they have an "absolute" validity which is mysteriously independent of ordinary sense-experience, but because they have no objective validity whatsoever . . .

—ALFRED J. AYER, *Language, Truth and Logic* (1950)

The statement "torturing children is wrong," in the context of emotivism, is neither true nor false. It is nothing more than the expression of a negative emotion or feeling toward torturing children—much like saying "yuck" when tasting a food that disagrees with one's palate. This means that someone's preference for torturing young children and another person's preference for a particular flavor of ice cream are both morally neutral.

This alliance between ethics and science (as interpreted by the positivists) proved fatal to ethics. If science is the only source of valid knowledge, then moral statements such as "killing unarmed people is wrong" and "torturing children is wrong" are meaningless, because they do not appear to correspond to anything in the physical world, as do statements such as "tigers have stripes" or "it was sunny at the beach yesterday."

British philosopher Mary Warnock (b. 1924) criticizes the positivists' separation of moral theorizing from concerns about human nature. She writes:

> One of the consequences of treating ethics as the analysis of ethical language is, as I have suggested earlier, that it leads to the increasing triviality of the subject . . . Deliberating, wishing, hating, loving, choosing; these are things which characterize us as people, and therefore as moral agents, and these are the things to which the emotive theory and its later developments paid insufficient attention.
>
> One aspect of this trivializing of the subject is the refusal of moral philosophers in England to commit themselves to any moral opinions.[21]

Emotivism was never widely accepted as a moral theory, and it fell out of favor following World War II. The horrors of the suffering wrought by the Holocaust forced some emotivists to reevaluate their moral theory and to commit themselves to the position that some actions are immoral: Genocide, like torturing children, is wrong—regardless of how one feels about it.

Philosopher Sandra Harding (b. 1935) also maintains that experience is an important component of knowledge; however, she disagrees with the emotivists that moral knowledge is impossible. Moral knowledge, she claims, is radically interdependent with our interests, our cultural institutions, our relationships, and our life experiences such as those based on gender and social status.[22] The "'hard core' of abstract reasoning thought most immune to infiltration by social values," she claims, stems from a particularly "male" perspective and way of experiencing the world. To rely solely on this male type of abstract reasoning, she argues, ignores other ways of experiencing the world and moral values within the world.

The moral theory of epistemologists such as Harding is not as "tidy" as those of the rationalists, but it does remind us that knowing cannot be separated from our position in society and from other practical pursuits such as working toward greater justice and equality. Moral knowledge and moral decision-making lie within the tension between the universal and the particular in our individual experiences. By emphasizing the importance of experience, feminist epistemology reminds us that we must listen to every-one's voice before forming an adequate moral theory—not just the voice of those, such as privileged white males who, Harding maintains, have "enjoyed cognitive authority."[23] This concern with experience has, in turn, led to an increased emphasis on multiculturalism in contemporary college education.

Exercises

1. Philosophers who believe that moral knowledge is intuitive argue that every-one (or almost everyone) would agree that causing pain to an infant for one's own amusement is morally wrong. How would you respond to someone who thinks that torturing infants is either morally right or, in the case of the posi-tivists, morally neutral?

2. Sandra Harding suggests that there may be different ways of knowing moral truths for different groups. Do you agree with her? For example, are there special "female," "Caucasian," "Asian-American," "crime-victim," or "Holocaust-survivor" ways of knowing? If there are, does this necessarily im-ply that moral truth is relative or simply a matter of propaganda? Or are there certain basic moral truths that transcend our particular experiences?

3. Do you agree with Alfred Ayer that moral judgments are nothing more than expressions of feeling and have no validity? If morality is simply an expres-sion of feeling, is there any such thing as moral responsibility? Does it matter anymore what we do or don't do? Are Gandhi and Hitler morally equivalent? Why or why not?

Philosophy and the Search for Wisdom

To do philosophy is to explore one's own temperament, and yet at the same time to attempt to discover the truth.
                                                                      —IRIS MURDOCH

In most North American and Western European universities, ethics is taught as a course in a philosophy department. Although some aspects of the study of ethics extend beyond the purview of philosophy, philosophical inquiry is at the heart of the ethical enterprise.

The word **philosophy** comes from the Greek words *philos,* meaning "lover," and *sophos,* meaning "wisdom." To be a lover (*philos*) entails not only having a positive attitude toward the object of our affection (wisdom, in this case) but also taking action, actively pursuing that object. This interplay of at-titude and action is reflected in the study of ethics. On the theoretical level, ethics includes theories regarding both attitudes and action. Ethics education also goes beyond theory by challenging us to live our lives consistent with moral values.

> The feeling of wonder is the mark of the philosopher, for all philosophy has its origins in wonder.
>
> —PLATO, "Theaetetus"

Philosophy, unlike most academic disciplines, involves the expansion and systematic nurturing of a basic human activity, rather than simply the accumulation of knowledge. Philosophy arises out of a natural sense of wonder and what many philosophers regard as a basic human need to find higher meaning and value in our lives. As very small children, we wondered and asked countless questions about the world around us. Indeed, child psychologists note that curiosity and ethical concerns about justice and sharing emerge spontaneously in children sometime between the ages of eighteen and thirty-six months, regardless of their culture and without prompting from adults.[24]

Wisdom begins in self-knowledge. According to British philosopher Philippa Foot (b. 1920), wisdom, unlike ordinary knowledge or cleverness, presupposes good ends and the search for values. We all share a common humanity, but how we proceed in our quest for wisdom and the good life will vary to some extent from person to person and from culture to culture, because we all have different personalities and different experiences. This does not imply, however, that wisdom is relative. Rather, it suggests that there are several paths to wisdom, just as there can be several paths to the top of a mountain.

Becoming Autonomous

In seeking answers to questions about the meaning of life and the nature of moral goodness, the philosopher goes beyond conventional answers. Rather than relying on public opinion or what others say, it is up to each of us, as philosophers, to critically examine and analyze our reasons for holding particular views. In this way, the study of philosophy encourages us to become more autonomous.

The word "autonomous" comes from the Greek words *auto-* (self) and *nomos* (law). In other words, an **autonomous moral agent** is an independent, self-governing thinker. A **heteronomous moral agent,** in contrast, is a person who uncritically accepts answers and laws imposed by others. The prefix *hetero-* means "other." Being an autonomous thinker is not the same as being independent, in the contemporary sense of living on one's own or being financially independent. In fact, many earlier philosophers, such as the ancient Greek philosophers and the Chinese philosopher Confucius, believed that community bonds are very important.

Because philosophy encourages people to be independent thinkers and to question the deeply held beliefs of their society, most people, as Socrates discovered, resist philosophy. Socrates, who is known as the "Father of Western Philosophy," was born in Athens, Greece, in 469 B.C.E. At that time, Athens was a flourishing city-state and a democracy. Socrates never wrote any books or papers on philosophy. What we know of him comes primarily from the writings of his famous student, Plato. Like most of the early philosophers, Socrates was not a career philosopher; he most likely made his living as a stone worker (his father's profession) or artisan. His real love was philosophy, however. As Socrates got older, he began hanging out more at the market and other places where people congregated, talking to the populace and questioning conventional answers to issues regarding justice and virtue.

According to Socrates, wisdom is important for achieving happiness and inner harmony as well as the intellectual and moral improvement of community. His approach to philosophy, known as the **Socratic method**, consists of a dialogue using questions and answers. The Socratic method is one of the most popular and productive methods used in philosophy.

The road to wisdom, Socrates believed, begins with the realization that we are ignorant. In his search for wisdom, Socrates would stop people on the street to ask them questions about things they thought they already knew. In doing this, he hoped to show people that there was a difference between Truth and what they felt to be true (their opinions). By exposing the ignorance of those who considered themselves wise, Socrates taught people to look at the social customs and laws in a new way. He taught them not to simply accept the prevailing views, but to question their own views and those of their society in a never-ending search for Truth and wisdom.

Not everyone appreciated having their views challenged by Socrates. People in positions of power were especially threatened and outraged by Socrates' habit of asking people to question existing laws and customs and encouraging them to think in new ways. At the age of seventy, Socrates was arrested and charged with blasphemy and corrupting the youth of Athens. He was found guilty and was sentenced to death by drinking poison hemlock.

Even as Socrates faced death, he did not cease being a philosopher. At his trial, Socrates is reputed to have said the following in a speech he made in his own defense before the 501 members of the jury:[25]

> I shall never stop practicing philosophy and exhorting you and elucidating the truth for everyone that I meet. I shall go on saying . . . Are you not ashamed that you give your attention to acquiring as much money as possible, and similarly with reputation and honor, and give no attention or thought to truth and understanding and the perfection of your soul?
>
> And if any of you disputes this . . . I shall question him and examine him and test him . . . I shall do this to everyone that I meet.

"The Death of Socrates," by Jacques-Louis David. Socrates (469–399 B.C.E.) was put to death by the state for blasphemy and corrupting the youth of Athens. Pictured here surrounded by his disciples as he drinks the poison hemlock, Socrates remained true to his principles right up to the moment of his death.

Self-Realization

Some of the most important philosophical questions are those regarding the meaning and goals of our lives. What kind of person do I want to be? How do I achieve that goal? Many philosophers define this goal in terms of **self-realization**—also known as self-actualization and enlightenment. Self-realization is closely linked to the idea of moral virtue. According to psychologist Abraham Maslow, self-actualized people are autonomous: They do not depend upon the opinions of others when deciding what to do and what to believe. Philosophers such as Socrates and Buddha exemplify what Maslow meant by a self-realized person.[26]

Self-realization is an ongoing process or way of life. People who are self-actualized devote their lives to the search for ultimate values. They are constantly searching for answers to questions like those we have raised in earlier sections of this chapter. People who are not honest with themselves will have a difficult time making good life choices. Being honest involves the courage to be different and to work hard at being the best one can be at whatever one does. People who are lacking in authenticity or sincerity blame others for their own unhappiness. This is the result of giving in to what French philosopher Simone de Beauvoir (1908–86) called "the temptations of the easy way."[27]

The man who is aware of himself is henceforward independent; and he is never bored, and life is only too short, and he is steeped through and through with a profound yet temperate happiness. He also lives, while people, slaves of ceremony, let life slip past them in a kind of dream. Once conform, once do what other people do because they do it, and a lethargy steals over all the finer nerves and faculties of the soul.

—VIRGINIA WOOLF, *The Common Reader* (first series) (1929)

People who are self-actualized, in contrast, are flexible and even welcome having their views challenged. Like true philosophers, they are open to new ways of looking at the world. They are willing to analyze and, if necessary, change their views—even if this means taking an unpopular stand. This process involves actively working to recognize and overcome the barriers to new ways of thinking; chief among these is cultural conditioning.

Skepticism

Philosophers try to approach the world with an open mind. They question their own beliefs and those of other people, no matter how obviously true a particular belief may seem. Rather than simply accepting established belief systems uncritically, philosophers first reflect on and analyze them. By refusing to accept beliefs until they can be justified, philosophers adopt an attitude of skepticism, or doubt, as their starting point.

The first [rule for seeking truth] was to accept nothing as true which I did not clearly recognize to be so: that is to say, carefully to avoid precipitation and prejudice in judgments, and to accept in them nothing more than what was presented to my mind so clearly and distinctly that I could have no occasion to doubt it.

—RENÉ DESCARTES, *Discourse on the Method of Rightly Conducting the Reason and Seeking Truth in the Sciences* (1637)

Skepticism, unlike cynicism, is grounded in wonder. The skeptic is always curious and open-minded, with an eye to the truth. Cynicism sometimes masquerades as philosophy; however, it is very different. **Cynicism** is closed-minded and mocks the possibility of truth; it begins and ends in doubt. Cynicism denies rather than analyzes. In this sense, cynicism is a means of resisting philosophical thought, because it hinders analysis. Most people are like the cynic: They resist having their ideas subjected to philosophical analysis because the truth is often at odds with their comfortable and entrenched worldviews.

Plato's "Allegory of the Cave"

Plato's "Allegory of the Cave" has been used to illustrate the nature of philosophical thought. Plato compares us to prisoners who have been chained and left in a cave since childhood. Our heads are held fast in place, so we face the back wall. When people and animals pass by the entrance of the cave, we see them only as shadows on the back wall. We hear the sounds of the outside world only as echoes.

Now, suppose that one of the prisoners has been unchained and turns to face the entrance of the cave. At first, the prisoner is frightened and blinded by the light. A guide, such as a philosopher or guru, comes to meet him. The guide tells the prisoner that everything he has seen before was a shadow. The prisoner will be confused at first and will probably not believe the guide. At this point most people will try to return to the comfort of the cave. But if our prisoner is forced or cajoled out of the cave into the light, his eyes will begin to adjust. Once the prisoner is out in the light and freed of the shackles of everyday opinion, he begins to see and learn about wonderful truths that he never before imagined.

After a period of study, he feels the urge to return to his fellow prisoners and share his knowledge with them. Each step back into the cave, however, is painful. He is ridiculed for his beliefs. At this point the budding philosopher has three options: (1) He can leave the cave again and return to the Light. In this case, his newfound wisdom will become irrelevant to the world of human experience. (2) He can give up the wisdom he has acquired and return to his old beliefs. By doing so, he gives in to public opinion rather than risk being unpopular. Or, (3) he can remain in the cave and persist in his quest to share his wisdom with others. This last option, according to Plato, is the path of the true philosopher.

Plato believed that truth was embodied in changeless universal forms that could be discerned by the use of reason. Other philosophers have a more organic and dynamic view of truth. They see truth, rather than being static and absolute, as constantly revealing itself to us. Truth is a vital living force that exists only in relationship to other things. Zen Buddhists, for example, speak of truth as being found in "the continued or repeated unfolding of the one big mind."

Some people believe that morality demands a sort of absolutist attitude; in other words, a person should stick to their "principles" no matter what. However, if we believe that truth is constantly revealing itself to us in our quest for moral wisdom, we must always be open to dialogue with each other and with the world at large. If we think at some point that we have found Truth and, therefore, close our minds, we have then ceased to think like a true philosopher. We will lose our sense of wonder and become rigid and self-righteous.

For a philosopher to stop seeking truth is like a dancer becoming frozen in one position because he thinks he has found the ultimate dance step or an artist stopping painting because she thinks she has created the perfect work of art. Similarly, to cease to be open-minded and to wonder is to cease to think like a philosopher. To cease thinking like a philosopher is to give up the quest for the good life.

Exercises

1. What is the difference, if any, between wisdom and knowledge? Which are you acquiring at college? How does one actively seek wisdom or live wisely? What is the connection between wisdom and morality? between knowledge and morality?

2. According to Socrates, the first step on the path to wisdom is to "know thyself." Discuss the following questions in light of this mandate.
   a. What is my goal or plan of life?
   b. What sort of person do I want to be?
   c. How close am I to my goal?

3. Sigmund Freud once wrote: ". . . it often seems that the poet's derisive comment is not unjustified when he says of the philosopher, 'With his nightcaps and the tatters of his dressing-gown he patches up the gaps in the structure of the universe.'"

   One of the challenges facing modern philosophy is to overcome these negative stereotypes and to reclaim our heritage. Discuss how philosophy can be made more relevant to modern life and the issues that are facing us.

*4. For those who are doing community service, how does your service fit in with or assist you in clarifying and achieving your life goals?

5. Do you agree that self-realization (self-actualization, enlightenment) is linked to virtue and to happiness? Explain why. To what extent are you a self-actualized or enlightened person? Is becoming self-actualized one of your goals in life? What barriers are holding you back from achieving self-actualization? What can you do to remove some of those barriers?

6. German philosopher Friedrich Nietzsche asks us to imagine what sort of life we would create for ourselves if we knew that it would be repeated over and over again for the rest of eternity. This is known as the theory of *eternal recurrence*. Nietzsche describes it as follows:

"What if, some day or night a demon were to steal after you into your loneliest loneliness and say to you: 'This life as you now live it and have lived it, you will have to live once more and innumerable times more; and there will be nothing new in it, but every pain and every joy and every thought and sign and everything unutterably small or great in your life will have to return to you, all in the same succession and sequence—even this spider and this moonlight between the trees, and even this moment and I myself. The eternal hourglass of existence is turned upside down again and again, and you with it, speck of dust!'

Would you not throw yourself down and gnash your teeth and curse the demon who spoke thus? . . . Or how well disposed would you have to become to yourself and to life to crave nothing more fervently than this ultimate eternal confirmation and seal?"[28]

How would you answer Nietszche's questions? Are you satisfied with the life you are now creating for yourself? If so, why? If not, what could you do to make it a better life, one that you would want to be repeated over and over ad infinitum? Would you prefer a life of self-actualization? Explain.

7. Discuss some of the other assumptions that underlie Western philosophy, or your own philosophy of life, that usually go unquestioned. How do these assumptions affect the way you or others treat other human and nonhuman beings? How do they affect your perception of your own place in society and in the world?

8. Discuss your own life in terms of Plato's "Allegory of the Cave." Where are you now in your journey? Are you still chained up in the cave? Have you had a glimpse of the light? How did you respond? Did you try sharing your insights with others? How did they respond?

Summary

1. **Ethics** is concerned with the study of right and wrong and how to live the good life.

2. **Descriptive statements** are about what *is*. **Prescriptive statements** are about what *ought* to be. Moral statements are prescriptive.

3. The two main subdivisions of ethics are theoretical and normative ethics. Theoretical ethics, or **metaethics,** is concerned with appraising the logical foundations of ethical systems. **Normative ethics** gives us practical guidelines for deciding which actions are right or wrong.

4. There are two types of *ethical theories.* **Noncognitive theories,** such as emotivism, claim that moral statements are neither true nor false. **Cognitive theories** claim that moral statements can be true or false. Cognitive theories can be further subdivided into relativist theories and universalist theories. *Relativist theories,* such as ethical subjectivism and cultural relativism, maintain

that right and wrong are creations of either individuals or groups of humans. *Universalist theories* claim that there are universal moral values that apply to all humans.

5. **Metaphysics** is the philosophical study of the nature of reality, including human nature.

6. **Metaphysical dualism** claims that reality is made up of two distinct substances: physical matter and nonmaterial mind. **Metaphysical materialism,** in contrast, claims that physical matter is the only substance.

7. **Sociobiologists** claim that morality is genetically programmed into humans and other animals. **Behaviorists,** on the other hand, claim that morality is shaped by our environment.

8. **Determinism** claims that all events, including human actions, are caused by previous events (predetermined) and that *free will* is an illusion. If there is no free will, then of course there is no such thing as moral responsibility.

9. **Epistemology** is the study of knowledge. Potential ways of knowing include reason, experience, feeling, and intuition. Most traditional Western philosophies emphasize reason as the primary source of moral knowledge; most non-Western and feminist philosophies emphasize intuition or sentiment.

10. **Emotivism** is the theory that moral statements are meaningless, because they do not correspond to anything in the physical world. Emotivism arose from an attempt by the **positivists** to scientifically legitimate the study of philosophy.

11. **Philosophy** is, literally, the "love of wisdom."

12. The **Socratic method** involves a dialogue in which a teacher questions people about things they thought they already knew.

13. Wisdom begins in self-knowledge, which in turn leads to **self-realization** or self-actualization.

14. True philosophers approach the world with an open mind. They begin the process of inquiry by adopting an initial position of **skepticism** or doubt.

15. *Plato's "Allegory of the Cave"* defines the task of the philosopher: moving out of our conventional mode of thinking (the darkness of the cave) into the light of truth. This experience of truth, in turn, should be shared with others who are still living in darkness.

CHAPTER 2

Moral Reasoning

*In a republican nation, whose citizens are to be led by reason
and persuasion and not by force, the art of reasoning becomes of
the first importance.*
  —THOMAS JEFFERSON

The Three Levels of Thinking

By sharpening our analytical skills, we can become more independent in our
thinking and less susceptible to worldviews that foster narrow-mindedness.
The thinking process used in philosophical inquiry can be broken down into
three tiers or levels: experience, interpretation, and analysis. Keep in mind
that this division is artificial and merely one of emphasis. We never have *pure*
experience or engage in *pure* analysis. All three levels overlap and interact
with one another (Figure 2.1). Experience provides the material for interpretation and analysis; analysis, in the end, returns to experience. If the results of
our analysis are inconsistent with our experience, then we need to start over
and fine-tune our analysis so that it takes into account all relevant experience.
Analysis also returns to experience in the form of action or *praxis*, a concept
we will discuss later in this chapter.

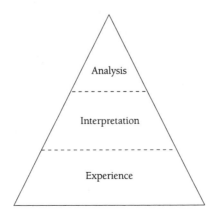

FIGURE 2.1   The Three Levels of Thinking

> Genuine philosophy leads to action and from action back again to wonder, to the enduring fact of mystery.
>
> —HENRY MILLER

Experience

Experience is the first level of thinking. Experience goes beyond the five senses: We notice certain events happening, we observe different feelings within ourselves, we have certain intuitions, and we receive information about the world by reading or hearing about the experiences of others. Experience forms the foundation of the philosophical enterprise. Without experience, there can be no thought.

At this level of thinking we simply *describe* our experiences. We do not, at least in theory, interpret or pass judgment on our experience. Here are examples of statements at the level of experience:

I feel angry when Mary lies to me.   The average annual income of men is higher than women's.

Interpretation

Interpretation involves trying to make sense of our experience in light of our other past experiences. This level of thinking includes individual interpretations of experience as well as collective or cultural interpretations. Some of our interpretations may be well informed; others may be based merely on our opinions or personal feelings. Upon analysis, an opinion may just happen to be true. Even opinions that make good sense and win the approval of others are still only opinions if we cannot support them with good reasons or factual evidence. Figure 2.2 provides some examples of statements at the level of interpretation.

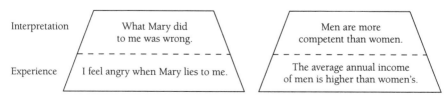

FIGURE 2.2   Statements at the Interpretation Level

The interpretations of our experiences taken together form what is known as our **worldview.** American physicist and philosopher Thomas Kuhn refers to our worldview regarding a particular aspect of our experience, such as science or morality, as a **paradigm.**[1] Paradigms provide an overall way of regarding and explaining phenomena in a particular discipline. Kuhn limited his discussion of paradigms to scientific worldviews; the concept of paradigms is also helpful in moral philosophy, however.

Most of us like to think that we came up with our worldview regarding morality on our own. In reality, our worldviews are strongly influenced by our upbringing and by cultural norms. Our experience contributes to our worldview, and our worldview also shapes how we experience the world. For example, in a study on stereotyping, college students were shown a picture of a white thug beating up a black man in a business suit. When students were later asked to describe what they saw, the majority reported that they saw a black thug beating up a white businessman! By not analyzing our worldview, we can get caught up in a sort of self-fulfilling prophecy, or vicious cycle, where our worldview is verified by our "experience" and our experience, in turn, further confirms our distorted worldview.

> Man is a thought-adventurer. But by thought we mean, of course, discovery. We don't mean by this telling himself stale facts and drawing false conclusions, which usually passes as thought. Thought is an adventure, not a trick.
>
> —D. H. LAWRENCE, *Selected Essays* (1950)

Analysis

People often blend fact and opinion. It is important, therefore, to learn to distinguish between the two. By learning how to critically analyze our worldview, we can break the vicious cycle we just described. **Analysis** of moral issues draws on the findings of other disciplines such as psychology, sociology, and the natural sciences; it also involves an examination of our worldviews, in light of fundamental moral intuitions, moral sentiments, and collective insights.

Analysis demands that we raise our level of consciousness and refuse to accept narrow interpretations of our experience. As such, analysis often begins with questions about the assumptions underlying our interpretations. Figure 2.3 includes examples of statements at the analysis level.

The process of moving from experience to interpretation to analysis and from there back to experience again is an ongoing one. Analysis is most

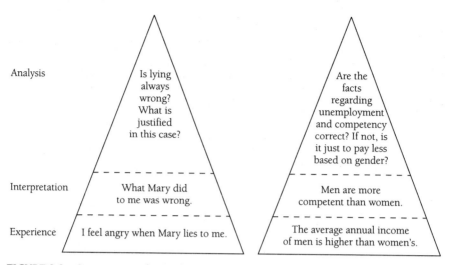

FIGURE 2.3   Statements at the Analysis Level

productive when it is done collectively, because people bring with them different experiences. At the same time, we cannot simply accept other people's interpretations of their experiences at face value.

Philosophers are like tightrope walkers: They walk a thin, and sometimes dangerous, line between acquiescing to uncritical public opinion and being irrelevant. Because philosophers, like all humans, are social beings who do not exist apart from a culture and a particular cultural worldview, it is all too easy for us to be lured into accepting cultural interpretations of reality as truth. Even well-trained philosophers can become captivated by the prevailing cultural worldview or the traditional philosophical interpretations of their professional colleagues.

[Traditional] philosophers, for their part, seem to take a perverse delight in shocking others by providing an analysis that appears to fly in the face of experience.

—SUSAN SHERWIN, "Philosophical Methodology and Feminist Methodology: Are They Compatible?" (1988), p. 21[2]

When philosophers succumb to the temptation to follow public opinion or simply accept traditional philosophical assumptions without question, they become maintainers of the status quo. As such, they can even become part of the problem. Analysis that ignores certain relevant aspects of experience can become distorted. The complicity of philosophers such as Martin Heidegger (1889–1976) in destructive ideologies like Nazism and the promotion of sexism and elitism in the name of philosophy are all instances of a philosopher accepting a prevailing worldview as truth without bothering to thoroughly analyze it.

Some liberation ethicists claim that certain groups of traditionally disempowered people, such as African Americans, women, and economically disadvantaged people, have **epistemological privilege.** Those who do not benefit from or are harmed by conventional interpretations of reality, it is argued, are the least likely to buy into or defend the interpretations that oppress them. Being the least biased in favor of traditional interpretation, they also have the least resistance to analyzing them. This is a reversal of the conventional wisdom that favors insight and the logical, abstract thinking processes used by well-educated white males.

To claim that those who lack power are epistemologically privileged is *not* the same as saying that they are sages or that they have special knowledge in all areas. Indeed, poverty often precludes having the leisure time or the resources to improve one's education, to engage in lengthy philosophical discussions, or to enjoy the arts and literature. The concept of epistemological privilege suggests that—rather than social policy being formulated and analyzed in isolation by people in positions of power like politicians—those who have the *least* power in society should be at the center of the process of analyzing and reformulating the social policy that adversely affects them.

Exercises

1. Select a "simple" experience, such as a man holding a door open for a woman or a student giving a dollar to a beggar on the street. In groups, discuss different interpretations of the experience, being careful not to let prejudice distort your interpretation or to make interpretations that are inconsistent with the experience.

2. Use the three-tiered model of thinking to discuss the following experience:

   While Black males represent only 6% of the U.S. population, they make up 50% of the prison inmates.[3]

   The interpretations you list do not have to be ones that you personally accept; you might also want to write down some interpretations that are common in our culture. Discuss how your interpretation of this experience has shaped your past experience and actions and how analyzing this issue might affect your future actions regarding the issue.

*3. Choose an experience from your community service work or your own personal life. Analyze this experience, using the three-tiered model. Relate your analysis back to the experience. Does the analysis take into account the relevant aspects of the experience?

*4. Do you agree that people who have the least power in a society—those who see the world from "below"—are epistemologically privileged? If you are doing community service with a group of people such as the homeless, the economically disadvantaged, or elderly people in nursing homes who have been marginalized in our culture, find out how they analyze our cultural traditions regarding homelessness and the elderly. Do you consider their analyses of issues relating to homelessness, medical care, and the treatment of the elderly, etc., to be better, more insightful, and more consistent with morality than those of people who are in positions of power? If so, how do you consider their analyses to be better?

Moral Analysis, Praxis, and Paradigm Shifts

The very truths you are now contending for, will, in fifty years, be so completely imbedded in public opinion that no one need say one word in their defence; whilst at the same time new forms of truth will rise to test the faithfulness of the pioneer minds of that age, and so on eternally; for truth will forever elaborate new forms by its creative energy, and thus furnish food for all growing minds.

— Angelina Grimke Weld to Elizabeth Cady Stanton (1861)

Moral Analysis and Praxis

The following story, which is attributed to Buddha, illustrates what is meant by praxis in moral philosophy: A group of people came across a man dying from a wound from a poisoned arrow. Instead of trying to save the man, the crowd stood around debating about where the arrow had come from, who had fired it, and the angle of the trajectory. Meanwhile, the man dies. The proper goal of the philosopher, according to Buddha, is to save the dying man, not to stand around engaging in speculation.

Today we overrate the rational values and behave as if thinking were a substitute for living. We have forgotten that thought and the intuition that feeds it only become whole if the deed grows out of it as a fruit grows from the pollen on a tree, and so everywhere in our civilized world there tends to be a terrible cleavage between thinking and doing.

— Laurens Van der Post, *The Lost World of the Kalahari* (1958)

Western philosophical methodology has traditionally focused primarily on one mode of analysis—abstract, logical reasoning—and ignored praxis. Although logical reasoning is very important in moral philosophy, it represents only one aspect of what is meant by analysis in moral philosophy.

In an article entitled "Shifting Perspective: A New Approach to Ethics," Canadian philosopher Sheila Mullett outlines a process for ethical analysis based on what she calls a feminist methodology. Mullett's approach to ethical analysis involves three steps or dimensions:

1. The first dimension, **moral sensitivity,** grows out of a collective consciousness-raising. Until we develop an awareness of the experience of violence, victimization, and pain that surrounds us, we will continue to inadvertently perpetuate it. Only through actually experiencing—directly or indirectly—"this consciousness of pain," Mullett argues, "can we begin to cultivate a new attitude towards the social arrangements which contribute to suffering."[4]

2. The second dimension is **ontological shock. Ontology** is the philosophical study of "being" or the nature of being. Ontological shock is something that shakes us to the very core of our being, thus forcing us to call into question our cherished worldview or standard interpretations of our experiences. Simply being aware of and lamenting the injustices and pain in the world is not sufficient to motivate us to do this. When we experience ontological shock, the worldview that we once took for granted is displaced, thereby forcing us to reanalyze our old assumptions.

3. The third dimension of analysis is **praxis.** Praxis refers to the practice of a particular art or skill. In ethics, praxis requires informed social action. True philosophical analysis always returns with an altered and heightened consciousness to the world of particular experiences. Ontological shock grows out of and nurtures moral sensitivity; until this spills over into praxis, social reform is not likely to occur.

One of the gravest obstacles to the achievement of liberation is that oppressive reality [worldview] absorbs those within it . . . To no longer be prey to its force, one must emerge from it and turn on it. This can be done only by means of *praxis*, reflection and action upon the world in order to transform it.

—PAULO FREIRE, *The Pedagogy of the Oppressed* (1970), p. 34

Liberation ethicist Paulo Freire, in his book *The Pedagogy of the Oppressed*, likewise writes: "This shift in consciousness includes a search for collective actions that can transform the existing unjust social structures . . .[5] Authentic thinking, thinking that is concerned about reality, does not take place in ivory tower isolation."[6] Indeed, genuine praxis demands a shift away from the manner in which an individual routinely sees the world, to viewing the world through the eyes of the collective "we." This involves expanding our moral community so that the "other" becomes part of the "we."

Analysis, in this broader sense, is interactive, interdisciplinary, and directed toward praxis or social action. We will use this broader definition of analysis throughout this text. This approach is not only richer and more inclusive but also more effective for promoting moral growth. Praxis demands that we also cultivate our own moral character. Until we overcome our own narrow interpretations of the world and incorporate these changes into our personal life, it is unlikely that we will be able to sustain our involvement in praxis.

> Thought without practice is empty, practice without thought is blind.
>
> —Kwane Nkruman, former president of Ghana

Paradigm Shifts

Paradigms do not exist in a vacuum but have real-life consequences. The definition of analysis as a purely abstract cerebral activity, for example, is embedded in a particular dualistic paradigm that sees reason as a function of a disembodied mind. Moral philosophers who regard reason as separate from action tend to focus on abstract problems—such as the relationship between free will and moral responsibility or the search for valid universal principles of ethics—rather than practical problems involving praxis. The prevailing paradigm also establishes limits on the ranges of acceptable answers to problems. The emotivists' view of morality, for example, was limited by the scientific paradigm and the belief that all knowledge is based on scientific observation. Because of this, the emotivists were unable to explain why the Holocaust was immoral.

If we get stuck in a particular paradigm, certain problems can seem unsolvable, whereas, if we could break "out of the box," a solution might be quite obvious. The exercise in Figure 2.4 illustrates what is meant by breaking out of a paradigm. Your goal is to connect all nine dots with four straight lines without lifting your pen from the paper. If you stick within the traditional paradigm of "staying within the box," there seems to be no solution. Only by breaking the prevailing concept of boundaries can new possibilities and new solutions be discovered. (By the way, the solution to this exercise can be found at the end of this chapter.)

·   ·   ·   FIGURE 2.4   Paradigm Exercise

·   ·   ·

·   ·   ·

In much of traditional Western moral philosophy, conclusions supported by logical analysis are considered acceptable, but those based on sentiment, intuition, or collective consciousness-raising are not. Logical analysis, in other words, becomes the "box." French philosopher Helene Cixous (b. 1937) refers to this paradigm in philosophy as "logocentrism." The importance of logic in Western thinking is reflected in the religious belief that a rational principle, the *logos,* created and governs the universe. Because of our identification of ultimate value and even the divine will with the *logos,* when logical analysis fails to arrive at a solution, the problem is generally written off as unsolvable. This is not to say that logical analysis is unimportant: Logic is very important. The problem arises when logic is seen as the *only* way to approach a problem.

According to Thomas Kuhn, challenges to traditional paradigms generally come from outside the profession or from people who are new to the profession. Those who question the prevailing paradigm or what is considered "normal" must generally work in isolation or join a "fringe group." Feminists, animal rights activists, and social reformers, for example, are often snubbed by academics as not being "real" philosophers.

New paradigms involve viewing the world in a radically different way. Paradigm shifts, such as that being advocated by feminist epistemologists, involve giving up our old worldview and adopting new ways of interpreting our experiences. This involves a complete reevaluation of traditional modes of philosophical analysis and the interpretations or worldviews they support, which generally takes several generations to achieve. Paradigm shifts often entail a shift in power. There is generally intense resistance from those who support the status quo, because of their heavy investment in the traditional paradigm.

Kuhn notes that paradigm shifts are more likely to occur in times of crisis—what Mullet called "ontological shock"—when the prevailing paradigm is unable to solve a particular pressing problem. The current environmental crisis, the population explosion, and the increase in human suffering throughout the world, despite advances in technology, may be just such a crisis. During times of crises, new approaches or paradigms, such as feminist epistemology and the approaches adopted by Eastern philosophies, are suggested and then tried out. When a paradigm shift occurs, heated debate and conflict are inevitable. Problems that were once considered trivial—such as the rights of women and indigenous peoples and, more recently, environmental ethics and animal rights—are now becoming central issues. Like Socrates, we should be willing to question the prevailing paradigms even when doing so may make us unpopular.

Exercises

1. Relate the notion of "ontological shock" to an event in your life where your worldview was shaken. How did you respond to the shock? Did it make you more morally sensitive and more likely to act upon your moral beliefs?

2. The civil rights movement in the United States in the 1960s involved the application of moral analysis to praxis. Malcolm X (1925–65) wrote about the importance of taking action in the ongoing struggle against racism in our country:

   > I believe in political action, yes. Any kind of political action. I believe in action period. Whatever kind of action is necessary. When you hear me say "by any means necessary," I mean exactly that. I believe in anything that is necessary to correct unjust conditions—political, economic, social, physical, anything that's necessary. I believe in it as long as it's intelligently directed and designed to get results.[7]

   What do you think Malcolm X meant when he said "by any means necessary"? Relate his comments to the concept of praxis, as opposed to uninformed action.

3. Looking back at the person you identified as your hero in Exercise 2, Chapter 1, page 7, is this person more willing than the average person to engage in serious analysis of his or her own and cultural worldviews? more likely to engage in praxis than most people? Explain, using examples to illustrate your answer.

*4. Discuss your choice of community service in terms of praxis. Relate your service learning to Mullett's three dimensions of ethical analysis.

Overcoming Resistance

Nothing strong, nothing new, nothing urgent penetrates man's mind without crossing resistance.
                                                    —HENRI DE LUBAC, *Paradoxes* (1969)

Most of us hate to be proven wrong. When a particular paradigm becomes thoroughly entrenched in our worldview, we may begin to see it as fact rather than an interpretation of experience, especially if we benefit by that particular worldview. For example, when slavery was legal, it was seen as a natural part of the world order by those who benefited from it. Few white people bothered to analyze or even to question the morality of the practice. Even President Abraham Lincoln did not always support the abolition of slavery in his public statements. In his first inaugural speech, Lincoln reassured the Southern voters that "I have no purpose, directly or indirectly, to interfere with the institution of slavery in the States where it exists. I believe I have no lawful right to do so, and I have no inclination to do so."[8] The Emancipation Proclamation of 1863 rather than clearly reflecting a moral repugnance toward slavery has been interpreted as a political move calculated to weaken the strength of the Confederate forces.

To avoid having our worldview challenged, we may use a type of defense mechanism known as resistance. **Defense mechanisms** are psychological tools, which we usually learn at an early age, for coping with difficult situations. Defense mechanisms can be divided into two main types: (1) coping and (2) resistance.

Healthy Defense Mechanisms

Coping, or healthy defense mechanisms, allows us to work through challenges to our worldview and to adjust our life in ways that maintain our integrity. Healthy ways of coping include logical analysis, objectivity, tolerance of ambiguity, empathy, and suppression of harmful emotional responses.

Immature Defense Mechanisms

Resistance, in contrast, involves the use of immature defense mechanisms that are rigid, impulsive, maladaptive, and nonanalytical. Isolation, rationalization, doubt and indecision, and denial are all examples of immature defense mechanisms.[9] Everyone uses these defense mechanisms at times to keep from feeling overwhelmed. Children from abusive backgrounds often find it necessary to construct rigid defenses to avoid being crushed by their circumstances. The problem arises, though, when people carry these once-appropriate defense mechanisms into their adult life, rather than substituting more mature forms of defense. When resistance becomes a habitual way of responding to issues, it acts as a barrier to any critical analysis of interpretations or worldview (see Figure 2.5).

The use of immature defense mechanisms or resistance impedes our moral development. Daniel Hart and Susan Chmiel, in a study of the influence of defense mechanisms on moral reasoning, found a strong relationship

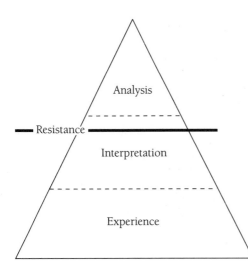

FIGURE 2.5   Resistance As a Defense Mechanism

between the use of immature defense mechanisms in adolescence and lower levels of moral development in adulthood.[10] Resistance also acts as a block against moving toward self-actualization. In Norman Bradburn's study of psychological well-being, he found that participation in novel experiences is positively correlated to happiness and a sense of well-being in a person.[11] The habitual use of resistance, on the other hand, entails avoiding novel experiences and ideas that challenge our worldview. This, in itself, can create both anxiety and a sense of boredom with life. Resistance can also numb us to the needs of others, immobilize us in the face of moral outrage, and prevent us from devising a plan of action.

Rather than being prisoners of our past, we can take steps to overcome immature defense mechanisms that stand in the way of our moral growth. This can involve putting our very identity at risk. Because giving up old ways of thinking can be both painful and confusing, people will rarely change without being challenged through *"knowledge perturbation,"* also known as **cognitive dissonance.** Knowledge perturbation occurs when our worldview is called into question, thus throwing us into a state of ontological shock. Socrates was a master at "knowledge perturbation." It is also practiced by some Eastern philosophers and masters.

Putting aside resistance often means experiencing uncomfortable feelings and ideas that we have been defending ourselves against. Breaking down resistance can create profound disequilibrium and confusion. For this reason, psychologists suggest that we do this in the context of a relationship where we are taken seriously and where we are emotionally supported during the period of confusion and vulnerability.[12]

Philosophy and the process of self-actualization is a social pursuit. Both the Socratic method and the traditional master-disciple relationship used in Eastern philosophy provide supportive context in which the student of philosophy can engage in self-examination. An experienced teacher, or supportive friends, can help us identify and work through our resistance by challenging us and offering constructive criticism.

In identifying our resistance, we may find that we rely primarily on one type of resistance, or we may have a repertoire of several types, depending on the situation. The following are just a few of the types of resistance that people are prone to use when their moral views are challenged.

Ignorance There are situations where we are ignorant simply because the information is not available. Sometimes, however, we avoid learning about particular issues because we just do not want to know. Some people think that not knowing excuses them from having to think about the issue or take a stand. As a result, problems continue to get worse. Ignorance is regarded as a vice and a hindrance to the good life in virtually all world philosophies. Socrates is reputed to have said, "The unexamined life is not worth living." Confucius taught that "ignorance is the night of the mind." "Ignorance," writes Hindu Yogi Swami Prabhavananda, "creates all the other obstacles."[13]

Avoidance   Rather than seeking out people who have different points of view, as Socrates did, we may avoid certain people and situations and instead hang out only with people who agree with us. Some people who hold very strong opinions about certain moral issues, yet are insecure in the face of challenges to their position, only read literature that supports their opinion and only attend social events, meetings, or rallies attended by people who agree with them. These gatherings are often referred to as "preaching to the converted." The tendency to avoid controversial situations or people with opinions unlike our own can lead to a serious lack of communication and even hostility between people who hold widely opposing points of view.

Denial   André Trocme, a leader in the French Resistance in World War II, defined denial as "a willingness to be self-deceived."[14] During World War II, most Germans tacitly supported the war effort by denying the cruelty of the Nazi policies. Similarly, parents may be in denial regarding their children's destructive lifestyles until it is too late. In its extreme form, mothers in incestuous families may fail to take action to halt the sexual abuse, not because they don't care about their children but because they have convinced themselves that such a terrible thing could not really be happening. Denial is also common in people who are addicted to alcohol or drugs. Denial keeps people from acknowledging and working on solutions to these pressing moral problems.

Anger   We cannot always avoid people who disagree with us. Some people respond by getting angry when they are confronted with a challenge to their views. Anger may be expressed overtly such as by physical violence or threats, or it may be expressed more subtly in angry phrases such as "don't force your views on me," an expression that implies, ironically, that the person challenging another's views is somehow threatening his or her autonomy. Anger as a form of resistance is most effective in thwarting disagreement when the angry person has greater social or physical power. Some men, for example, feel that they are entitled to be right and to have the last word. Prison or the threat of prison may be used by authority figures to oppress dissent or stifle social reform.

Clichés   "Don't force your views on me." "It's all relative." "To each his own." "Things always work out for the best." "I have a right to my own opinion." Hannah Arendt writes, in her book about Nazi war criminal Adolf Eichmann, that when Eichmann was challenged to analyze the contradictions of his society, he became "genuinely incapable of uttering a single sentence that was not a cliché."[15] Used sparingly, clichés can be useful for illustrating a point; however, the habitual use of clichés in responding to challenges to our worldview works as a barrier that keeps us from having to think seriously about issues.

Conformity/Superficial Tolerance Many people are afraid that they will not be accepted by their peers if they disagree with them. Even though they may actually disagree, they go along with the group rather than risk rejection. For example, suppose that someone at a party makes an offensive ethnic or sexist joke. Rather than speaking up or leaving the room, some people will either laugh or say nothing, thus tolerating and perpetuating the bigotry.

> Many people fear nothing more terribly than to take a position which stands out sharply and clearly from prevailing opinion. The tendency of most is to adopt a view that is so ambiguous that it will include everything, and so popular that it will include everyone.
>
> —MARTIN LUTHER KING, JR.

Some people who engage in superficial tolerance really do not have a point of view of their own. The expression "I can see both sides of the issue" often masks a reluctance to analyze the various, often contradictory, sides of a moral issue. Italian poet Dante (1265–1321) had a dim view of people who use this sort of resistance. In his *Divine Comedy,* he reserved "the darkest places in Hell" for those who decide to remain neutral when confronted with a moral conflict.

"I'm Struggling" During the Nazi occupation of France in World War II, the 3,500 people of the village of Le Chambon provided refuge for Jews who were fleeing the Nazis. In doing this, the villagers took tremendous risks. Many years later, they were asked by a television reporter from the United States why they did this while other people in France were still struggling with the issue. One elderly gentleman replied: "Those who struggle don't act; those who act don't struggle." It is appropriate to wrestle with moral issues before reaching at least a tentative stand, but for some people the "struggle" is used to avoid taking a stand while still creating an appearance of being concerned.

Distractions The use of distractions is a very popular means of blocking out conflicting thoughts. Indeed, certain enterprising people have become very wealthy marketing distraction to the American public. Some people hate silence and being alone with their thoughts. They turn on the television or have loud music playing whenever they are home alone. Or else they use alcohol, drugs, food, partying, work, or shopping for things they don't really need as a means of keeping their minds off of their problems.

The constant drive to accumulate more knowledge can also serve as a distraction. Mental hindrances, according to Buddhist teaching, keep us from having clear understanding. For this reason, most Eastern philosophies emphasize the importance of stillness and quiet contemplation for achieving wisdom.

> Right contemplation (*samma samadhi*) stands for the clear and composed mind that is a prerequisite for the understanding that leads to moral perfection. Right contemplation is no doubt much needed by contemporary humanity; we are constantly bombarded by a dizzying variety of sensuous stimuli from our material environment, driving us to the brink of insanity. Those who have had the unsettling experience of sensory overload and excessive sensuous gratification suffer subsequent spells of boredom and depression, leading them to seek solace in psychedelic drugs that promise temporary states of altered consciousness, rapture, or mental ecstasy.
>
> —P. Don Premasiri, "The Relevance of the Noble Eightfold Path
> to Contemporary Society"[16]

Doublethink

Because most people resist analyzing their worldview they may, unwittingly, get caught up in "doublethink," a term coined by author George Orwell. **Doublethink** involves holding two contradictory views at the same time and believing both to be true. Orwell's novel *1984* was written in 1948, in part, as a warning that, unless we recognize the insidious role of doublethink in our society, we will continue to head down the path toward destruction.

When young people come to college, they often hold certain contradictory worldviews regarding morality. In Allan Bloom's book on U.S. colleges and universities, *The Closing of the American Mind*, the author claims that most students believe morality is relative and that there are no universal moral values. At the same time, however, these students profess to believe that human equality and tolerance are universal moral values!

> There is one thing a professor can be absolutely certain of: almost every student entering the university believes, or says he believes, that truth is relative . . . Students nowadays are unified only in their relativism and in their allegiance to equality . . . The danger they have been taught to fear from absolutism is not error but intolerance . . . The point is not to correct the mistake and be really right; rather it is not to think you are right at all.

Doublethink often takes the form of supporting double standards. For example, surveys indicate that most college students believe that women should be the primary caretakers of children, but these students will just as vehemently argue that they believe in equality and freedom of choice for all humans in regard to lifestyle and career. Many people also claim that they believe in animal rights. They may support their position by pointing out that they are morally opposed to hunting or to the mistreatment of pets. Yet, they have no qualms about eating meat or wearing animal products such as clothing (leather or fur coats).

Sometimes doublethink involves a conflict between our expressed worldview and our actual actions. We've all heard the expression "actions speak louder than words." In coming to "know ourselves," in the philosophical sense, we must be willing to take a good look at our own lives and how we treat ourselves and others. For example, almost all teachers, even those who claim to be ardent feminists, treat their female students differently than their male students. They call on the boys more often, praise their accomplishments more often, and are more tolerant of their disruptive behavior.[17] Yet, when teachers are told this, the great majority will deny that it happens in their classroom. When teachers are shown videotapes of their classes, most are shocked at the extent to which they ignore the girls in the classroom and downplay their abilities.

Doublethink often goes unnoticed because almost everyone around us— our professional colleagues, members of our religion, and our peers—accepts it. For this reason, it is important to be always on the alert for doublethink in our own lives. This involves learning what type of resistance we are most likely to use when our contradictory views are challenged. It may seem that, by avoiding conflict, life will be more tranquil and enjoyable; in fact, habitual resistance takes a lot of energy. When we shut out ideas and experiences that conflict with our cherished worldview, we also shut out much of the richness of life.

Exercises

1. Name some of your healthy coping mechanisms. What can you do to strengthen these? What type of resistance are you most likely to use when one of your cherished moral views is challenged? Illustrate your answer with a specific example of a time when you used this type of resistance during a discussion about a moral issue. What can you do to make yourself less prone to use this type of resistance?

2. Studies focusing on the college experience have found that college freshmen are particularly influenced by peer opinion. Do you think that you were more of a conformist when you first entered college? Has the college experience

changed you in this regard? How did this tendency to conform affect your views on morality?

*3. If you are doing community service work as a class requirement, how did you respond when you first learned that it was required, or when you first started your service work? Did you engage in any resistance? If you did, discuss why and how you overcame your resistance.

 4. Do you agree with Allan Bloom that the morality espoused by most students involves doublethink? Why or why not? What about the popular belief that morality is relative? How might this theory itself involve doublethink?

*5. If you are doing community service, has it helped you to strengthen your healthy coping mechanisms and to overcome your immature coping mechanisms (resistance)? If so, give specific examples.

Recognizing and Constructing Moral Arguments

The very first lesson that we have a right to demand that logic shall teach us is how to make our ideas clear; and a most important one it is, depreciated only by minds who stand in need of it.   —CHARLES SANDERS PIERCE

Logic

The ability to analyze arguments and to recognize faulty reasoning is important to the study of ethics. **Logic,** the study of correct and incorrect reasoning, provides us with the methods and skills to formulate sound moral arguments and to distinguish good arguments from poor arguments. **Reason** is defined as "the power of understanding the connection between the general and the particular."[18]

Logic enables us to analyze the logical consistencies of various ethical theories. Logic also helps us to make better moral decisions. Without correct reasoning, even a person with good intentions can end up actually causing more harm than good. This happens because, although people may be strongly motivated to do what is right, they cannot always figure out *what* is the best course of action to take to accomplish this goal.

Much of what passes for moral reasoning is, in fact, **rhetoric**—a type of incorrect reasoning where a person has an opinion and then attempts to persuade others that that opinion is correct. Some people are so emotionally invested in certain opinions on moral issues that they may, unknowingly, manipulate their arguments to "prove" a conclusion that does not logically follow from the premises. Many opinions seem to make good sense and can win a person's approval, but they are still merely opinions until they are supported with good reasons or evidence. It is our responsibility to learn how to use reason so that we can discriminate successfully between logic and rhetoric.

There may be times when we know that a person's argument is faulty, but we refrain from speaking out because we cannot figure out exactly what is wrong with the argument. When we are unable to figure out why an argument is faulty, we are more likely to back down on our own position or even adopt the other person's interpretation and then do something that we may later come to regret. When a person fails to take appropriate moral action or makes a moral decision that they later regret, we call it a **moral tragedy.** A knowledge of logic helps people to break through patterns of resistance— their own and those of others—and thus avoid moral tragedies.

Recognizing Moral Arguments

The Components of an Argument   To distinguish between correct and incorrect reasoning, we need to be able to recognize arguments. An **argument** is made up of two or more propositions; one of these is claimed to follow from or be supported by the others. A **proposition** is a statement that expresses a complete thought. It can be either true or false. The **conclusion** is the proposition that is affirmed or denied on the basis of other propositions in the argument. The **premise** is a proposition that supports or gives reasons for accepting the conclusion. An argument can have one or many premises.

In an argument, we move from the premise(s) to the conclusion through a process known as *inference*:

$$\text{Premise(s)} \longrightarrow \text{Inference} \longrightarrow \text{Conclusion}$$

Ethical arguments may contain different types of observations. The truth or falsehood of a proposition can be based on **empirical** facts, those based on scientific observation and the use of our five senses. The statement "AIDS is currently one of the leading causes of death of young adults in the United States" is an empirical fact. A proposition can also be a lexical definition of a key term. The proposition "lying is any intentionally deceptive message that is stated" gives us a lexical definition of "lying." We determine the truth or falsehood of a lexical definition by looking for the term in a dictionary. The first two types of propositions are descriptive. Other propositions contain **prescriptive statements** regarding moral truths. The statement "it is wrong to hurt other people for our own amusement" is an example of a moral proposition.

Different sentences can be used to express the same proposition. For example, the statements "torturing children is wrong," "it is wrong to torture children," and *"Kinder zu quälen ist unmoralisch"* are all the same proposition, because they all express the same thought. A proposition can also appear in the form of a rhetorical question. Several propositions can also be found in one sentence. French philosopher René Descartes' famous *cogito* argument can be summarized in one sentence, "I think, therefore I am," which contains two propositions: "I think" and "I am."

Premise and Conclusion Indicators Some arguments contain terms known as *premise indicators* and *conclusion indicators* that can help us to identify the conclusion and the premises. Words such as "because," "since," and "for" can serve as premise indicators. The words "therefore," "thus," "hence," "so," "as," and "consequently" are examples of conclusion indicators. Indicators signal that a premise or conclusion follows. In the argument "I think, therefore I am," the word "therefore" tells us that the conclusion is "I am."

The bad news is that not all arguments contain indicators. Also, words such as "since," "for," and "as" can serve as premise or conclusion indicators in one context but not in another context. The terms "because" and "therefore" can also be used in explanations. In the statement "Ying stole the food because his children were starving," we are not trying to prove that Ying stole the food; rather, we are explaining why he stole the food. When breaking down an argument into its components, if there are no premise or conclusion indicators, it is usually easiest to identify the conclusion first. To do this, we should ask ourselves: What is the argument trying to prove? What position is the argument trying to defend?

To get practice in breaking down arguments, let's look at the following argument from a 1927 article by Dr. Joseph Collins entitled "Should Doctors Tell the Truth?" [19]:

> Every physician should cultivate lying as a fine art . . . Many experiences show that patients do not want the truth about their maladies, and that it is prejudicial to their well-being to know it.

There are three separate propositions in this argument. Bracket and number each of the propositions, as shown:

> 1. [*Every physician should cultivate lying as a fine art*] 2. [*Many experiences show that patients do not want the truth about their maladies*] and 3. [(many experiences show) *that it is prejudicial to their well-being to know it* (the truth).]

This argument is more difficult to analyze than some, because there do not appear to be any conclusion or premise indicators. If you cannot identify the conclusion, try inserting a conclusion indicator, such as "therefore," before the proposition(s) that you suspect might be the conclusion. Or try inserting a premise indicator, such as "because," before the proposition(s) that you think might be the premise(s). If the argument is not essentially changed by the addition of an indicator, this means that the indicator is in the right place.

> 1. [*Every physician should cultivate the fine art of lying*] because, 2. [*Many experiences show that patients do not want the truth about their maladies*] and 3. because [(many experiences show) *that it is prejudicial to their well-being to know it* (the truth).]

In the preceding argument, the first proposition is the conclusion, and propositions 2 and 3 are the supporting premises. The first premise is a proposition about an empirical fact. In this case, we might want to find out how many patients were surveyed and whether they constituted a representative sample. The second premise is also an empirical statement. The claim is that knowing the truth will bring harm to the patient in the form of anguish and earlier death. (Studies conducted after this article was written have found that this proposition, like the preceding premise, is false.)

If the premises are false or logically unrelated to the conclusion, as they are in this argument, then we have a poor argument. However, when a particular conclusion is poorly argued or supported by premises that are false, this does not necessarily mean that the conclusion itself is false or worthless: It is simply unsubstantiated.

As we noted earlier, not all premises are stated in an argument. It is sometimes assumed that certain beliefs are so generally accepted that there is no need to state them. In the preceding argument, there is an unstated third premise regarding a moral principle, the principle of non-maleficence, also known as the "do no harm" principle. You may be surprised to learn that premises about general moral principles or sentiments are often the least controversial of the premises—an observation that runs contrary to the popular belief that morality is relative and varies from individual to individual.

Rhetoric   Now that we've learned how to recognize and break down arguments, we can move on to constructing our own arguments. Many people mistake rhetoric for logical arguments. Rhetoric is a means of defending a particular worldview rather than analyzing it. In logical arguments, we end with the conclusion. Rhetoric, in contrast, begins with a pseudo-conclusion or an opinion. Rhetoricians use only statements that support their particular opinion and disregard any statements that do not. The purpose of rhetoric is to win your opponents over through the power of persuasive speech; the purpose of argumentation is to discover the truth.

When constructing an argument about a particular moral issue, we begin by making a list of premises. When coming up with premises, it is generally most productive to work with others, especially those who disagree with us. According to Socrates, it is through the process of dialogue that we are given an opportunity to try out our views and, hopefully, come closer to discovering the truth.

Constructing Moral Arguments

The following is a summary of the steps for constructing an argument:

1. *Come up with a list of premises.* In a good argument, the premises will be relatively uncontroversial and should be acceptable to all or most reasonable people. Much of the disagreement in moral arguments stems not from disagreement about basic moral principles but about empirical

facts or the definitions of ambiguous key terms. It is important to be able to identify relevant moral principles and ideals; in addition good moral reasoning depends on first getting the facts straight, rather than relying on unsupported assumptions or opinions. Any ambiguous key terms should be clearly defined and used in a consistent manner throughout your argument.

2. *Eliminate irrelevant or weak premises.* After coming up with a list of premises, go back over these, and eliminate any that are weak or irrelevant. Resist the temptation to eliminate premises that do not mesh with your particular opinion regarding the moral issue. Also, make sure that there are no obvious gaps in the list of premises. When constructing arguments, it is also important that there are no fallacies in the premises. We will learn how to recognize some of the more common fallacies later in this chapter.

3. *Come to a conclusion.* The last step in constructing a moral argument is drawing the conclusion. The conclusion should take into account the information contained in the premises but should not state more than what is contained therein. Conclusions that are too broad include more than the premises say; conclusions that are too narrow ignore certain premises.

4. *Try out the argument on others.* The final step is to try out your argument. When doing this, be careful not to become rigid and slip into rhetoric. Remember, the mark of a good philosopher is to be open-minded. If your argument is weak, you should be willing to revise it in your ongoing search for wisdom.

Exercises

1. Break down the following arguments into their premises and conclusion. It is usually easiest to first bracket the propositions. Then circle the conclusion indicator and the premise indicators. Next identify the conclusion, and then identify the premise(s). In each of the arguments, ask yourself whether there are other premises that might strengthen the argument. Also think of premises that might be unstated but simply assumed in each of the arguments.

   a. Racism and sexism are wrong, since all people deserve equal respect.

   b. It is immoral to use rabbits in cosmetic experiments, because causing pain is immoral, and animals such as rabbits are capable of feeling pain.

   c. People need to pass a driving test to get a license to drive a car. People should also have to take a test and get a license before they can become a parent. After all, parenting is a greater responsibility and requires more skill than driving.

d. We have an obligation to become the best person we can. One of the primary purposes of education is to make us better people. Therefore, colleges should seriously consider having a community service requirement for graduation, since community service has been shown to increase students' self-esteem and facilitate their moral development.

2. Choose a controversial moral issue such as euthanasia, capital punishment, mandatory AIDS testing, abortion, or banning drinking on campus. Brainstorm with others to come up with a list of relevant premises. Try to remain open-minded and avoid using resistance if some of the premises seem to run contrary to your cherished worldview.

   After completing your list of premises, ask yourself, "What conclusion follows from these premises?" Once you have completed your argument, try it out on someone else in the class. What were the weaknesses in your argument? How can you make your argument stronger? This may involve revising your conclusion. Continue this process until you feel satisfied with your argument. Save a copy of your final argument and the list of premises you devised through brainstorming, because we will return to this in our following discussion "Avoiding Logical Fallacies."

3. Look back at the argument you constructed in the previous exercise. To what extent were you tempted to engage in rhetoric instead of logical analysis by using only those statements that supported your particular opinion on the topic? Did working in a group make it easier for you to avoid rhetoric? Explain why.

Avoiding Logical Fallacies

> . . . *arguments, like men, are often pretenders.* —PLATO

There are several ways in which an argument can be weak or invalid. When an argument is psychologically or emotionally persuasive but logically incorrect, it contains what logicians call an informal **fallacy.** We are more likely to use fallacies when we are unsure of our position. Fallacies can be used as a form of resistance to keep us or others from analyzing our position. The use of fallacies can be effective in the short run, but thoughtful people will eventually begin to question the reasoning behind the fallacious argument. It is important to be able to recognize and identify fallacies, because this will make us less likely to fall victim to them or to use them unintentionally in an argument.

Many different types of fallacies can occur in an argument over a moral issue. In this section, we will look at some of the fallacies that are most likely to appear in moral arguments. As you read through the following descriptions of these fallacies, consider which fallacy or fallacies you are most likely to fall victim to or use in an argument regarding a moral issue.

Fallacy of Equivocation

Some words or terms have several definitions. Most often, the context in which a particular word or phrase is used lets us know which definition is intended; however, this is not always the case. When the meaning of a particular term is unclear from its context or when it could have any of several meanings in a given context, we refer to it as an *ambiguous* term. The **fallacy of equivocation** occurs when an ambiguous word changes meaning in the course of an argument. For example:

> *Hans:*   All people have a right to a minimal level of health care.
>
> *Beth:*   That's not true. Our constitution says nothing about people having a right to health care; therefore, as taxpayers we have no obligation to provide it.

In this argument, Hans and Beth are using differing meanings of the word "right," which has several different meanings. The *Webster's Encyclopedic Unabridged Dictionary* gives sixty-two different meanings of "right"! By taking a closer look at their respective arguments, we can see that Hans is most likely talking about rights in terms of moral or human rights, while Beth is using the term to refer to legal rights.[20] Their first task in resolving their disagreement is to agree upon which definition of "right" they will use.

Appeal to Force

This fallacy occurs when we use or threaten to use force—whether physical, psychological, or legal—in an attempt to coerce another person to accept our conclusion. This fallacy is used most often by people in positions of greater power. The phrase "might is right" summarizes the reasoning (or lack of reasoning) behind this fallacy. The use of this fallacy is illustrated in the following argument:

> Don't disagree with me because if you do I'll slap your #@& face. I'll show you who's in charge around here!

Although most people would not be taken in by such overt threats of violence, others such as children may actually come to believe that might does make right and begin to identify with the views of the person who threatens them. At other times, the intimidation is more subtle. There may be an implied threat to withdraw affection or favors if the other person does not come around to our way of thinking. However, there is no logical connection between being right and having the power to hurt someone else or to withhold affection or desired objects.

This is a particularly dangerous fallacy, not only because it can lead to injury or even death, but because we are taken in by it a lot more often than most of us like to admit. People who have financial, social, or political power over others may come to believe that they deserve their privileged status. This is particularly troublesome when people who lack power start to agree with their oppressors and become resigned to or even blame themselves for their own oppression and inferior status. The disempowered person may also internalize the message that "might is right" and, in turn, attempt to impose his or her views on others by using force against those that are even more socially disenfranchised. We see this in gang warfare, where groups of relatively powerless people turn on each other, seeking power by terrorizing and oppressing those with even less power.

Abusive Fallacy

This fallacy occurs when we disagree with someone's conclusion, but, instead of addressing their argument, we turn and attack the character of the person who made the argument. By doing so, we attempt to evoke a feeling of disapproval toward the person who made the argument, so that disapproval of the person overflows into disapproval of the person's argument. The **abusive fallacy** is also known as the **ad hominem** fallacy.

> *Lila:*   I think abortion is morally wrong.
>
> *Chloe:*   You pro-lifers are just a bunch of narrow-minded, anti-choice, religious fanatics who think they have a right to force their religious morality on others.
>
> *Lila:*   Oh, yeah? Well you pro-choice people are nothing but a bunch of selfish baby-killers who are out to destroy the family and all it stands for!

In the preceding conversation, the issue of the morality of abortion has been completely sidetracked. Instead, Lila and Chloe got caught up in slandering the character of the people who hold the opposing view. When we call people "narrow-minded," "fanatic," or "selfish baby-killers," we are simply dismissing their views without ever analyzing them.

Virtually all great thinkers and reformers, because they challenge us to rethink our cherished worldviews, have had detractors who have tried to discredit their ideas through character assassination. What distinguishes great thinkers is their ability to remain focused on their position and not to be distracted by critics' use of fallacies against them. Elizabeth Cady Stanton and Lucretia Mott, for example, first met in 1840 at the World Anti-Slavery Society convention in London, England, where both of their husbands were attending as delegates.[21] The women delegates from the United States were denied seats at the convention because of the strenuous objections of some male delegates from the United States. Mott, in response, demanded that she be treated with the same respect accorded any man—white or black. During these discussions, Stanton, who was then a young newlywed, marveled at the way that Mott, a woman of forty-seven, held her own in the argument, "skill-fully parried all their attacks . . . turning the laugh on them, and then by her earnestness and dignity silencing their ridicule and jeers."[22] This meeting and Mott's refusal to back down in the face of ridicule and attacks upon her char-acter led to the first woman's rights meeting in U.S. history.

Circumstantial Fallacy

The **circumstantial fallacy** occurs when we argue that our opponent should accept a certain position because of special circumstances, such as his or her lifestyle or membership in a particular group based on race, ethnicity, gender, nationality, or religion. This fallacy, like the previous one, is a type of ad hominem fallacy, because it entails attacking one's opponent rather than ad-dressing their argument. Here is one example:

> Granted, you may be a vegetarian, but you certainly can't argue against the killing of animals. After all, you do wear leather shoes and use products that were tested on animals.

As in the preceding example, someone can use animal products and still argue against the very practice in which they engage. Parents who are heavy drinkers or smokers, for example, can certainly give their children sound ar-guments regarding the evils of alcohol and drug abuse. Being a hypocrite or engaging in doublethink does not invalidate arguments against the evils that one knows firsthand, such as alcohol and drug abuse. We can avoid having to respond to our opponents' arguments by focusing on their circumstances, or hypocrisy, as the case may be.

Appeal to Inappropriate Authority

In an argument, it is appropriate to use the testimony of someone who is an expert in the field or area that is being debated. We commit a fallacy, how-ever, when we appeal to an expert or authority in a field other than the one under debate. Young children, for example, often see their parents as author-ities on every subject. As adults, we may regard people in certain professions as all-around authority figures. The assumption is that someone who is an au-thority in one field must also be knowledgeable in all other fields. This is sometimes called the "halo effect." Here's an example:

> My priest says that genetic engineering and in vitro fertilization are dangerous. Therefore, all experimentation in this field should be stopped immediately.

In this example, the person cited as providing support for the conclusion ("all experimentation in this field should be stopped immediately") is not an expert in the medical field; he is simply someone who is admired as an expert in his particular field of theology. Titles such as Doctor, Professor, President,

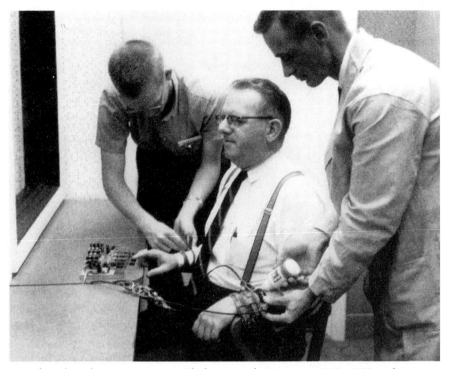

Scene from the Milgram experiment on obedience at Yale University, 1960–1963. In this experiment, subjects were led to believe that they were delivering real electric shocks to the learner. In fact, the learner was an accomplice in the experiment. Despite the fact that they thought they were causing harm to the learner, about two-thirds of the subjects continued delivering the shocks at the urging of the experimenter.

and Lieutenant and the visual impact of uniforms such as white lab coats and police or military uniforms all increase our perception of a person's authority. We tend to believe and obey these authority figures even when they overextend their authority to the point where it would be more appropriate to question their authority.

Most of us like to think that we would not follow orders that would require us to cause grave harm to innocent people, such as what happened during the Holocaust. Evidence suggests that the opposite is true, however. In 1960, Stanley Milgram of Yale University placed an advertisement in the newspaper asking for men to participate in a scientific study on memory and learning. The participants were told that the purpose of the experiment was to study the effects of punishment (electric shock) on learning. In fact, the real purpose of the study was to see how far people were willing to go in obeying an authority figure. Although no shock was actually being delivered, the "subject" responded with (apparently) increasing anguish as the shocks supposedly increased in intensity. Despite repeated pleas from the learner to be released from their obligation, two-thirds of the participants administered the requested 450 volts, simply because an authority figure (a man in a white lab coat) told them to continue.[23]

Popular Appeal

This fallacy occurs when we appeal to popular opinion to gain support for our conclusion. **Popular appeal** can take several different forms. The most common one in moral arguments is the "bandwagon" approach, where a certain conclusion is assumed to be right because "everyone" is doing it or "everyone" believes it. The following is an example of this bandwagon approach:

> Seventy percent of Americans are in favor of capital punishment. So it must be morally acceptable.

This example is based upon the assumption that the majority of us know what is right. One of the dangers of living in a democracy, however, is what English philosopher John Stuart Mill (1806–73) referred to as the "tyranny of the majority." Historian Alexis de Tocqueville, after visiting the United States in 1826, made the observation that, although democracy liberates us from tradition, the great democratic danger is enslavement to public opinion. "Repugnance at the power of the people," he noted, is rare in a modern democracy. In fact, studies show the majority of U.S. citizens define morality in terms of what the majority believe to be right and wrong.[24] Young people often simply accept the norms of their peer group; adults are more likely to uncritically adopt the established norms of the wider community or nation. However, a particular position or conclusion is not necessarily correct just because the majority of people agree with it. After all, the majority of people once believed that the Earth was flat and slavery was natural.

Hasty Generalization

When used properly, generalization can be a valuable tool for gathering information in both the physical and social sciences. The fallacy of **hasty generalization** occurs when we use only unusual or atypical cases to support our conclusion. In doing so, we hastily generalize to a rule or conclusion that fits only these unusual cases, rather than the whole group. For example, early doctors such as Joseph Collins hastily generalized from their experience with a few patients with terminal cancer to the faulty conclusion that no one with a terminal condition really wants to know the truth about their condition.

Unusual cases ───────────────────→ Odd rule about a whole group
  (Premises)   (Hasty generalization)   (Conclusion)

Stereotypes and *prejudices* are often be based upon hasty generalizations. A woman who has been abused by her father or boyfriend may hastily generalize from her limited experience to reach the conclusion that all men are abusers. During wartime, governments will intentionally create negative stereotypes of the enemy, thus justifying the dehumanization and destruction of that enemy. Negative stereotypes can lead to an unconscious devaluation of whole groups of people, particularly when not much interaction exists between the different cultural groups.

Fallacy of Accident

This fallacy occurs when we apply a rule that is generally accepted as valid to a particular case whose exceptional or accidental circumstances render the rule inappropriate. The **fallacy of accident** is the opposite of hasty generalization. In this fallacy, we start with the rule and apply it to an unusual or accidental case or circumstance:

Good rule ─────────────────────────→ Exceptional or accidental cases
(Premise)   (Inappropriate application of rule)   (Conclusion)

The vast majority of rules, including laws and moral principles, have exceptions. However, rather than spelling out all the circumstances that might produce an exception, people are expected to use their powers of discrimination and reason to decide when a rule should be applied and when it is inappropriate.

Following are examples of people taking a rule to be absolutely binding that was never intended to be so.

> Going through a red light is illegal. Therefore, Wanda should be given a ticket for going through that red light on the way to the hospital with her dying child.

Almost everyone would accept the legal rule "stop at red lights" to be a reasonable law. This law is good for *most* cases, but that does not mean it is appropriate in all cases. In the preceding case, preventing the child's death—the moral duty of non-maleficence—should take precedence over obeying the law about stopping at red lights. Indeed, a police officer who pulled Wanda over and gave her a ticket would be considered overly rigid in interpreting the law as well as remiss in his or her moral duties.

Like legal rules, moral rules can also have exceptions:

> You should keep your promises. You promised to pay back the money I loaned you today. So give it to me—I need it to buy the last few parts for my bomb.

As with the law "stop at red lights," most reasonable people consider "keep your promises" to be a good moral rule. However, circumstances can render a normally good moral rule inappropriate. The duty not to abet a malevolent action is more important than the duty to fulfill one's promise to pay back the money on time.

A rule that is universally accepted as a good rule need not be absolute. When applying both legal rules and moral principles, we need to consider the context in which the rule is being considered. People who rigidly apply moral rules regardless of the circumstances are known as **absolutists.** Some people, in their rejection of absolutism, swing to the opposite extreme, moral relativism. These people believe that, because moral rules have exceptions, all rules should be thrown out. Indeed, many college students respond to the plethora of new ideas that they encounter when they first come to college and the realization that these rules are not absolute by subscribing to moral relativism.

Fallacy of Ignorance

Ignorance, in this fallacy, does not indicate that we are stupid. It simply means that we are ignorant of how to go about proving something. The **fallacy of ignorance** is committed whenever it is argued that our conclusion is true simply because it has not been proven false, or that it is false simply because it has not been proven true. However, suppose that we are ignorant of how to prove the existence of something such as UFOs or free will; this does not mean that they do not exist. When we lack proof of a particular phenomenon, the most that we can logically conclude is that we do not *know* whether or not it exists.

> *Kwesi:*   God is clearly the creator of the moral order. Try as hard as they may, ethicists have been unable to come up with any other explanation of the source of universal moral principles or why moral principles are binding on us.
>
> *Mercedes:*   You're clearly mistaken. The fact that no one can come up with a proof or even a testable theory regarding the source of universal moral principles just goes to prove, on the contrary, that there are no universal moral principles and that so-called morality is really just a matter of personal opinion.

In this example, both Kwesi and Mercedes are guilty of using the fallacy of ignorance in their arguments. Kwesi makes the claim that his conclusion must be true because the opponent cannot prove it false. Mercedes, on the other hand, also commits the fallacy of ignorance when she counters with the argument that, if we cannot identify the source of universal moral principles, then they are not "real" or binding on us.

The ultimate source of universal moral principles has been a source of puzzlement to many ethicists. This does not mean, however, that universal moral principles do not exist. We also don't know the source of the laws of physics, but this ignorance on our part neither proves that God *must* have created the universe and the laws of physics nor diminishes the hold that the laws of physics have upon us as physical beings.

Begging the Question

Begging the question is also known as circular reasoning. This fallacy occurs when a premise and conclusion are actually rewordings of the same proposition. In other words, when making the argument, we simply assume the truth of our conclusion rather than offering proof for it.

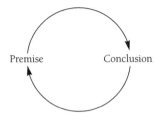

This fallacy is sometimes difficult to recognize, because the premise and the conclusion are worded differently. The premise may be just a definition or synonym of a key term in the conclusion. At first glance, it may appear to us that the person using this fallacy has an airtight argument, because the premise seems to support the conclusion so perfectly. However, upon closer inspection it will become clear that this is so because, despite differences in language, the premise and conclusion both express the same idea and, in fact, are the same proposition:

> Voluntary euthanasia is morally acceptable because people have the right to choose when and how they will end their lives.

The conclusion of this argument is a rewording of the premise. Rather than offering proof that voluntary euthanasia is morally acceptable, the premise simply *assumes* that it is morally acceptable. If we reverse the conclusion and the premise, we are left with exactly the same argument: "Voluntary euthanasia is morally acceptable; *therefore,* people have the right to choose when and how they will end their lives."

This fallacy can be very frustrating if we fail to recognize it, because there is no way to disprove the person's position. The best way to recognize this fallacy is to reverse the premise and conclusion. If this can be done without changing the essence of the argument, then chances are the argument contains the fallacy of begging the question.

Irrelevant Conclusion

In one sense, all the conclusions in fallacious arguments are logically irrelevant. However, in the fallacy of **irrelevant conclusion,** the conclusions are irrelevant in a particular way. This fallacy is committed when we support or reject a conclusion using premises that are, in fact, directed at a different conclusion. In other words, we change the topic to a related but different subject that we feel more comfortable discussing.

Sometimes, people will avoid a specific topic that makes them feel uncomfortable by changing the topic to something more general or less controversial. A politician, instead of discussing a universal health care plan, may change the topic to the desirability of being healthy, a premise with which almost everyone would agree. In this way, the politician avoids addressing the question about his specific plan to achieve this goal (which not everyone would support).

Irrelevant conclusion in a moral argument can also take the form of changing the topic from what one *ought* to do (a prescriptive question) to what we *would* do (a descriptive question). In one study, twenty percent of the teenagers interviewed did not seem to understand questions about "what ought (or should) you do?" They chose to reframe them instead as "what would you do?" Another twenty percent of these teenagers were unable to engage in any sort of discussion when asked about what they ought to do.[25]

> *Rosa:*   "Don't you think that it was wrong for Michael to copy the test answers from the person sitting next to him?"
>
> *Katrina:*   "Oh, I don't know about that. If I had been in his situation, I probably would have done the same thing."

In this example, Katrina answers Rosa as though the question were about what she *would* do, rather than what she thinks a person *ought* to do in a similar situation. In doing so, Katrina changes the topic from a prescriptive *ought* statement about moral value to a descriptive statement about a *would*. To say that a student probably *would* cheat on a test, if they had the opportunity, is not the same as saying that they *ought* to cheat on the test. Indeed, we often do things that we know we ought not do.

Naturalistic Fallacy

The **naturalistic fallacy** is a specific type of irrelevant conclusion. G. E. Moore (1873–1958) argued in his *Principia Ethica* that "good" is not based on any observations about the world but is intuitively known, or self-evident. According to Moore, we commit this fallacy when we go from an *is* to an *ought* statement. We cannot assume, because something *is* the case, that it is morally acceptable or *ought* to be that way. We may not agree with Moore that nature, or what *is,* is entirely irrelevant for determining what is morally good; however, the following example illustrates that nature is certainly not the sole determinant of what is good.

Only women are physically capable of bearing and nursing children. Therefore, women ought to be the primary caretakers of children.

Women are physically capable of bearing and nursing children but men are not (what "is"); this does not mean, though, that women have a moral obligation to be the primary caretakers of children (what "ought to be"). On the other hand, nature sets the limits of what "ought to be." We cannot argue that men ought to share equally in the bearing of children because men, by nature, are incapable of bearing children!

People who use the naturalistic fallacy may refer not only to human nature but also to the natural activities of other animals. But the fact that other animals eat meat or that they sometimes kill and eat their young or that most animals have several sexual partners (and a few even eat their partner after mating!)—all of this does not indicate that it is morally acceptable for humans to do so. The morality of these behaviors must be evaluated on grounds other than that it is natural.

Appeal to Tradition

This fallacy also goes from an *is* to an *ought* statement. Whereas the naturalistic fallacy points to what is natural, this fallacy appeals to tradition or cultural norms as a reason for continuing a certain practice. People who are prone to these last two fallacies often refer to themselves as *realists,* as opposed to *idealists,* because they base their moral decisions on what *is* rather than a conception of an ideal.

The Negro has never been recognized as a person in this country or by the U.S. Constitution. Therefore, slavery should remain legal.

People who use the **appeal to tradition** may argue, as in the above example, that a certain practice is moral because it is constitutional. However, the U.S. Constitution is a legal rather than a moral document. Our constitution has allowed slavery and prevented women from voting and, to this day, allows people to own handguns, but this does not necessarily mean that these traditions are moral. On the contrary, the provisions of the constitution itself should be judged in the light of moral principles.

The fallacy of appeal to tradition is used primarily by cultural relativists to maintain and to legitimate the status quo. Once a practice becomes a tradition, people begin to accept it as normal and natural, even in the face of overwhelming evidence that it harms people. Our current attachment to the prison system is a good example of how appeal to tradition inhibits us from thinking of creative alternatives. The traditions of other countries, such as lack of legal and social protection for women and children, has also been used as excuses for exploiting people living in those cultures.

Exercises

1. Which fallacy are you most likely to use in a discussion about a moral issue? Give an example of a time when you used this fallacy. Which fallacy are you most likely to fall victim to in a discussion about a moral issue? Give an example of a time when this fallacy was used on you. What can you do to make yourself less prone to using or falling for these particular fallacies?

2. Consider the argument that you constructed in Exercise 2 on page 59. Are there any fallacies in your argument? Look at the premises you discarded. Do they contain any fallacies? If so, which ones? If necessary, rework the argument so it is fallacy-free. After doing this, try out your original argument on someone else in the class, to see whether he or she can recognize the fallacies.

3. The Bill of Rights was put forth to protect minorities or dissenters from the "tyranny of the majority." Is the Bill of Rights working? To what extent should those in the minority be protected from the dictates of the majority? Or should the will of the majority always prevail in a democratic nation? If not, why not?

*4. Discuss some of the common stereotypes of groups found on your campus. Are these based on hasty generalization? How do these stereotypes harm or diminish the autonomy of the people who are members of the group being stereotyped? If you are a member of one of these groups, what effect do the stereotypes of your group have on your own life? What steps could you and others on campus take to overcome these stereotypes?

   Contact with diverse groups of people has been found to decrease a person's tendency to stereotype or prejudge people in general. If you are doing community service work, discuss how, if at all, your work has helped you to overcome certain negative stereotypes about people such as senior citizens and the homeless.

*5. Some students protest the use of community service as a course requirement, on the grounds that it is not a traditional way to teach a course. Discuss whether this is a good reason for rejecting a community service requirement.

Resolving Moral Dilemmas

Moral conflicts are neither systematically avoidable, nor all soluble without remainder.
                                    —BERNARD WILLIAMS, *Problems of Self* (1973), p. 82

In the movie *Sophie's Choice,* a guard in the Nazi internment camp tells Sophie, who is standing in a line with her two children, to make a choice. She can choose to have one of her children killed and save the other; or she can choose not to choose, in which case both children will be killed. The choice facing her is especially agonizing, because she is not sure if the guard is serious or if he is playing a cruel mind game with her.

What Is a Moral Dilemma?

Situations where we have a conflict between moral values are known as **moral dilemmas.** We do *not* have a moral dilemma when the conflict is between moral values and nonmoral values such as economic success, popularity, or good grades. In a moral dilemma, no matter what solution we choose, it will involve doing something wrong in order to do what is right. Solutions to moral dilemmas are not right or wrong, only better or worse. In deciding what to do, like Sophie, the best we can hope for is to find the solution that causes the least harm.

The great majority of moral decisions are straightforward. Moral decision-making is such a normal part of our everyday life that we generally don't even give it a second thought. We don't struggle about whether we should run down a pedestrian, even though he or she is jaywalking. Instead, we stop or at least try to avoid hitting them. We don't kill a person, even though we may want to, because they irritate us. Nor do we clobber the person sitting next to us in class and take their textbook, simply because we forgot ours. We wait our turn, learn to share scarce resources, apologize if we hurt someone, refrain from stealing from our friends, and, for the most part, get along with others without having to think too much about it.

Sometimes, however, we encounter a situation where the right thing to do is not so clear-cut. Most of us have struggled with moral dilemmas at one time or another. Fortunately, the moral dilemmas we usually encounter are not nearly as devastating as the one Sophie faced. We may be torn between our loyalty to a friend and telling the truth—particularly when it involves bad news. Or we may have to decide whether to leave a relationship with a friend or relative who is engaged in abusive or destructive behavior, such as alcoholism or drug abuse. Many of us will also be faced someday with the difficult decision of whether to place an elderly and ailing parent or grandparent in a nursing home or continue caring for them at home.

Most people try not to let troublesome problems get out of hand, but this can occur if we do not have the requisite skills for resolving moral dilemmas when they first arise. Even worse, we may not recognize a situation as a moral dilemma. Family violence, homelessness, and hunger in many big cities in the world have become major problems, because many of us deny that these are problems since we tend to avoid situations where we may have to acknowledge those who are abused or homeless. Because of resistance or inability to resolve moral dilemmas, problems can continue to accumulate and get worse until we find ourselves in a crisis.

Many people do not like conflict and build up strong defense mechanisms to avoid it. When confronted with a moral dilemma, our first reaction is often discomfort. Educational psychologist William G. Perry found that college freshmen tend to see the world in black and white: right and wrong. Dilemmas illustrate that, although the world is not always black and white, right and wrong (or at least morally better and worse), answers can still be found in the grey area.

Practice at resolving moral dilemmas has been found to be an effective means of improving our skill at moral reasoning. Moral and personal growth requires that a person be willing to give up their old ways of solving problems. Dilemmas, by their very nature, demand that we sort out and take a closer look at moral values and learn how they are relevant to making decisions about our lives. In a study of moral reasoning and the college experience, discussion of real-life dilemmas was found to be more effective in promoting moral reasoning than the acquisition of knowledge in specific content areas, such as the study of different ethical theories.[26]

> Judging is not in general simply accepting one or two ready-made alternatives as the right one. It cannot be done by tossing up. It is seeing reason to think and act in a particular way. It is a comprehensive function, involving our whole nature, by which we direct ourselves and find our way through a whole forest of possibilities . . . We are always moving into new territories.
>
> All the same, some explicit maps and some general guidelines for explorers do exist and can be referred to. There is the constant use of rationality; the area is cognitive; we can know things. We are not just guessing or gambling.
>
> —MARY MIDGLEY, *Can't We Make Moral Judgements?* (1993), p. 25

Steps for Resolving Moral Dilemmas

Resolving a moral dilemma is similar to constructing an argument. It begins with the collection of relevant facts and moral principles and ends with a proposed solution or conclusion. As with moral argumentation, it is important to resist the temptation to start with a "solution" and then rationalize it by selecting only the facts and principles that support it. Also, coming up with a satisfactory resolution to a moral dilemma is generally easier when it is done with someone else or in a group.

Describe the Facts   The first step in resolving a moral dilemma is to arrive at a clear description regarding the facts of the case. Avoid the use of emotional or biased language in describing the dilemma. This description of the facts, which can be as short as a paragraph or two, is similar to the premises in an argument which contain empirical statements. When putting together this description, facts may come to light that we did not initially realize were relevant. In the process of gathering together the facts, we may discover that what at first appeared to be a moral dilemma was not a dilemma after all. For example, doctors who used to routinely lie to cancer patients realized that lying in general was wrong, but they also believed that the conflicting moral principle of "do no harm" was more compelling, in these cases. However, once they found out that telling the truth was actually more beneficial to their patients, the conflict between the two principles disappeared.

List Relevant Moral Principles and Sentiments   The next step in resolving a moral dilemma is to identify the relevant moral principles and sentiments. The duty to tell the truth, sympathy for the patient, loyalty in the physician–patient relationship, and a duty to do no harm were all relevant in the preceding case about the physicians. Our relationships with the people involved and our individual temperaments and circumstances all affect how much weight we give to each of the conflicting moral values.

List Possible Courses of Action   Once the first two steps are complete, begin listing possible alternative courses of action. This is a time to brainstorm. List any possible actions that come to mind. Some ideas that may seem silly at first might work well in combination with another.

Devise a Plan of Action   Since none of the solutions will be completely satisfactory, the proposed course of action needs to be examined to determine which actions or combination of actions takes into account the greatest number of important moral concerns. Highlight the courses of action that seem the best, and delete the others. Your final plan of action can include a combination of some of the alternative courses of action, just in case your first plan of action doesn't work.

Carry Out the Plan of Action   Finally, as with any type of moral reasoning, you must be motivated to put the chosen plan of action into effect. Even the best-thought-out plan is useless if it's not carried out. Moral reasoning that is unrelated to action or praxis, as we have already noted, becomes a mere academic exercise.

Exercises

1. Give some examples of moral dilemmas in your life. Since starting this course and thinking about morality, do you now see some situations as moral dilemmas that you did not see as dilemmas before? Discuss.

2. Think of a time in your life when a decision you made, or failed to make, resulted in a moral tragedy. How might you have avoided that moral tragedy? How might knowing how to break down and construct arguments have been helpful to you?

3. Choose one or more of the following dilemmas and resolve it, using the method outlined in the previous section. Each of these moral dilemmas is based on a real-life case.

   a. On May 19, 1994, the yacht *Mignonette* sailed from England for Sydney, Australia, where it was to be delivered to its new owner. There were four persons aboard: Dudley, the captain; Stephens, the mate; Brooks, a seaman; and Parker, a seventeen-year-old cabin boy and apprentice seaman. The yacht capsized in the South Atlantic during a storm, but the crew managed to put out in a 13-foot lifeboat. They drifted for twenty days in the open boat. During this time, they had no fresh water except rainwater and, for the last twelve days, no food. They were weak and facing starvation. The captain called them together to make a decision about their fate. What should they do?

   b. Prosenjit Poddar, a student at the University of California in Berkeley, fell in love with a fellow student, Tatiana Tarasoff, whom he met at folk dancing classes. When Tatiana rejected him, he fell into a deep depression. He decided to seek treatment at the Cowell Memorial Hospital, which was affiliated with the university, after the depression began to interfere with his health and his studies. During his course of treatment, he confided to a hospital psychologist, Dr. Lawrence Moore, that he was going to kill a girl after she returned from spending the summer in Brazil. Although he didn't name the girl, it was clear that he was referring to Tatiana. What should Dr. Moore do?

   c. You live in a climate that is cold and hostile. Every fall and spring you need to move camp to find enough food. Winter is coming, and it is time to move camp again and head south with your family. Your family consists of your spouse, your three children (ages six to twelve), and your aged father. Your father, who was once a proud seal hunter, is now blind and in poor health. The journey would be very hard on him, and it is possible he would not survive it. Also, he would slow down the progress of the group, and it is very likely that you would not be able to reach your winter camp in time to avoid the first winter storms and starvation. What should you do?

*d. You are answering a hotline for the local Women's Resource Center, as part of a community service project required of all psychology majors. An eighteen-year-old high school junior calls and asks if she can get into a shelter. She tells you that she has run away from home because she is afraid her father will beat her when he finds out about her poor grades. She agrees to give you her name and permission to call her father and tell him that she is okay, as long as you promise not to tell her father where she is. As it happens, her father is head of the psychology department at your university, and you need a recommendation from him to get into graduate school. What should you do?

Would your solution be any different if the girl's father were also chairman of the local United Way, which provides most of the funding for the Women's Resource Center?

e. A homeless person comes up to you on the street and asks you for money. What should you do?

*4. Choose an unresolved moral dilemma from your own personal life or from your community service. Using the method outlined in this chapter, find a solution to your dilemma. Carry out your proposed solution. Report on the results of your decision.

A Final Word

Between us and the universe there are no "rules of the game." The important thing is that our judgments should be right, not that they should observe a logical etiquette.

—WILLIAM JAMES (1842–1910)

We should avoid the use of fallacies and rhetoric. However, it is important to remember that logic or moral reasoning is a tool, rather than an end in itself. Moral reasoning is only one of the components of moral development. Moral sentiments like sympathy and intuitive truths are also important for ethical decision-making. Indeed, just as a person who is deficient in moral reasoning can make decisions that they later come to regret, so too can people who are rational but lack sympathy inadvertently behave in cruel and unfeeling ways.

Summary

1. The thinking process used in moral philosophy can be divided into three levels. The first level is *experience*. The second level involves *interpretation* of these experiences. These interpretations or worldviews can be based on either opinion or fact or a combination of the two. The third level of the thinking process is **analysis** of the interpretations. Analysis includes logical

reasoning as well as examination of these interpretations in light of moral intuitions and sentiments, consciousness-raising, and collective insights.

2. Sheila Mullett outlines three dimensions in the process of ethical analysis. The first is the development of **moral sensitivity** through collective consciousness-raising. The second dimension is **ontological shock,** or awareness of the pain and injustice in the world. The third dimension is **praxis,** or informed social action.

3. A **paradigm** is an overall way of looking at and explaining a phenomenon in a particular discipline, such as science or ethics. *Paradigm shifts* occur when enough people disagree with a prevailing or traditional paradigm to get it overthrown.

4. **Resistance** is a type of immature defense mechanism that acts as a barrier to critical analysis of our interpretations of the world.

5. *Ignorance, avoidance,* anger, conformity, and the use of clichés or distractions are all examples of resistance, or immature defense mechanisms.

6. **Doublethink** involves simultaneously holding two contradictory views and believing both to be true.

7. A **moral tragedy** occurs when we fail to take appropriate moral action or when we make a moral decision that we later come to regret.

8. An **argument** is made up of propositions. **Propositions** are statements that express a complete thought. They can be either true or false. The **conclusion** in an argument is a proposition that is supported by one or more propositions known as **premises.**

9. In an argument, we move from the premises to the conclusion by the use of *inference.*

10. *Premise indicators* are words such as "because" and "since," that signal that a premise follows. *Conclusion indicators* are words such as "therefore" and "thus," that signal that a conclusion follows. Not all arguments contain indicators.

11. When *constructing arguments* in moral discourse, we first create a list of premises and from there move to our conclusion.

12. **Rhetoric** is a type of pseudo-argument in which people begin with a position and then use only statements that support their particular position.

13. A **fallacy** is a type of argument that is psychologically persuasive but incorrect. Many different types of fallacies can occur within a moral argument.

14. The fallacy of **equivocation** occurs when an ambiguous term shifts meaning during the argument.

15. **Appeal to force** occurs when a person uses or threatens to use force to get another person to accept their conclusion.

16. With the **abusive fallacy,** instead of addressing the conclusion of someone's argument, we turn and attack their character instead.

17. A **circumstantial fallacy** occurs when it is argued that someone should accept a particular conclusion because of their special circumstances such as lifestyle, ethnic group, gender, or religion.

18. **Appeal to inappropriate authority** involves using the testimony of someone who is an expert or authority in another field than the one under discussion.

19. **Popular appeal** occurs when someone appeals to the opinion of the majority or the opinion of the elite to gain support for his or her conclusion.

20. **Hasty generalization** occurs when only unusual or atypical cases are used to support a conclusion. This fallacy is often found at the root of prejudice and *stereotypes.*

21. The **fallacy of accident** occurs when a person applies a good rule to an exceptional case where the circumstances render the rule inappropriate.

22. In the **fallacy of ignorance**, it is argued that a conclusion is true simply because no one can prove it is false or that a conclusion is false because no one has proved it is true.

23. In **begging the question,** the conclusion and premise are rewordings of each other.

24. An **irrelevant conclusion** occurs when the premises of an argument are directed at a conclusion other than the stated one.

25. A person commits the **naturalistic fallacy** in going from what *is* to a conclusion about what *ought* to be.

26. An **appeal to tradition** occurs when it is concluded that a particular practice or worldview is right simply because it is a custom or tradition.

27. A **moral dilemma** is a situation with conflicting moral values. In resolving a moral dilemma, we should (1) describe the facts, (2) list the relevant moral principles and sentiments, (3) make a list of possible courses of action, (4) come up with a plan of action, and (5) carry out the chosen plan of action.

28. *Logic* or *moral reasoning* is a tool and only one aspect of morality.

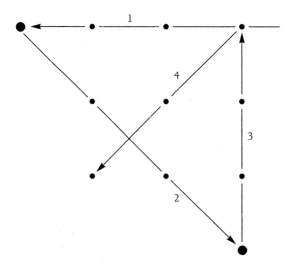

Solution to Exercise on Page 45.

SECTION II

Ethical
Relativism

Except for those rare individuals who have led a completely cloistered life, we have all experienced moral disagreement in some form or another, whether on a personal or a cultural level. You may believe in abortion rights; your best friend may be pro-life. The majority of people in the United States are in favor of capital punishment, yet capital punishment is considered immoral in just about every other Western nation. In some cultures, beating one's spouse is considered morally repugnant and cowardly; in others it may actually be expected under certain circumstances, such as punishment for adultery. Why the disagreement? Who is right and who is wrong?

Our inquiry will begin with a look at *ethical relativism*. According to ethical relativists, ethical values are created by, or are relative to, the people who hold the beliefs. Humans, either individually or collectively, are the ultimate judges of right and wrong. Ethical subjectivism states that morality is simply the expression of individual opinions. Cultural relativism, on the other hand, claims that societal norms, rather than the opinions of isolated individuals, form the basis of morality.

Egoism is sometimes included under the rubric of ethical subjectivism. Like ethical subjectivism, egoism looks to the individual for standards of right and wrong; however, ethical subjectivism asks what the individual desires or approves of, while egoism asks what will most benefit the individual. Because egoism subscribes to self-benefit as a universal moral principle, this theory will be discussed in the section on universal moral theories.

Some people argue that morality is grounded in or relative to religion. *Divine command* theorists, for example, argue that an act is moral because God commands it. *Natural law* ethicists, on the other hand, maintain that God commands something because it is right. Both of these theories have major implications for the nature of God and the nature of moral obligations.

Moral theories do not exist in isolation. Each of these theories has broad implications, not only for how we define morality, but for how we define moral community and, consequently, how we treat each other.

As people develop morally, they tend to expand their moral community. The process of moving from a concept of moral community that includes only oneself to one that includes all humans is gradual and proceeds in stages. Each stage entails examining and rejecting the reasoning of the previous stage. Before moving on to universalist theories, we will look at theories of moral development. The study of moral development not only enhances our *own* moral development; it also helps us to place the various types of ethical theory and our own style of moral decision-making in context.

The relativist theories contain several weaknesses and logical inconsistencies. This does not mean, though, that the study of ethical relativism is pointless or going nowhere. Discovery and exploration flourishes given the freedom to engage in speculation.

For example, in the sciences, speculation tends to run wild in astrophysics—one of the branches of science that has currently gone through a paradigm shift, moving from the old Newtonian model of the universe to one that incorporates both the theory of relativity and chaos theory. As such, astrophysics is still relatively flexible and open to new ideas. Even though most theories in astronomy are eventually found to be false or unworkable (in many cases by the very people who proposed them in the first place), it is still one of the most exciting and most rapidly advancing fields in science. Even theories that are eventually discarded usually contain a seed of truth that can be salvaged. Science often makes the greatest progress by discarding an inadequate theory and replacing it with one that overcomes its predecessor's weaknesses. The same is true in the study of ethics.

CHAPTER 3

Ethical Subjectivism
Morality Is Just a Matter
of Personal Feeling

What I feel is right is right. What I feel is wrong is wrong.
—JEAN-JACQUES ROUSSEAU

Morality is a private choice.
—CRAIG PRICE (convicted serial killer)

There is one thing a professor can be absolutely certain of:
almost every student entering the university believes, or says
he believes, that truth is relative . . .
—ALLAN BLOOM, *The Closing of the American Mind*

What Is Ethical Subjectivism?

Ethical subjectivism is perhaps the weakest of the moral theories that we will study in this text. Despite its many weaknesses and inconsistencies, however, many people believe, or claim to believe, in this theory. Many, if not most, college students say they believe that morality is relative.[1] For this reason, it is important that we study ethical subjectivism to analyze its weaknesses—and its strengths.

Ethical subjectivism makes the claim that people can never be mistaken about what is morally right or wrong, because there are no objective or universal moral standards or truths; instead, there are only opinions. An **opinion** expresses what a person believes. It does not have to be backed up by reasons or facts. What is right or wrong for one particular individual is simply a matter of personal taste, rather like our preference for particular foods or hairstyles. What is right for you may be wrong for another, depending on each of your respective feelings or opinions. I may like broccoli; you might think it is quite disgusting. You may like wearing your hair long; I find long hair does not suit me and, hence, is wrong for me.

Do not confuse ethical subjectivism with the obviously true and therefore trivial statement that "whatever a person believes is right for him or her is what that person believes is right for him or her." Subjectivism goes beyond this by claiming that sincerely believing or feeling that something is right *makes* it right (or true) for that person.

Referring back to the analogy of the blind men and the elephant, an ethical subjectivist could be compared to a person who notices that everyone seems to be coming up with a different description of the elephant. Hearing these apparently incompatible descriptions, the ethical subjectivist concludes that there is no such animal as an elephant. The "elephant," instead, is simply a creation of each person's imagination or feelings. "Elephant" is thus whatever you believe it to be—a winnowing basket, a granary, a post, a plow pole, or perhaps a column. Or maybe you missed the elephant completely and are still wandering around looking for it; in this case, you may conclude like the emotivist that any concept of elephant at all is pure illusion.

Now just as an "elephantness subjectivist" might argue that there are no objective standards by which to judge the various descriptions of the elephant, so too do ethical subjectivists argue that there are no absolute standards by which to judge a person's moral preferences. If a person sincerely believes something to be morally correct for him or her, then this in itself causes it to be morally true.

For example, no one could rightfully accuse Louisiana state senator David Duke of being insincere about his opinions on morality. As a defender of the Nazi ideology, Duke has expressed great admiration for Nazi war criminals Rudolf Hess and Dr. Josef Mengele. The latter, to name just one of his many atrocities, performed experiments on twins at Auschwitz. As a member of the Ku Klux Klan (KKK), Duke also believes that blacks have "inherited tendencies . . . to act in anti-social ways." It is irrelevant that he cannot support this assumption. What is important to an ethical subjectivist is simply that he or she personally believes something to be true. Political analyst George Will writes that, as a true believer, "his [Duke's] reputation is supposedly redeemed, at least a little bit, by 'sincerity,' considered inherently virtuous in an age so committed to subjectivism that it firmly believes only in believing."[2]

The great majority of moral philosophers disagree with ethical subjectivism. These philosophers maintain that there are fundamental moral standards by which we can judge people like David Duke. Philosopher Renford Bambrough (b. 1926), for example, claims that almost all of us would agree that it would be immoral to perform a painful operation on a small child without an anesthetic, because we intuitively know that torturing children is wrong. There is no need to prove to someone that torturing children is wrong; it is already self-evident.

Now, an ethical subjectivist would disagree with Bambrough's conclusion. If Dr. Josef Mengele felt good about seeing Jewish children in extreme pain, operating without an anesthetic would then be the morally correct action for him and for other surgeons with similar feelings. Similarly, persecuting Jews and blacks is the morally correct action for Duke, simply because he believes it is right. In fact, if we want to carry ethical subjectivism to its logical conclusion, it may even be immoral for Duke to *refrain* from doing so.

The statements "it is good to torture children" and "it is right to persecute Jews and blacks" are no different to ethical subjectivists than statements such as "I enjoy walking on the beach." Therefore, it makes no more sense to use reason to convince someone who feels that it is right to torture children that he does *not* actually enjoy torturing children than it does to try to convince our beachcomber that she does not enjoy walking on the beach.

Of course, ethical subjectivists may instead have a desire or preference for preventing people from torturing children or persecuting Jews and blacks. But to them this preference is not backed by any objective moral standards that they can expect the torturer or KKK member to accept. Personal tastes or feelings are the only standard. If it feels right, do it. There are thus no universal moral truths, only individual moral truths based on each person's own opinion and feelings.

Exercises

1. Since 1995, more than three hundred African-American churches in the United States have been destroyed by fire. According to a federal investigation, most of the arsons are the result of hate crimes. Is the burning of these churches morally acceptable, and perhaps morally required, if the arsonist sincerely believes that African Americans are inferior and have no right to live in this country as free people? Support your answer. Is your answer consistent with ethical subjectivism?

2. Do you agree with Bambrough that there are moral truths that do not require proof? Do we intuitively know that it is wrong to torture children? that pain is bad and pleasure good? that all humans are created equal? Are there any other self-evident moral truths? If these moral truths are self-evident, how would you respond to someone who believes that it is morally acceptable to torture children or to treat other humans as morally inferior?

3. Khalil Sumpter, a sophomore at Thomas Jefferson High School in Brooklyn, New York, was afraid that two other students were planning to beat him up. These two students, Ian Moore, a senior, and Tyrone Sinkler, a junior, had had a falling-out with Khalil that had escalated into picking on Khalil and making threats against him. So, Khalil brought a .38 caliber pistol to school one morning, and he shot and killed both Ian and Tyrone at point-blank range in the school hallway.[3]

   Was this shooting morally justified? Why or why not? Support your answer. How did Khalil's personal feelings regarding the morality of the killing influence your decision? Would it have made a difference if Khalil had shot Ian and Tyrone simply because he felt like it or because he didn't like the way they dressed? If you think it would make a difference, try to explain why. What if Khalil later came to believe that what he had done was wrong? Would this have any effect on your decision regarding whether the shooting was morally justified? How might an ethical subjectivist respond to these questions?

4. Make a list of general guidelines that you use to make moral decisions, including those you used to determine the morality of Khalil Sumpter's actions in the previous exercise. Where did you get these guidelines? How relevant were your private and personal feelings in coming up with these guidelines?

What Ethical Subjectivism Is Not

What we mainly need to notice here is that this exaltation of individual freedom apparently is itself a moral judgement, and that the arguments supporting it are moral arguments.
—MARY MIDGLEY, *Can't We Make Moral Judgements?* (1993), p. 17

Ethical subjectivism is a relatively straightforward theory, but despite its simplicity, it is often confused with other positions—a confusion that may account for its popularity among some people.

Many people confuse ethical subjectivism with an ethics of tolerance and respect for others' lifestyles—an ethics that is often summed up by the phrase "live and let live." However, ethical subjectivism does not necessarily entail tolerance. If a person, such as a Nazi or a member of the Ku Klux Klan, does not want to be tolerant of others, then this person has no moral obligation to tolerate others' opinions—or their existence, for that matter.

> Tolerance is good for all or it is good for none.
>
> —EDMUND BURKE, in a speech (1773)

Tolerance is a universal moral principle. The statement "live and let live" implies a universal duty to respect others, regardless of how we personally feel toward them, and a duty not to harm them either directly or by interfering with their rights to pursue their own interests. According to ethical subjectivism, though, universal moral duties do not exist. If an ethical subjectivist does not feel that others are worthy of respect or simply dislikes them, then that person doesn't have to respect them or to refrain from harming them.

Some people confuse ethical subjectivism with the obviously true observation that individuals *do* hold different views about what is morally right and morally wrong. In the presence of moral disagreement, when asked if a particular person is right, some people will reply: "Well, they believe they are right." When people say this, they are changing the topic from what a person *ought* to do to what a person believes *is* the case—thus committing the fallacy of irrelevant conclusion. Ethical subjectivism is a moral theory and it is prescriptive—that is, it is about what a person *ought* to do. The statement that a person believes something to be right, on the other hand, is descriptive. Ethical subjectivism, however, goes beyond the merely descriptive by claiming that sincerely believing or feeling that something is right *makes* it right (or true) for that person. By doing this, ethical subjectivism fails to recognize the distinction between descriptive and prescriptive statements.

Moral Uncertainty

Ethical subjectivism is not the same as moral uncertainty. Occasionally, people seem to retreat into a position of ethical subjectivism when they are confronted with a moral dilemma—a situation where there seems to be no clearly right or wrong answer. For example, a friend may tell you that she saw the boyfriend of one of your mutual friends holding hands with another woman in a restaurant. What should she do? "Well," you reply, "there seems to be no clearly right answer to this." So, you may advise your friend: "In this situation, do what you feel is right." But saying this does not necessarily mean that morality is relative. Rather, we are most likely to give this advice when we trust someone to make a morally acceptable decision. However, if your friend was wielding a gun and was on the verge of killing the seemingly unfaithful boyfriend, you probably would not tell her to do whatever feels right for her.

In other words, don't confuse trusting someone's moral judgment in a particular situation with ethical subjectivism. It is also logically inconsistent to claim that morality is a matter of opinion in one case but not in another. If all moral values are simply a matter of individual preference, as the ethical subjectivist claims, then morality is relative in *all* situations, not just for moral dilemmas.

We are sometimes uncertain, to be sure, but this does not imply that morality is simply a matter of opinion. Disagreement about moral values, in itself, does not imply that objective moral truths do not exist. Some astronomers believe that there is a planet beyond Pluto; other astronomers say that there is no planet beyond Pluto. However, the fact that these people disagree about the existence of a planet does not mean that *both* astronomers are correct in their claims. Similarly, the existence of disagreement about the morality of torturing children does not mean that both positions are morally correct.

Some people also confuse ethical subjectivism with the metaphysical position that individuals are ultimately responsible for their own moral decisions; however, the latter position is about free will. An ethical subjectivist does not necessarily believe that humans have free will, simply that a person's feelings and opinions are the source of moral truth. Indeed, moral responsibility, in terms of assigning moral blame or praise, becomes a moot issue with ethical subjectivists, because there are no objective standards against which to measure the morality of a person's actions; ethical subjectivism therefore precludes passing judgment on other people's or even on our own actions.

Ethical subjectivism is also sometimes mistaken for ethical skepticism or emotivism. There are, however, important differences between these three theories. Both ethical skepticism and emotivism deny knowledge of moral truth. Ethical subjectivism, on the other hand, claims that there are moral truths, but that these vary from person to person.

Ethical Skepticism

Ethical skepticism, rather than denying the existence of universal moral principles, states that it is difficult, if not impossible, to know whether moral truths exist or what these truths are: Maybe there *are* universal moral standards, maybe not; we just don't know. Agnosticism, for example, is a type of religious skepticism. An agnostic believes that we have no way of knowing, at least in our present limited human condition, whether or not God really exists. This uncertainty, however, does not imply that God does *not* exist; the most we can say is that we just do not know. Similarly, an ethical skeptic maintains that the existence of moral truths canot be proved. Ethical subjectivism, on the other hand, claims that universal moral truths do not exist but that moral truths *do exist* for each individual.

Adopting an attitude of skepticism as part of our method of inquiry provides a good starting point for developing a theory of moral knowledge. By calling into doubt prior interpretations regarding the existence and nature of moral truth, we can proceed to analyze these interpretations with a more open mind and, presumably, develop a more unbiased theory. Ethical skepticism, however, makes skepticism the end point of the search rather than a method of inquiry. In doing so, it—like ethical subjectivism—closes off further inquiry into the nature of universal moral standards.

Emotivism

Emotivism goes beyond the uncertainty of ethical skepticism by stating that there are no moral truths. Because we cannot quantify and examine moral

TABLE 3.1 Summary of the Three Theories

	ETHICAL SKEPTICISM	EMOTIVISM	ETHICAL SUBJECTIVISM
Premises	People disagree about what is morally right and wrong.	People disagree about what is morally right and wrong.	People disagree about what is morally right and wrong.
	People do not agree on a set of objective standards for resolving moral differences.	People do not agree on a set of objective standards for resolving moral differences.	People do not agree on a set of objective standards for resolving moral differences.
	There is no convincing evidence that such moral standards exist.	There is no convincing evidence that such moral standards exist.	There is no convincing evidence that such moral standards exist.
		All moral statements are opinions or expressions of a person's feelings.	All moral statements are opinions or expressions of a person's feelings.
		Opinions are neither true nor false.	Moral truths exist.
			Moral truths are not based on universal standards.
Conclusions	*Therefore,* we cannot know with certainty whether or not objective moral standards exist.	*Therefore:* All moral statements are meaningless.	*Therefore:* Individual feelings must provide the standard of moral truth.

statements like we can examine scientific statements, emotivists conclude that there are no moral truths, only moral feelings or opinions. Like emotivism, ethical subjectivism also claims that morality is a matter of personal opinion; however, unlike emotivism (which denies the existence of moral facts), ethical subjectivism claims that there *are* moral facts or truths and that these moral facts are based on each individual's feelings about a particular action or group of people. According to ethical subjectivism, feeling or believing that something is right *makes* it right for the person who is having those feelings.

Exercises

1. Mohandas Gandhi once wrote: "The golden rule of conduct, therefore, is mutual tolerance, seeing that we will never all think alike and we shall see Truth in fragments and from different angles of vision. Conscience is not the same thing for all. Whilst there, it is a good guide for individual conduct, imposition of that conduct upon all will be an insufferable interference with everybody's freedom of conscience."[4]

   How would an ethical subjectivist respond to Gandhi's words? Is Gandhi arguing from a position of ethical subjectivism or ethical objectivism? Support your answer.

2. A *New York Times* article published in 1986 by college president Norman Lamm expresses concern that today's generation of college students are being permitted, in the name of scientific objectivity and value neutrality, ". . . to grow up as ethical illiterates and moral idiots, unprepared to cope with ordinary life experiences." Lamm argues that, instead of being taught how to make effective moral judgments, students are being told that morality is all relative or a matter of personal opinion. According to Lamm, "a counsel of despair," which is often "impressed on students under the guise of tolerance," is taking its toll on our young people."[5] Do you agree with the author? Explain why or why not.

3. Ethical skepticism, emotivism, and ethical subjectivism each share some common premises, but they all arrive at different conclusions about the existence and nature of moral truths.

   Discuss the strengths and weaknesses of each of these three arguments. Are any of the premises questionable or weak? If so, which ones and why? Are there any premises that you would add? Do fallacies exist in any of the arguments? If so, what are they?

*4. If you are doing or have done community service, what were your reasons for doing it? What do you do when you do not feel like going to your site? Do you have a moral obligation to not turn up on those days? Discuss your answer in light of the theory of ethical subjectivism.

Jean-Jacques Rousseau: The Roots of Ethical Subjectivism in Romantic Sentimentalism

Nature made man happy and good, and society deprives him and makes him miserable.
—JEAN-JACQUES ROUSSEAU, *Emile* (1762), p. 253

Ethical subjectivism is, for the most part, a Western phenomenon and an outgrowth of the romantic sentimentalism that thrived from the late eighteenth through the mid-nineteenth century. Romantic sentimentalism, which em-

Jean-Jacques Rousseau (1712–78), Swiss philosopher. A romantic sentimentalist and ethical subjectivist, Rousseau exalted feeling over reason. He believed that we can discover goodness by retreating to pure inner feelings.

phasizes the inner person, is based upon the assumption that humans are by nature good. Unlike Enlightenment philosophers who regarded reason as the path to truth, romantic sentimentalists such as philosopher Jean-Jacques Rousseau believed in the "law of the heart." According to the law of the heart, we can discover true goodness by retreating to pure inner feelings. Only in this radical subjectivism does true moral goodness abide.

Jean-Jacques Rousseau (1712–78) was born in Geneva, Switzerland. His mother died when he was an infant. Rousseau wrote regarding his birth, "I was born weakly and sick. I cost my mother her life, and my birth was the first of my misfortunes."[6] His father, an eccentric watchmaker, cared for him sporadically over the next ten years. Most of his care was provided by an aunt whom Rousseau described as "an amiable and sensible woman." His father taught him how to read, but he did not teach his son much about social conventions, and the boy grew up to be undisciplined and quarrelsome.

When Rousseau was ten, his father wounded a man in a duel, and, fearful of being arrested, he fled Geneva, leaving his family behind. Rousseau was placed in the home of a kindly local pastor. Despite these setbacks, Rousseau recalled his childhood as one of idyllic innocence, free of societal restraints. This recollection had a profound influence on the development of his moral philosophy; however, his paradise came to an end when he was apprenticed out to a violent and boorish engraver.

At the age of sixteen, Rousseau ran away from the engraver and took up the life of a vagabond before settling in Paris at the age of twenty-nine. Here, he kept house with an illiterate washerwoman, Therese Lavasseus, although they did not marry until almost thirty years later. Together, they had five illegitimate children, all of whom were sent to foundling homes. In Paris, Rousseau entered the society of the Enlightenment thinkers. As a sentimentalist,

Rousseau had frequent and sometimes bitter disagreements with them. In 1749, Rousseau wrote a prizewinning essay that catapulted him into fame. *Emile,* his treatise on education, was published in 1761, but because of its negative depiction of society and the establishment, *Emile* was condemned by the Paris Parliament in 1762, and Rousseau was forced to flee France. He eventually returned to Paris, where he died in 1778.

Rousseau was a highly emotional and sensitive person, who believed in the natural goodness of people. Rousseau also believed that virtue and society stand in opposition. In his book *Emile,* Rousseau argued that the negative influence of society could be remedied by early education. Education should be mainly concerned with removing the obstacles to a child's natural development and innate goodness. Feelings alone, Rousseau argued, not society or abstract principles, inform us of what is right and wrong. Society forces upon us masks of hypocrisy and deceit. The purpose of moral education, therefore, is not to train people to fit into society; rather, it is to help us to remove these socially imposed masks to reveal the authentic openness and innocence that is our true essence.

Romantic Sentimentalism

Romantic sentimentalism is currently popular among some child psychologists and educators. Penelope Leach, for example, in her best-selling book *Your Baby and Child* (1989), advises parents to be "child-centered" so that the child's natural creativity and impulses can be expressed without being stifled by too much discipline.[7] According to romantic sentimentalists, we should try to understand and encourage children in whatever they are doing, rather than discipline them or attempt to guide their behavior.

In more formal ethics education, romantic sentimentalism usually takes the form of the "values clarification" or "value-neutral" approach, where students are encouraged to express their opinions without fear of censorship or judgment. Values are considered to be something one clarifies rather than discovers. Moral truths are based on inner feelings, rather than on a shared objective reality. Any opinion is just as valid as any other.

Unfortunately, though, this popular approach to moral education has been shown to have no effect on a student's actual moral development and, in fact, can even retard their development. This approach may have failed partly because incorporating the "law of the heart" into a moral theory involves a contradiction. Like Rousseau, romantic sentimentalists wish, and even expect, others to share their sentiments. Rousseau seemed to believe that, with the proper upbringing, everyone will share the same moral sentiments, including sympathy, compassion, generosity, and forgiveness. This expectation involves doublethink on the part of ethical subjectivists, however. Given the obviously true observation that people do have different opinions about right and wrong, who are we to say that the feelings of those who disagree with us,

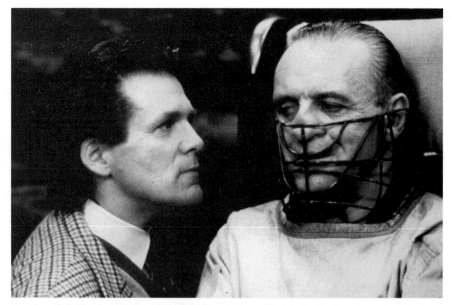

Dr. Hannibal "the Cannibal" Lector (played by Anthony Hopkins) with the prison psychologist in the 1991 movie The Silence of the Lambs. *As a psychopath, Hannibal Lector exemplifies the ethical subjectivist—a person who listens only to his or her inner feelings without any regard for social norms.*

even if they are influenced by social values, are any less valid for them than our feelings are for us?

Ethical subjectivism, by its very definition, cannot provide or even acknowledge universal moral standards, even those based on so-called natural moral sentiments, because it denies that universal moral standards exist. Instead, romantic ethical subjectivists are isolated in their own inner feelings—they are torn between the desire to see certain sentiments universalized and the contradiction involved in expecting people to acknowledge universal moral values.

Besides the logical contradiction in the moral theory of romantic sentimentalists, their claim that society corrupts us is surely an oversimplification of the presence of moral evil. The belief that we are all good by nature but corrupted by society is blatantly contradicted by the phenomenon of the psychopathic or antisocial personality.[8]

Ironically, the psychopath is perhaps the person who is most like Rousseau's "natural" person, as opposed to someone who has been oversocialized and corrupted by society. Psychopaths, also known as "moral idiots," seem oblivious to any attempts to indoctrinate them with social values. They have no concern for the social good or the welfare of others. Psychopaths are radically isolated, on a psychic level, from the rest of society; they listen only to their own "inner feelings" and have no desire that their feelings and beliefs be universalized as moral principles. Indeed, it is because of their consistent ethical subjectivism that psychopaths are so dangerous and socially disruptive. They were not *mis*-educated: Their lack of moral values or empathy for others, at least in the case of true psychopaths, seems to be unrelated to either their education or their upbringing. Of course, Rousseau, like Aristotle, could argue that psychopaths are not true humans, because they lack a soul or a conscience. But then, who among us is a true human, possessing an absolutely pure nature?

The Value of Romantic Sentimentalism

Despite some of the logical inconsistencies in the assumptions underlying romantic sentimentalism, the theory has much to offer the study of ethics. Its insistence on innate moral sentiments as the heart of morality, rather than abstract reasoning, provides a much-needed balance to the rationalism that dominates so much of Western ethics. Rousseau's idea that education should aim to nurture a person's natural moral development has also influenced theories of moral development.

On the other hand, Rousseau's overly optimistic view of human nature and his unsubstantiated assumption that human nature can be separated from society led him to neglect the importance of active interventions or ethics education to guide the unfolding of an individual's moral character. Rousseau's assumption that pure moral sentiments can exist outside of any social context also seems to be unrealistic. Indeed, this naive assumption caused him to overlook the power of social convention for shaping human behavior, even in very young children.

> Woman was made especially to please man . . . This is the law of nature. If woman is formed to please and to live in subjection, she must render herself agreeable to man instead of provoking his wrath; her strength lies in her charms.

Rousseau lambasted society as oppressive to the development of a virtuous character and denounced the education system as being too rigid and formal, but he did not bother to question the extent to which his own feelings and ideas about the different natures of men and women were culturally conditioned or whether they placed obstacles in the way of women's moral development. Rather than taking into consideration the influence of socialization on gender identity, Rousseau simply assumed that men and women have different natures. A boy's education, he claimed, should prepare him to be a member of society (in the best sense of the term). A girl's education, on the other hand, should be designed to prepare her to be an obedient wife and mother and to make "life easy and agreeable for men."[9]

Exercises

*1. Do you agree with Rousseau's premise that people are good by nature and that society corrupts us? Use examples from your own experience and your community service work to illustrate your answer.

2. Rousseau's beliefs about the different natures of males and females are shared, at least tacitly, by many contemporary teachers. These teachers believe they are right. Does this morally justify their preferential treatment of male students in certain areas that involve intelligence and reason, and female students in areas that involve feelings and social graces?

Mary Wollstonecraft: Critic of Rousseau's Ethical Subjectivism

For man and women, truth, if I understand the meaning of the word, must be the same.
—MARY WOLLSTONECRAFT, *A Vindication of the Rights of Woman* (1791)

English philosopher Mary Wollstonecraft (1759–97), one of the most promising philosophers of her time, wrote the *Vindication of the Rights of Woman* (1791) partly in response to Rousseau's belief that men and women are by nature different. Wollstonecraft was an avid opponent of ethical subjectivism and disagreed with Rousseau's exaltation of feeling and sentiment over reason. Like men, she argued, women's "first duty is to themselves as rational creatures." At that time, married women were not even recognized as a separate legal entity. Women could not enter a legal complaint or appear in court. Because of the prevailing belief that women lacked the capacity to reason, women were denied the educational opportunities to develop their intellectual potential.

Unlike Rousseau, who remembered much of his childhood as a period of idyllic innocence, Wollstonecraft came from a violent and troubled home. Born in 1759, she was the eldest daughter of a silk weaver, whose "violent temper and extravagant turn of mind," she wrote in a letter to a friend, "was the principle cause of my unhappiness and that of the rest of my family."[10] In 1778, she left home, presumably because it had become impossible for her to continue living at home.

Wollstonecraft later went to work for publisher James Johnson until 1792, when she left England to witness the French Revolution. After returning to England, she became part of a radical group of thinkers that included William Blake, Thomas Paine, William Wordsworth, and William Godwin. In 1797, Wollstonecraft married William Godwin. Godwin was a radical philosopher and writer, and he appreciated Wollstonecraft's intellect and ideas. Godwin later became her biographer.

Mary Wollstonecraft (1759–97), English philosopher, author, and feminist. Unlike Rousseau, Wollstonecraft believed that morality is based on reason rather than feeling. An advocate of equal rights for women, she also disagreed with Rousseau that morality is different for men and women because of their different natures.

Wollstonecraft argued that men and women are intellectual and moral equals. Because women's nature is essentially the same as men's, Wollstonecraft advocated coeducation, a radical concept that was ridiculed by the male thinkers of her time. Furthermore, she maintained that to claim that there are two different moral systems—one for men and one for women—is to make a mockery of the concept of virtue. "How can women be just or generous, when they are the slaves of injustice?" she asked.[11] Moral truths, such as human equality, must therefore be the same for everyone. Unless human equality is upheld as a moral principle, there can be no genuine relationships between men and women. Following is an excerpt from her book *A Vindication of the Rights of Woman* (1791):

> [I]t seems almost impertinent to illustrate truths [about the rights and duties of man] that appear so incontrovertible; yet such deeply rooted prejudices have clouded reason, and such spurious qualities have assumed the name of virtues, that it is necessary to pursue the course of reason as it has been perplexed and involved in error . . .
>
> Impressed by . . . the misery and disorder which pervaded society, and fatigued with jostling against artificial fools, Rousseau became enamoured of solitude . . . Raised on a false hypothesis his arguments in favour of a state of nature are plausible but unsound . . .
>
> It is the pestiferous purple which renders the progress of civilization a curse, and warps the understanding, til men of sensibility doubt whether the expanse of the intellect produces a greater portion of happiness or misery. But the nature of the

poison points out the antidote; and had Rousseau mounted one step higher in his investigation or could his eye have pierced through the foggy atmospheres, which he almost disdained to breathe, his active mind would have darted forward to contemplate the perfection of man in the establishment of true civilization, instead of taking his ferocious flight back to the night of sensual ignorance.

Wollstonecraft pointed out that romantic sentimentalism, with its focus on inner feelings at the expense of reason, provides an incomplete description of morality. Moral development does not thrive on the free expression of opinions or feelings, as Rousseau claimed, but rather seems to flourish when our ideas and worldviews are challenged rather than simply uncritically affirmed. Our feelings or sentiments are often good guides for making moral decisions, although they can sometimes lead us astray and actually contribute to bigotry and oppressive social structures. According to Wollstonecraft, because of this, our feelings and ideas about what is moral should also be held up to the light of reason.

Wollstonecraft died in childbirth at the age of thirty-eight. Her daughter, novelist Mary Wollstonecraft Shelley, was the author of the classic novel *Frankenstein.*

Exercises

1. In her book *The Vindication of the Rights of Woman,* Wollstonecraft argued that Rousseau's romantic sentimentalism leads to prejudice and clouds the mind. Morality, and moral education, must instead be based on reason and universal moral principles. Do you agree with Wollstonecraft? Support your position, using examples from your own life.

2. Relate Rousseau's and Wollstonecraft's theories of moral education to your own moral development. What events in your childhood had the greatest influence on your moral development? Were these times when you were left alone to spontaneously develop your own morality, or were these times when your views and feelings were challenged? Illustrate your answer, using examples. Given your own experience, what suggestions would you give parents and teachers regarding moral education?

The "Kitty Genovese Syndrome"

It is tempting to deny the existence of evil since denying it obviates the need to fight it.
—ALEXIS CARREL, *Reflections on Life*

Non-resistance to evil which takes the form of paying no attention to it is a way of promoting it.
—JOHN DEWEY, *Human Nature and Conduct* (1922)

Kitty Genovese was attacked by a man with a knife in this alley outside of her apartment in Queens, New York, in 1964. Despite her cries for help, not one of the thirty-eight people who lived nearby and heard her screams called the police.

Ethical theories do not exist in abstraction. Ethical theories inform and motivate our real-life decisions and actions. They shape the way that we define ourselves, as well as our community and our ideas of community responsibility. Ethical subjectivism, however, by retreating into pure inner or subjective feelings, neglects to take into account the social context that gives moral sentiments their value in the first place. To remove morality from the social realm is to condone isolation and apathy in the face of others' pain.

Some social commentators believe that the prevalence of ethical subjectivism in our society may contribute to what has come to be known as the "Kitty Genovese syndrome." The *"Kitty Genovese syndrome"* is characterized by an attitude of moral indifference to another person's distress and cries for help.

In 1964, twenty-eight-year-old Kitty Genovese was murdered outside her New York apartment building. Her killer left twice when other people in the building turned on their lights. Yet, during the half hour that elapsed during the attack, none of Kitty's thirty-eight neighbors, who heard her repeated cries for help, even bothered to call the police. The third time the killer returned to the scene, he finished her off.

More recently, in August 1995, thirty-three-year-old Deletha Word jumped to her death from the Belle Isle Bridge in Detroit to escape her attacker—a nineteen-year-old man who savagely beat her after a fender bender. Dozens of spectators stood by and watched, some even cheering on the attacker. One man, who arrived at the scene just after Word had gone off the bridge, jumped into the river and tried, unsuccessfully, to save her. He later told a reporter that the crowd was "standing around like people taking an interest in sports."[12]

How would ethical subjectivists respond to these two preceding events? To be consistent, they would have to reply that, if the people in the crowds watching Genovese and Word being bludgeoned to death felt like simply standing around, then that was the right thing for them to do. Only personal feelings matter in ethical subjectivism. If Martell Welch, Word's attacker, felt that it was morally acceptable to beat another motorist to death for nicking a fender, then it was morally right, and perhaps even obligatory, for him to do so. As for the man who tried to save Word, of course this was the right thing for him to do, but it would have been the wrong thing for the others to do.

With ethical subjectivism, there are no objective values regarding helping others or refraining from harming or even killing others. There are only individual opinions or feelings on the issue. Beating someone to death may be wrong for you, but it may be right for me. Calling the police may be right for you, but cheering on the assailant or ignoring a dying person's cries for help might be morally right for me. After all, morality is just a matter of personal opinion.

Exercises

1. Do you agree with the ethical subjectivists that each person who witnessed or participated in the deaths of Kitty Genovese and Deletha Word did the morally correct thing for themselves? Or do you think that some of the people involved acted in a way that was morally blameworthy? If so, why? Is assigning moral blame in these cases compatible with being an ethical subjectivist? On an individual and societal level, what are some of the consequences of not assigning moral blame in cases like these?

2. Discuss a situation where people used ethical subjectivism to justify their failure to take action to prevent harm, or to justify actions that harmed you or others. How did you, or how could you, respond to their argument?

3. Discuss the following case studies. Discuss how you would respond to each of the people in the case studies. Relate your answers to how an ethical subjectivist might view these cases. How do your answers differ from those of an ethical subjectivist?

   a. JoAnne, a sophomore at State University, has just found out in the course of giving blood to the Red Cross that she is HIV positive—that is, in all likelihood she is infected with the AIDS virus. JoAnne is quite distraught, as a result of this news. She is currently somewhat interested in Doug, a classmate of hers. That evening, Doug tells JoAnne that his parents are out of town and invites her over to his house for the weekend. She has not told him the test results, nor does she intend to. JoAnne does not want to be alone tonight and would find spending the night with Doug greatly comforting. As an ethical subjectivist, JoAnne feels that this is morally acceptable for her. She tells you of her plan and asks you, an ethics student, what you think of it. How do you respond?

b. Jeff, who lives in your dormitory, is already selling drugs on campus but would like to expand his market. He has heard that drug use among children is increasing, and he would like to cash in on the market by selling cocaine to the children at a local elementary school. He doesn't particularly like children, and he also has no qualms about selling drugs to young children. He tells you of his plan. How do you respond?

*c. Chris is doing community service work at a nursing home. He started working there as part of a class requirement, but because Chris enjoys working with elderly people, he is considering continuing to volunteer there throughout the summer. How do you respond when Chris tells you this?

d. Some parents bear children specifically to use them to make kiddy porn films, a very profitable business. Does the parents' apparently sincere belief that this practice is morally acceptable (or at least so these parents claim) make this morally acceptable and perhaps even morally obligatory for them? Why or why not?

If you doubt the parents' sincerity that this practice is morally acceptable, on what grounds do you doubt them? Is your doubt regarding their sincerity, despite their claims to be sincere, consistent with ethical subjectivism?

Critique of Ethical Subjectivism

A system of morality which is based on relative emotional values is a mere illusion, a thoroughly vulgar conception which has nothing sound in it and nothing true.

—SOCRATES, quoted by Plato in the *Phaedo*, 68c

1. *Ethical subjectivism incorrectly assumes that moral disagreement necessarily implies that there are no universal moral standards.* According to ethical subjectivists, it makes no more sense to try to convince someone who enjoys torturing children that what they are doing is wrong than to try to convince a chocoholic that they don't really like chocolate.

But these two situations are not comparable. It does not make sense logically to try to convince a chocolate lover that they really hate chocolate, because love and hate, at least when it comes to food, are contradictory feelings. In contrast, most people *do* believe that it makes good sense to try to convince people that they ought not torture children, even though they may believe it is right to do so. Most people also believe that we can give good reasons for why people should not torture children. We might, for example, cite the principle of non-maleficence or respect for the rights of others. Or we could appeal to their sense of compassion. In each of these instances, we do this because we have the expectation that the person we are trying to convince acknowledges the same basic moral values that we do.

In fact, the majority of people who commit heinous acts, with the notable exception of psychopaths, justify their actions by referring to generally accepted moral principles and sentiments. For example, almost all child abusers agree that it is wrong to initiate sex with a child or to beat a child for no good reason. Rather than deny the existence of moral standards such as non-maleficence, liberty rights, and compassion for others, abusers will often justify their actions by claiming that the child seduced them or actually enjoyed the sexual encounter. A person who beats their children may justify it on the grounds that the children brought the beating upon themselves because of their "naughty" behavior. Some abusers even claim that they were beating a child for the good of the child, as a form of discipline.[13] Thus, what is often interpreted as disagreement about basic moral principles is instead disagreement about the application of these principles in particular situations.

2. *Ethical subjectivism is based on the incorrect assumption that we cannot be mistaken in our moral beliefs.* However, people often pass judgment on their own past feelings and on actions that were based upon those feelings. When our tastes change, such as our taste for a particular kind of food, we do not regard our former tastes as wrong—just different. As a child I disliked broccoli; now, it is one of my favorite foods. In contrast, though, when our moral views change, we do regard our former views as mistaken.

This is inconsistent with ethical subjectivism. According to ethical subjectivists, to claim upon further reflection that we were wrong for lying to a friend in the past is as absurd as claiming that we were mistaken about disliking broccoli as a child. Of course, ethical subjectivists might respond to this criticism by saying that a person who comes to regard a past action as wrong does not understand that morality is simply a matter of taste and, hence, is simply confused in labeling past actions as "wrong."

3. *We do pass judgment on our feelings and actions.* At times we judge that it would be immoral to act upon certain feelings or desires. We may feel a strong desire to punch out someone who annoys us, or ram into a motorist who has cut us off in traffic. Most of us, however, do not try to beat someone to death simply because they accidentally dented our fender. Instead, we refrain from doing so, even when we may have a powerful urge to strike out, and even though no more compelling feelings such as fear are restraining us,

because we realize that acting on these feelings is wrong. If morality is the same as feeling, then it makes no sense to restrain ourselves from acting on our feelings. To restrain ourselves only makes sense if we are using moral criteria or principles that are *independent of our feelings*.

4. *In real life, we regard acting on certain feelings and desires as immoral.* Although moral evaluation can take a person's feelings into account, for the most part we judge an action to be moral or immoral independently of the agent's feelings. The desire to hurt others solely for one's own pleasure and feeling disgust or hatred toward certain groups of people are not generally seen as morally justifying actions based on these feelings.

When we passed judgment on Hitler's actions, for example, we did not ask how he felt about killing Jews. Nor did we judge his actions to be moral because he personally believed that he was doing the right thing. Rather than consider members of the Ku Klux Klan, the Nazis, child molesters, and serial killers as highly moral people just because they acted on their deeply held inner feelings, we generally regard their actions as even more immoral and horrific precisely *because* they believed what they did was morally acceptable.

5. *Ethical subjectivism is disastrous for the weak and defenseless.* People's desires frequently clash. Feeling that something is right does not necessarily mean that we will have the power or opportunity to act upon that feeling. The strong are able to fulfill their desires at the expense of the weak, while those who lack power, such as children, often have no choice but to suppress their desires. Furthermore, if we accept ethical subjectivism, there is no such thing as a victim, because there is no universal moral principle that says we must respect other people's "right" to put their desires into action. Ethical subjectivism, rather than encouraging tolerance, denies the existence of universal moral values. Thus, slavery, rape, child abuse, and genocide can all be justified, using this theory.

6. *Ethical subjectivism can lead to social chaos and disintegration.* In the 1970s and early 1980s, many people thought that ethical subjectivism would liberate us from restrictive, "absolutist" moral principles. "Freedom," "choice," and "private" became the buzzwords in discussions of moral issues. But, rather than freeing up young people to live their lives as they see fit, ethical subjectivism can contribute to an atmosphere of despair and aimlessness. Simply advising people to act "authentically" is not very helpful. After all, wasn't Hitler being "authentic," in terms of being true to his feelings?

Almost all moral theories contain at least a grain of truth, but the problem with many theories arises when they mistake this grain of truth for the whole truth. Ethical subjectivists, for example, are correct in noting that morality begins with the individual experience and that these experiences are sometimes at variance with one another. Ethical subjectivists' belief in the basic goodness of human nature and that our sense of morality is innate may also contain more than just a grain of truth.

But moral experience and moral growth do not end with our limited individual experience. Nor are we as humans infallible in discerning the moral voice within us. There seem to be other voices, from both within and without, that compete with our conscience or sense of morality. For us to develop morally, our sense of what is right and wrong must be nurtured, as well as challenged, by our community. Like the blind men and the elephant, ethical subjectivism does not see beyond our private feelings. Rather than engaging people in dialogue to see whether there is a common thread to our experiences or, when put together, if the various descriptions form a more integrated picture, ethical subjectivists see us only as isolated individuals.

No one, with the possible exception of psychopaths, really lives as though ethical subjectivism is valid. Ethical subjectivism, rather than being a workable moral theory, amounts to little more than lazy thinking or a type of resistance: "If I don't question or pass judgment on anyone else's views, then my views won't be challenged either." Thus, ethical subjectivism can become a defense mechanism that people can use to avoid having to analyze or defend their worldviews.

> The humbug lies in pretending that both the world and our own lives are now—in this modern age—so well designed that neither we nor anybody else has any obligation to do what they don't wish to. The pretence is produced by a wholly admirable attempt at producing the reality—at making the world paradisal . . .
>
> What this means is that morality has not been put out of date in the simple way that has always looked so attractive—by making life so good that morals are not needed. Angels, it may reasonably be supposed, do not need a morality, because they never wish to do anything but what they ought to do. In such a situation, duty and obligation lose their meaning. But that situation is not ours.
>
> —MARY MIDGLEY, *Can't We Make Moral Judgements?* (1993), pp. 154–155

Ethical subjectivism, if taken seriously, is a dangerous theory. It not only isolates the individual but permits people to exploit and hurt others without ever having to justify their actions or stand in judgment. Romantic sentimentalism, which supports ethical subjectivism, is based on a sadly incorrect view of the absolute and unwavering goodness of human nature. Ethical subjectivism, as promoted by the romantic sentimentalists, seems to be a moral theory fit only for angels and saints.

Exercises

*1. Ethical subjectivism is more popular among people who are members of traditionally powerful socioeconomic groups and thus have the opportunity to act on their feelings and desires. How do the people you work with in your community service feel about this theory? Do they agree or disagree with it? What reasons do they give for agreeing or disagreeing with ethical subjectivism?

2. In his article "Student Relativism," Stephen Satris argues that the relativism of most college students is intended not as a philosophical theory but rather as an "invincible suit of armor" to "prevent or close off dialogue and thought." Do you agree with Satris? Why or why not? Relate your answer to the concept of resistance discussed in Chapter 2.

3. Convicted serial killer Craig Price, when asked if he thought he had done anything wrong, replied that he hadn't, because "[morality] is a private choice." How would you respond to Price?

Summary

1. **Ethical subjectivism** states that what is morally right and wrong is simply a matter of personal opinion. What may be right for you may be wrong for me, depending on our respective feelings.

2. An **opinion** is a statement that expresses how a person feels.

3. Ethical subjectivism is not an ethics of tolerance for individual differences. *Tolerance* is a universal moral principle, and ethical subjectivists reject the existence of universal moral principles.

4. Ethical subjectivism is not the same as observing that people do disagree on moral issues. The existence of disagreement, in itself, does not imply that there is no objective truth.

5. **Emotivism** states that all moral statements are meaningless and that there are no universal standards of moral truth; ethical subjectivism states that individual feelings provide the standards of moral truth.

6. **Ethical skepticism** states that we cannot know with certainty that there *are* objective moral truths; ethical subjectivism claims that there are no objective moral truths.

7. *Romantic sentimentalism* emphasizes the inner person and the innate goodness of people. *Jean-Jacques Rousseau's* ethical subjectivism was based on romantic sentimentalism.

8. The "values clarification" or "values neutral" approach in ethics education is based on the assumptions underlying romantic sentimentalism and ethical subjectivism.

9. *Mary Wollstonecraft* disagreed with Rousseau's romantic sentimentalism. She argued that reason is more important to morality than individual feelings and that there *are* universal moral principles.

10. The *"Kitty Genovese syndrome"* involves the failure of people to help another person in distress. Some people suggest that the popularity of ethical subjectivism in our society has contributed to the breakdown of concern for others.

11. Ethical subjectivism not only contains logical inconsistencies as a moral theory but also justifies domination of the weak by the strong and leads to the breakdown of community.

CHAPTER 4

Cultural Relativism
Is Morality Dependent on Culture?

*For if anyone, no matter who, were given the opportunity of
choosing from amongst all the nations of the world the set of
beliefs which he thought best, he would inevitably, after careful
consideration of their relative merits, choose that of his own
country. Everyone without exception believes his own native
customs . . . to be the best.*
  —HERODOTUS, *The Histories* (c. 500 B.C.E.)[1]

*We recognize that morality differs in every society, and is a
convenient term for socially approved habits.*
  —RUTH BENEDICT, "Anthropology and the Abnormal"
  (1933)

What Is Cultural Relativism?

The great majority of moral philosophers throughout the world reject cultural
relativism, although it has been a popular moral theory among nonphilosophers since antiquity. According to developmental psychologists, ninety percent of adults in the United States equate morality with cultural norms of
right and wrong.

Like ethical subjectivism, **cultural relativism** looks to people for standards of right and wrong. Subjectivists claim that individuals create their own
moral standards; cultural relativists argue that moral standards and values are
derived from groups of people or cultures. Public opinion, rather than private
opinion, determines what is right and wrong. There are no objective universal moral standards that hold true for all people in all cultures. Morality, instead, is regarded as nothing more than socially approved customs.

Cultural relativists point out that something regarded as morally wrong
in one culture may be morally praiseworthy in another culture. Head-
hunting, for example, flourished in certain cultures well into the twentieth
century and was even considered a courageous act.[2] In some cultures, a

young man could not marry until he had taken his first head. However, a young man in the United States who tried to impress his girlfriend's family by displaying his collection of shrunken heads would be quickly locked up and labelled not only morally deviant in the extreme but mentally ill as well.

The great diversity of marriage habits has also been used to illustrate differences in cultural values. Polygamy is morally acceptable in some African and Asian cultures. In Muslim cultures, the number of wives is limited to four. In other cultures, the limit is set only by the husband's ability to support a large household. For example, King Mtessa of Uganda is said to have had seven thousand wives! In our culture, polygamy is illegal; however, "serial polygamy," where marriages end in divorce and are followed by a new marriage, is now morally acceptable.

Cultural variations in norms also exist within different historic time frames. Like laws and fashions, cultures change over time. One hundred years ago, "serial polygamy" was not morally acceptable in North America; now it is. Polygamy used to be morally acceptable among the Mormons; now it is not. Two hundred years ago, slave ownership was morally acceptable and even a status symbol in some parts of the United States; now, slavery is considered highly immoral.

> Our researchers into Public Opinion are content
>
> That he held the proper opinions for the time of year;
>
> When there was peace, he was for peace; when there was war, he went.
>
> —WYSTAN AUDEN, *The Unknown Citizen*

According to cultural relativists, because morality is nothing more than custom, we have no grounds for judging the moral practices of another culture or another time. If two cultures disagree about what is morally right but there is no disagreement about the facts or definitions of key terms, then there is no rational means for continuing the discussion or reaching agreement. We have no grounds for passing judgment on or disagreeing with our own cultural values, because our culture is the source of our moral values. To know what is right or wrong, we need only ask what the norms and customs of our culture or society are at this point in history.

Cultural relativists do not argue merely that *some* moral values are relative to the culture. Rather, they maintain that *all* moral values are nothing more than cultural customs. Slavery *was* morally correct in the United States 150 years ago; anti-Semitism *was* the morally correct attitude for Germans 60 years ago.

Excusing

Cultural relativism is not the same as excusing certain cultural practices, such as slavery, on the grounds that the people of that culture sincerely believe that what they are doing is morally acceptable. *Excusing* entails granting an exemption or pardon from *wrongdoing*. A person or group of people can be excused for several reasons: Either they were not aware at the time that what they were doing was wrong; they were misinformed about the nature and consequences of their actions; they had no control over the situation; or they have made appropriate amends for their wrongdoing.

For example, cultures where head-hunting was practiced generally believed that the soul matter was concentrated in the head. By preserving or eating the brain of the enemy, the soul matter of their own group was increased and the power of the enemy proportionally weakened. Consequently, head-hunting was regarded as important to the survival of the culture. These cultures have since come to understand that this belief was mistaken. Thus, rather than condemn the headhunters for their past actions, we may *excuse* the behavior on the grounds that their actions were based on misinformation or incorrect beliefs.

Cultural relativists, in contrast, claim that these practices were actually morally right for the members of that culture. They would see no reason to excuse these behaviors, because the headhunters did nothing wrong in their view. And in the case of slavery, if anyone deserved to be excused, it would be the abolitionists, who acted against cultural values.

Tolerance of Cultural Diversity

Cultural relativism is not the same as tolerance of cultural diversity. Nowadays, making moral judgments is out of fashion. One often hears the admonishment not to be "judgmental" or "impose your values on others." Instead, we are advised to be tolerant of others' beliefs and value systems. In this nonjudgmental climate, cultural relativism is sometimes advocated on the grounds that it promotes tolerance and acceptance of cultural diversity.

To defend cultural relativism as a theory that champions tolerance and multicultural diversity, however, is to misinterpret the theory. By advocating tolerance, we acknowledge the existence of universal, transcultural moral standards. But, like ethical subjectivism, cultural relativism is committed to *denying* the existence of universal moral standards—including tolerance. Cultural relativists, however, cannot both deny the existence of universal moral standards and also defend the existence of a universal moral standard. To be consistent, cultural relativists can only say that tolerance is a norm valued by our culture. Because being tolerant is currently valued in our society, or at least among certain subcultures of our society, *we* as a society ought to be tolerant of people and cultures that hold different values. However, if another culture values intolerance, then according to cultural relativists,

Ku Klux Klan lynching, Indiana, 1930. The Ku Klux Klan was founded in the South in 1866 and officially disbanded in 1869. It was reorganized in 1915. By the 1920s the Ku Klux Klan had five million members and had expanded its reign of terror to the Northern states as well.

that is the moral value that members of that culture are morally bound to follow.

Tolerance and respect for the integrity of other cultures has not always been one of the moral norms in the United States. During the early and mid-nineteenth century, the doctrine of Manifest Destiny was used to justify the United States' expansionist policy and the takeover of lands belonging to Mexico and to Native Americans. Between 1845 and 1853, Mexico lost about one half of its territory to U.S. expansionism. "The right to our Manifest Destiny to overspread and to possess the whole continent," wrote a nineteenth-century journalist, "[is a right] which Providence has given us for the development of the great experiment of Liberty and federated self-government entrusted us."[3] Some groups opposed expansionism as immoral and racist, but these groups were small and found little support among the majority, who approved of expansionism and our right to occupy and annex the lightly populated land belonging to Mexico.

The increasing emphasis in this country on freedom of speech and non-critical tolerance of diversity since the 1970s has been accompanied by a concomitant growth in organizations such as the Ku Klux Klan. Indeed, some people believe that intolerance is once again becoming the norm in our culture and that we may be facing an "epidemic of hate." This increasing hatred is expressed in the popularity of white supremacist ideas, the rash of hate crimes, and the growing antagonism against Mexican immigrants, Asian Americans, Jews, Muslims, gay men, and lesbians.[4]

Some people will temporarily switch to principled moral reasoning when faced with a situation where cultural relativism does not seem to work—such as trying to make sense of the Holocaust or slavery in the United States. Or, if they disagree with their own culture's moral standards, they may temporarily become ethical subjectivists. However, we cannot claim that morality is ultimately derived from culture and simultaneously believe that it is also just a matter of personal opinion or that universal moral standards exist. To do so is to engage in *doublethink.*

Cultural Relativism Versus "American Values"

A cultural relativist may hold similar beliefs to those of who believe in universal, transcultural moral standards. For example, cultural relativists in the United States generally believe in human equality and universal human rights. However, the justifications for these beliefs differ from those of philosophers like Thomas Jefferson and John Locke. Jefferson and Locke rejected the cultural norms of their time that privileged members of the aristocracy.

In contrast, for most of us, beliefs in equality and universal human rights are based upon the view that these are "American values." As such, the concept of equal human rights is seen as a *creation of Western culture.* Some cultural relativists even go so far as to say that the development of the concept of equal human rights and dignity could occur *only* within the context of Western thinking. Jefferson and Locke, on the other hand, claimed that the moral principle of equal human rights is not a creation of one culture or of Western culture in general but is *self-evident to all humans,* whether they be Englishmen or Australian aborigines.

Exercises

1. Discuss some examples of moral values or practices, other than those already mentioned in the text, that differ from culture to culture. Do these differences necessarily reflect differences in basic moral standards?

2. Many colleges actively promote multiculturalism through their curriculum as well as their hiring and admission processes. Is this a desirable trend?

   Sometimes cultural norms come into conflict, such as those of Neo-Nazi students versus those of Jewish and African American students: or those of American women versus men from cultures where women are regarded as chattels. Should we just look the other way rather than pass judgment when a conflict erupts on campus? How would a cultural relativist answer this question? Are you satisfied with their answer? Explain with specific examples to support your answer.

3. Name some customs or ideals in our culture that reflect moral values. Name some customs or ideals that reflect nonmoral values. What criteria can we use to distinguish between these two types of values?

4. Make a list of some of the primary moral values in our culture. Now make a list of some of your own moral values. Are the two lists in agreement? If not, how might you explain the disagreement?

5. Psychologist Lawrence Kohlberg found that most college students—despite their theoretical allegiance to ethical subjectivism—are cultural relativists when it comes to making real-life moral decisions. As cultural relativists, college students are very dependent on the opinions and values of their peers. Right and wrong are defined primarily in terms of prevailing norms and values. Indeed, as Steven Satris pointed out in Chapter 3, the widespread belief in ethical subjectivism among young people is not so much a well-thought-out philosophical position as a case of people simply adopting the prevailing view of their peer culture.

   To what extent are the moral values you listed for yourself in Question 4 the same as those of your peers? Discuss the potential problems of relying on peer opinion for one's moral values.

Distinguishing Between Cultural and Sociological Relativism

It is often said that one cannot derive an "ought" from an "is" . . . Put in more contemporary terminology, no set of descriptive statements can entail an evaluative statement without the addition of at least an evaluative premise. To believe otherwise is to commit the naturalistic fallacy.   —JOHN SEARLE, *Speech Acts,* p. 51

Cultural relativism is not the same as sociological relativism. Cultural relativism is a theory of *philosophical ethics.* As such, it is concerned with what *ought* to be. **Sociological relativism,** in contrast, is a theory in *descriptive ethics,* a branch of sociology that is concerned with what *is.* **Descriptive ethics** aims to discover and describe the moral beliefs of a given society. Sociological relativism, in contrast, is simply the *observation* that there is disagreement among cultures regarding moral values. Unlike cultural relativism, sociological relativism draws no conclusions; it makes no judgments about the rightness or wrongness of different cultural standards. Cultural relativists presuppose that sociological relativism is true, but sociological relativists do not necessarily accept cultural relativism as true.

Almost everyone, including moral philosophers, accepts sociological relativism as a description of the way things are. Because sociological relativism does not draw any conclusions about the correctness of moral standards, unlike cultural relativism, it leaves open the possibility that one society could be mistaken about its moral beliefs and that there might be transcultural moral

standards against which to judge conflicting cultural standards. Cultural relativists, in contrast, claim that differences in moral practices necessarily imply
that there are no universal moral standards.

Disagreement regarding moral practices between cultures, however, can
stem from a variety of factors, some of which are situational. Just as scientists
using the same aeronautic principles can come up with very different designs
for an airplane based on the needs of the various people who will be using the
airplane, so too people from different cultures may disagree widely about the
application of different moral principles, while agreeing on the principles
themselves.

A parallel can also be found in the field of linguistics. According to one
school of thought, the grammatical structures found in language are relative
to each culture. This theory, like cultural relativism, gained popularity in
light of the tremendous cultural diversity in languages found by anthropologists. Supporters of a more recent school of linguistics, in contrast, argue that
universal grammatical structures underlie *all* human languages. This universal linguistics theory notes that, on the surface, each culture's language, like a
culture's moral practices and values, appears to be completely different from
all others. Deeper analysis of the various human languages, however, reveals
a deep grammatical or linguistic structure that is independent of culture and
appears to be common to all human languages.[5]

Deeper analysis of the differences in moral practices between cultures
also reveals many similarities in the fundamental moral principles. The following description of the Kabloona, an Eskimo culture living in the Canadian
Arctic, was published in 1941 by Gontran de Poncins.

> One observer was told of an Eskimo who was getting ready to move camp and was
> concerned about what to do with his blind and aged father, who was a burden to
> the family. One day the old man expressed a desire to go seal hunting again, some-
> thing he had not done for many years. His son readily assented to this suggestion,
> and the old man was dressed warmly and given his weapons. He was then led out to
> the seal grounds and was walked into a hole in the ice into which he disappeared.[6]

This description of de Poncins' is an example of sociological relativism. It
does not contain any value judgments upon the morality of the act. A cultural
relativist would go beyond the merely descriptive and say that, because the
customs are different, the two cultures—ours and the Kabloona—have different basic moral standards. However, must we accept this conclusion? Let's
analyze this interpretation of the disparate findings regarding the treatment of
the elderly in these two cultures.

On the surface, it certainly appears that our moral standards are simply
different and even in conflict with those of the Kabloona. In the United States,
if we walked our elderly parents into a hole in the ice, we would surely be
regarded as highly immoral! But is this the only possible interpretation of the

experience? Perhaps this was the aberrant act of one deranged son, perhaps a son who had never resolved his childhood Oedipus complex. If so, then maybe Kabloona values are not so different from ours. However, if we read on, we will discover that this was a custom of the Kabloona and other Eskimo cultures at that time. What the son did was considered morally acceptable by his culture. His father probably did the same thing to *his* father, and his son will probably do it to him when he is old and sickly.

It may be tempting at this point to throw up our hands and accept cultural relativism. But let's not give up our quest for a common moral understanding so easily. Let's push on with our analysis. As we noted earlier, situational factors play an important role in shaping how a culture translates fundamental universal moral standards into particular cultural values: What is the culture like? Is it sedentary or nomadic? What are their religious beliefs and family customs? How does their environment determine their needs and shape the way they honor moral standards? How does our situation in the United States differ from that of the Kabloona?

As modern Americans, we can care for our elderly parents at home. If we are working full-time, we can hire someone to come in and take care of them, or we can take our elderly parent to an adult day care center. If caring for an elderly and ailing parent becomes too burdensome for the family, we can place him or her in a nursing home. If our family does not have the resources to pay for a nursing home, public funds can be used to cover the cost.

Now compare our situation to that of the Kabloona. At the time that de Poncins lived and studied among the Kabloona, they were nomadic people living in a cold and hostile environment. "Home" did not mean a permanent structure with a spare bedroom for grandma or grandpa. There were no adult day care centers, home care nurses, or nursing homes. *None* of the alternatives now available to us were available to the Kabloona. As nomadic people, their very lives were dependent on moving camp regularly to follow the seal herds, their primary source of food. To take a blind and ailing parent on one of these treks could have resulted in the starvation and death not only of the parent but of the rest of the family as well.

It is now apparent that much of what initially appeared to be disagreement about basic moral standards may instead be simply the result of situational differences. It is interesting that this practice ceased among the Kabloona once the Eskimos had permanent settlements.

Very few ethicists believe that morality is completely autonomous—that is, independent of its particular context. As moral decision-makers, we live in a world of particulars. Social settings, individual circumstances, cultural values, environmental conditions, and religious beliefs vary tremendously from culture to culture. Acknowledging the influences of these factors in shaping the particular moral practices and values of a culture does not imply that there are no underlying basic universal moral standards. Universal moral standards, rather than determining the exact content of a culture's moral values and customs, instead provide general guidelines and set limits upon the values and customs that are morally acceptable within their particular context.

Exercises

1. Discuss some examples of sociological relativism, such as variations in marriage practices, which do not necessarily imply that the basic underlying moral principles are different. What are the common underlying moral principles?

2. In most Western cultures, suicide is regarded as immoral. In the Japanese tradition of hara-kiri, on the other hand, suicide is regarded as an honorable and moral action. Do these differences in attitudes toward suicide reflect a fundamental difference in basic moral principles regarding the intrinsic value of human life? Or can the differences be explained as a reflection of non-moral cultural values rather than as a difference in basic moral values? Support your answer.

3. In the case of the Kabloona, can you think of any other relevant moral principles or sentiments? Was walking the aging father into a hole in the ice the morally best option for the Kabloona? Discuss your answers, using the procedure for resolving moral dilemmas discussed in Chapter 2.

*4. Community service puts us in contact with people who hold different values or worldviews than those we've come to accept as normal and natural and thus creates social dissonance. As we learned earlier, people respond to social dissonance either by putting up resistance or by analyzing and attempting to make sense of the new information.

   Discuss a situation in your community service where this occurred. What were the conflicting values? How did you react when you encountered values that were at odds with your own? How would a cultural relativist react? Could you resolve or make sense of this difference in values? How?

Social Darwinian Ethics: The Concept of Moral Progress

The leading moral laws are seen to follow as corollaries from the definition of complete life carried on under social conditions . . . in civilized societies more than in savage societies . . . the justice is greater.   —HERBERT SPENCER, *The Principles of Ethics* (1897), p. 35

[The savage] has no moral feelings of any kind, sort, or description; and his "mission" may be summed up as simply diabolical . . .   —CHARLES DICKENS, "The Noble Savage"[7]

Two events in the late nineteenth century led to a dramatic rise in the popularity of cultural relativism among intellectuals. The first was the publication of Charles Darwin's theory of evolution. The second was the increased use of fieldwork by cultural anthropologists.

Darwin's publication of *The Origin of the Species* (1859) and, several years later, *The Descent of Man* (1871) precipitated a period of upheaval and a "crisis of conscience"; during this time, ethicists and other intellectuals were challenged to reexamine their deeply held assumptions about human culture and human nature.[8] According to Darwin, human instincts, including the moral sense, are nothing more than response structures that have in the past contributed to the survival of the species. The concept of the "good," instead of being something peculiar to human nature or part of our "divine" nature, is simply a means of the perpetuation of the species.[9] Morality, in other words, does not exist in some abstract realm but is a part of the natural world and is intimately linked to our struggle for survival within it.

Social Darwinists, such as biologist Thomas H. Huxley (1825–95) and philosopher Herbert Spencer (1820–1903), took evolutionary ethics one step further: Spencer, who was primarily a self-educated man, was one of the leading Victorian philosophers. Although Darwin spoke of evolution as adaptation to changing environments, rather than progress per se, belief in progress had become firmly entrenched in the Western psyche during the eighteenth century Period of Enlightenment. Rousseau's romantic notion of the "noble savage," the natural person unaffected by the restrictions of modern society, was never generally accepted and was easily usurped by the view of savages as a lower form of human life.

Much of what we attribute to Darwin, such as the idea of the evolution as progress and the "survival of the fittest," came from Spencer and the social Darwinists. According to Spencer, just as animals "progress" or evolve over time from lower life forms, so too does humanity evolve culturally over time from the ignorant savage cultures to the intelligent and morally civilized Christians—what God (or nature) intended humans to be. Human culture progresses from "lower" to "higher" forms of society just as animals, at least according to Spencer's interpretation of Darwin's theory, pass through intermediary stages on their way to higher, more evolved forms. Within a culture, Spencer believed, those who were successful were better suited to survival—a belief that fostered a paternalistic and degrading attitude toward the poor.

Spencer argued that, as human cultures become more civilized, the life of peaceful cooperation begins to take precedence over the life of antagonism that characterizes primitive societies. The assimilation of social Darwinism into the social sciences "scientifically" validated the prevailing Victorian worldview that the so-called savage was morally inferior to the civilized European. A linear model of cultural progress was developed, using modern "savages" to illustrate the early prehistoric stages of human cultural development. Following is an excerpt from sections 51 and 52 of Spencer's book *The Principles of Ethics* (1897):

> For each kind and degree of social evolution determined by external conflict and internal friendship, there is an appropriate compromise between the moral code of enmity and the moral code of amity . . . This compromise, vague, ambiguous, illogical, though it may be, is nevertheless for the time authoritative . . . But such [inconsistent] moralities are, by their definitions, shown to belong to incomplete conduct; not to conduct that is fully evolved. We saw that the adjustments of acts to ends which, while constituting the external manifestations to life conducive to the continuance of life, have been rising to a certain ideal form now approached by the civilized man.

Because of Spencer's lack of formal education, his ideas were initially derided by the academic establishment of his time, although his ideas tended to be more popular among the intellectuals in the United States. His optimistic idea that evolution is synonymous with progress, however, eventually won him a large popular following.

Even Charles Dickens (1812–70), who championed the rights of the downtrodden workers in England during the industrial revolution, unquestioningly accepted the social Darwinian view of "savages" as morally inferior. During the mid-nineteenth century, adventurers would bring back "savages" from their travels to put on exhibit. After Dickens attended an exhibition of Zulus from Africa at a gallery in London, he wrote:

> I have not the least belief in the Noble Savage. I consider him a prodigious nuisance and an enormous superstition . . . he is a savage—cruel, false, thievish, murderous; addicted more or less to grease, entrails, and beastly customs; a wild animal with the questionable gift of boasting; a conceited, tiresome, bloodthirsty, monotonous humbug . . .
>
> He has no moral feelings of any kind, sort, or description; and his "mission" may be summed up as simply diabolical . . .[10]

Spencer's moral philosophy may seem imperialistic and elitist to us today, but it had a tremendous influence on philosophical thought during the late nineteenth and early twentieth centuries. Social Darwinism was used to justify the long-term takeover and colonization of "primitive" societies by Europeans, in the name of evolutionary progress. The ideas of social Darwinism are still evident in the moral philosophies of sociobiologists and the ethical egoism of U.S. philosopher Ayn Rand.

Exercises

1. Do you agree with Herbert Spencer that civilization and moral progress go hand in hand? Are people from First World nations, for example, more moral

than people from Third World nations? On a wider scale, are humans as a species becoming more moral as we progress technologically? Support your answer using examples.

2. Social Darwinism has been used to morally justify competitive economic individualism as "survival of the fittest." To what extent have the ideas of social Darwinism been used to support the view that those who are economically successful are morally better people than the poor?

Ruth Benedict: Cultural Relativism as a Protest Against Social Darwinism

> *We recognize that morality differs in every society, and is a convenient term for socially approved habits.* —RUTH BENEDICT, "Anthropology and the Abnormal," p. 73

The modern version of cultural relativism emerged as a protest against social Darwinism and the imperialism that it supported. In the early twentieth century, several notable anthropologists and sociologists—including William Graham Sumner, Emile Durkheim, Franz Boas, and Ruth Benedict—spoke out against this degrading view of "primitive," simpler cultures.

Ruth Benedict was born Ruth Fulton in New York City in 1887. She attended Vassar, where she studied English literature, and from there went on to teach English in a girls' school. After her marriage to biochemist Stanley Benedict in 1914, she became interested in the New School for Social Research and decided to go to Columbia University, where she completed a Ph.D. in anthropology in 1923 under the direction of Franz Boaz. At the time, Spencer's ideas were enjoying great popularity in U.S. intellectual circles.

In her landmark book *Patterns of Culture,* published in 1934, Benedict uncovered the inconsistencies in the social Darwinists' claim that Western society is at a higher level of moral, religious, and social evolution. She claimed that Darwin's evolutionary theory does not imply that morality is found in a greater degree in civilized societies.

> Early anthropologists tried to arrange all traits of different cultures in an evolutionary sequence from the earliest forms to their final development in Western civilization. But there is no reason to suppose that by discussing Australian religion rather than our own we are uncovering primordial religion, or that by discussing Iroquois social organization we are returning to the mating habits of man's early ancestors.
>
> Since we are forced to believe that the race of man is one species, it follows that man everywhere has an equally long history behind him. Some primitive tribes may have held relatively closer to primordial forms of behavior than civilized man, but this can only be relative and our guesses are as likely to be wrong as right. There is no justification for identifying some one contemporary primitive custom with the original type of human behavior.

Ruth Benedict (1887–1948), American anthropologist. In her book Patterns of Culture, *Benedict used examples from her field-work to support the theory of cultural relativism.*

Although this new breed of anthropologists questioned and critically analyzed the assumptions of the social Darwinists, they simply accepted at face value the stories being told about bloodthirsty practices such as cannibalism and bizarre sexual practices in certain cultures; most of these stories later turned out to be unsubstantiated or untrue.[11] Benedict and her colleagues rejected offhand the possibility of transcultural or universal moral standards altogether, rather than at least look for a common moral sentiment or standard among all humans. Like the social Darwinists they opposed, the new cultural relativists instead focused on the differences between Western and non-Western cultures.

The morality of a group at a time is the sum of the taboos and prescriptions in the folkways by which right conduct is defined.

—WILLIAM GRAHAM SUMNER, *Folkways* (1906)

Benedict argued that morality is historical, institutional, and empirical, rather than universal or based on individual feelings. Each culture, Benedict argued, should be seen as a functioning whole that cannot be evaluated by outside standards. According to her, cultural customs cannot be evaluated internally by transcultural standards because such standards do not exist. Support for this apparent internal consistency in moral values was bolstered by claims that, within any particular culture, there is general agreement regarding moral values. The popularity of cultural relativism was further promoted by the psychological theory of the time, which regarded morality as simply the internalization of cultural values.

In other words, there are no objective, transcultural moral standards or rational criteria to analyze divergent worldviews regarding the morality of a particular custom. Because of this, interpretation rather than analysis stands at the top of the "thinking" pyramid. Our culturally shaped interpretations or worldviews about what is right and wrong *are* our reality. We thus have no grounds, other than cultural norms, for judging the morality of a practice such as cannibalism. Anthropologists such as Benedict and Sumner were not simply promoting sociological relativism. They were not just saying that cannibals believed that eating other humans was right: This is simply stating the obvious. Instead, the cultural relativists claimed that cannibalism was, in fact, morally right for cultures such as the Dobu of New Guinea (who were rumored to have been cannibals before the arrival of the Europeans).

> The "right" way is the way which the ancestors used and which has been handed down. The tradition is its own warrant. It is not held subject to verification by experience. The notion of right is in the folkways, whatever is, is right. This is because they are traditional, and therefore contain in themselves the authority of the ancestral ghosts. When we come to the folkways we are at the end of our analysis.[12]
>
> —WILLIAM GRAHAM SUMNER, *Folkways* (1906)

By advocating cultural relativism, however, these anthropologists ceased to be social scientists describing sociological phenomena and instead began to do exactly what they claimed to be avoiding—making value judgments about what is morally right and wrong. According to cultural relativists, a hypothetical kindhearted Dobu who tried to protect a stranger from her anthropophagous (man-eating) kinfolk was doing something that was *morally wrong*. She *ought not* to have protected the stranger.

Now, we may acknowledge that our kind and gentle Dobu would have been regarded as deviant and perhaps mentally deranged in her own culture, but it is much more difficult to agree that she was an immoral person in the wider scheme of things. Indeed, today we generally regard a person who refuses to follow cultural mores that cause pain and harm to others as highly moral. This is true not only when passing judgment on people from other cultures, but also when passing judgment on the behavior of people within our own culture.

Once we begin to examine cultural relativism, it becomes clear that the early advocates of this theory did not completely think through all the implications of their position. Like the social Darwinists who used evolutionary ethics as a means to legitimate European imperialism, cultural relativists also had a political agenda. By advocating cultural relativism, anthropologists such as Benedict wanted to stop imperialist practices and replace them with greater respect for and tolerance of cultural differences.[13] If moral values are relative to each culture, then no culture's values can be superior to those of any other culture. And if no culture's values are superior to those of any other, they reasoned, then Western cultures have no justification for imposing their morality on other cultures.

As caring people, we may sympathize with the intention of these anthropologists to promote tolerance and respect; however, this does not mean that their reasoning was correct. Their conclusion—that we should not impose our Western values on other cultures—does not logically follow from cultural relativism. The cultural relativists had no grounds to support the belief that laissez-faire ("live and let live") moral values are any better than those of the imperialists that they opposed. Indeed, by opposing imperialism, they were going against the cultural mores of their wider culture, and by doing so, they were encouraging immorality. To be consistent, they should have accepted, if not encouraged, imperialism and colonization as the morally correct behavior for Europeans at that time!

According to the cultural relativists, since we cannot pass judgment on the moral values of other cultures, neither do we have any grounds for criticizing or protesting the traditions of other cultures, no matter how despicable these traditions may appear to us. Indeed, U.S. slave traders justified the slave trade by emphasizing that the slave trade was already an established African custom, with criminals and prisoners of war being sold as slaves by their fellow Africans as part of their punishment.[14] Today, the use of workers in poorer nations as a source of cheap labor has been justified on the grounds that low pay for long hours and even child labor are traditions, and hence morally acceptable, in those cultures.

Exercise

*1. Do you agree with the cultural relativists that a person who deviates from cultural norms (such as our kind Dobu) is immoral, but the conformist is, by definition, moral? Support your answer, using examples from our own culture and from your community service work.

Cultural Relativism and the Moral Community

Each group nourishes its own pride and vanity, boasts itself superior, exalts its own divini-
ties, and looks with contempt on outsiders. Each group thinks its own folkways are the only
right ones, and if it observes groups that have other folkways, these excite its scorn. Oppro-
brious epithets are derived from these differences. "Pig-eater," "cow-eater," "uncircum-
cised," "jabberers," are epithets of contempt . . .[15]

—WILLIAM GRAHAM SUMNER, *Folkways* (1906), p. 13

Variations in cultural norms are sometimes due to differences in how cultures define their moral communities instead of differences in basic moral standards. Cultural relativism defines the moral community in ethnocentric, rather than universal, terms. There are no universal or natural human rights. Someone, or something, has moral value only because their society grants them this status. There is no source of moral value other than one's culture. Those who are granted moral status by their culture receive the protection and support of the community.

If we consider the concept of moral community when examining the moral values and practices of another culture, we can find far more commonality among cultures. The existence of cross-cultural values does not, in itself, prove cultural relativism; however, the presence of these apparently universally accepted values does strengthen the argument against cultural relativism.

The Moral Community

American anthropologist Clyde Kluckhohn (1905–60) claimed that there are basic universal, transcultural moral standards that are recognized in all cultures and that are binding upon all members of a particular culture's moral community. "In no human group," he notes, "is indiscriminate lying, cheating or stealing approved."[16] Incest, too, is prohibited or strictly controlled in all cultures. Every culture makes some provision for mating and the rearing of children. Random violence against other members of the community is also prohibited in all cultures. For example, in head-hunting cultures, only people outside of the cultural community were targeted as victims.[17] Among the Papuans of New Guinea, a wife who comes from within the group has full status; wives who have been captured during enemy raids do not come from within the group and, hence, are fair game for headhunters!

When violence does occur within the community, it must be justified. The bombing of "enemy" civilians of another culture—particularly a non-Western culture—is regarded with relative unconcern by most Americans. However, the same type of violent actions within the borders of our community, whether carried out by police officials or antigovernment groups, such as the Oklahoma bombing in 1995, are met with unmitigated horror.

Some cultures are more inclusive and less hierarchical than others in their definition of moral community. The Dobu have a very exclusive definition of moral community. The Buddhist moral community, on the other hand, is very inclusive and egalitarian. Since Buddhist ethics supports a universalist ethics rather than cultural relativism, all living beings are encompassed within their moral community—not simply members of their particular culture. Many Native American cultures also include other humans and nonhuman animals in the moral community. The Pawnee Indians, for example, address "all of life as a 'thou'—the trees, the stones." [18] All beings were seen as objects of reverence and value. While the Pawnee recognize that it may be necessary to kill living beings for one's own survival, this must be done with respect and only when necessary. Other animals are not a resource for humans but co-dwellers.

The only mythology today that is valid is the mythology of the planet—and we don't have such a mythology. The closest thing I know to a planetary mythology is Buddhism, which sees all beings as Buddha beings . . . The only task is to know what is, and then to act in relation to the brotherhood of all these beings . . .

Now brotherhood in most of the myths I know of is confined to a bounded community. In bounded communities, aggression is projected outward.

For example, the ten commandments say, "Thou shalt not kill." Then the next chapter says, "Go into Canaan and kill everybody in it." That is a bounded field. The myths of participation and love pertain only to the in-group, and the out-group is the total other.

—Joseph Campbell, *The Power of Myth* (1988), p. 22

The moral community of a culture can be represented by using a mandala. **Mandala** is the ancient Sanskrit word for a circle that symbolizes the cosmic order.[19] The mandala includes within its borders all that is sacred or, in moral terms, all that has intrinsic moral value. When using a mandala to represent a culture's moral community, beings who have the greater status in that culture are placed toward the center of the mandala. As one moves further toward the edges of the mandala, one's moral value diminishes. Beings that are outside the moral community are placed outside the circle.

Using a mandala, the moral community in the United States in 1800 might be represented as in Figure 4.1.

Cultural relativists such as Ruth Benedict were concerned about members of "primitive" cultures being exploited by more powerful cultures. However, not everyone living within a particular culture is a member of that

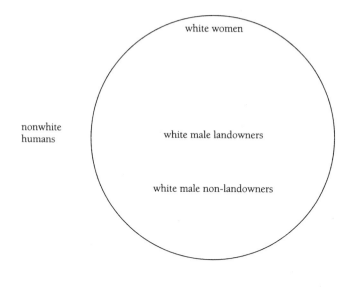

nonwhite
humans

non-human animals

FIGURE 4.1   Mandala of the U.S. Moral Community in the Early 1800s

culture's moral community. This means that exploitation can also occur within the culture.

Slavery and the Holocaust

Slavery was legal for more than two centuries in the United States. Yet, as any historian can tell you, respect for human equality and a belief in justice *were* pre–Civil War American values. These values were even written into the U.S. Constitution. What has changed between now and then is *not* the basic moral principles, but the definition of moral community. Slavery could only be morally justified by excluding the victims of slavery from the moral community. By excluding African Americans, our cherished values of equality and justice did not apply to them. This definition of the moral community was reaffirmed by the U.S. Supreme Court in *Dred Scott v. Sanford* (1857).

> In the opinion of the court, the legislation and histories of the times, and the language used in the Declaration of Independence, show, that neither the class of persons that have been imported as slaves, nor their descendants, whether they had become free or not, were then acknowledged as part of the people, nor intended to be included in the general words used in the memorable instrument . . .
>
> They had for more than a century before been regarded are beings of an inferior order; and altogether unfit to associate with the white race, either in social or political relations; and so far inferior that they had no rights which the white man was

bound to respect; and that the negro might be lawfully reduced to slavery for his own benefit . . .

This opinion was at that time fixed and universal in the civilized portion of the white race. It was regarded as an axiom in morals as well as in politics which no one thought of disputing, or supposed to be open to dispute . . . The state of public opinion has undergone no change [from] when the Constitution was adopted . . .

Now the right of property in a slave is distinctly and expressly affirmed in the Constitution. . . . He is himself property in the strictest sense of the term. And the Government in express terms is pledged to protect it in all future time, if the slave escapes from his owner . . .[20]

The "natural inferiority" of Africans was affirmed not only by popular opinion and the U.S. Supreme Court but also by the medical profession. Dr. W. H. Holcombe of Virginia wrote, in the *Southern Literary Messenger,* in 1861: "The negro is not a white man with a black skin, but of a different species, . . . the hopeless physical and mental inferior [of the white, and] organically constituted to be an agricultural laborer in tropical climates—a strong animal machine."[21] Women, likewise, because they were not regarded as fully rational, were relegated to the fringes of the U.S. moral community until 1920, when they were given the right to vote. Indeed, women still don't enjoy the same status as men do in the community.

In Nazi Germany, the Jews were also excluded from the moral community by an action of that country's supreme court and by public opinion. The exclusion of the Jews from the German moral community legitimized the Holocaust. Because Jews were nonpersons and outside the moral community, fundamental moral principles did not apply to them.

. . . the Jew is only a rough copy of a human being, with humanlike facial traits but nonetheless . . . lower than any animal . . . otherwise nothing. For all that bear a human face are not equal.

—GERMAN SUPREME COURT (1936)

The cultural definition of moral community is fluid; it can change over time and even, in the case of agism, over the course of a lifetime. For example, African Americans who were once outside the moral community are now inside, albeit at the margins. Jews are now part of the moral community in Germany. Unborn humans, who were once inside the moral community and protected by law, are now outside. Our animal companions and endangered species enjoy some protection from the moral community. Farm animals, insects, and wild animals who are not cute and cuddly, on the other hand, are excluded from our culture's moral community and may be squashed, poisoned, shot, experimented upon, or raised in the most confining and cruel conditions without the slightest fear of censure from those at the center of our moral community.

Marginalized Groups

Just as some beings—both human and nonhuman—can be outside of the moral community or mandala, other groups may be relegated to the fringes or margins of the moral community. We refer to these groups as **marginalized.** It is not morally acceptable to kill or torture those who are marginalized, but they don't receive the respect and cultural protection or have access to the same opportunities as those who are closer to the center of the community.

When a member of a marginalized group transgresses cultural norms, they are not given the same protection as are those in power. For example, in the United States African Americans and women receive harsher penalties and longer prison sentences than white males who commit the same crimes. Members of marginalized groups have also been used, without their consent, in medical experiments. Between 1930 and 1953, for instance, the United States Department of Health Services conducted a study on syphilis, known as the Tuskegee study, using poor black men living in Macon County, Alabama, as subjects. Despite the discovery in the late 1940s that penicillin could cure syphilis, treatment was withheld from the nearly three hundred men participating in the study. As a result, many of the men died for the sake of scientific knowledge although their lives could have been saved. According to a 1973 investigation into the study, "there is no evidence that informed consent was gained from the human participants in this study."[22] Medical experiments with contraception have also been conducted in the United States on poor Mexican-American women without their knowledge or informed consent.[23]

The cultural definition of moral community is, to a large extent, politically and economically motivated. Cultural relativism, in other words, supports a definition of the moral community that serves primarily to maintain the status quo. By doing so, cultural relativism protects the interests of those in power while morally sanctioning the marginalization and exploitation of other groups, thereby promoting ethnocentrism and legitimating hatred and discrimination as morally acceptable.

During the mid-nineteenth century, thousands of Chinese immigrated to the Western United States to work on the transcontinental railway and in the gold mines. Many employers preferred Chinese workers because they worked hard for lower wages and they refused to join unions. An anti-Chinese campaign, fueled by the new labor movement, quickly spread throughout the West and gave rise to demonstrations and violence. In 1879, the state of California adopted a provision to its constitution which forbade the employment

During World War II thousands of Japanese-American families were forced to give up their jobs and homes to go to internment camps such as the one in this photo, taken April 29, 1942 at the Tanforan Assembly Center—just two days after its opening—in San Bruno, California. The evacuees are lined up because only one mess hall was in operation at the time. (Photo by Dorothea Lange.)

of any "Chinese or Mongolian [in] any state, county, municipal, or other public work, except in punishment for crime." These sections of the California Constitution were not repealed until 1952.

This California law was followed by one enacted by the United States Congress in 1882, and revised in 1888, which asserted that ". . . the coming of Chinese laborers to the country endangers the good order of certain localities with the territory thereof: . . . the coming of Chinese laborers to the United States [will] be . . . suspended . . . hereafter no State court of the United States shall admit Chinese to citizenship."

The hostility toward and internment of Japanese-American citizens and Japanese immigrants (but not Americans of German descent) during World War II is just one more example of the marginalization of nonwhite people in the U.S. moral community.

The Vicious Cycle

When cultural relativism defines the moral community in a hierarchical manner, it creates large groups of needy people who do not have full access to the opportunities and resources available to those who are closer to the center of the moral community. This, in turn, can lead to a vicious cycle, where those who are neediest come to be seen as unworthy, lazy, or bad and deserving of their degraded status. As such, they are regarded by those in the dominant position with suspicion and intolerance.

The U.S.-Mexican border *es una herida abierta* [is an open wound] where the Third World grates against the first and bleeds. And before a scab forms it hemorrhages again, the lifeblood of two worlds merging to form a third country—a border culture. Borders are set up to define the places that are safe and unsafe, to distinguish *us* from *them*. A border is a dividing line, a narrow strip along a steep edge. A borderland is a vague and undetermined place created by the emotional residue of an unnatural boundary. It is in a constant state of transition. The prohibited and forbidden are its inhabitants. *Los atravesados* live here: the squint-eyed, the perverse, the queers, the troublesome, the mongrel, the mulato, the half-breed, the half dead; in short, those who cross over, pass over, or go through the confines of the "normal." Gringos in the U.S. Southwest consider the inhabitants of the borderlands transgressors, aliens—whether they possess documents or not, whether they're Chicanos, Indians or Blacks. Do not enter, trespassers will be raped, maimed, strangled, gassed, shot. The only "legitimate" inhabitants are those in power, the whites and those who align themselves with whites. Tension grips the inhabitants of the borderlands like a virus. Ambivalence and unrest reside there and death is no stranger.

—GLORIA ANZALDUA, *Borderlands/La Frontera: The New Mestiza* (1987)

If moral value is derived only from our culture and morality is synonomous with cultural norms, then the exclusion of whole groups of people from the moral community should be fairly uncontroversial. Those in power should have no need to try to convince themselves that certain groups "deserve" a lower status. However, this is rarely the case. When a culture excludes or removes a group of people from the moral community, the culture often feels compelled to justify its actions even to the point of engaging in blatant doublethink. Indeed, the group in power may even justify the exclusion of another group as being for their "own benefit."

In 1830, with the encouragement of President Andrew Jackson, the United States Congress passed the "Indian Removal Act." With the passage of this law, there was a shift in the moral community; Native Americans became further marginalized. No longer was peaceful coexistence the official policy. Despite the sanction of the U.S. Congress, those in charge of the removal still felt compelled to morally justify their actions. The "removal" of the Indians from their homeland was justified by the European Americans as being in the Indians' best interests. Despite the fact that the Seminoles in Florida fought off the United States for seven years before finally giving up, the 1832 U.S. "treaty" that forced them off their homeland read as follows:

> The Seminole Indians [regard] with just respect the solicitude manifested by the President of the United States for the improvement of their condition, by recommending a removal to a country more suitable to their habits and wants than the one they at present occupy in the territory of Florida.[24]

Slavery was also defended by many prominent white Southerners as saving the slaves from "the horrible consequences of emancipation." Without slavery, it was argued, "the blacks would rapidly degenerate into a primitive barbarism" and the whole "fabric of civilization and liberty . . . would be completely demolished by the relentless fury of ignorant barbarians."[25] Even Thomas Jefferson, who was morally opposed to the slave trade, owned several slaves. United States humanist Margaret Fuller wrote in 1843 regarding the doublethink involved in slavery:

> Though the national independence be blurred by the servility of individuals; though freedom and equality have been proclaimed only to leave room for a monstrous display of slave dealing, and slave keeping; though the free American so often feels himself free, like the Roman, only to pamper his appetites and his indolence through the misery of his fellow beings, still it is not in vain, that the verbal statement has been made, "All men are born free and equal." There it stands, a golden certainty, wherein to encourage the good, to shame the bad.[26]

Fuller's observation is a good illustration that people, for the most part, *know* what is morally right. However, cultural norms and self-interest can modify how we apply moral knowledge in real-life situations. Martin Luther King, Jr., once said that the "universe bends toward justice." King was a strong opponent of cultural relativism, and he believed that the call of justice in our hearts cannot simply be overridden by legal decrees or cultural norms. There are times in all of our lives when, upon reflection, we realize that we can do more toward making this a more compassionate and just world.

Exercises

1. Make a list of the criteria that our culture uses for including or excluding humans and non-human animals as well as the environment from the moral community. To what extent do these criteria reflect cultural norms? Do any

of these criteria conflict with each other? Do you consider these criteria acceptable? If not, why not? How do you define the moral community? Draw a mandala of your moral community. Is it the same as the U.S. moral community? If not, how can you explain the discrepancy?

2. Thomas Jefferson wrote the following indictment against the King of England for encouraging slavery and the slave trade: "He has waged cruel war against human nature itself, violating its most sacred rights of life and liberty in the person of a distant people who never offended him, captivating and carrying them into slavery in another hemisphere, or to incur miserable death in their transportation thither."[27] Was Jefferson immoral for denouncing the cultural norms and laws of his time? How would a cultural relativist respond to his indictment? Are you satisfied with this response? Explain.

On the other hand, Thomas Jefferson was a slave owner himself. How did he justify this? Was he engaged in doublethink? If so, how was this discrepancy explained, if at all, by your teachers in school and in U.S. history books?

3. Where are you in our cultural mandala? In what ways do cultural definitions of where you fit in the moral community affect your life? How do they affect the way you treat others? Are you content with your place in the mandala? Why or why not?

4. In Northern India and China, the birth of a female is often regarded as a great tragedy. Many women undergo amniocentesis to determine the gender of their fetus. An estimated eight to ten thousand fetuses were aborted in Bombay alone between 1978 and 1982 simply because they were female. In the United States, the selective abortion of females is legal and probably occurs more often than most people realize; nevertheless, the majority of us consider amniocentesis for sex selection to be immoral. However, we generally have few qualms about using amniocentesis to detect Down's syndrome or spina bifida in the fetus so it can be aborted.

Discuss selective abortion in light of cultural variations in definitions of moral community. Do cultural differences in definitions of moral community justify these practices? How does the "weeding out" of female infants in India and infants with birth defects in the United States affect the treatment of women and handicapped people in these two cultures?

5. Using the mandala of our current moral community that you drew for Question 1, discuss how our moral community is politically motivated and works to benefit those with the most power. How is the status quo maintained through custom, language, and the use of resistance? What effect does support for a hierarchical definition of moral community have on society in general?

*6. Which particular groups of people are most likely to need help from community service organizations in our culture? Is there any relationship between the populations most in need in our culture and their position on the mandala of the U.S. moral community? If so, discuss why this might be so. Relate this to the concept of ethnocentricity.

Has your community service work influenced your concept of the moral community at all? If so, explain how.

Are Some Cultures More Moral than Others?

One of the first features which mark the distinction between a civilized, and a rude nation, is the value attached to human life, and the protection given it by the former . . . Respect for human life, and vigilant protection of it, is a feature of civilization sadly absent in this country [the United States].

—FREDERICK DOUGLASS, "Contradictions in American Civilization" (1861)

The anthropologists who promoted cultural relativism in the late nineteenth and early twentieth century were concerned about Europeans and Americans passing negative judgment on the moral values of "primitive" societies. Cultural relativism, if one subscribes to it, does prevent Europeans and Americans from claiming that they are morally superior, but it also precludes non-European cultures from pointing out their moral superiority. Cultural relativism, in other words, ignores the possibility that other cultures can teach Westerners valuable lessons in how to live the good life.

Like most philosophers, both Aristotle and Plato rejected cultural relativism. They argued that societies should be judged according to how well they live up to a certain transcultural moral ideal. In Plato's *Republic,* he sets forth a plan for a republic that he believes would be most conducive to the promotion of justice and virtue in its citizens. The structure of this properly ordered and just city-state, Plato maintains, is similar to that of the properly ordered person. Just as a good or just person promotes goodness and justice all around, so too does a just society promote justice and virtue in its individual citizens. According to Plato, the just society is based upon the principles of mutual need and specialization. This society not only meets the needs of its people but is structured so that each person is encouraged to specialize in the field for which he or she is best suited.[28] The ideal society would be ruled by philosopher-kings (and queens) who, because of their training in philosophy, would be more just and less open to false ideologies.

Ibn Khaldun

North African philosopher Ibn Khaldun (1332–1406) also rejected cultural relativism. Ibn Khaldun was born in Tunisia to Yemenite Arab parents. His family had immigrated from Spain in the eighth century, with the decline of Muslim rule in Spain. Muslim immigrants from Spain were considered part of the aristocracy, and the Khaldun family was well known for their scholarship and statesmanship.

When Ibn Khaldun was still in his teens, he entered the service of Egyptian ruler Sultan Barquq. Khaldun remained in the service of the sultan only a short time, deciding instead to pursue his education further. His career as a scholar, however, was made difficult by ongoing political rivalries, so he decided to take refuge in a small village in Algeria. He remained there for three years, completing the first volume of *The Muqaddimah,* his definitive work on world history and philosophy. Contemporary historian Arnold Toynbee called it "undoubtedly the greatest work of its kind that has ever yet been created by any mind in any time or place." Khaldun returned to Egypt, where he remained until his death in 1406. There, he lectured at the Al-Azhar University and served as Chief Malakite Judge.

In his book *The Muqaddimah,* Khaldun argued that nomadic cultures are morally superior to sedentary, urban cultures. The customs of nomadic cultures, he noted, enhance our good traits such as courage, cooperation, and striving for justice; the customs of sedentary and urban cultures encourage immorality. Among the Bedouins, he pointed out, the importance of community, group solidarity, and harmony with the environment promotes the development of virtues and behavior such as courage, peacefulness, and striving for justice. Sedentary people, on the other hand, are more concerned with their own individual ends and the indulgence in worldly pleasures. This preoccupation, Ibn Khaldun suggested, leads to moral evils such as injustice, mutual aggression, greed, and lack of courage.

John Fire Lame Deer

Sioux Indian philosopher John Fire Lame Deer likewise regards the European-American lifestyle as morally unacceptable. He argues that the anthropocentric definition of moral community characteristic of the morality of whites is destructive not just to the environment but to the humans who are part of this environment. This destructive attitude of whites toward nature and our environment, he argues, is based upon the misconception that the earth, the wind, the rocks, and the water are dead or inert. For the Sioux, these elements are "very much alive."[29] We are all physical matter. Matter, in all its forms, has its own consciousness and life force.

Can we learn from philosophers such as Ibn Khaldun and John Fire Lame Deer? A cultural relativist would simply dismiss what they say as being right only for them, but not for us, because there are no transcultural moral standards. Plato, Ibn Khaldun, and John Fire Lame Deer, on the other hand, claim that there *are* universal moral standards that we can use to pass judgment upon other cultures. Rather than simply dismissing a culture's values as relevant only to the people living within that culture, a universalist view of morality encourages us to listen to other points of view and to attempt to understand other people. We should also be willing to analyze and, if necessary, revise or reject our own cultural values in light of our new understanding.

Harriet Tubman

Even more troubling to the cultural relativist than cross-cultural criticism is criticism of cultural norms coming from within that culture. Harriet Tubman was one of the thousands of fugitive slaves who sought sanctuary in another culture: Canada. Tubman rejected the United States' definition of moral community and instead regarded Canada's more inclusive moral community as superior. By making this judgment, she rejected the U.S. norm that she, as a black woman, did not have the same right to liberty as a white person.

Tubman was born Harriet Ross in Bucktown, Maryland, around 1820. She served as a slave under several masters—some of whom beat the free-spirited girl several times a day. Despite her unhappy and abusive childhood, Tubman never gave up hope. In 1849, she escaped through the Underground Railroad, a network of antislavery activists who helped slaves escape to freedom in the Northern states and in Canada. Tubman later became a "conductor" on the Underground Railroad, leading more than three hundred slaves, including her own parents, to their freedom.

Social Reform

The belief that there is a morality that stands above society and to which society is responsible has been a recurring theme throughout world history. Like Tubman, most social reformers, rather than urging people to be more culture-maintaining, claim that cultural laws and norms are morally binding only when they respect and nurture human dignity and, in the case of animal rights and environmental activists, what they perceive to be the dignity of all beings. In doing so, social reformers maintain that they are not simply being arbitrary in their demands but that they are judging their culture in light of a transcultural standard of the ideal society.

Because those at the center of the moral community benefit most from promoting cultural relativism, social reformers are more likely to come from the ranks of those who are oppressed by the prevailing cultural mores. In South Africa, for example, great moral reformers such as Desmond Tutu, Steve Biko, Allan A. Boesak, and Winnie and Nelson Mandela emerged not out of the white leadership of South Africa but out of the oppression of apartheid.

In Mexico, the January 1994 Chiapas Rebellion was led not by middle- and upper-class Mexicans but by the Chiapas Indians, a relatively marginalized group of Mexicans. Their rebellion was fueled by long-standing grievances regarding economic injustices in Mexico and the need for land reforms.

A child operative in the spinning room of a Fall River, Massachusetts, mill, c. 1900. During the nineteenth and early twentieth centuries children as young as eight years old worked in the mills. In 1900 an estimated 25 percent of the mill operatives in the textile mills of New England were children fourteen years and younger. Photograph courtesy of the Fall River Historical Society.

Similarly, Cesar Chavez, Mexican-American labor reformer and organizer of the United Farm Workers of America, started out as a poor field-worker rather than as a member of the establishment.

> It has now come to be accepted that rule of law can only be effective in a country provided the conditions are such that the dignity of the human personality and the liberty of the individual are respected. Law cannot function in a vacuum. If sections of society are deprived of the benefits of law and treated as second class citizens, or if the law does not protect the liberty of the individual, then it would be meaningless to say that the rule of law prevails.[30]
>
> —MAHOMEDALI CURRIM CHAGLA, former Indian ambassador to the United States

Children have also been marginalized in many cultures and hence been made fair game for exploitation. Child labor used to be common practice in the United States and is still prevalent in many parts of Southeast Asia. In India, as many as 20 to 50 million young children are employed in factories. World-wide estimates of "child slavery" are over 200 million. Child rights activist Iqbal Masihn of Pakistan was sold at the age of four to a carpet manufacturer who often kept him chained to a loom. For six years, he worked making carpets mainly for Western markets. At the age of ten, with the support of labor rights groups, Masihn began touring to different countries and speaking out against child labor. In 1995, at the age of twelve, he was gunned down and killed under mysterious circumstances in his village of Muridke.[31]

If morality is the same as cultural norms, then not only is the notion of moral progress meaningless, but social reformers such as Harriet Tubman, Nelson Mandela, Cesar Chavez, and Iqbal Masihn are nothing but common criminals. Most of us do distinguish between reformers and criminals, though, which demonstrates that, in practice, we do distinguish between cultural and moral norms.

Exercises

1. On October 24, 1995, in Pocatello, Idaho, a Fort Hall police cruiser parked across the railway tracks to block a train from passing through the Fort Hall Indian Reservation. The train, which was carrying radioactive nuclear waste material, was on its way to the Idaho National Engineering laboratory. By taking this action, the police were breaking the law. Was their action morally justified? If so, on what grounds?

2. English psychologist and author Havelock Ellis (1859–1939) wrote: "It has always been found a terrible matter to war with the moral system of one's age; it will have its revenge, one way or another, from within or from without, whatever happens after." Think of a time when you took a moral stand against the norms of your peer group. Did the group try to get "revenge" on you? How did you respond?

    Read about the lives of some of the moral reformers, such as Iqbal Masihn in Pakistan and Martin Luther King, Jr., in the United States. Discuss this quotation in light of the fate of moral reformers who dared to take a stand against the cultural norms of their time.

3. Ibn Khaldun's belief that urban culture is destructive to morality and that we should return to a simpler lifestyle has also been part of the American dream since the time of Thomas Jefferson, who referred to farmers as "the chosen people of God."

    Do you agree with Ibn Khaldun's assessment of the effect of urban culture on people's morals? Discuss your answer in light of your own life and experiences.

4. In 1516, Sir Thomas More published a book entitled *Utopia*. His book envisions an ideal society where everything is ordered for the best of humankind and where evils, such as poverty and bigotry, have been eliminated. Since then, several other books have been written about utopias—and anti-utopias—including Samuel Butler's *Erewhon* (1872), Edward Bellamy's *Looking Backward* (1888), Charlotte Perkins Gilman's *Herland* (1915), Aldous Huxley's *Brave New World* (1932), B. F. Skinner's *Walden II* (1961), and Margaret Atwood's *A Handmaid's Tale* (1986).

   Discuss the ideas about the nature of utopia, in light of one of these books or your own conception of an ideal society. Compare this ideal to our own culture.

5. In a democracy, the majority determines the moral norms that everyone is expected to follow. A democratic culture thus tends to reinforce an ethics of cultural relativism or conformity and the oppression of the individual conscience. In the book *On Liberty* (1859),[32] British utilitarian and libertarian John Stuart Mill (1806–73), while not arguing that we should do away with democracy, nevertheless criticized it as being the "Tyranny of the Majority" and the "Tyranny of Custom."

   Do you agree with Mill? If so, does this necessarily imply that a democracy is a morally inferior type of society? What steps can we take, both as individuals and as a society, to make ourselves less vulnerable to majority opinion?

6. In our international economy, our life is affected daily by other cultures. Many of the products we use—clothing, athletic equipment, teddy bears, jewelry, home accessories—are made in sweatshops by child labor in Third World countries. Some of these children are slaves; others are blinded or maimed for crying or for trying to return home.

   On a television show, in the summer of 1996, Kathie Lee Gifford tearfully confessed that her Walmart outfits were made in Honduras by children earning 31 cents per hour. She vows that she will try to be more responsible in the future. Michael Jordan, who earns as much as $20 million per year endorsing Nike sneakers that are allegedly made in sweatshops in Indochina, disclaims any moral responsibility. Does it bother Jordan that Nike might be exploiting child labor? "My job with Nike," he told *Time* magazine, "is to endorse the product. Their job is to be up on that."[33] Others argue that workers, including child labor, in Third World sweatshops actually benefit from their own exploitation, because at least they will not starve to death.

   Do we as individuals have a moral responsibility to avoid buying products that are produced by child labor? Does our moral responsibility end there? Does our ignorance of the origin of the products we purchase excuse us? Do U.S. companies have a moral responsibility not to place orders with companies—either U.S. or foreign—that exploit their workers? If child labor is a cultural norm in a given culture, does that make it morally acceptable to purchase goods made by exploited children in that country?

7. Read the following excerpt, "Why Bosnia Matters to America," from a speech given by President Clinton regarding U.S. intervention in Bosnia.

> Over the last four years, the world has witnessed images we thought had been banished from Europe forever: sunken-eyed prisoners; defenseless men shot down into mass graves. Bosnia-Herzegovina, once a symbol of multicultural tolerance, has been Europe's bloodiest battleground since World War II.
>
> But now, in Dayton, Ohio—where the presidents of Bosnia, Croatia, and Serbia are beginning negotiations aimed at ending the brutality— horror is giving way to hope. America has led the way to the best chance for peace since the war began . . .
>
> Peace in Bosnia matters to America—to our values and our interests. We have an urgent stake in stopping the slaughter, preventing the war from spreading, and building a Europe at peace.
>
> The war in Bosnia has been waged chiefly against innocent civilians who have suffered mass executions, ethnic cleansing, terror, and systematic rape. Murder in the markets and the playgrounds of Sarajevo has outraged our nation and our conscience—for the violence done to the Bosnian people does violence to the principles on which America stands.[34]

Is it right for us to impose our moral principles upon other countries? If rape and mass murder are a normal part of a culture, are these practices then right for that culture? Should we interfere by trying to impose the "principles on which America stands" on their culture? Why or why not? How would a cultural relativist answer these questions? How about someone who believed in universal moral principles and sentiments?

8. Seventeen-year-old Fauziy Kasinga fled her native home in Togo, Africa, and is seeking asylum in the United States to avoid an arranged marriage and genital mutilation, which are both customs in her culture. Female genital mutilation involves cutting the clitoris and sometimes other genital tissue to curtail the woman's sexual pleasure. No anesthetic is used, and the procedure sometimes causes serious health problems or even death. Currently, asylum is granted in the United States to people who can show that they have a well-grounded fear of persecution based on race, religion, nationality, political belief, or membership in a social group. Can asylum for Kasinga be morally justified using the principles of cultural relativism? Should the United States grant asylum to Kasinga or to anyone who is fleeing the oppressive customs of their culture?

Although female circumcision has been banned in most states of the United States since 1985, male circumcision (which was initially introduced to discourage masturbation) is still customary. Routine circumcision of males has been discontinued in all other Western nations and is even illegal in some; still, in the United States about half of all newborn infant boys undergo routine nontherapeutic circumcision, a procedure that can be traumatic and very painful. Is this custom morally justified? Why or why not?

The Holocaust and Disillusionment with Cultural Relativism

Power, like a desolating pestilence,
Pollutes whate'er it touches; and obedience,
Bane of all genius, virtue, freedom, truth
Makes slaves of men, and, of the human frame,
A mechanized automaton.

—PERCY BYSSHE SHELLEY, *Queen Mab* (1813), III

Postwar Sentiments

Cultural relativism fell out of favor with social scientists after World War II. Faced with the horrors of the Holocaust, it became harder and harder to maintain the belief that there are no standards of right and wrong outside of cultural norms. Anti-Semitism was a cultural norm supported by the majority of Germans before and during the war, rather than a conspiracy of a few deranged and power-hungry men. This cultural perception is discussed in the following excerpt from Daniel Goldhagen's book, *Hitler's Willing Executioners* (1996):

> The men and women who became the Holocaust's perpetuators were shaped by and operated in a particular social and historical setting. They brought with them prior elaborate conceptions of the world, ones that were common to their society . . . The Holocaust was the defining aspect of Nazism, but not only of Nazism. It was also the defining feature of German society during its Nazi period . . . No analysis of German society, no understanding or characterization of it, can be made without placing the persecution and extermination of the Jews at its center. The program's first parts, namely the systematic exclusion of Jews from German economic and social life, were carried out in the open, under approving eyes, and with the complicity of virtually all sectors of German society, from the legal, medical, and teaching professions, to the churches, both Catholic and Protestant, to the gamut of economic, social, and cultural groups and associations . . .
>
> The killings [of the Jews] met with general understanding, if not approval. No other policy (of similar or greater scope) was carried out with more persistence of zeal, and with fewer difficulties, than the genocide, except perhaps the war itself.

Not only were the majority of Germans at that time anti-Semitic, but Jews were legally considered nonpersons in Germany and therefore had no substantial rights. Thus, to take a stand against the Holocaust necessitated taking a stand against cultural relativism.

The United Nations chose to reject cultural relativism. In 1945, the tribunal at the United Nations Nuremberg Trials put forth a list of universal standards of justice that established parameters on the norms of civilized behavior. The primary purpose of officially acknowledging a transcultural standard of justice was to prevent mass murderers and other "war criminals" from avoiding judgment and punishment by hiding behind their cultural norms. The tribunal maintained that these standards—which prohibited "crimes against humanity," "torture," "waging or preparing for an unjust war"—were not a cultural creation but universal moral standards and, as such, binding on all people everywhere. According to the charter, we each have an individual moral responsibility not to take refuge in any laws or customs of our culture that run contrary to universal moral standards.

Between 1945 and 1949, almost 200 war criminals were tried under this new charter. Of these, 161 were found guilty and 37 were sentenced to death. How can we reconcile these men's actions with the theory of cultural relativism? The belief that the Nazis were ruthless totalitarians who cared little about public opinion was far from the truth. The first people slated for Hitler's "humane euthanasia" program were the mentally ill and "incurably sick persons [who] should be granted a mercy death."[35] However, the gassing of the mentally ill was stopped because of protests from the public and a few church dignitaries. When the program was switched to the Jews, there was no similar outcry. Hitler and the Nazis, rather than being "deviants," had the support of the wider community. Indeed, what was perhaps most disconcerting about these war criminals, with a few exceptions, was their normalcy.

Political scientist Hannah Arendt refers to this cultural phenomenon, in her book about Adolf Eichmann, as the "banality of evil."[36] Like the slaveholders in the United States, and the cavalrymen who hunted down and massacred thousands of American Indians, the Nazis were, for the most part, "good" family men and upstanding members of their community. Although the official claim was that only "a relatively small percentage" of Germans had been Nazis or Nazi sympathizers, in fact, the exact opposite was the case.[37] After the defeat of Germany in World War II, prominent Nazi officials held prominent public offices in post-War Germany and were pillars of the community.

Adolf Eichmann as "Everyman"

Nazi Adolf Eichmann represented the quintessential cultural relativist. He was, in terms of his moral reasoning, "everyman." He was a medium-built, bespectacled bureaucrat, who worked as Minister of Transportation in Nazi Germany; his job was to arrange for the collection and deportation of all Jews. Following the war, because he was sought by international officials for his role in the Holocaust, Eichmann fled to Brazil with his family. In May 1960, he was abducted by representatives of the Israeli government and deported to Jerusalem, where he was charged with crimes against the Jews with intent to destroy the people.[38] He was found guilty of these crimes and sentenced to death by hanging on May 31, 1961.

At his trial, Eichmann pleaded "not guilty in the sense of the indictment" to each of the counts brought against him. He had been a good, law-abiding

Adolf Eichmann (1906–62) in a bulletproof witness stand during his 1962 trial in Jerusalem. As Minister of Transportation in Nazi Germany, Eichmann was responsible for the collection and deportation of Jews to the concentration camps. Eichmann was found guilty of crimes against humanity under the principles of the Nuremberg Charter and sentenced to death.

citizen. In a police examination, he stated that he would have sent his own father to his death if that had been what the law required. Unlike with a common criminal, Eichmann's thinking and that of his society were in perfect harmony.

Not until September 1939 did the Nazi government change its policy and, instead of expelling Jews from the country, began deporting Jews to concentration camps. Eichmann was horrified and repulsed by his first visit to one of these camps. He even told the SS commander about his feelings. Why then did he and other Nazi officials continue to follow orders? Members of extermination squads had quit their jobs without any serious consequences. Eichmann could also simply have asked to be switched to another high-paying job. At his trial, Eichmann said that, although he did initially have doubts about the extermination program, these doubts were put to rest when he realized that all his friends and professional colleagues supported the program. After all, he thought, "Who am I to judge?" Nobody, not even his pastor, ever reproached him for what he did in the performance of his duties.[39]

As for the majority of his fellow countrymen, Eichmann's chief standard was the "good society," as he knew it. Arendt writes:

> His conscience was indeed set at rest when he saw the zeal and eagerness with which everyone in the "good society" reacted as he did. He did not need to "close

his ears to the voice of conscience," as the judgment has it, not because he had none, but because his conscience spoke with a "respectable voice," with the voice of respectable society around him.[40]

If justice is a cultural creation, we then have no justifiable grounds for labeling Eichmann and the Nazi culture unjust or immoral. All we can say is that the Nazi culture was no better or no worse than our culture, just different.

Exercises

1. Do you think that it was morally acceptable for the United Nations to punish the Nazis for following the norms of their culture? Should U.S. actions during World War II be judged in light of the same moral standard? Why or why not?

2. A 1995 Gallup poll found that approval of dropping the atomic bomb on Hiroshima is high among men, whites, older, and college-educated Americans. However, a "substantial" number of Americans, "particularly those who are younger, female and non-white, say they disapprove of the decision." On what grounds might these young people protest the dropping of the atomic bomb? How might a cultural relativist respond to their protests?
   Discuss the difference in approval rates and the concept of moral community between the two groups.

3. Following the sentencing of Adolf Eichmann, his defense lawyer, Dr. Servatius, responded: "The accused had carried out 'acts of state,' what happened to him might happen in the future to anyone; the whole civilized world faces this problem." Do you agree with Dr. Servatius? Could a similar Holocaust happen in this country? How do you think you would respond if our government asked you to carry out acts that would bring about the suffering or deaths of people that were outside the moral community, as defined by our culture?

4. The United Nations and other international humanitarian groups, such as Amnesty International, frequently respond to what they perceive to be moral atrocities in other countries. In Rwanda, Doctors Without Borders reports that "it appears that every adult [Tutsi] woman and every adolescent girl spared from a massacre by militia [from the former Hutu-dominated government's genocidal campaign against the minority Tutsis in 1994] was then raped." Many of the women are HIV positive as a result of the rapes and two to three thousand women have given birth.[41]
   Is it wrong for humanitarian groups from other cultures, whether governmental or volunteer, to step in and interfere by helping the Tutsi women and infants? By helping them and not the Hutus, are these groups imposing their own cultural mores and passing moral judgment on Rwandan moral

norms? Since the Hutus are in the majority, shouldn't their moral norms prevail?

*5. To what extent, if at all, do you think that the widespread acceptance of cultural relativism as a moral theory allowed horrific events such as the Holocaust and the genocide in Rwanda to occur? How does acceptance of cultural relativism by most Americans allow, and perhaps even encourage, actions that are harmful to minority groups, under the guise of "the American way"? Relate your answer to your community service work.

6. "Who am I to judge?" During his trial, Nazi Adolf Eichmann was asked if he had ever questioned the orders of his commanders. He replied that it was not his place to judge his superiors.[42] The response "Who am I to judge?" is often heard—usually in conjunction with a shrug of the shoulders and an effort to change the topic—when people are faced with norms that differ from their own or when someone questions the norms of their culture. Of course, the question is generally rhetorical; no answer is expected. Discuss an instance when you said, "Who am I to judge?" when faced with conflicting moral viewpoints. Answer the question.

A Critique of Cultural Relativism

Conventionality is not morality . . . To attack the first is not to assail the last.
—CHARLOTTE BRONTË, *Jane Eyre* (1847), preface

And to say it once more. Public opinions—private laziness.
—FRIEDRICH NIETZSCHE, *Human, All-Too-Human* (1878)

The concept of moral reform, which is found throughout the world, provides a strong argument against cultural relativism. Moral reform, by its very nature, presumes that there are moral ideals that transcend cultural norms. However, the concept of moral reform is not the only inherent weakness in the theory of cultural relativism. The following is a summary of some of the other problems with this theory:

Cultural Relativism Is Illogical

Disagreement among cultures does not prove that objective, transcultural moral standards do not exist. To claim that they do *not* exist is to commit the fallacy of ignorance. At the most, we can adopt an initial position of ethical skepticism regarding the existence of objective moral standards. By claiming that sociological relativism (what *is*) implies cultural relativism (what *ought to* be), cultural relativists are guilty of committing the naturalistic fallacy.

The assertion that moral values are created by consensus within a particular culture is also highly questionable. Indeed, it is even questionable whether the "primitive" cultures that anthropologists studied were really as simplistic as they were portrayed. Because visitors to foreign cultures generally talk primarily to people in positions of power, what is reported as cultural unanimity is often just the values held by those in the dominant group. When viewing a culture from the eyes of those in power, we may come away with a one-dimensional view of the cultural values and remain unaware of the discontent of the people who are marginalized and often invisible to those passing through. Appealing to tradition to justify moral norms can also lead to rigid conformity, a distrust of change, and a disdain for those who do not adhere to tradition.

Cultural Relativism Does Not Work in a Pluralist Society

In today's world, it is much harder to accept the claim of anthropologists like Ruth Benedict that there is general agreement within each culture regarding moral values. In modern cultures, pluralism is generally an acknowledged fact: The definition of what constitutes a culture can vary from subculture to subculture and even from person to person, and almost all of us are members of several cultures. Because of this, cultural relativism becomes unworkable in a pluralistic society. Which values should we follow when the values of our various subcultures are in conflict? For example, I could be a member of the Cambodian-American culture, the Roman Catholic culture, the Democratic Party, and my college culture. Cultural relativism, rather than offering moral guidance, leaves us hopelessly confused with no standard for deciding between conflicting moral values.

Cultural Relativism Confuses Custom with Morality

Most of us distinguish between moral values and customs or nonmoral values such as marriage customs, food preferences, religious rites, lifestyles, and preferences in fashion and music. By identifying morality with custom, cultural relativists draw behavior into the moral realm that may be outside the scope of morality. A custom that is inconvenient or even offensive is not necessarily immoral. Nude bathing, cross-dressing, and use of obscene language in our own society, for example, are not necessarily immoral even though they may offend some people and run contrary to the norms and even the law in some places.

Because cultural relativism does not need to offer any justification for imposing a particular cultural value on people—other than to say that it is the way things are done—it can become legalistic and oppressive. Cultural norms, masquerading as moral duties, can become particularly oppressive during times of conflict or when a society feels itself threatened. Conformity may be demanded not only in terms of avoiding criminal behavior, but in dress, speech, and ideology as well.

People Act More Morally When Others Are Not Around

If culture were the ultimate source of moral values, then people would probably behave most morally when in a group of people, just as we tend to use better manners when we are out in company than when we are home alone. However, research indicates the opposite. It suggests that the source of our moral guidance does not lie solely in imposed cultural values.

Consider the case of Kitty Genovese. Genovese was stabbed to death in front of her apartment. No one bothered to call the police. Many people interpreted the lack of action on the part of the bystanders as personal apathy and urban anonymity. However, a study in which "emergencies" were staged in various locations in the city revealed that a person who is *alone* is much more likely to help the victim than someone who is a part of a crowd of bystanders. Social groups, rather than encouraging us to behave morally, actually seem to inhibit helpful behavior. Our primary motivation for helping others, the researchers concluded, seems not to be social pressure or cultural norms, but a sense of personal responsibility that tends to be diffused, rather than reinforced, when one is part of a crowd.

Even the best of people are not immune to the potentially demoralizing effects of being "part of the crowd." As a young man, Gandhi secretly smoked, ate meat, and told lies when in the company of his boyhood friends—all actions he personally felt were immoral. He suffered tremendous feelings of guilt as a result of these incidents. The resulting resolutions he made about resisting such social pressure lasted for life.

> Individual men may be moral . . . They are endowed by nature with a measure of sympathy and consideration for their kind . . . Their rational faculty prompts them to a sense of justice which education may refine . . . But all these achievements are more difficult, if not impossible, for human societies and social groups. In every human group there is less reason to guide and to check impulses, less capacity for self-transcendence, less ability to comprehend the needs of others and therefore more unrestrained egoism than the individuals, who compose the group, reveal in their personal relationships.[43]
>
> —REINHOLD NIEBUHR, *Moral Man and Immoral Society* (1932)

Sometimes cultural norms, in the form of a role or a profession assigned to us by our community, can take us over. One of the most famous examples to illustrate the "anti-moral" power that cultural norms regarding roles can have over us is the prison simulation experiment conducted at Stanford

University in 1973. This experiment involved twenty-one male volunteers who were judged to be stable, mature, and socially well-developed. Some of the volunteers were assigned the role of guard and others the role of prisoner. The basement of one of the buildings at Stanford was converted to resemble a prison.

Great care was taken to make the prison situation as realistic as possible. The "guards" and "prisoners" wore appropriate uniforms for their roles. The guards were expected to turn up for work, and the prisoners remained confined in the prison twenty-four hours a day. As the experiment progressed, the guards became increasingly aggressive and authoritarian, and the prisoners became more and more passive and dispirited. Five prisoners actually had to drop out of the experiment because of acute stress reactions. Finally, after six days, the experiment had to be called off because of the atrocious and immoral behavior that the guards were exhibiting toward the prisoners.

Cultural Relativism Does Not Correctly Describe How We Make Moral Judgments

We do pass judgment on the "moral" norms of our own and other cultures. When we make a judgment, we do not do so by examining the customs and laws of, say, South Africa or by checking the latest polls to see how the majority of people in that country feel about a certain practice. Nor do we necessarily judge other cultures in light of our own norms. In fact, we can conclude that a subtle form of apartheid is very much a part of U.S. culture and that we ought to end racism here as well. When we make these judgments, we generally do so by appealing to transcultural values such as justice and respect for human dignity rather than to cultural norms.

The explanation used by cultural relativists about how morality develops in people also does not fit with prevailing psychological theory on moral development. The emergence of children's awareness of moral principles, as opposed to the awareness of social mores, appears to follow a different course. Around the age of three, children are already aware of the difference between a moral issue, such as stealing and lying, and a social custom, such as how to dress or eat. "Even with their limited conceptual powers," writes psychologist Tom Kitwood, "they can grasp the point that moral issues do not depend on the nature of social rules."[44] Only later, as people enter the conventional stage of moral development, do some people begin to confuse custom and morality.

There Are Moral Values that Seem to Exist in All or Most Known Societies

The degree of variance among moral values is not as extreme as cultural relativists claim. Many extremes of behavior—such as cannibalism, human sacrifice, and unrestricted sexual activity among children—that have been used to illustrate the irreconcilable differences between moral values in Western and "primitive" cultures have never been documented by reliable sources.[45, 46] Indeed, many people, when they first come into prolonged contact with people from different cultures or subcultures are surprised at the extent of shared values. Although the presence of universal moral norms does not disprove cultural relativism, the cross-cultural agreement on certain moral values strengthens the case against this theory and places the burden of proof on the cultural relativists to explain how this has occurred.

Cultural Relativism Is Divisive and Creates a We/They Mentality

As such, it legitimates the oppression and even the extermination of certain groups of people. The belief that people from other cultures do not have the same basic moral standards that *we* have, such as respect for human life and human rights, can lead to distrust. If morality is simply the creation of each culture, people from other cultures may even have dangerous values. Thus, rather than encouraging tolerance, cultural relativism gives rise to distrust and "-isms" such as nationalism, racism, sexism, and ethnocentrism.

Because cultural relativism rules out the possibility of rational discussion between cultures, when cross-cultural values come into conflict and rhetoric or persuasion fails, groups may resort to either apathy and isolationism, when the other culture's values do not threaten theirs, or violence, when another culture's values or actions impinge on or threaten them. The latter happens on an international level, in the case of war, and on a national level, in the case of gang warfare and racial, gender, and ethnic violence.

As we noted earlier, almost all theories contain at least a grain of truth, even though it may be blown out of proportion and a part can be mistaken for the whole. Cultural relativism begins with the correct observation that our culture affects our interpretation of moral values and that these interpretations vary from culture to culture. However, from there cultural relativism makes the unwarranted conclusion that morality equals custom.

Looking predominately to our culture or to our peers for our moral values is a normal and healthy stage in a young person's moral development. Culture nurtures us and gives our lives significance within a historical context. As humans, we cannot exist outside of a culture. Respect for and obedience to cultural authorities and laws is the mechanism that cements us together as a society and gives us a common political purpose. However, as adults, we must move beyond moral heteronomy and dependence upon others for our moral values.

Given our tremendous dependence on culture, is it really possible to step outside of culture and look at our customs and mores impartially? Perhaps not completely. There is little doubt that culture shapes the way we interpret the most basic moral principles. But we need to be discerning and to develop our analytical skills. Cultural relativism, when taken seriously, is a dangerous theory. By throwing out universal moral standards, cultural relativists also throw out the proverbial baby with the bathwater. In their well-meaning effort to debunk European and American claims of racial and moral superiority, they also throw out the possibility of common, transcultural moral standards. The outcome has been the promotion, not of tolerance and rational dialogue, but of suspicion and intolerance.

> When you think of the long and gloomy history of man, you will find more hideous crimes have been committed in the name of obedience than have ever been committed in the name of rebellion. If you doubt that, read William Shirer's *Rise and Fall of the Third Reich.* The German Officer Corps were brought up in the most rigorous code of obedience . . . in the name of obedience they were part to, and assisted in, the most wicked large scale actions in the history of the world.[47]
>
> —C. P. Snow, "Either-Or" (1961)

Instead of viewing each culture as a separate entity, morality—and, indeed, human survival itself—is better served by viewing the world in terms of a web of life that incorporates not just our own culture, nor even the totality of human cultures, but the whole world. Being part of the universal web gives the greatest moral value to our lives and to the lives of all peoples.

Exercises

*1. Has your community service work made you more aware of the common values shared by all people? Or has it confirmed the cultural relativists' belief that people from various cultures are just different when it comes to basic moral values? Explain, using specific examples.

2. Just as the social Darwinists encouraged rumors of cannibalism to justify Western imperialism, societies often focus on differences (real or imaginary) between cultures in order to promote their political and military ends. Make a list of other stereotypes that you've heard regarding the practices and moral values held by people of other cultures, and by different subcultures within our society, that differ sharply from those of your own culture or subculture. Are these stereotypes realistic?

3. Slogans are frequently used in times of war and social unrest to maintain loyalty to the culturally accepted ideology. For example, segregation was main-

tained with the slogan "separate but equal." Can you think of any slogans that are popular now that serve to keep us from examining certain inconsistencies in our own cultural norms?

Summary

1. **Cultural relativism** is the metaethical theory that moral standards and values are created by groups of people or cultures and that morality is nothing more than socially approved customs.

2. Cultural relativism is *not* the same as *excusing* behavior.

3. Cultural relativism is *not* the same as *tolerance* for multicultural diversity.

4. **Sociological relativism** is the observation that there is disagreement among cultures regarding moral values. It is not a moral theory; it does not conclude that value systems are necessarily relative.

5. *Social Darwinists,* such as philosopher *Herbert Spencer,* claimed that people from "primitive" cultures were less morally developed than those from European cultures.

6. Anthropologists, such as *Ruth Benedict* and *William Graham Sumner,* disagreed with the social Darwinists, arguing instead that morality is relative to each culture.

7. Cultural relativists define the moral community in terms of cultural ideas regarding who has moral worth, rather than in terms of transcultural moral standards such as dignity and human rights. Thus, cultural relativism can be used to justify the **marginalization** or exclusion of certain groups of people from the moral community.

8. The *Holocaust* led to disillusionment with cultural relativism.

9. The *Nuremberg International Military Tribunal* declared that, rather than morality being relative to each culture, there are universal, transcultural moral standards. Several Nazi war criminals, including *Adolf Eichmann,* were tried and found guilty using these standards.

10. Most philosophers, including *Aristotle, Plato, Ibn Khaldun,* and *John Fire Lame Deer,* claim that some cultures are more moral than others because they offer more opportunities for people to fulfill themselves.

11. According to cultural relativism, there is *no* such thing as *moral progress or moral reform.* Social reformers are thus no better than common criminals.

12. Research has found that people tend to behave more morally when they are alone than when part of a group.

13. Cultural relativism is *illogical* because it is based upon **the fallacy of ignorance, the fallacy of popular appeal**, and **the fallacy of appeal to tradition.**

14. Cultural relativism is *not a correct description* of how people actually make moral judgments.

15. Cultural relativism cannot work in a *pluralistic society.*

16. There are universal moral values which seem to exist in all or most known societies. These include a sense of moral community, *provisions for mating and rearing of children,* a *taboo against incest,* a *sense of justice and fair division of labor,* and *limits on violence.*

17. When conflicts exist between cultures, the only alternatives that cultural relativism provides for resolving these conflicts are *isolationism* and *armed conflict.*

CHAPTER 5

Is Morality Grounded in Religion?

*The God of the Bible . . . is a God who not only governs history,
but who orientates it in the direction of establishment of justice
and right. He is more than a provident God. He is a God
who takes sides with the poor and liberates them from slavery
and oppression. His might is at the service of justice. His power
is expressed in the defense of the rights of the poor.*[1]
    —GUSTAVO GUTIERREZ, *The Power of the Poor
    in History* (1993)

*The religious perspective is the conviction that the values one
holds are grounded in the inherent structure of reality, that between the way one ought to live and the way things really are
there is an unbreakable connection.*[2]
    —CLIFFORD GEERTZ, *Islam Observed* (1968)

*A list of virtues or duties drawn up by a Buddhist would not dif-
fer very greatly from one drawn up by a Christian, a Confucian-
ist, a Muhammadan or a Jew. Formally all of the ethico-religious
systems are universalist in scope.*
    —MORRIS GINSBERG, *Reason and Unreason in Society*
    (1947), pp. 307–8

Religion and Morality

Religion is an institutionalized system of beliefs and values shared by a group
and grounded in faith and the worship of a supreme transcendent Being(s).
During worship, people praise that which has the highest worth or value.[3]
God is worshipped because God represents perfect goodness and the highest
values. By imitating God, believers express their morality. Worshipping re-
affirms these moral values.

Many people look to their clergy not only as religious authorities but also
as moral authorities. People come to the clergy with ethical problems such as

147

marital problems and personal conflicts. Most hospital ethics boards have at least one clergy member. Clergy are also asked to testify before Congress on moral issues ranging from the use of nuclear weapons to health care. Clergy are exempt from active duty in the military because of the prevalent belief that their high moral sensibilities would not allow them to kill even in wartime.

The concept of God in the major world religions—Judaism, Christianity, Hinduism, and Islam—is so intimately connected to the concept of moral goodness that the moral code is incorporated right into the doctrine of these religions. The study of sacred scriptures is important, in part, because it teaches right from wrong. However, this by itself does not imply that religion or scripture is the only source of moral guidance or that morality is relative to religion. In the Jewish religion, Roman Catholicism, and mainstream Protestant religions, the basic moral principles are also held to be universal and discoverable through other means such as the use of reason or intuition.

In contrast, Islam, like fundamentalist Christianity, maintains that ethics is inseparable from religion and is built entirely upon it. An action is right simply because God commands it. Religion informs not only the Muslim's personal life but also the basis of public policy. The sovereignty of Allah [God] is the starting point of Islamic political philosophy and law.[4] In many Muslim countries, such as Saudi Arabia and Morocco, the law of the sacred texts—the *Qur'an*—is the law of the land and applies to everyone (Muslims and non-Muslims) living in that country. Humans are not expected to discern right from wrong but simply to submit unquestioningly to God's Will.

> The authority rests with none but Allah. He commands you not to surrender to any one save Him. This is the right way (of life).[5]
>
> —*Qur'an*

Not all religions are monotheistic (believe in one God) or regard God as a divine entity with whom we humans can have a personal relationship. Gandhi, who considered himself an orthodox Hindu, believed there was no God other than Truth. Because God is not a person but Truth, and because Truth is universal and all-pervasive, Gandhi believed that we must learn to love and respect even the lowest of living beings.

> To see the universal and all-pervading Spirit of Truth face to face, one must be able to love the meanest of creation as oneself.[6]

Buddhism and Jainism, which developed out of Hinduism, also had a major influence on Gandhi's moral philosophy. Neither Buddhism nor Jainism is strictly speaking a religion (although they are sometimes referred to as "sectarian religions"), because belief in God or a transcendent being is not part of either worldview. Confucianism, which is also sometimes considered a religion, is actually a philosophy.

Exercises

1. How have your religious beliefs shaped your morality? Is there a difference between religious and secular morality in your life? If so, what are the differences? If there are differences, how do you resolve a conflict between religious and secular morality?

2. When religious people use the words "right" and "wrong," are they using these words in a different sense than someone who is an agnostic or an atheist? Discuss the differences and similarities.

3. Is "God" just another word for "good"? If so, why bring God into discussions of morality at all? Why not just say "To know good is to do justice"?

4. In a survey of attitudes about religion in the United States, more than half of the people surveyed responded that religion should remain separate from social and political matters. Do you agree?

    If you agree that religious morality is different from secular morality, what role should religious morality play in forming public policy? Is religious morality morality at all, if it is irrelevant to our public life?

The Divine Command Theory

> *There is no Good save obedient behavior, save the obedient will. But this obedience is rendered not to a law or a principle which can be known beforehand, but only to the free, sovereign will of God. The Good consists in always doing what God wills at any particular moment.*
> —EMIL BRUNNER, *The Divine Imperative* (1947)

In Plato's *Euthyphro,* Socrates asks: "Do the gods love holiness because it is holy, or is it holy because the gods love it?" The divine command theory claims the latter: Something is holy or moral because God loves it.

The divine command is a type of ethical relativism. According to this theory, morality is dependent upon or relative to God. Morality does not exist independently of God's Will. Just as morality for the cultural relativist is relative to cultural norms and commands, for the divine command theorist morality is relative to what God commands or wills. There are no independent, universal moral standards by which to judge God's commands. No other justification is necessary for an action to be right other than that God commanded it.

Abraham and his son, Isaac. As a test of his faith and obedience, God commanded Abraham to sacrifice his son, Isaac. According to the narrative in Genesis 22 of the Holy Bible, God spared Isaac in return for Abraham's obedience.

The divine command theory could be compared to a "parental command theory." Our parents tell us to do something that may seem unfair by our standards. So we ask, "Why?" The reply is, "Because I said so!" And that's the end of the conversation. Your parents' saying so makes them right. Similarly, with the divine command theory, God does not have to have any reasons to back up "His" commands. God's command is right simply by virtue of God having commanded it.

Thus, to say that God is "good" is not to attribute any particular characteristic to God. To say that God is good is simply to say that "what God wills, God wills." God's reasons are ultimately unknowable to humans, and therefore, we must accept God's commands—whatever they are—on faith. To question God's commands or to demand independent nonreligious reasons for accepting a divine command shows lack of faith.

If God doesn't exist, everything is permissible.

—FYODOR DOSTOYEVSKY, *The Brothers Karamazov* (1880)

The biblical story of Abraham and Isaac, in which God orders Abraham to take his son, Isaac onto the mountain and sacrifice him, is sometimes used as an example of the divine command theory.[7] According to this interpretation, Abraham did not question God's command; nor did he look to universal

moral standards, such as "thou shalt not kill," since God, being omnipotent and the source of all morality, can change the moral rules at any time simply by an act of Will. Abraham's righteousness stemmed from his unquestioning obedience to the Will of God.

Examples of Divine Commands

According to Dostoyevsky, if morality is reducible to or relative to the Will of God, then without God there can be no morality. However, the divine command theory does not offer a much better alternative to Dostoyevsky's bleak prognosis for a godless world. If God *does* exist, and if morality is dependent upon God's Will, then morality is arbitrary. Anything—rape, murder, genocide, killing one's own children—is permissible *as long as God wills or commands it.*

Several years ago, a woman put her baby in a microwave oven and turned it on. When she was arrested for murdering her child, she defended herself on the grounds that God had commanded her to carry out the action. Did God command her to kill her child? How are we to know what was in the mind of God? To simply dismiss her claim as a symptom of a deranged mind is to sidestep the whole issue of faith and its relation to morality. After all, we do not regard Abraham as deranged but as a righteous man of great faith, yet he was also willing to kill his son for God.

More recently—on November 4, 1995—a 27-year-old Israeli law student, Yigal Amir, carried out what he likewise perceived to be the Will of God. Amir shot and killed Israeli prime minister Yitzhak Rabin as Rabin was leaving a peace rally. When Amir was tackled by police immediately after firing the shots, he told them, "I acted alone on God's orders and I have no regrets."[8]

If we respond to these examples by arguing that God would not have commanded these people to do such terrible things, we are implying that there are independent moral standards that we can use to appraise the morality of God's commands. If this is the case, then we should judge Abraham to be immoral, because it is generally believed that parents have a moral duty to protect their children. The fact that God substituted a lamb at the last minute and saved Isaac from death at his father's hand does not negate Abraham's willingness to kill his son.

The divine command theory leaves us without any criteria for judging whether the actions of Abraham, or of Yigal Amir, were morally justified or an expression of God's Will. Of course, this by itself does not disprove the divine command theory; a believer in the theory can reply that no proof is needed—that it's a matter of personal faith, not reason. For us to respond in turn that, without proof, the theory is false would be to fall prey to the fallacy of ignorance.

The Theory Debunked

Unlike Dostoyevsky, philosopher Kai Nielsen says that, as far as morality is concerned, it does not really matter whether God is dead or alive.[9] The divine command theory, Nielsen argues, is logically unsound. God cannot be used as a fundamental criterion for moral goodness, nor is God necessary for morality. Instead, the claim that what God wills is good *is dependent on a previous belief that there exists a being worthy of worship.* Thus, rather than God being the foundation of morality, a belief in God is dependent on our *already* having a concept of moral goodness. Morality, in other words, does not literally come from God but instead represents what people already believe to be moral *independent* of their belief in God. For example, most people would reject a voiced command to kill their children as not being the "voice of God." In other words, we do not depend on religion but rather on reason and other nonreligious criteria to discern right from wrong. We accept the ethical teachings in the scriptures as the revealed word of God precisely *because* they are consistent with what we already believe to be moral. According to Nielsen, although a moral code is incorporated into the doctrine of most religions, moral controversies can be resolved without appealing to religion.

> The Sages clearly recognized that the ethical moment of [Jewish Law] consists of commandments which, "Had they not been written, it would have been proper that they be written." Thus [one Rabbi] states that in the absence of a revealed Torah "we should have learned modesty from the cat, aversion to robbery from the ant, marital faithfulness from the dove, and conjugal deportment from the rooster."[10]
>
> —F. ROSSNER and J. DAVID BLEICH, *Jewish Bioethics* (1985)

Exercises

1. Does morality depend upon the existence of God? Do you agree with Dostoyevsky that "if God doesn't exist, everything is permissible"? Why or why not? What, if anything, would be different about your morality, if there was no God? Explain, using specific examples.

2. Traditional Christian theology teaches that we, as humans, are made in the image of God and, as such, have the same moral inclinations as God. If we accept this as true, does it necessarily follow that our inclinations reflect or are an expression of the Will of God? Discuss.

3. Discuss a case where someone justified an action that most people would have regarded as immoral on the grounds that God commanded him or her to carry out this action. How would you respond to this person?

Thomas Aquinas: Natural Law Theory

> *God approves of the good because it is good and eschews the evil because it is evil.*
> —KWAME GYEKYE, *An Essay on African Philosophical Thought:*
> *The Akan Conceptual Scheme* (1987)

> *Human law has the aspect of law to the extent to which it is in accord with the correct norm; and from this viewpoint it is evidently derived from the eternal law.*
> —THOMAS AQUINAS, *Summa Theologica,* Bk. I, Pt. II, Qu. 93, Art. 3

Natural Law Ethics

Natural law ethicists disagree with the divine command theorists. Instead of an action being right *because* God commands it, natural law theorists maintain that God commands an action *because* it is moral *beforehand and independently of God's commanding it.* Variations of natural law theory are found in moral philosophies throughout the world.

African philosopher Kwame Gyekye is a member of the Akan tribe in Ghana. Akan moral philosophy is a blend of natural law ethics and utilitarian ethics (which we will study in a later chapter). In response to Socrates' question in Plato's *Euthyphro,* Gyekye writes:

> . . . the response of the Akan moral thinker would be that God approves of the good because it is good. The reason is, if something is good because God approves of it, how would that good thing be known to them? How would they know what God approves of in a nonrevealed religion? On the contrary, their ascription of moral attributes to God and the sanctions that he is believed to apply . . . in the event of a breach of the moral law clearly suggest the Akan conviction that God approves of the good because it is good and eschews the evil because it is evil.[11]

According to natural law theory, morality is grounded in "nature" rather than being relative to God's commands (divine command theory), human feelings (ethical subjectivism), or cultural norms (cultural relativism). By this, natural law theorists do not mean laws in terms of physics and the biological sciences. By "nature," they mean *human nature.* Unlike physical nature, human nature is seen as nonmaterial and rational. Physical nature is fixed and determined, according to most natural law theorists. Human nature is free and autonomous.

Accepting natural law theory does not entail that we know the origin of natural law. Not all physicists agree on the origin of the laws of physics; not all natural law ethicists agree on the origin of natural law. Some natural law philosophers, such as Thomas Aquinas, maintain that moral law was created by God as part of His divine plan for the universe. Others, such as Aristotle, argue that the moral law has always existed as part of the natural order. Whatever the source of the moral law, natural law theorists all agree that it lies outside of cultural norms and laws and that the moral laws embedded in our nature as humans take the form of a universal code that we all ought to follow.

Natural law ethicist and Jewish scholar Lippman Bodoff, for example, interprets the story of Abraham and Isaac as a conflict between blind obedience (divine command theory) and moral choice (natural law theory). Bodoff argues that God, rather than expecting blind obedience, was "testing Abraham to see if he would remain loyal to God's moral law . . . even when divinely commanded to break it." Abraham was also testing this "new" God to see if He was worthy of worship. A God who was worthy of worship would not allow Abraham to kill his son, because this was contrary to the moral law. In the end, both Abraham and God passed the test. Abraham showed moral courage as well as strong religious faith.

The morality of the Nazis, on the other hand, was found sadly wanting

Thomas Aquinas (c. 1225–74), Italian philosopher and theologian. One of the leading moral philosophers of the medieval period, Aquinas' natural law theory has had a profound impact on the moral teachings of the Catholic Church.

according to natural law ethics, at least as interpreted by the United Nations. According to the U.N. Nuremberg Charter, rulers and citizens—regardless of their particular religious affiliation or lack thereof—are responsible "under God and [natural] law." These natural laws, the charter continues, include prohibitions against "crimes against humanity," "torture," and "waging or preparing for an unjust war." Each person has an individual responsibility not to take refuge in the laws or customs of their culture. Because of our ultimate responsibility to a universal moral code, people can be tried for doing so under international law when these cultural laws are contrary to natural law.

Thomas Aquinas

Italian philosopher and theologian Thomas Aquinas (c. 1225–74) is one of the foremost Western natural law philosophers. He also lived what he believed—placing moral or natural law above the demands of his culture and his family. Aquinas was born into nobility. He was a precocious child and an independent thinker. At the age of fourteen Thomas entered the University of Naples. After graduating in 1244, he joined the newly established evangelical Dominican Order. His parents were distressed by this turn of events—especially after the zealous Dominican monks refused to let the mother visit her son—so they arranged to have his brothers kidnap him.

Thomas remained locked in a tower in his parents' castle for one year. Even imprisonment by his own parents did not dissuade young Thomas from his chosen calling, however. His family eventually released him, and he returned to the Dominicans in Naples. In 1256, he was appointed Professor of Theology at the University of Paris. His most important scholastic work, the *Summa Theologica,* brings together Christian doctrine and the teachings of Aristotle.

According to both Aquinas and Aristotle, we function best as humans when we are perfecting our human capacities, reason being the highest or most important of these capacities. Because moral law is embedded in human reason, our actions do not depend upon our perception of God's Will or His commands at any particular moment.

Although natural law theorists do not necessarily believe in God, most Western versions of natural law theory accept Aquinas' concept of human nature as a creation of God. Because God is the perfectly rational being, according to these natural law theorists, rationality constitutes the divine spark within humans; it is our essence. It is only because God made us rational beings—in His image—that we can discern right from wrong. Moral principles, therefore, can be discovered not only through a study of religious doctrine but through the "light of natural reason," which is part of our human nature. Through the light of natural reason with which God endowed human beings, we are able to discern good from evil.

> Conscience is the dictate of reason . . . If an action is in accord with the reasonable order of conduct, then it will be a good kind of action . . . [If an action] is repugnant to reason it is a bad kind of action.
>
> —THOMAS AQUINAS, *Summa Theologica,* Bk. I, Pt. II, Qu. 19, Art. 3

Natural law theory is also **teleological.** This means that it is grounded in a specific view of the purpose or goal of the natural order. According to Aquinas, God as the most perfect and rational Being furnishes the end toward which the universe is directed. The moral or natural law is our human way of participating in and actively working toward that vision. Both Christian and Jewish natural law ethics look toward a messianic age when human law will be in perfect harmony with natural law. When this happens, true peace will finally be realized and "the lion shall lie down with the lamb."

In his hierarchy of laws, Aquinas recognizes four types of laws. Eternal law is the highest law; human law is the least binding upon us.

1. *Eternal law* is the uncreated reason of God that guides the universe as it moves toward a particular goal or end.

2. *Divine law* directs humans and other creatures to their supernatural end, which consists of a vision of God and eternal blessedness.

3. *Natural law,* or moral law, is the special way that rational creatures, such as humans, participate in eternal law and are thereby directed toward their earthly happiness.

4. *Human law* is at the bottom of the hierarchy of laws; it is law, such as legislation or cultural norms, that is derived by humans from natural law.

Moral Laws and Rules

Natural laws exist in the form of general or formal guidelines—such as "respect for other persons" and the Golden Rule. Aquinas formulates the basic principle of natural law as "do good and avoid evil." Philosopher H. L. A. Hart argues that "the minimum content of natural law" must also include the assumption that human survival is good.[12] These very general moral laws are contained within the moral codes of all major religions.

> There are some general principles in the holy books of all religions that teach love, charity, liberty, justice and equality for all the human family, there are many grand and beautiful passages, the golden rule has been echoed and re-echoed around the world.
>
> —ELIZABETH CADY STANTON, *The Woman's Bible* (1895), Pt. 1, p. 13

Normative moral rules, on the other hand, contain specific content and guidelines for action: "homosexuality is immoral," "honor your mother and your father," "do not commit adultery," "do not steal." These specific rules are derived from natural law, by use of reason. Because normative rules are interpretations of natural law, they are subject to human error and cultural biases. Therefore, they are open to analysis in light of more general moral principles as well as reinterpretation or rejection.

Reason is key in natural law theory, for discerning natural law and for knowing how to apply it. Because the application of natural law can change as we humans progress toward our natural or divine end, it is incumbent upon us to use reason to decide how to apply these general guidelines in a specific situation and at specific times in our history. For example, a specific rule prohibiting the use of artificial birth control may have been the fulfillment of natural law at one time (promoting the survival of the human race), but the present human condition may now require that this rule be rescinded. Indeed, the appropriateness of a rule against contraception is an issue that is currently the subject of much debate among Catholic natural law theorists.

To summarize natural law theory, natural law ethicists answer "no" to the question "Is morality relative to religion?" Natural law is universal and applies to all rational beings: God and humans, religious people and atheists alike are all bound by the same moral principles and sentiments. We act morally for the same reasons that God does.

Exercises

1. Do you agree with Aquinas that there is a higher law than human law? Why or why not? If there is a higher moral law, is it necessary for the concept of God to explain or validate this law? Support your answer. How would Aquinas and Kai Nielsen, respectively, respond to your answer to this question? How would Aquinas respond to Nielsen's criticism of natural law ethics? Which philosopher do you think has the strongest position? Support your answer.

2. Many of the Africans who were brought to North America by slave traders came from the Akan tribe in Ghana, which is on the west coast of Africa.[13] To what extent, if at all, does the moral code embraced by the African-American churches and members of these churches reflect the natural law ethics of the Akans rather than divine command theory or cultural relativism?

3. Discuss which interpretation of the story of Abraham and Isaac—Bodoff's or that of the divine command theorists—is most consistent with your understanding of morality.

4. As philosophers, we are called on to be autonomous thinkers rather than simply followers. However, it is sometimes difficult to tell whether a person chose a particular path in life based on well-thought-out reasons, or whether they chose their path simply as a reaction to their parents' lifestyle, because it was a fad, or because it fulfilled some lack in their life. How would you have reacted if you had been Aquinas' parents? How would you have reacted if you had been Aquinas locked away in your parents' house for a solid year? Justify your reactions, and relate your answers to natural law theory.

5. Some people claim that we should keep our religious morality and public morality separate. For example, a Catholic politician may believe that abortion is immoral, but this does not necessarily mean, the argument goes, that abortion should be illegal or that abortion is wrong for non-Catholics. Does this argument make sense? If natural or moral law is universally binding upon everyone, how can we separate our religious ethics from our secular

ethics? Aren't they both the same? If one's "religious" morality does not apply in public life, then is it really morality at all? Isn't it one of the characteristics of morality that it takes precedence over all other demands in our life? Discuss.

6. Natural law ethics have been used to both condone and condemn practices such as voluntary euthanasia, abortion, slavery, homosexuality, and birth control. Choose one of these issues, and discuss it in light of natural law theory. Remember that natural law ethics gives only very general guidelines; resist the temptation to bring in personal feelings or to use cultural norms and definitions of moral community to support your position.

Religion, Natural Law Theory, and Civil Disobedience

> *If the law is of such a nature that it requires you to be an agent of injustice to another, then*
> *I say, break the law.* —HENRY DAVID THOREAU, "Civil Disobedience" (1849)

Members of animal liberation groups break into laboratories to set the animals free; antiabortionists block women from entering Planned Parenthood clinics; before the legalization of abortion, women formed cooperatives to assist other women in getting abortions; workers stage illegal strikes to protest unfair working conditions; antinuclear activists block roads leading to nuclear power plants and military establishments; during the Vietnam War, college students openly burnt their draft cards to protest the war; thousands of parents refuse to send their children to school because they are opposed to state-mandated schooling; and in the back of his Volkswagen van, Dr. Jack Kevorkian—despite repeated warnings from the courts—continues to assist terminally ill people to end their lives. Are these people justified, on the grounds of a higher moral law, in breaking the law of the land?

Natural law ethicists answer with a qualified "yes." A person is justified in breaking a human law if the law they are breaking conflicts with natural law and if breaking the unjust human law does not create more harm that obeying it would cause. There are several ways in which a human law can be unjust. For example, a law may be unjust because it has one of the following characteristics:

1. *It is degrading to humans.* The laws that permitted slavery and laws that allow the torture of prisoners of war are degrading to humans.

2. *It is discriminatory.* Laws that apply to one group of people but not to another may also be unjust. For example, the fourteenth amendment of the U.S. Constitution gave men, but not women, the right to vote. The laws that supported apartheid in South Africa and the caste system in India are also unjust, because they were discriminatory.

3. *It is enacted by an authority that is not truly representative.* The cry "no taxation without representation," which sparked the American Revolution, was a protest over this type of unjust law.

4. *It is unjustly applied.* Search-and-seizure laws in this and other countries, for example, are intended to protect citizens from dangerous people; however, these laws are sometimes unjustly applied simply to harass a person or to punish political dissenters or other controversial figures.

Civil Disobedience

Because natural law is higher than human law, when human laws or cultural norms conflict with natural law or any of the higher laws, civil disobedience may be not only morally acceptable but morally required. **Civil disobedience** involves the refusal to obey certain government laws for the purpose of trying to bring about a change in legislation or government policy.

> [Human] laws can be unjust because they are contrary to the divine good, for example, the laws of tyrants which promote idolatry or whatever else is against divine law. In no way is it permissible to observe them.[14]
>
> —THOMAS AQUINAS, *Summa Theologica*

Most people who break laws are not engaged in civil disobedience, because most criminals are not interested in social reform. A person may break a law simply because it is an inconvenience to obey it—we exceed the speed limit, drive through red lights, sneak in the back door of the movie theater, and lie about our age at the local bar.

On the other hand, some people may break a law with good intentions; yet, they may be mistaken in their interpretation of natural law. Most Roman Catholic theologians, for example, believe that natural law prohibits suicide. If this is the case, then what Dr. Kevorkian is doing is morally wrong. However, both Kevorkian and these theologians agree that we have a higher moral duty to respect and treat other humans with dignity. In other words, they agree on the general content of moral or natural law. What they disagree on is the *application* of this higher law in a specific context. Whether this higher moral law precludes the use of voluntary euthanasia is still being debated. The morality of homosexuality is another issue that is still under debate among natural law ethicists. Of course, as in the case of euthanasia, it may sometimes be difficult to decide who is mistaken, particularly since our idea of morality is so bound up with our cultural norms and subjective feelings rather than with reason.

Protest in Beijing, China, 1989. According to natural law ethicists, civil disobedience may be morally justified in the face of injustice. Civil disobedience and questioning cultural norms, however, can be dangerous. In 1989 demonstrators protesting China's totalitarian government were massacred in Beijing's Tiananmen Square.

Henry David Thoreau

Another factor to be considered is how we should protest an unfair law. We may agree on the content of natural law and its application to a particular situation, but we can still disagree about how to protest an unjust human law that conflicts with the requirements of natural law in a particular situation. Henry David Thoreau (1817–62) believed that petitions to elected representatives and other indirect democratic processes are insufficient to bring about social change. He argued that we also have a moral obligation to take direct nonviolent action in the face of an unjust law. When Thoreau refused to pay his taxes, as a protest against the evils of slavery, the authorities threw him in jail.

Thoreau's essay on "Civil Disobedience" (1849) continues to be one of the most prominent works in the field. When breaking an unjust human law, Thoreau wrote, we must do so in a way that is consistent with natural law, as follows:

1. *Use only moral and nonviolent means* to achieve our goals. These methods include boycotting, illegal picketing and blocking traffic, nonviolent resistance, and nonpayment of taxes.

2. *First make an effort to bring about change through legal means.* Most people who engage in civil disobedience continue to try to change the unjust law through legal means as well.

3. *Be open and public* about our actions. If no one knows we are breaking the law, then it is unlikely that our actions will have much impact on law-makers!

4. Be willing to *accept the consequences of our actions*—such as prison sentences, fines, deportation, loss of a job, or social disapproval.

Martin Luther King, Jr.

During the Montgomery boycotts in 1956, civil rights leader and natural law ethicist Dr. Martin Luther King, Jr., called for civil disobedience of the local segregation laws. King was born in 1929 in Atlanta, Georgia, the grandson of a sharecropper. Despite the constant oppression of racism and segregation, King remembered his childhood as a happy one. His father, a respected Baptist minister, and his mother, Alberta King, taught their three children that they could overcome the humiliation of segregation.

King returned to the South after completing a Ph.D. from the Boston University School of Theology. He soon became one of the driving forces behind the civil rights movement in the 1950s and 1960s. Beginning with the bus boycott in Montgomery, he and other civil rights leaders such as Rosa Parks deliberately violated Southern segregation laws as a means of protesting injustice. Because of his protest, King, like Thoreau, was arrested and sent to jail.

On August 28, 1963, King organized a march on Washington to raise the nation's awareness of civil rights and to encourage congress to pass President Kennedy's civil rights bill. At this peaceful demonstration, attended by more than 200,000 people, King delivered his famous "I have a dream" speech. The following year, King won the Nobel peace prize (the youngest person ever to do so) for his role in leading nonviolent demonstrations.

King's antiestablishment teachings made him the target of violence from white racists. In 1968, he was assassinated by James Earl Ray in Memphis, Tennessee, where he had gone to speak out on behalf of striking sanitation workers.

The life and writings of Indian philosopher Mohandas Gandhi had a profound influence on King. Like King, Gandhi believed in a higher moral law against which human laws could be judged. Gandhi used the term *Satyagraha* to describe civil disobedience based on passive resistance and noncooperation. *Satyagraha* embodies deep respect and love for *all* living beings, even oppressors.

Feminist Civil Disobedience

Natural law ethicists who engage in civil disobedience often come into conflict with the law because of their rejection of cultural relativism and their belief in a higher moral law. The early feminists in the United States used civil disobedience, based on natural law theory, to protest human laws that denied

Martin Luther King, Jr. (1929–68) delivering his famous "I have a dream" speech in Washington, D.C., 1963. King organized the bus boycott in Montgomery, Alabama, in 1955. In 1964 King received the Noble peace prize for his work in civil rights and racial equality.

women certain basic rights. Many early feminists were arrested and jailed as a result of their civil disobedience. Susan B. Anthony was arrested in 1872 for registering and voting in an election, a right enjoyed only by men at the time. During her trial, she urged all women to refuse to accept unjust laws that discriminate against women: "I shall earnestly and persistently continue to urge all women," she told the judge, "to the practical recognition of the old revolutionary maxim, that 'Resistance to tyranny is obedience to God.'"[15]

Exercises

1. List some examples of unjust laws. Explain why they are unjust.

2. Discuss the following case studies. Which are examples of civil disobedience? If they are not examples of civil disobedience, explain why and discuss what type of civil disobedience a person could engage in to protest the law.

   a. Mary Beth believes it is unfair that faculty and staff have better parking facilities on campus than commuter students. She frequently has to park in a commuter lot that is almost a half mile from her classes. Meanwhile, there are plenty of empty spots in the faculty lots. The other day, while cutting through one of the faculty lots on her way to class, Mary Beth noticed that one member of the faculty had left their car unlocked. A parking decal was sitting on the dashboard. Mary Beth checked to make sure that no one was around, and then she took the pass and placed it in on the windshield of her own car.

b. In some states it is legal for landlords to discriminate against prospective tenants on the basis of their sexual orientation. Greg and Jorge, a gay couple, were frustrated in their attempt to find an apartment near campus. With the permission of the local police, they set up a picket line in the public park across from their apartment building. Here, they passed out brochures and collected names on a petition to get the existing law changed.

c. Brice is opposed to animal testing. Last night, he and two of his friends broke into the laboratory in the pharmacology building on campus. They released the lab animals and then destroyed the laboratory equipment that was used for animal experimentation. The next morning they turned themselves in to the campus police.

d. The Unabomber, alleged to be former University of California math professor Theodore Kaczynski, believes that our current dependence on technology is immoral and destructive to both humans and the environment. To voice his protest, between 1978 and 1996, when Kaczynski was arrested, the Unabomber mailed sixteen bombs to people who are prominent in the development of technology. The bombings have claimed three lives and left twenty-three people injured.

e. Native American activists Russell Means and Dennis Banks organized a nonviolent protest demonstration in Washington, D.C., in 1972 to protest the broken promises made to Native Americans by the United States Bureau of Indian Affairs and to lobby for reforms within the Bureau of Indian Affairs.

f. When the demonstration in Washington (described in "e") did not yield satisfactory results, Means and Banks led about five hundred Native Americans in a six-day takeover of the Bureau of Indian Affairs.

g. During the Vietnam War, many Americans who were opposed to the war emigrated to Canada to avoid the draft.

h. The notorious pirate Anne Bonny was born in Ireland in 1700 as the illegitimate daughter of a wealthy lawyer and a servant. Because of the scandal of adultery, her family was forced to move to South Carolina. Here, Anne, described as a high-spirited girl, rebelled against her father. She entered a life of piracy by dressing up as a man, because women were then not allowed to be crew members on ships.

3. Martin Luther King, Jr., in his "Letter from a Birmingham Jail," responds to the criticism that he should have waited before engaging in civil disobedience such as the bus boycotts. He writes that the advice "wait" until the time

is right are the words of the oppressors. The right time to fight oppression is now, even if that requires using illegal means. Do you agree with King's decision to engage in civil disobedience? Was he wrong in using illegal means to bring about social change?

King used Socrates' refusal to stop publicly teaching and discussing philosophy as an example of an act of civil disobedience. Do you agree with King? Support your position.

How would a cultural relativist respond to the civil disobedience of people such as Martin Luther King, Jr., Socrates, Susan B. Anthony, and Gandhi?

4. Do you agree with Thoreau that, besides the usual democratic processes, we are morally required to take more direct action against an unjust law? Does the democratic process encourage compromise on social issues? The fourteenth amendment to the U.S. Constitution, which gave *all* men the right to vote but did not grant the vote to women, was a compromise between universal suffrage and expanding the right to vote to all men—black and white. Should we protest compromises like these as unjust, as some feminists did, even though in general more people benefit from them?

Relate your answer to a time in your own life when you chose to compromise on a moral issue. Were you and the other parties involved satisfied with the compromise? Why or why not?

*5. Under what circumstances, if any, would you engage in civil disobedience? Would you be more likely to engage in civil disobedience since becoming involved in community service? Discuss.

Robert Bellah: Civil Religion and Cultural Relativism

Whatever may be conceded to the influence of refined education on minds of peculiar structure, reason and experience both forbid us to expect that National morality can prevail in exclusion of religious principle.   —GEORGE WASHINGTON's "Farewell Address"

Religion is the sign of the oppressed creature, the heart of a heartless world, just as it is the spirit of spiritless conditions. It is the opium *of the people.*   —KARL MARX

Religion, like cultural norms, offers powerful external motivations for behaving morally. We are expected to behave morally because it pleases God. Eternal damnation awaits those who fail to heed religion's moral commands; prison or social ostracism awaits those who break cultural norms. Those who are obedient to their religion's moral code can look forward to eternal salvation and reward; similarly, those who adhere to social norms get their rewards, such as social approval and economic prosperity, here in this life. The melding of these two sets of sanctions together—religious and cultural—can make religion a powerful force in our lives.

Religion as the Worship of Society

French sociologist and philosopher Emile Durkheim (1858–1917) argued, in his 1915 landmark work *The Elementary Forms of the Religious Life,* that God stands in the same relationship to worshippers as society does to its individual members. God is the symbol of society, and each society creates God in its own image. God thus becomes a symbol of cultural unity. Religion is the worship of society, thereby acting as a mechanism for justifying the moral norms of a particular culture.

Socialization, according to Durkheim, involves getting people to *want* to do what they *must* do for society to survive. Rather than human law being judged in light of a universal transcultural natural law or moral law, it is "rewritten" to be consistent with human law. By sacralizing cultural norms and values, religion gives these cultural norms a transcendent authority that they would otherwise lack.

> [In American slavery] men convince themselves that a system which was so economically profitable must be morally justifiable. They formulated elaborate theories of racial superiority. Their rationalizations clothed obvious wrongs in the beautiful garments of righteousness . . . Religion and Bible were cited to crystallize the status quo . . .
>
> —MARTIN LUTHER KING, JR., *The Strength to Love* (1963), p. 41

To account for the special position that a particular society and its cultural norms play in the scheme of things, people attribute creative power to God, however, God is not only the author of their moral code. Members of that society—or group of societies in the case of more "universal" religions—see themselves as all descended from one father—God, the father (or mother, as the case may be). Those who are descended from God have moral value; those who are not are nonpersons and have only instrumental value. The following argument, for example, was used to justify slavery in the United States:

All men are made in the image of God;
God, as everyone knows, is not a Negro;
Therefore, the Negro is not a man.[16]

Unlike Durkheim, who admired how religion united people around a common set of values, Karl Marx denounced religion as a destructive force. Marx argued that religious institutions, rather than uniting people in a common interest, exist primarily for the purpose of maintaining the status quo and legitimating the interests of the ruler class by deifying their norms. According to Marx, religion, rather than motivating us to work toward a more just society, serves as the "opiate of the people" by lulling us into a sense of false security. Religion also prevents those who are oppressed from overthrowing their oppressors, by extolling meekness and submissiveness.

Both Kai Nielsen and Sigmund Freud have interpreted belief in God as a longing for an all-protecting father and a fear of the "dreadful freedom that gives [us] human dignity." Nielsen notes, "That because we have feelings of dependence does not mean that there is something on which we can depend."[17] He viewed such a hope as an illusion—an illusion that entails a sacrifice of our autonomy.

Robert Bellah's Moderate Stance

United States sociologist Robert Bellah (b. 1927) takes a more moderate position than either Durkheim, Marx, or Nielsen. Like Durkheim, Bellah suggests that the primary role of modern religion is the creation of a sense of cultural or national identity and purpose. Bellah maintains that Christianity and Judaism are no longer the dominant religions in the United States; a new form of religion has emerged. He calls this new religion American civil religion; following is an excerpt from his essay "Civil Religion in America":

> . . . [In American civil religion,] though much is selectively derived from Christianity, this religion is clearly not itself Christianity. For one thing, neither Washington nor Adams nor Jefferson mentions Christ in his inaugural address; nor do any of the subsequent presidents, although not one of them fails to mention God. The God of the civil religion is not only rather "unitarian," he is also on the austere side, much more related to order, law, and right than to salvation and love . . . He is actively interested and involved in history, with a special concern for America.

American civil religion defines the significance of the United States in relation to the transcendent. However, rather than supporting universal transcultural moral values, most U.S. religious denominations support and celebrate cultural relativism, or what is known as the "American way of life." In *American Civil Religion*, Bellah writes, America is the "new Israel, the promised land" where "God has led his people to establish a new sort of social order that shall be a light unto all nations."[18] This new social order is identified with transcendent moral law and our human progression toward moral perfection.

The presence of the U.S. flag in the sanctuary of most places of worship in this country serves as a powerful symbol of this civil religion and the moral claims that the "American way of life" has on us. In American civil religion, ethical principles—including those found in the Bible—are altered and reinterpreted to serve our national ideals and mission. This should come as no surprise given that ninety percent of Americans are cultural relativists. The words of Washington and Jefferson, with their strong emphasis on personal freedom, rather than biblical ethics, form the heart of moral scriptures in the United States.

Because the ethics of civil religion are primarily relative to the culture, the ethical ideals of civil religion do not apply as stringently to those outside of the U.S. moral community. Indeed, Bellah points out that our ethical standards tend to be quite different on the international scene:

> With respect to America's role in the world, the dangers of distortion are greater and the built-in safeguards of the tradition weaker. The theme of the American Israel was used, almost from the beginning, as a justification for the shameful treatment of Indians so characteristic of our history. It can be overtly or implicitly linked to the idea of manifest destiny that has been used since the early nineteenth century. Never has the danger been greater than today . . . we have been overtaken by a third great problem that has led to a third great crisis, in the midst of which we stand. This is the problem of responsible action in a revolutionary world, a world seeking to attain many of the things, material and spiritual, that we have already attained.[19]

Bellah notes that a "theme that lies very deep in the American tradition [is] the obligation, both collective and individual, to carry out God's will on earth. This was the motivating spirit of those who founded America, and it has been present in every generation since . . ."[20] However, because God is the symbol of America and the "American way," God's Will on Earth is interpreted in an ethnocentric manner.

"Without an awareness that our nation stands under higher judgment," Bellah writes, "the tradition of civil religion would be dangerous indeed. Fortunately the prophetic voices have never been lacking." Bellah maintains that the spirit of civil disobedience and the belief in a higher moral law are very much alive today. This, he notes in *Essays on Religion in a Post-Traditional World* (1970), is found in the creative tension in American civil religion between cultural relativism, or uncritically deifying the "American way," and the belief that we have a responsibility toward a higher transcultural moral law:

> . . . since the American civil religion is not the worship of the American nation but an understanding of the American experience in the light of ultimate and universal reality, the reorganization entailed by such a new situation need not disrupt the American civil religion's continuity. A world civil religion [based on universal moral principles] could be accepted as a fulfillment and not as a denial of American civil religion. Indeed, such an outcome has been the eschatological hope of American civil religion from the beginning. To deny such an outcome would be to deny the meaning of America itself.

Does this more universalistic ideology of "eschatological hope" justify American civil religion? As Bellah illustrates in his writings on civil religion, there is no doubt that many religiously motivated actions are noble and consistent with philosophical morality. However, grounding moral values in religion encourages dependence upon outside authorities for moral guidance.

This will thus encounter the same pitfalls as grounding moral values in cultural norms.

Just as our dependence on cultural norms and the opinions of our peer group for moral guidance can stunt our moral development, studies of college students have also found that a "conservative Christian focus may actually inhibit moral development especially if it adopts an ideological answer-oriented approach which discourages autonomous principled reasoning."[21] On the other hand, grounding moral values in universal transcultural moral values provides a person with the motivation to do what is morally right *even when it goes against the teachings of one's religion and culture.*

Exercises

1. Why do you behave morally? Would you behave any differently if there was no divine judgment or no Heaven and Hell?

2. Religions have different concepts of God. Discuss some of the concepts of God in your own and other cultures. How, if at all, do these various concepts of God reinforce cultural values? Relate your discussion to Durkheim's statement that God is the symbol of society.

3. Do you agree with Robert Bellah that there is basically only one religion in America—American civil religion? Is religion simply a means of deifying cultural norms and legitimating an ethics based on cultural relativism? Are patriotism and belief in God closely linked? Give examples. To what extent do your own religious beliefs support the status quo?

4. Slavery was morally justified by American civil religion. Are there any cultural practices nowadays that you believe conflict with the demands of morality but that are justified under American civil religion? Explain.

Religion and the Moral Community

God created man in his own image, in the image of God he created them; male and female he created them. And God blessed them and God said to them, "Be fruitful and multiply, and fill the earth and subdue it: and have dominion over the fish of the sea and over the birds of the air and over every living thing that moves upon the earth."

—Genesis 1:27–28

Then I was standing on the highest mountain of them all, round beneath me was the whole hoop of the world . . . I was seeing in the sacred manner of the shape of all things of the spirit and the shapes as they must live together like one being. And I say that the sacred hoop of my people was one of many hoops that make one circle, wide as daylight and starlight . . . And I saw that it was holy. —BLACK ELK, *The Sacred Hoop*

The metaphysical assumptions of different religious traditions regarding the nature and purpose of humans in this world have a profound influence on our definition of moral community. Just as cultural relativism defines moral community in cultural terms, religious ethics tends to define moral community in relation to God. The more a being is like God, the greater that being's moral value.

The teachings of the scriptures in Western religion not only affirm human dignity but also imply a special moral bond between God and humans and a special role for humans in creation. In Judaism, because humans are created in the image of God, to kill a person is to diminish the likeness of God and the reality of God's own self. Because humans bear the greatest likeness to God—having been created in God's image—humans have the highest moral value. Other creatures, in contrast, exist only to satisfy the needs of humans.

Besides placing humans above other animals, religion has been used to support a hierarchy of moral values within humanity, based on racial differences and the "different natures" of males and females. Thomas Aquinas, by formulating his natural law ethics, simply accepted Aristotle's theory that humans are by nature intended to be male and that women are "misbegotten males." As defective versions of men and an "inferior mix," women are not as rational as men and, lacking men's moral self-control, are more prone to disorder and sin. When Aquinas was asked why God, who is Himself apparently a single male, allows women to exist, he concluded that women exist for the sake of procreation; however, because men have a special, higher spiritual nature, it is proper that men rule over the naturally inferior. Only through submission to men can women be redeemed.

Thus, Christian theology, as traditionally interpreted, legitimates discrimination against women as morally and theologically acceptable. Because God in Western religion is male, writes theologian Rosemary Radford Ruether, men "as the monopolizers of theological self-definition project onto women their own rejection of their 'lower selves.' Women's essential nature is seen as having less of the divine image and more of the physical nature."[22]

Carol Christ, in her essay "Why Women Need a Goddess," likewise argues that patriarchal religions centering on the worship of a male God create an atmosphere and worldview "that keep women in a state of psychological dependence on men and male authority, while at the same time legitimating the political and social authority of fathers and sons in the institutions of society."[23] This, in turn, has led to unjust social structures and the marginalization of women in society. Christ suggests that women need to celebrate the symbol of the Goddess to reclaim their power and self-respect.

Theologian James Cone points out that the portrayal of God as a white man has also had a demoralizing effect on the psyche of African Americans. He rejects the "white American 'Christianity' that is built on racism," calling for the dissolution of current Christianity and its God, and a "revaluation of all values." "Being black in America," he writes, "has very little to do with skin color. To be black means that your heart, your soul, your mind, and your body are where the dispossessed are."[24]

By calling for a reevaluation of traditional Christian values, Cone asks for a recognition of our common humanity and a rejection of our racist and hierarchical concept of the moral community that rotates around a white-skinned God. Liberation from the oppression of traditional Christianity, Cone suggests, entails the development of a black theology, a theology for those who are oppressed and marginalized.

Black Elk

The portrayal of God as a white male has also contributed to the degradation of non-Europeans, including the military massacres of Native Americans. For many Native Americans, the whole Earth is sacred and contained with the moral community.[25] Their non-Western view of what constitutes the moral community has led to antagonism and conflict between them and the European Christians who settled here—particularly around the concept of private ownership of land. Because the Earth is sacred or has intrinsic moral value, in many Native American philosophies, it cannot be owned or sold. To do so is to treat the environment as having only instrumental value.

During his life, Black Elk (1863–1950), a Sioux holy man and philosopher, saw his people all but destroyed by European settlers. As a child, Black Elk began having visions that tormented him, calling him to bring his people back into the sacred hoop where they could be happy and prosperous again. His visions worried his parents, who consulted a medicine man. The medicine man told Black Elk that he must enact his vision of a more inclusive moral community for the people on Earth. At the age of twenty-two, Black Elk joined Buffalo Bill's Wild West Show, hoping that he could learn from the experience how to help his own people; however, when he returned home in 1889 he found his people in a state of despair. Black Elk was confused and fearful that he would be tempted to give up his vision for a lesser one, so he resumed his nomadic life.

His journey took him to Pine Ridge, South Dakota, where in December 1890, the starving Sioux Indians had gathered to surrender. Instead of accepting the surrender, twenty-five white soldiers killed almost three hundred Indians that day at Wounded Knee. Black Elk, armed only with his sacred bow, managed to escape into the Badlands. Black Elk eventually returned to Pine Ridge, where he lived the rest of his life with his broken dreams. In the 1930s Black Elk's visions were written down by John Neihardt. His book, *Black Elk Speaks,* is widely acclaimed as one of the greatest books about American Indian life and religion.

The Yanomamo Protest, Brazil, 1989. The Yanomamo Indians lived in the Amazon rainforests of Brazil and Venezuela. Dubbed "the keepers of the forest" by anthropologists, the Yanomamo have taken a strong public stand against the destruction of the rainforests and the takeover of their homeland by commercial interests. In 1993, seventeen Yanomamo Indians were massacred in Venezuela by gold miners.

Native American Attitudes

Much of contemporary Native American religion is a countercultural movement against the traditional Judeo-Christian depiction of the moral community. "The universally agreed-upon tenets of American Indian spirituality," writes Amanda Porterfield,

> include condemnation of American exploitation of nature and mistreatment of Indians, regard to precolonial America as a sacred place where nature and humanity lived in plentiful harmony, certainty that American Indian attitudes are opposite to those of American culture and morally superior on every count, and an underlying belief that American Indian attitudes toward nature are a means of revitalizing American culture.[26]

The American Indian Religious Freedom Act of 1978 served as an acknowledgment by the United States Congress that certain places are sacred space to many Native American tribes. Although all of the Earth and those upon it are sacred, a sacred space has special spiritual power or significance—it is a place were human beings experience a strong sense of being connected to the universe. The notion of sacred spaces in nature is also found in many other religions. For example, in Japan Mount Fuji is considered a shrine; Ayers Rock is a sacred space for Australian aborigines.

The Judeo-Christian concept of moral community, in contrast, places humans outside of and above nature. This has led to a corresponding moral degradation of nonhuman animals and the environment. Environmental ethicist Lynn White writes that "by destroying pagan animism, Christianity made it possible to exploit nature in a mood of indifference to the feelings of natural objects."[27] In the traditional Western religions, food and food production are not considered to be part of the moral community (sacred) but instead a commodity or a form of "natural capital."[28] The destructive effects of the exclusion of nonhuman animals and the environment from our moral community have only recently begun to be realized.

Eagle Man, an Oglala Sioux lawyer and writer, warns us that "the plight of the non-Indian world is that it has lost respect for Mother Earth, from whom and where we all come."[29] The environmental destruction and pollution we are now experiencing, he says, are a warning from Mother Earth that we must change our attitudes and lifestyle. This change, however, can only come through a radical paradigm shift regarding our definition of the moral community.

Exercises

1. Draw a mandala of the moral community of your religion or one of the major religions in this country. What criteria are used for the inclusion and exclusion of different beings? How are these criteria justified? How does the mandala of the religion's moral community resemble and differ from that of the moral community in the United States?

2. The belief that we, as humans, are all children of God and share a common parent—God, the father—has been a powerful force for motivating people to respect the dignity and rights of other humans and to work toward social justice for all humans. Is the belief that humans are special necessary to motivate people to respect others? Would a belief in the equal dignity of all living beings, such as that espoused by many Native American and Eastern philosophers, weaken the moral value of humans, including ourselves?

*3. How do religious depictions of God affect a society's concept of the moral community and its treatment of different groups of people? Relate your answers to your community service work. Do you agree with the solutions proposed by James Cone and Carol Christ?

4. Traditional religious views of the moral community privilege white ablebodied males. To what extent, however, has placing men at the top of the hierarchy actually harmed men by restricting their opportunities to speak out against the establishment, to pursue a lifestyle not oriented toward material achievement, or to achieve self-realization?

    Relate your answer to some of your own experiences. Share your experiences with others in the class who have had different experiences because they belong to another gender, for example, or a different race, ethnic group, or sexual orientation.

5. Do you agree with Lynn White that the anthropocentric moral community supported by Christianity has been the primary culprit in our current ecological crisis? Why or why not? Relate your answer to the philosophy espoused by Black Elk and Eagle Man. Do you agree with them that we can only find peace by expanding our moral community to include "all things in this world"? Discuss how this would change your lifestyle.

God and the Problem of Evil

God would never have allowed evils to subsist in his creation, were it not that he might find
in them the occasion to produce good things unique in kind, and dependent for their unique
character on the character of the evils in question.

—AUSTIN FARRER, *Love Almighty and Ills Unlimited:*
An Essay on Providence and Evil (1952), p. 163

I can't combine faith in God with Auschwitz. Either there is no God, or I don't belong
to him.   —MILAN MACHOVEC (Polish Marxist philosopher)[30]

The presence of apparently senseless suffering and evil in the world is one of the primary reasons why people lose faith in God. We have all experienced evil that causes suffering or prevents us from enjoying cherished values and achieving worthy ends. Both secular and religious ethics have difficulty explaining the presence of evil, but the problem is most difficult to overcome for those, such as Western theologians, who believe in a personal, omnipotent, and perfectly good God. If God is all-powerful and perfectly good, why does God allow the existence of so much pain and suffering in the world?

Although much of our suffering is the result of human foibles or ignorance, suffering is sometimes the result of forces that lie outside the control of humans, either individually or collectively. Each year millions of humans and other living creatures either die or have their lives devastated as the result of natural disasters—floods, droughts, hurricanes, earthquakes, genetic disorders, plagues, and epidemics.

Also problematic for the religious ethicist are cases of moral evil when it is not the person who causes the evil who ends up suffering. Much of the suffering in the world—child abuse, genocide, rape, and even many cases of starvation—is the result of other people's immoral actions. Why would a God who is both omnipotent and perfectly good allow people to torture and slaughter their fellow humans? Even minimally decent parents would at least step in to try to save their children from someone who is torturing them.

One reply is that God does not prevent these atrocities because this would interfere with human free will or choice. This reply is problematic, however. God, by simply standing back and allowing Nazis and child abusers to freely ravage, torture, and murder their victims, is allowing the victims' freedoms to be destroyed forever.

The response that the victims of these atrocities have not been permanently harmed, since they will go to Heaven, also has a troubling implication for ethical theory. If murder and torture and genocide no longer have any moral implications, since no one has really been harmed, then these actions cannot be considered morally wrong. Instead, these actions simply become vehicles for sending others to Heaven. Indeed, it might even be argued that we have a moral obligation to kill as many people as possible—an extreme position that was actually used to some extent to justify the carnage associated with the Crusades.

Another proposed solution to the problem of evil is the supposed existence of two opposing cosmic forces in the universe—a good force, or God, and a demonic force. However, this leaves one question unanswered: Why would a good and omnipotent God allow such an evil presence to continue to exist and torment humans and other creatures?

Can God Coexist with Evil?

Some philosophers, such as utilitarian John Stuart Mill, argue that there is no God because of the "absolute contradiction" involved between the existence of evil in the world and a perfectly good and all-powerful God.[31] By denying the existence of such a God, the problem of reconciling the existence of evil in the world with the existence of a good God disappears. The expectation of some religious people that God should have intervened in events such as the Holocaust is, in other words, based on a mistaken view of reality. Reality, or nature, is instead morally neutral.

In Peter De Vries' book *The Blood of Lambs,* the main character, Wanderhope, is asked by another patient in the tuberculosis sanitarium whether he is praying for her. He responds in the negative. He explains to her:

> That would mean that the one I was addressing had done this to you to begin with, which I find hard to believe anybody would . . . I simply mean that asking Him to cure you—or me, or anybody—implies a personal being who arbitrarily does us this dirt. The prayer then is a plea to have a heart. To knock it off. I find the thought repulsive. I prefer to think we're the victims of chance to dignifying any such force with the name of providence.[32]

Philosopher David Hume (1711–76) likewise concluded in his *Dialogues Concerning Natural Religion* (1779) that God, if He exists, cannot be omnipotent and perfectly good, because He created a world that contains evil. The other alternative, Hume points out, is to deny the existence of evil in the world. However, Hume rejects this line of reasoning on empirical grounds, pointing out that there clearly is evil and suffering in this world. Therefore,

God did not pick the best course. Furthermore, if such a malevolent or impotent God exists, He is hardly worthy of our worship:

> Is he [God] willing to prevent evil, but not able? Then he is impotent. Is he able, but not willing? Then is he malevolent. Is he both able and willing? Whence then is evil? . . . The only method of supporting Divine benevolence . . . is to deny absolutely the misery and wickedness of man.[33]

The Best of All Possible Worlds

Gottfried Leibniz (1646–1716) chose a different tack than Mill and Hume. Leibniz attempted to save God's good name by arguing that this is the "best of all possible worlds." By doing this, Leibniz denies the existence of evil except that which is necessary for the accomplishment of the divine purpose. God, who freely chose to make this the most perfect world possible, Leibniz argues, is like a clockmaker who preestablished the harmony in the world. Everything goes its own way according to its own nature and laws but in such a way that everything is synchronized. The world, including human "choices," is ordered so that it moves toward the establishment of "a moral world within the natural world." Following is an excerpt from Leibniz's "A Vindication of God's Justice":

> There is much complaint that in this life human nature is exposed to so many evils. Those who feel this way fail to consider that a great part of this evil is the effect of human guilt . . .
>
> Others are particularly dissatisfied with the fact that physical good and evil are not distributed in proportion to moral good and evil, or in other words, that frequently the just are miserable while the unrighteous prosper.
>
> To these complaints there are two answers: the first, given by the Apostle, namely, that the afflictions of this life are nothing compared with the future glory, which will be revealed to us. The second, which Christ Himself has suggested, in an admirable parable: If the grain falling to the soil did not die, it would not bear fruit.
>
> Thus our afflictions not only will be largely compensated, but they will serve to increase our felicity. These evils are not only profitable, but indispensable.

The loss of human free will in Leibniz's solution to the problem of evil is unacceptable to most theologians. Bishop Joseph Butler (1692–1752) rejected the idea that everything in this world is predetermined. To explain the presence of evil in the world, Butler describes our present life as a trial—a state of probation or a testing ground for a future life.[34] Evil and temptation exist in this world as part of our test. As such, this life provides humans, who are inferior creatures in need of perfection, with opportunities for both good and immoral behavior. Humans, who are under the "moral government of God," will receive their reward and punishment in the Hereafter. Thus, at times we must forego our earthly happiness for the sake of our future happiness.

In another variation on this theme, John Hicks refers to this world with its sufferings and tribulations as a "vale of soul-making."[35] The purpose of suffering is the perfection of our souls. This world is not intended to be a paradise where we are sheltered from all dangers and challenges like a pet in a comfortable cage where all its needs are provided for. Only by participating in the "hazardous adventure in individual freedom," an adventure that involves suffering and overcoming temptations, can we become the perfected, moral creatures God wants us to be. Hicks points out that there are striking examples, the most notable being the crucifixion and resurrection of Christ, of good being brought triumphantly out of evil. Hicks is also aware that evil and suffering can lead to bitterness, fear, and mental and emotional breakdown. Because of this, the business of soul-making and striving after moral perfection must continue in the afterlife.

The Eastern Concept of Karma

The concept of "soul-making" is also found in Eastern philosophies and religions, where it is generally tied in with the notion of **Karma.** One of the fundamental principles of Hinduism and Buddhism is that happiness should be proportional to goodness. This fundamental principle of justice is expressed in Karma, a natural, impersonal law of cause and effect that applies universally to everyone.

Unlike Hicks' solution, the law of Karma is not connected to the idea of a supreme Being or God. Instead, people work toward moral perfection through reincarnation, which involves being reborn in the world into a succession of bodies. Nor is suffering seen as redemptive, as in the Christian religion. According to the law of Karma, a person's condition in this life is the result of his or her actions in previous lives. Thus, Karma can be used to explain why some people suffer more in this life or have lower socioeconomic status. Similarly, our actions in this life will affect our status in future lives. Only by attaining the spiritual state of bliss or moral perfection known as Nirvana can a person finally be liberated from the cycle of suffering and rebirth.

Exercises

1. How do you explain the presence of evil—both natural evil and moral evil— in the world? Are you satisfied with any of the theories that attempt to reconcile evil with the traditional Judeo-Christian view of God as omnipotent and perfectly good?

2. How would you respond to Wanderhope's reply to the patient in *The Blood of the Lamb?* What does Wanderhope see as the relationship between God and morality? Do you agree with him? Support your answer.

3. The concept of Karma has been used to blame people for their own victimization. This is captured in the expression "What goes around comes around." Is this true?

Does Morality Need Religion?

The love of other human beings and the ethical life in general are autonomous in that they justify themselves, requiring no support from religion. But there is a religious dimension to life and it has its effect on the whole life. On the religious view it is God's concern, as it were, how man behaves towards his fellow and the love of the neighbor is the love of God.[36]

—LOUIS JACOBS, "The Relationship Between Religion and Ethics in Jewish Thought" (1996)

. . . the way of life of such an individual, after he has achieved this apprehension [of Him], will always have in view loving-kindness, righteousness, and judgment.

—MOSES MAIMONIDES, *The Guide of the Perplexed* (12th century)

Religion has been credited with inspiring people—such as Susan B. Anthony, Martin Luther King, Jr., Mother Teresa, and Bishop Tutu of South Africa—to reach a higher moral standard than that required by everyday life. Morality that is beyond what is normally expected of an individual is known as **supererogatory.** Acts such as giving away one's belongings to the poor, or risking one's life in the name of a moral cause, are examples of supererogatory actions. Some religious ethicists claim that it is faith in God that inspires people to engage in supererogatory actions. Evolution and the laws of (physical) nature, they argue, do not have the same moral force as do the laws created by God. The belief that God is the creator of moral law gives morality its authority and motivates the believer to behave in accordance with moral law even when it conflicts with human laws.

Whether or not he recognizes his situation, [the atheist] is confronted by the problem of good, which is at least as difficult for him as the pervasiveness of evil is for the theist. In a godless universe, how are we to account for the manifest fact that high values are sought for and realized? How can we reconcile with an absurd, meaningless cosmos that cares nothing for human striving the patent reality in human experience of the pursuit and discovery of truth, the creation and appreciation of beauty, and the quiet strength of self-sacrificial love?[37]

—PAUL SCHILLING, *God and Human Anguish* (1977)

As we have already noted, there is no shortage of examples of social re-form movements and courageous acts of civil disobedience that have been in-spired largely by faith in God. On the other hand, belief in God does not seem to be necessary to motivate someone to place morality above human law and to engage in supererogatory moral acts. Some natural law ethicists do not be-lieve in God, thinking it unnecessary to postulate a God to justify the exis-tence of a natural (moral) law.

Gandhi did not believe in a personal God. For Thoreau, discovery of the natural law came through the individual's dialogue with nature—in the form of the woods and lakes—rather than through dialogue with God. Yet, this lack of faith did not weaken the commitment of these two to the moral law. The nineteenth-century feminist movement had religious underpinnings; the current women's liberation movement, however, has been a secular move-ment and even at times antireligious. The animal liberation movement and environmental movements have also, for the most part, eschewed religion and adopted philosophical ethics as the basis of their beliefs.

Also, although there are many stories of great and courageous deeds car-ried out in the name of God, there is no shortage of atrocities committed in the name of religion and God. Slavery in the South was supported by the ma-jority of white Christians at the time as morally acceptable and part of God's natural law. Likewise, the church in Nazi Germany, for the most part, ratio-nalized the inhumane treatment of the Jews as consistent with natural law. Herbert Spencer's contention that civilized Christians are more peaceful than their "primitive" non-Christian counterparts is hard to substantiate in the light of the many wartime atrocities committed in the name of God. The Cru-sades of 1095–1272, which were carried out in the name of God and the Christian faith, and the Inquisition that followed the Crusades cost countless lives and created untold misery.

On an individual level, religious people are no more likely to engage in acts of moral heroism than are nonreligious people. Surveys of Americans, in-cluding those who claim that religion is very important to them, show that re-ligion has little effect on people's everyday moral values or on their ideas of social morality.[38] Even being a member of the clergy does not guarantee ex-emplary moral behavior, let alone a willingness to engage in acts of civil dis-obedience in the face of social injustices. Indeed, our faith can be shaken to its foundation when we hear reports of clergy being involved in acts such as child molestation, sexual harassment, and theft.[39,40]

The failure of religion to keep people on the straight and narrow path of righteousness has traditionally been explained in terms of human weakness and sin. We know what is right but sometimes choose what is wrong. Some sociologists, such as Robert Bellah and Karl Marx, however, suggest that the moral failure of religion may have little to do with faith in God and a lot more to do with the culture-maintaining role of most traditional religions.

Spirituality Versus Religiosity

Discussions of morality and religion should be separate from discussions of the role of spirituality in morality. In Western thought, spirituality is generally associated with being religious. In Eastern philosophies, spirituality is not associated with being religious—at least in the Western sense of being religious. Religion is a social phenomenon involving the institutionalization of a particular set of beliefs about a transcendent God. **Spirituality,** on the other hand, is an inner attitude of reverence or deep respect for the ultimate moral worth or sacredness of oneself and others, independently of a belief in a transcendent God or any particular religious or cultural doctrine. Spirituality does not imply a belief in metaphysical dualism or the existence of a non-material afterlife

Some religions encourage spirituality; others do not. Some people who are nonreligious or even antireligion regard themselves as highly spiritual. Kenneth Ring, for example, in his study of near-death experiences (NDE) found that, following the NDE, most experiencers become less religious yet, at the same time, more strongly disposed toward spirituality and the universalism of Eastern philosophies as well as more concerned with doing what is morally right.[41]

Gandhi, as we already noted, did not believe in a personal God. Yet, he was a highly spiritual person who believed in the power of the soul-force. Gandhi maintained that this soul-force gives people the moral strength to persevere in nonviolent action and to love our oppressors and to engage in nonviolent action to overthrow unjust social structures and to overcome evil.

> Truth is soul or spirit. It is, therefore, known as soul-force.
>
> —MOHANDAS GANDHI, *Non-Violent Resistance*[42]

Being religious, on its own, does not encourage moral behavior. Indeed, studies show that church members, as a group, are *more racially prejudiced* than nonmembers. (For example, the Ku Klux Klan considers itself a Christian organization.) On the other hand, studies have also found that the most active members of the church are the *least* prejudiced of both church members and nonmembers.

Psychologist Gordon Allport explained this discrepancy by making a distinction between intrinsically religious people and extrinsically religious people.[43] *Intrinsically religious people* join churches because faith is meaningful to them as an end in itself. Because of this they are more likely to be active in their church. Intrinsically religious people, studies find, are also more autonomous and *committed at the moral level.* Like nonmembers, they are comfortable with being nonconformists and are more likely to reject or protest cultural norms when these conflict with universal moral principles.

Extrinsically religious people, on the other hand, join churches because of the secular benefits, such as social status. Although these people are likely to be "indiscriminately pro-religious," their religious faith does not usually translate into being a "nuclear church member." These are the heteronomous moral reasoners who uncritically accept the tenets of civil religion—including its narrow view of moral community.

In a study of the differences between people who helped to rescue Jews during World War II and those who did not, it was found that religious affiliation was not a major factor. However, one's *interpretation of the nature of their religious commitment* was important. Rescuers were more likely to define their moral community broadly to include all of humanity, whereas non-rescuers were more likely to use narrower cultural definitions of moral community.[44] Truly moral people, unlike heteronomous moral reasoners, strive to live the good life and to be a certain kind of person—compassionate and just—not because God or their religion orders them to do so, but because it is the right thing to do.

Morality Is Independent of Religion

Most philosophers, as well as most theologians, agree that morality exists independently of religion—that religious ethics is not fundamentally different from philosophical ethics. When people who are religious use the terms "right" and "wrong," they mean the same thing as someone who is not religious.

Religious differences tend to fall away in most serious discussions of moral issues, such as slavery and abortion, not because religion isn't important to the participants but because moral disputes can be discussed and even resolved without bringing religion into the equation. For example, many people initially regarded the protest against slavery as a religious issue. Most of the early petitions regarding slavery were presented by members of the Society of Friends (Quakers) and were, for the most part, dismissed by Congress as the "mere rant and rhapsody of meddling fanatics"[45] trying to force their religious views on Southerners. People living in the South particularly resented the "very indecent attack on the character" of the slave states and slave owners by these religious fanatics. "Abolitionism," wrote John Calhoun in 1837, "originated in that blind fanatical zeal which made one man believe that he was responsible for the sins of others."[46] Analogies were made between the Quakers and the fanaticism of witch-hunters of the Puritan period who "tied the victim that it could not convert to the stake."[47] As the debate over slavery moved further into the public arena in the 1840s and 1850s, however, the discussion shifted from religious differences to the moral issues involved.

When debating moral issues that are associated with the doctrinal positions of specific religious groups, therefore, we must take care not to commit the circumstantial fallacy by assuming that a person must hold one particular view simply because they are a member of a particular religion. The current abortion debate, for example, is regarded by some people as a specifically Catholic issue; however, the debate can be carried on without any reference to religion. Indeed, according to the Gallup polls, Catholics are just as likely to be pro-choice as Protestants, although people who are not affiliated with any religion are split about whether abortion should always be legal or whether there should be restrictions.[48] Some religions take an official stand regarding different moral issues—such as slavery, abortion, and pacifism—but this does not imply that these issues are specifically religious rather than moral issues. In debating these and similar issues, we must be careful to separate the moral issues involved from religious doctrine.

Religious ethics that are not securely moored in autonomous universal ethics but rather demand uncritical acceptance of official doctrines on various moral issues promote heteronomous moral reasoning. It is easy for religious ethics, once set adrift, to become grounded on the rocky shores of cultural relativism. When this happens, religion can become a destructive force by sanctifying cultural customs that are unjust and limiting one's conception of the moral community.

Exercises

1. Can science and our everyday existence give our life meaning? Or do you agree that without God there is no purpose or meaning in life and, consequently, no reason why we should be moral? Support your answer.

2. What is the difference between religious faith and spirituality? Is spirituality necessary for moral autonomy? Why or why not? Does spirituality play a role in your moral life? If so, what role does it play?

3. What do you think Gandhi meant by the "soul-force"? Relate the concept to your own life and moral behavior.

4. Think of some highly religious people you know—either personally or as public figures—who are moralistic but who commit acts that are highly immoral. Discuss ways in which these people are either intrinsically or extrinsically motivated.

5. Choose a controversial issue, such as homosexuality, that is sometimes regarded as a religious issue. Can the debate over the morality of homosexual-

ity be carried on without using religious doctrine? If not, what happens when a religious principle seems to conflict with a moral principle? Or is such a conflict even possible?

Summary

1. *Religion* is an institutionalized system of beliefs and values shared by a group and grounded in faith and the worship of a supreme transcendent Being(s). *Worship* involves lifting up and praising that which has the highest worth. God is worshipped because He represents perfect goodness and the highest values.

2. In some religions, such as *Islam*, morality is dependent upon religion.

3. The *divine command theory* states that an act is moral because God commands it.

4. *Natural law theory* states that morality is autonomous; that is, it is independent of religion and God's commands.

5. The natural law theory of *Thomas Aquinas* has had a major influence on modern Catholic teachings. Aquinas lists four types of law: *eternal, divine, natural* (moral), and *human* (legal laws and cultural norms).

6. When a human law is unjust and conflicts with moral law, we have a moral obligation to engage in **civil disobedience.**

7. *Emile Durkheim* argued that God is the symbol of society and religion is the worship of society.

8. *David Hume* and *Karl Marx* regarded traditional religion as destructive to morality.

9. Sociologist *Robert Bellah* suggests that the primary role of modern religion is to create a sense of national unity. *American civil religion* is the dominant religion in the United States.

10. The traditional Western religious concept of God is *anthropocentric, patriarchal*, and racially biased. This, in turn, affects our definition of **moral community.** Several philosophers, such as *Rosemary Radford Ruether, Carol Christ, James Cone, Black Elk,* and *Eagle Man,* suggest that we need to move beyond a definition of moral community that is based on Judeo-Christian concepts of moral worth.

11. The presence of *evil* and suffering in the world is one of the major reasons that people lose faith in the concept of a perfectly good God.

12. Various *solutions* have been proposed to the *"problem of evil."*

    • Postulate two *cosmic forces:* God and a demonic force.

    • Deny the existence of *an omnipotent, perfectly good God* (Mill, Hume).

- Suffering is essential for our moral perfection (*Leibniz, Butler, Hicks*)
- The *universe is basically just,* and therefore, happiness in the long run will be proportional to goodness in the final scheme of things. The concept of **Karma,** found in *Hinduism, Buddhism,* and *Jainism,* states that justice is a natural, impersonal law of cause and effect.

13. A **supererogatory** action is one that is above and beyond everyday morality. There is no evidence that religious people are more likely to engage in supererogatory acts.

CHAPTER 6

Conscience and Moral Development

Let a man not do what his own sense of righteousness tells him
not to do, and let him not desire what his sense of righteousness
tells him not to desire;—to act thus is all he has to do.
 —MENCIUS, *The Book of Mencius,* 7A17

The fruit of conscience is humility, and the fruit of humility
is love.
 —The Ethiopian *Book of the Philosophers* (c. 9th century)

Ethics and the Study of Human Development

Immanuel Kant once said that the basic questions of philosophy—including the question "What ought I to do?"—are all fundamentally related to anthropology, or "What is man?"[1] The study of moral development takes place at this juncture of philosophical theory and the social sciences. Although some purists do not want these two disciplines to overlap, any adequate theory of morality must take into consideration the relevant facts about human nature and human behavior.

If we agree with Aristotle that the primary reason for studying ethics is to make us better people, then an examination of our development must be part of that process. This is not to say that we can determine what our moral values ought to be by looking at what people do. Instead, a study of human development helps us to better understand how people discern moral principles when making moral judgments.

Most of us know what is good, at least in principle. The difficulties arise in living what we know and in the application of general moral knowledge to particular contexts. Self-knowledge can help us toward this goal. By learning about the psychological mechanisms that govern our moral development, we can actually advance our moral growth.

One of the assumptions underlying developmental theories, in both philosophy and psychology, is that humans have an innate desire to grow and to fulfill their potential. The belief that human nature strives toward the good life is consistent with the philosophies of Kant and Aristotle as well as many non-Western philosophies such as Confucianism and Buddhism. Cognitive-development theorists also claim that people who live up to their potential and lead good lives will be happier, experience greater inner peace and harmony, and be more satisfied with their moral decisions.

Exercise

What do you think of when you hear the word "conscience"? Take a few minutes to draw a picture of your conscience or make a list of words describing your conscience.

Conscience: Culturally Relative or Universal?

> *Some good must come by clinging to the right. Conscience is a man's compass, and though the needle sometimes deviates, though one perceives irregularities in directing one's course by it, still one must try to follow its direction.*
> —VINCENT VAN GOGH, *Dear Theo: An Autobiography of Vincent van Gogh*

For most people, a well-developed conscience is the essence of the moral life. What seems to differentiate the saint from the psychopath is not so much the norms of their culture, their religious affiliation, or their power to impose their desires upon others: Rather, it is the vitality and strength of their conscience. Conscience is clearly assumed to be guiding the majority of our actions, so acting in accordance with our conscience is hardly newsworthy. Acts of violence and degradation, on the other hand, are newsworthy precisely *because* they are so unusual. Despite the centrality of the concept of conscience in our lives, the concept itself has received little direct attention from philosophers and psychologists.

Philosopher Georg Hegel defined "true conscience [as] the disposition to will what is absolutely good."[2] The English word "conscience" comes from the Latin words *com* ("with") and *scire* ("to know"). Conscience, in other words, provides us with *knowledge* about what is right and wrong. However, conscience is more than just a passive source of knowledge. Conscience involves *reason* and critical thinking; it also involves *feelings*. Conscience not only *motivates* us; it *demands* that we act in accord with it.

In most religions, conscience is intimately linked to who we are. Many Christians view the conscience as divine guidance or "the voice of God" speaking through our hearts. In Judaism, worshipping and following one's conscience are inseparable: "When our conscience is not at one with the actions of our body, then our worship of our Creator is imperfect."[3] The

Ethiopian *Book of the Philosophers* compares conscience to an inner light in the soul that not only bears the fruit of love for one another, but also gives us the "wisdom that distinguishes what should be."[4] The comparison of conscience with light or energy is found in many other philosophies.

Psychologist Carl Jung, like the Buddhists and the Hindus, believes that morality is a basic law of consciousness. As such, conscience involves both our conscious and unconscious thought processes, including our dreams. The Hindu *Upanishads* locate the conscience in the deepest levels of the mind, beyond ordinary reasoning. Meditation, consequently, is an important tool for getting in touch with our conscience. Kant also believed that the good will—which is the expression of our true conscience, though it may be affirmed by "ordinary rational knowledge"—has its source beyond ordinary reason.[5]

Among the ancient Greek philosophers, Plato defined conscience as an activity of the soul that directs us toward the good. Acting in accordance with conscience or "reason" is thus essential to our functioning as human beings. A human without a conscience, according to Plato, is not a person and lacks moral standing in the community. Because psychopaths are not persons, Plato makes a provision in his *Republic* for the execution of these people or those "whose souls are incurably evil."[6]

Sometimes other messages get confused with those from our true conscience. One of the popular images associated with conscience is that of a little angel on one shoulder, whispering into one ear, while on the other shoulder perches a little demon gleefully telling us to do the exact opposite. Those who are heteronomous moral reasoners or cultural relativists, in particular, may describe their conscience as a voice coming from "outside" of them—from God, or their parents, or society, or peers. German philosopher Friedrich Nietzsche (1844–1900), in his book *Beyond Good and Evil,* refers to this heteronomous "morality" that is shaped by and caters to outside forces as "herd [or] slave morality."[7]

> Being nationalistic in the sense in which it is now demanded by public opinion, would, it seems to me, be for us who are more spiritual not mere insipidity but dishonesty, a deliberate deadening of our better will and conscience.[8]

This image of conscience as both good and evil captures one of the paradoxes of conscience. Although the basic structure of our conscience may be innate, like language, the specifics are culturally shaped. This, combined with our social nature and desire to be liked by others, leaves the uncritical or unanalytical conscience vulnerable to public opinion and outside forces that want to control us in the name of "morality."

There are three main forces that contribute to the shaping of our conscience: (1) heredity or biological factors, (2) learning or environmental factors, and (3) conscious moral direction.

Heredity or Biological Factors

Altruistic Behavior   Confucian philosopher Mencius believed that human nature is basically good. People, he pointed out, will rush to save a child, not because they think about it first or because they expect a reward, but out of an innate feeling of benevolence that is essential to humans. Most developmental psychologists and sociobiologists concur with Mencius. As with language, there are certain biological requirements that must be present for conscience to become fully developed. University of California professor James Q. Wilson refers to this predisposition as the "moral sense." Sociobiologists, such as E. O. Wilson, speak of an "altruism gene" that genetically predisposes us to care for and help others. Aristotle refers to this aspect of our conscience as "natural virtue."

> What is striking about the newer findings of child psychologists is that the emergence of a moral sense occurs before the child has acquired much in the way of language. The rudiments of moral action—a regard for the well-being of others and anxiety at having failed to perform according to a standard—are present well before anything like morality could occur.
>
> —JAMES Q. WILSON, *The Moral Sense* (1993), p. 130

According to psychologist Robert Katz, the capacity for altruistic behavior or sympathy seems to be inborn and involves both "non-logical and instinctive," or intuitive, components.[9] Sympathy is visible as early as ten months after birth, when a baby gets upset in response to another baby's distress. The expression of sympathy appears to follow a predictable developmental path, going from egocentric empathy to empathy for others' feelings to empathy for others' life conditions.[10]

Studies also show that the level of an individual's sympathy and generosity tends to remain relatively stable over the years, suggesting that this capacity is to a large extent part of our innate disposition.[11] In some children, the capacity for sympathy is strong but in others it is weak or nonexistent. Florence Nightingale "was so ready with her sympathy for all who suffered or were in trouble," even as a teenager, that people referred to her as an "angel in the homes of the poor."[12] Frederick Douglass, as a child of six, was already deeply troubled by the injustices of slavery. Yet, he displayed an inordinate sympathy and love for those who profited by the system.[13] Gandhi also displayed an unusual degree of moral sensitivity, from the time that he was a young child, and was often called on to act as mediator in disputes among his playmates and his family.

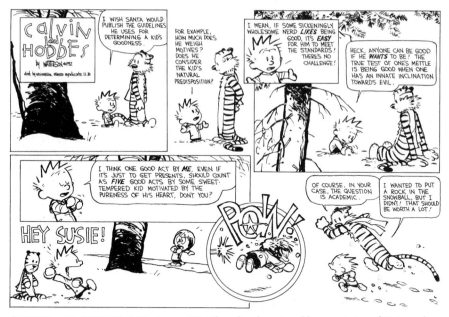

(CALVIN AND HOBBES © Watterson. Distributed and reprinted by permission of Universal Press Syndicate, Inc.)

Anyone who comes from or has a family with siblings is likely well aware that questions relating to justice as fairness appear at an early age—even though the recognition of the duty of fairness is initially limited to issues regarding the child's own fair treatment and an adult's duty to treat him or her fairly. The sense of moral indignation or outrage at one's own unfair treatment likewise emerges at a very young age. Even very young children will protest their unfair treatment despite their parents' or society's attempts to impose "unjust" cultural norms upon them. This suggests that a basic sense of justice is also, to some extent, inborn rather than learned.

The Frontal Lobes There is strong evidence that the frontal lobe cortex in the brain plays a key role in moral decision-making. Most of the work in this area has been with *psychopaths*—people who apparently lack a conscience or moral sense. A study of prisoners found that, when psychopaths were compared to non-psychopathic criminals, the former had specific deficits associated with frontal lobe functioning.[14]

One of the most fascinating studies of the relation between the brain and morality was carried out by a team of scientists led by Hanna Damasio on the skull of Phineas Gage.[15] In 1848, Phineas P. Gage was drilling holes and blasting rock to make room for a railway track in Vermont, when one of the explosives accidentally went off. The impact sent a long metal rod through his skull just behind his left eye. The rod passed through the frontal lobes of his brain and landed several yards away.

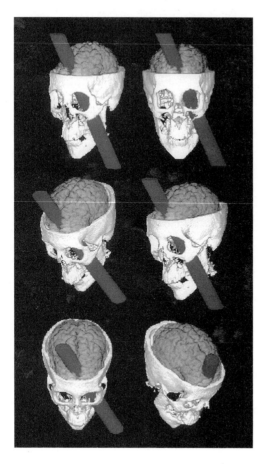

Computer images of the skull of Phineas P. Gage showing the most likely path of the rod that passed through his brain. Gage was injured by a flying rod during an explosion while blasting rock for a railroad track in Vermont in 1848. Following the accident, Gage was unable to make moral decisions.

After Gage recovered from the trauma of the accident, his intellectual and motor skills were found to be unaffected; however, he no longer seemed to be capable of making moral decisions. Before the accident Gage had been well liked, responsible, and hardworking, whereas afterward he was untrustworthy, obscene, and unable to make the simplest moral decisions. This and similar studies of the behavior of people with frontal lobe damage has led scientists such as Damasio to the conclusion that this part of our brain plays a critical role in our moral behavior.

Psychopaths are generally intelligent, rational, and outwardly normal. However, they have a deficit in the affective, or emotional, side of their brain. Psychopaths can mimic emotions such as concern and moral indignation, but apparently they do not actually feel them. Psychopaths are unable to sympathize with or imagine the feelings of others; therefore, they are completely self-centered. They can lie, cheat, maim, and kill without feeling the slightest remorse. In other words, they are ethical subjectivists acting only on their own desires and whims. They have no interest in passing moral judgment on others, nor do they pay any heed to judgment from others.

Natural moral dispositions are apparently present at the time of birth in most people, though this is not enough to ensure the development of moral character—just as the capacity for language at birth is in itself insufficient for its development. Without community and nurture, neither capacity can develop. On the other hand, if we are lacking an innate moral sense, or if there is damage or a deficit in our brain, we will never be able to develop a conscience, no matter how nurturing and virtuous our society at large.

Learning or Environmental Factors

Our conscience is also shaped through the interactions of our natural moral disposition and temperament with our early experiences and our environment (family, religion, nation). Culture is not the source of our most basic moral sense, but it does help to establish the boundaries and guidelines within which our moral sentiments and principles express themselves. Sometimes, however, cultural norms run contrary to the basic demands of morality. In these cases, our conscience helps us to discern which cultural norms are consistent with the demands of morality.

Of course, cultural relativists would disagree. To them, to be morally well-adjusted is to act in conformity with others' expectations. The view of conscience as purely a product of our environment was reinforced in the early 1900s by behaviorists, who regarded moral behavior as nothing more than imitation or social conditioning.

Sigmund Freud also regarded conscience as a product of our environment. Freud placed the conscience in the middle of the battleground between the irrational id (our instinctual nature) and the voice of public opinion. The Freudian concept of conscience as an internalized tyrant imposed on us by our parents and by society has dominated most of the contemporary literature on the subject. According to Freud, the "conscience" or **super-ego** develops as a reaction formation against our childhood Oedipus complex. The task of the super-ego is to repress the Oedipus complex, which stems from the id. The super-ego keeps us from carrying out our wish to murder our same-sex parent, who is perceived as a "rival" or obstacle to the fulfillment of our sexual desires for our other parent. The repression of these desires, Freud claimed, is accomplished by internalizing parental commands and taking on the character of the rival parent. The parental commands not only provide us with an ego ideal: "You ought to be like this (like your father)." They also prohibit certain behaviors: "You may not be like this (like your father)—that is, you may not do all that he does; some things are his prerogative."[16] These prohibitions are reinforced by societal norms.

Although Freud maintained that the conscience or super-ego is necessary for life within society, he also argued that the conscience could become oppressive and that people with the strongest consciences are also the most repressed. The Freudian notion that our conscience is a relentless slave master

Sigmund Freud (1856–1939), Austrian neurologist and psychoanalyst. Freud believed that the conscience, or super-ego, developed as a reaction against our childhood sexual attraction to our opposite-sex parent.

that must be overcome or at least toned down, if we are to be happy, has not been borne out by empirical studies.[17]

> . . . The super-ego retains the character of the father, while the more powerful the Oedipus complex was and the more rapidly it succumbed to repression (under the influence of authority, religious teaching, schooling and reading), the stricter will be the domination of the super-ego over the ego later on—in the form of conscience or perhaps of an unconscious sense of guilt.[18]
>
> —SIGMUND FREUD, *The Ego and the Id* (1923)

The belief that morality is wholly a product of learning and our environment is no longer accepted by most psychologists. Many philosophers and psychologists acknowledge that there is something like a super-ego or heteronomous conscience, but they distinguish between the super-ego and true conscience. In most cases, the super-ego reinforces the conscience; however, on occasion, the demands of the super-ego conflict with those of the true conscience. There is an obvious connection between environment and moral character, yet we have the ability to rise above our environment. Children brought up in a loving home are more likely to be caring and virtuous, but many people, such as Harriet Tubman, grew up in very abusive environments yet became caring adults. Some of our most vicious serial killers, in contrast, have come from intact families that seemed to be loving and supportive.

Conscious Moral Direction

Autonomous Moral Reasoning   Although innate and external forces can influence our conscience, the exercise of the conscience demands active participation on our part through the use of conscious and responsible deliberation. On September 3, 1995, the *Providence Journal* published a story about Penny Cullerton, a high school teacher in New Ipswich, New Hampshire, whose inner conscience conflicted with social norms. Cullerton chose to listen to her conscience. She decided to use two books in her literature class: Mary Sarton's *The Education of Harriet Hatfield,* a novel about lesbian love and "coming out," and E. M. Forster's *Maurice,* a novel about two young men who meet at college and fall in love. In making her decision, Cullerton used her conscious moral direction. Because she listened "to the voice within, not to others," Cullerton was dismissed from her job.

The great majority of world philosophers have held that true conscience is autonomous. Most people like to think of themselves as autonomous moral reasoners. Collective morality, however, exerts a much greater influence over people than most of us realize, as demonstrated by the Holocaust and slavery here in the United States. Many people, unlike Penny Cullerton, back down when cultural norms and other nonmoral values, such as job security or popularity, conflict with their conscience. We readily internalize cultural norms such as "Jews are bad" or "homosexuals are perverts." Because of our readiness to uncritically accept cultural norms, it is important for us to develop autonomy through conscious moral direction.

> Nature prepares in us the ground for their [moral virtues] reception, but their complete formation is the product of habit.
>
> —ARISTOTLE, *Nicomachean Ethics,* Bk. I, Ch. 1

Aristotle emphasized the importance of **habituation**—practicing virtuous behavior. Confucian philosophy also teaches that, although inborn moral sentiments are important, only through conscious reflection can we achieve perfect goodness. The ability to engage in conscious moral direction—to be a morally mature person—entails accepting responsibility for our actions, rather than simply reacting to our environment. One of the basic assumptions of moral philosophy is that humans have at least some free will. As free agents, we can overcome a lack of early moral training or negative influences.

1. The way of greater learning lies in keeping one's inborn luminous Virtue unobscured, in renewing the people, and in coming to rest in perfect goodness.

2. Knowing where to come to rest, one becomes steadfast; being steadfast, one may find peace of mind; peace of mind may lead to serenity; this serenity makes reflection possible; only with reflection is one able to reach the resting place.[19]

—*The Greater Learning* (Ta-Hsueh)

Determinism   Determinists claim that there is no such thing as conscious moral direction. Freud tells us to blame our parents for our shortcomings. If we are nothing more than products of our environment or our genetic inheritance, then we are no more to blame for our behavior then a computer would be.

In 1892, two young men, Nathan Leopold and Richard Loeb—both described as coming from "good homes"—decided to see whether they could commit the perfect murder. They killed Loeb's fourteen-year-old cousin, Bobby Franks, and hid his body in a storm drain. The body was soon found, and the two boys were arrested. In the boys' defense, attorney Clarence Darrow argued that they were not responsible for their actions; therefore, they could not be blamed for their crimes. The killing of Loeb's cousin, Darrow claimed, was simply part of a causal chain of events beginning with early childhood influences and honed by the two boys' fascination with detective stories.

Most defense lawyers do not claim that the actions of their clients are fully determined, but there has been a trend in the hundred years since the Loeb trial for defense lawyers to try to excuse their clients' criminal actions by claiming that they were determined by prior traumas. Thirty-two-year-old Willie Bocket lives in New York's Woodbourne Correction Center in a Plexiglas cell fit for the likes of "Hannibal, the Cannibal." When Willie was nine, he was sent to reform school. At the age of fifteen, he murdered two people on a New York City subway. Willie says it is wrong to hold him responsible for his actions—that he is, to use his own words, "a monster created by the system." His biographer, Fox Butterfield,[20] also argues that Bocket is the product of a three-hundred-year tradition of violence that began with a brutal system of slavery and culminated in our currently out-of-control urban youth violence and poverty.

In extremely oppressive societies, to do what we know is right can cost us our lives. Sometimes, our options are so limited—especially if we are a member of a marginalized group—that it is extremely difficult to act autonomously. Indeed, this failure to acknowledge the restrictions that social norms place upon people is one of the main criticisms of philosophical traditions that regard people as completely autonomous and self-sufficient beings who can determine their own lives independently of social forces. On the other hand, even though our options may be limited, this does not justify harming others. Indeed, it is a tribute to the power of the human conscience that more people from terribly cruel and oppressive backgrounds do not choose to travel the path of Willie Bocket.

We should certainly be wary of uncritical social conformity, but leading a moral life is not the same as simply going against the crowd or ignoring social conventions. British philosopher Mary Midgley writes about the social role of private conscience:

> . . . those who have struggled, as Mill and Kant did, to liberate the individual conscience from social pressures have been aiming, not just to make individuals free and happy, but also to make them capable of undertaking this work of moral creativity—of generating new practical concepts. They wanted the kind of inner freedom in which the conscience can be much more than a mere conformist superego—more than an internalized parent-figure policing traditional standards. They wanted it to find strength to act critically and rationally so that it could create new ones.
>
> When this is actually done, however, the new ideas in their turn become public property. They do not remain as private playthings of those who first conceived them. Morality—like art—thus continues to have both a public and a private aspect, and this public function seems to be unavoidable.[21]

A Delicate Balance

As beings who are both free and embedded in society, we live under the constant tension of balancing our social nature and our freedom. We cannot, nor would we want to, deny the role that society plays in shaping our conscience. However, nor do we want our identity and our conscience to be absorbed by society. On the other hand, we are not simply passive computers receiving direct instructions from our conscience. The exercise of the conscience involves willpower or action on our part. Because conscience is much more than gut feelings or a list of instructions about how to behave, to make use of it, we also need to develop our powers of discernment and to cultivate our moral sentiments.

Exercises

*1. Discuss how your conscience influences your moral decisions. For example, did it influence your choice of a community service site, or perhaps your decision not to cheat on a test or to steal from the bookstore, or a decision to refrain from hurting someone who was really irritating you, or to help someone in need?

*2. Do you agree with Mencius that we are born with a moral sense? If you are doing community service with young children, illustrate your answer with examples.

3. If a person acts virtuously because they are naturally virtuous, are they truly being moral? What about small children or nonhuman animals who, according to most Western philosophers and psychologists, act altruistically simply out of "instinct" rather than from an act of the will? Are children and nonhuman animals behaving morally?

4. To what extent is your conscience shaped by what Nietzsche calls "herd morality"? Illustrate your answer with specific examples. Does your conscience sometimes demand that you act contrary to the cultural norms? If so, where do you think these demands come from, if not from your own personal desires? Explain, using examples.

5. Discuss a time when you went along with the crowd—either actively or as a passive bystander—even though you knew that what they were doing was morally wrong. How did you feel afterward? What thoughts went through your mind? Relate your answer to the concept of conscience.

6. Jean-Jacques Rousseau claimed that modern society distorted humans and made us hateful and violent. He said that this behavior does not come from our true human nature but is an artifact of a hierarchical and alienating society. Psychologist Erich Fromm also refers to "normalcy" in modern industrial societies as pathological.[22]

 Other philosophers, such as Thomas Hobbes, argue that humans have a natural tendency to be violent and self-seeking and, therefore, need society to control their destructive impulses. Which position do you agree with? Support your answer.

7. Penny Cullerton claims that she did what she did because it was the right thing to do. How do you think she came to this conclusion? Do you agree that she did the right thing? Would a cultural relativist agree with Cullerton's decision? Why or why not? Support your answer.

 What would you have done if you had been in Cullerton's position? To what extent do you use conscious moral direction to determine what is moral and immoral, rather than relying upon guidance from those around you? Illustrate your answer.

8. Discuss the following quote from Hillary Rodham Clinton's book *It Takes a Village* (1996): "Nothing is more important to our shared future than the

well-being of our children. For children are at our core—not only as vulnerable beings in need of love and care but as a moral touchstone amidst the complexity and contentiousness of modern life. Just as it takes a village [community] to raise a child, it takes children to raise up a village to become all it should be."[23]

9. What do you think that Mary Midgley meant when she said that morality has both "a public and private aspect"? Relate your answer to your own conscious moral direction.

The Affective and Cognitive Sides of the Conscience

The bodhisattva is one who possesses the dual nature of wisdom (prajna) and compassion (karuna), which are, in many respects, two aspects of the same reality of a perfected being.
—Kenneth Inada, "The Buddhist Perspective on Human Rights" (1982)

Early childhood experiences interacting with innate temperamental differences may create a disposition to give greater emphasis to one or the other of the several moral senses. One person may be more inclined to emphasize justice, fairness, and duty, another to stress sympathy, care, and helping.
—James Q. Wilson, *The Moral Sense* (1993), p. 179

Conscience can be broken down into two elements: (1) affective (moral sentiments), and (2) cognitive (moral reasoning). This division is artificial and is primarily a tool for trying to better understand how our conscience works. Our affective or feeling side almost always contains a cognitive aspect to it, and our reasoning is almost always informed to some extent by our feelings.

The Affective Element of Conscience

Moral sentiments are emotions that move us to feel moral approval or disapproval. These sentiments include, among others, sympathy, "helper's high," indignation or resentment, and guilt.

> If we compare all these circumstances, we shall not doubt, that sympathy is the chief source of moral distinctions . . .
>
> —David Hume, *A Treatise of Human Nature* (1739), p. 593

Sympathy and Compassion   *Sympathy* is "the capacity for and inclination to imagine the feelings of others."[24] Sympathy is regarded as an important moral sentiment in virtually every ethical system in the world. To many philosophers, sympathy is the greatest virtue and the cultivation of sympathy and compassion our primary moral duty. *Compassion,* a more active form of sympathy, is the combination of sympathy with praxis.

The moral principle of universal compassion and love is found in moral teachings throughout the world: In Buddhism, it is known as *metta.* In Indian philosophy, universal compassion is called *ahimsa.* In Christianity, it is called *agape.*

You have heard that it was said, "You shall love your neighbor and hate your enemy." But I say to you, Love your enemies and pray for those who persecute you . . .

If you love those who love you, what reward have you? Do not even the tax collectors do that? And if you greet only your brothers, what more are you doing than others? Do not even pagans do that? You, therefore, must be [morally] perfect, as your heavenly Father is perfect.

—Matthew 5:43–44; 46–48

Sympathy expresses itself as both tenderness and joy at another's happiness and sadness or indignation at another's misfortune or mistreatment. Through sympathy, we move beyond our own small world by feeling for and establishing connections with each other. Without sympathy, true intimacy and a genuine sense of community would be impossible.

As we have no immediate experience of what other men feel, we can form no idea of the manner in which they are affected, but by conceiving what we ourselves should feel in the like situation . . . [When we sympathize] by the imagination we place ourselves in his situation.

—ADAM SMITH, *The Moral Sentiments* (1759), p. 5

Like most human sentiments, sympathy must be nurtured to develop properly and to flourish. However, sympathy by itself, without the collaboration of moral reasoning and other moral sentiments, could even lead us to behave immorally. As humans we seem to have a strong natural urge to be among people who are like us and to distrust people who are different. It is, therefore, easy for us to sympathize with those who are like us at the expense of those who are different. Conscious moral direction requires us to grow beyond our natural tendency to sympathize only with those who resemble us.

"Helper's High"   According to Plato, we behave justly not only because it is the right thing to do but because of the positive effect it has upon us.[25] The reward Plato mentioned was not in a heavenly afterlife but happiness in the here and now. Feminist care ethicist Nel Noddings likewise notes that caring for others is often accompanied by a sense of joy.[26] The association of morality with happiness and a sense of well-being is found in moral philosophies throughout the world. Buddhist ethics teaches that joy comes only through the desire to help others.[27] When we help others, we generally come away from the experience feeling better about ourselves and energized by the experience. Our conscience, in other words, "strokes" us when we act in accordance with it. Psychologists call this feeling "helper's high."

> The more joy we have, the more nearly perfect we are.
>
> —BENEDICT DE SPINOZA, *Ethics*

There is considerable medical evidence that doing good for others has more than just psychological benefits. According to the Institute for the Advancement of Health, community service work has a positive effect on our overall sense of physical and emotional well-being. Hans Seyle, author of *The Stress of Life,* suggests that people engage in altruistic projects as a means of reducing stress. The helper's high that accompanies volunteer work results from an increase in the release of endorphins—morphine-like chemicals that occur naturally in the body. The release of endorphins, in turn, is followed by a longer period of increased relaxation and improved self-esteem.[28]

Is an action moral if it is done simply so that we can feel better about ourselves? Most philosophers would say "no." Conscience and morality are far more complex. Unlike true moral acts, helping others just to experience helper's high does not stem from a respect for others and the moral law but from self-interest. Feeling good about what we are doing can make helping others easier, although feeling good in itself is not enough to sustain our good actions.

Moral Outrage   Not all moral sentiments make us feel warm and fuzzy, however. Moral outrage occurs when we witness a violation or transgression of the boundaries of moral decency. As such, our outrage is oriented toward justice and motivates us to correct the situation by demanding that justice be done. Moral outrage can take two forms: The first, **resentment,** is the anger that one feels by having been personally injured. **Moral indignation,** on the other hand, is the anger that one feels at the sight of others being harmed.

Moral outrage in the form of resentment appears very early in childhood, when children believe that they have been treated unfairly. Moral indignation appears later, as our sense of moral community expands to include others besides ourselves. In each case, moral outrage involves passing judgment upon someone else's behavior. This involves the use of the cognitive side of our conscience, in conjunction with the affective.

Just as moral indignation is the morally appropriate response in the face of the abuse and oppression suffered by others, so too is the display of resentment appropriate in the face of one's own abuse and oppression. Resentment is a "form of personal protest which expresses our respect for self, for others, and for morality."[29] By sending a message to the abuser that we will not tolerate such treatment, resentment serves to affirm our moral worth and to protect us from future abuse. To put aside resentment or moral indignation and forgive in the face of ongoing abuse, on the other hand, serves to absolve oppressors of any need to change their behavior.

People who never feel resentment or moral outrage—such as servile people—also do not recognize injustice. Instead, they believe that they, or other groups who are being oppressed, deserve to be harmed or treated with contempt. Moral outrage fosters community by encouraging victims and their sympathizers to work toward justice and moral reform.

> . . . people who are not angered by the right things, or in the right way, or at the right times, or towards the right people, all seem to be foolish . . . Since he is not angered, he does not seem to be the sort to defend himself; and such willingness to accept insults to oneself or to overlook insults to one's family and friends is slavish.
>
> —ARISTOTLE, *Nichomachean Ethics,* Bk. IV, Ch. 5, 1126a

Our sense of moral duty is often roused by a sense of anger or moral outrage directed at an event or a person. When Gandhi was a young lawyer working in South Africa, he was prohibited from sitting where he wanted to on the train and even from walking beside his "non-colored" friends. Rather than acquiesce to the cultural norms, he reacted with resentment and moral outrage. This moral outrage sparked one of the most effective nonviolent moral reform movements in the history of the world.

Rosa Parks (b. 1932), American civil rights activist. Parks was arrested in 1955 after refusing to give up her seat to a white man on a bus in Montgomery, Alabama. The ensuing case went all the way to the United States Supreme Court, which ruled that segregation on public transportation was unconstitutional.

On December 1, 1955, Rosa Parks, an African-American woman living in the South, also refused to stifle her moral outrage. After a long, tiring day at work, she climbed aboard a crowded bus and sat down in the middle section. A few stops later, a white man got on the bus. The bus driver ordered Parks to give up her seat; she refused. The white people on the bus were horrified at her impertinence. How dare she think she was above the law! The bus driver threatened to call the police, to which she replied, "You may do that." Her defiant action, her resentment at her disrespectful treatment, and her demand that she be treated with dignity acted as a catalyst in the civil rights movement.

Like sympathy, moral outrage can be a powerful motivation. A study of why some people are "Good Samaritans" and will go to the aid of a crime victim, while others do not, found that the people who did intervene were also the quickest to anger and the most temperamentally aggressive. Most said they acted reflexively, without rational deliberation or reflection upon their sympathy for the victim.

> Anger is not only inevitable, it is necessary. Its absence means indifference, the most disastrous of human failings.
>
> —Arthur Ponsonby, *Casual Observations*

One might wonder whether the "Kitty Genovese syndrome"—where people passively stand by and watch with indifference as another person is being beaten, raped, or even killed—is, at least in part, the result of years of learning to stifle our moral outrage. This taboo on displays of anger may be, in part, because in our "live-and-let-live" society passing judgment on others is considered to be disrespectful and even arrogant. "Who are *you* to pass judgment?" we are admonished. Given this "nonjudgmental" atmosphere, it is not surprising that the moral outrage that often accompanies moral judgment is often regarded as a "bad" feeling that we should work to get beyond.

> The world needs anger. The world often continues to allow evil because it isn't angry enough.
>
> —Bede Jarrett (historian)

Ressentiment Cultural norms generally serve to maintain the status quo. In a hierarchical society, those who control the wealth and the power are the most likely to be judged, while those who are oppressed are the most likely to feel moral outrage. The effects of suppressed or misdirected moral outrage are now becoming apparent in our culture. Friedrich Nietzsche, and later Max Scheler (1874–1928), used the term **ressentiment** to describe this phenomenon. Unlike resentment, ressentiment occurs when we suppress or redirect our resentment. Resentment, denied its proper expression, degenerates into ressentiment, which eventually leads to a "self-poisoning of the mind" by saturating the entire personality with repressed feelings of "revenge, hatred, malice, envy, the impulse to detract, and spite."[30] Desire for revenge, in turn, leads not only to self-blame and self-loathing, but also the search for a scapegoat to blame for one's suffering.

Our scapegoats are often members of even more oppressed groups. Women who continue to live with an abusive husband are far more likely to beat their children than they are if they leave the abusive husband.[31] The movie *Boyz N the Hood,* about African-American youths growing up in a south central Los Angeles neighborhood, is a vivid depiction of how morally outraged young black men can turn against each other instead of the system that is oppressing them. Thus, moral outrage can become destructive when it drifts loose from its cognitive mooring in justice.

Guilt and Shame **Guilt,** as a moral sentiment, has also gotten a bad rap—but undeservedly so. As a culture, we have a love/hate relationship with guilt. We generally regard a person who feels no guilt—such as Hannibal "the Cannibal" Lector in the movie *Silence of the Lambs*—as either inhuman or a monster. At the same time, in our "if-it-feels-good-do-it" society, guilt is often regarded as a barrier to freedom and human liberation. The bad reputation that guilt has acquired is due, in part, to the Freudian psychoanalytic view of guilt as a symptom of neurosis, and hence, in need of a cure.

It is also due to a confusion of guilt with shame. The word "guilt" is frequently used broadly to include shame as well; however, it is important to distinguish between the two. **Shame,** which is heteronomous, is aroused as a result of a social blunder or the violation of social norms. The super-ego, which is governed by external sanctions, is associated with shame. Shame leaves us feeling inadequate, embarrassed, and humiliated before others. Shame can be beneficial, to the extent that it motivates us to be polite and considerate of others; it can also become destructive when its dictates conflict with those of our true conscience. Teenagers who are gay or lesbian, for example, can develop a deep sense of shame for not living up to their family's and church's expectations, but they do not generally feel moral guilt.

Feelings of moral or autonomous guilt result from the violation of a moral norm.[32] As cultural relativists, most adults have learned to include the two feelings under one rubric; however, studies show that children as young as seven are able to distinguish between the shame that often accompanies the breaking of a nonmoral social custom and the guilt that occurs as the result of transgressing a moral norm.[33] Guilt not only demands that we accept moral responsibility for our actions but that we make reparation to those we have harmed and, if necessary, change ourselves to make a repeat of the harmful behavior less likely. However painful and unpleasant guilt may be, it seems to be essential to our well-being and that of others. Both pain and guilt act as damage control. Physical pain occurs when we damage our bodies, as a signal for us to take steps to fix the damage or remove the cause of the harm. In the same manner, guilt lets us know when something is morally wrong so that we can take steps to correct the situation.

> A guilty conscience is a form of punishment for wrongdoing which any normal wrong-doer cannot escape and so it is better to stop doing wrong and do good.
>
> —Ewe proverb of Africa

Having a guilty conscience is more than just a mental state. Our whole autonomic nervous system is disrupted when we experience feelings of guilt. Because of this, polygraph devices—popularly known as "lie detectors"—can determine whether a person is lying by measuring changes in his or her heart, lungs, and sweat glands. A lie detector, though, is useless for determining whether a psychopath is lying, because such a person has no conscience. Consequently, a psychopath has no physiological reaction to lying.

Guilt not only results from actual wrongdoing; it also motivates us to avoid harming ourselves and others. A study of AIDS risk–perception among college students found that avoiding behavior that could lead to infection with the AIDS virus was better predicted by feelings of guilt about possibly getting the virus and infecting others than by being very well informed about the risks of AIDS.[34]

Guilt, rather than being a private experience with no social consequences, is very important in maintaining relationships.[35] Studies show that adults with the strongest conscience and the strongest sense of guilt have the strongest affiliations with others. Guilt motivates us to pay attention to other people. The single biggest cause of guilt is not spending enough time with family and loved ones. Guilt also serves to equalize power in a relationship because, for a morally sensitive person, misuse of power leads to feelings of guilt. Guilt also motivates us to restore relationship by making up for the harms that we have done to the relationship.[36]

The Cognitive Element of Conscience

The cognitive side of our conscience is involved in making rational judgments about what we *ought* to do. The current emphasis on moral relativism has been accompanied by a rejection of what has been perceived as rigid absolutist and traditional Western rationalistic moral theories. This, in turn, has led to a backlash against principled moral reasoning and a focus instead on caring and moral sentiments at the expense of analytical reasoning.

If we neglect or fail to develop the critical cognitive side of our conscience, however, our moral sentiments can get us into trouble or even lead us to commit immoral actions. Moral sentiments by themselves are uncritical. People who are uncritically sympathetic, for example, may be easy targets for people who would take advantage of their kindness. Other people feel overwhelmed with guilt but are unable to discern why or to devise a plan of action to remedy the situation that gave rise to the guilt in the first place.

The affective and cognitive elements of conscience are inseparable. The critical importance of moral sentiments for moral reasoning is particularly evident with psychopaths. Psychopaths are quite capable of complex reasoning; however, because they lack the ability to sympathize with others, psychopaths are apparently incapable of using their cognitive abilities in the service of morality.

Studies suggest that moral reasoning is not something that must be taught or that develops only when children have achieved a certain level of rationality. Like sympathy and moral outrage, children begin making moral judgments at a very early age—even before they have a command over language. Young children seem to possess a standard of moral judgment within themselves and look to this standard for direction, rather than being taught what is right and wrong or looking to authority figures.[37]

> People with bad consciences always fear the judgment of children.
>
> —MARY MCCARTHY, *On the Contrary*

About half of children between eighteen and thirty-six months of age will spontaneously—without any prompting from a parent or other adult—offer to share things such as food, a pacifier, or a toy with another person. According to psychologist William Damon, by the age of four children are "already in possession of active, flourishing conceptions of fairness."[38] This phenomenon has been observed cross-culturally: It is found in North American babies and the infants of African bushmen.[39]

Although many young children possess a concept of fairness, they tend to engage in moral judgments in an egocentric manner. Most young children are concerned only with how others' actions affect them and are less concerned with how their own actions affect others. As we grow older, our sense of fairness and justice, like our feelings of sympathy, extends to encompass a wider and wider moral community.

A well-developed conscience demands that we treat ourselves and others with respect. When we behave in ways that violate basic moral principles, the cognitive side of our conscience asks us to justify our actions. To say that we felt like hurting someone else or enjoyed inflicting harm does not satisfy our conscience. Instead, we must offer justifications based on higher moral claims. An uncritical conscience is likely to resort to rationalization. **Rationalization** involves the use of rhetoric, fallacies, and resistance, rather than logical analysis. People who rationalize their harmful actions suffer from what is known as weakness of the will or a weak conscience. Weak-willed people place nonmoral values such as popularity or economic success above moral values and the demands of their conscience.

Conscience not only has a powerful influence in shaping both our conduct and our character; it is also an essential part of who we are as individuals. Acting in good conscience seems to be necessary for maintaining our sense of personal *integrity*. Our conscience compels us to question cultural norms that require us to be insincere or to pretend that we are someone we are not. To be at odds with our conscience is to be out of harmony with our very being.

Exercises

*1. Psychologists have found that one of the best means of cultivating our feelings of sympathy and expanding our moral community is to place ourselves in situations where we come face to face with people who are different from us. In what ways, if any, has your community service work affected the development of your capacity to sympathize with others?

2. Many parents believe that it is their duty to shield their children from experiences that set them apart from the group. Do you agree? Why or why not? Thinking back to your own childhood, what experiences contributed most to the development of your sympathy for others?

*3. In an interview conducted shortly after the death of Jerry Garcia, the lead guitarist for the Grateful Dead, Carlos Santana said of Garcia's life: "You can only get high serving people." Discuss this statement in light of your own experience.

   How does "helper's high" sustain or motivate you in your community service? Is service a moral action if it is done only to make ourselves feel better? Why or why not?

4. Discuss the following quotation from Irish poet W. B. Yeats: "Hate is a kind of 'passive suffering,' but indignation is a kind of joy."

5. Jesus taught that we should "turn the other cheek" and "love our enemies." Discuss this in light of the quotation from Aristotle regarding the moral value of resentment and indignation in the face of our own mistreatment. Do the teachings of Jesus preclude resentment and indignation? Support your answer.

6. Malcolm X referred to himself as "the angriest black man in America."[40] How did his anger and the indignities and despair suffered by black people in the United States motivate him to seek justice? Discuss a time when your moral outrage, either in the form of resentment or moral indignation, motivated you to seek positive change.

7. Oceans of outrage are currently flooding our talk shows and newspapers. Are expressions of moral outrage becoming more acceptable? Are these outpourings really expressions of genuine moral indignation and resentment, or are they expressions of ressentiment and bitterness? Illustrate your answer with specific examples.

8. Cultural relativists tend to confuse shame with guilt. Discuss examples of both from your own experience. Compare and contrast the two experiences.

9. How do you respond to guilt? Discuss the types of defenses, especially immature defenses or resistance, that you sometimes use when you feel guilty. How might you substitute mature defense mechanisms for resistance?

10. Buddhist philosopher Kenneth Indara claims that "an all-knowing person must necessarily be an all-loving person, and an all-loving person must necessarily be an all-knowing person." Do you agree with him? Support your answer.

*11. Do you agree that we have an innate tendency to be fair? Discuss your answer in light of your own childhood experiences. How did you respond, as a child, when you were treated unfairly? when someone else was treated unfairly? Has your sense of fairness changed as you've matured? How? If you are doing community service work with young children, relate your answer to your community service.

12. Should children who commit crimes—such as Willie Brocket, Nathan Leopold, and Richard Loeb—be held morally responsible for their actions in a court of law? If so, to what extent should they be held responsible? What about adults who have either a weak conscience or no conscience at all?

13. Philosophers such as Gandhi and Martin Luther King, Jr., argue that violence can never be justified by moral outrage. Instead, we need to use our moral reasoning to devise nonviolent strategies for responding to violence. Do you agree? Why or why not?

Lawrence Kohlberg: The Stage Theory of Moral Development

> *Ethics is a stage in evolution. That which is common to all stages is the urge . . . towards self-expression.* —THE SRI AUROBINDO ASHRAM, *The Life Divine* (1970)

> *Moral thought, then, seems to behave like all other kinds of thought. Progress through the moral levels and stages is characterized by increasing differentiation and increasing integration, and hence is the same kind of progress that scientific theory represents.* —LAWRENCE KOHLBERG, *The Philosophy of Moral Development* (1971)

Swiss child psychologist Jean Piaget (1896–1980) was one of the first psychologists to systematically study moral reasoning in children. Piaget saw children as moral philosophers. Children, he noticed, go through distinct stages in their moral development. The first stage he labeled the **stage of heteronomy.** This stage is based on a "morality of constraint." The second stage, the **stage of autonomy,** is based on a "morality of cooperation."[41] Although Piaget regarded moral development as part of human nature, he also believed that interrelationships between the individual and society are essential to nurture this development. A sense of moral duty does not come from principle alone but rather develops within a relationship characterized by mutual respect. According to Piaget:

Communal life alters the very structure of consciousness by inculcating into it the feeling of respect.[42]

In his research, Piaget also distinguished between theoretical and practical morality. **Theoretical morality** is reasoning and judgment dissociated from actual deeds or any need to act. It comes into play when a person ". . . is called upon to judge other people's actions that do not interest him directly or to give voice to general principles regarding his own conduct independently of his actual deeds."[43] **Practical morality,** in contrast, involves motivations and a sense of obligation. "Effective moral thought" leads us to the formulation of moral judgments that guide us in particular cases.[44] Practical morality, according to Piaget, is mainly intuitive and is more deeply rooted within the person than is theoretical morality.

In the 1950s, developmental psychologist Erik Erikson (1902–90) likewise found that people go through different stages in the development of a healthy personality. Like Piaget, Erikson believed that the gradual unfolding of personality through these stages is part of an inherent "plan of growth" or "ground plan."[45]

Kohlberg's Stages

Because of the domination of modern psychology by behaviorism—whose natural corollary in moral philosophy is cultural relativism—Piaget's research on moral development received little attention until relatively recently. In the 1970s, the work of Harvard psychologist Lawrence Kohlberg caught the public's attention. As a psychologist, Kohlberg was primarily influenced by Piaget; philosophically, he was strongly influenced by moral philosophers such as Socrates, Immanuel Kant, and John Rawls—all philosophers whose works, he believed, exemplified a high stage of moral reasoning.

Kohlberg's ideas about moral development became popular in the wake of the Vietnam War protests and the civil rights movement, both of which gave rise to dissatisfaction with ethical relativism. The analytical movement in moral philosophy had culminated in the theory of emotivism, which completely removed morality from any connection with the real world. Kohlberg wanted to return to a more synthetic approach in which theory and practical experience came together.

According to Kohlberg and other developmental theorists, there are innate cognitive structures that are fundamental to all humans. These structures include—among others—causality, time and space, and moral excellence. Although the specific content of moral codes can vary, depending on a person's culture, the difference is only on the surface. The conceptual structures from which these specific codes are formulated are universal:

> As soon as we talk with children about morality we find that they have many ways of making judgments that are not "internalized" from the outside and that do not come in any direct and obvious way from parents, teachers, or even peers.

Lawrence Kohlberg (1927–87), American educator, psychologist, and director of the Harvard University Center for Moral Development and Education. Kohlberg maintained that moral development occurs in stages going from self-centered to acting according to universal moral principles. His contribution to the psychological study of moral development has had a major impact on ethics education.

According to Kohlberg, humans, with the exception of psychopaths and other severely impaired people, have an inherent potential for growth from the lower (earlier) to higher stages of moral development. These stages are universal or transcultural and represent "transformations in the organization of thought, rather than increasing knowledge of cultural values."[46] These stages are sequential, much like stairs. Each stage, according to Kohlberg, represents a different pattern or system of logic for deciding what is the just or right way to solve a moral dilemma. Each stage is distinct and reflects a level of moral judgment that is more complex than that of the preceding stage.[47] We do not skip stages. Gains that are made in moral judgment tend to be retained. The lower stages are not so much replaced by higher stages as incorporated into them—much like elementary school arithmetic becomes part of our way of understanding calculus.

Kohlberg identified three main levels of moral development, each with two distinct stages (see Table 6.1). In the preconventional stages, moral duty and moral community are defined primarily in terms of oneself. Young children are preconventional reasoners. The majority of adults in the United States (about ninety percent) are in the conventional stages of moral reasoning. These are heteronomous moral reasoners who look to outside sources—their peers or cultural norms—for moral guidance. Less than ten percent of American adults ever reach the postconventional stage of being autonomous moral reasoners.

TABLE 6.1 Kohlberg's Stages of Moral Development[48]

STAGE	DESCRIPTION
Preconventional	
1. Punishment and obedience	Avoid punishment; submit to authority. Fear of punishment is the primary motive.
2. Egoist	Satisfy one's own needs; only consider the needs of others if it benefits you: "You scratch my back, I'll scratch yours."
Conventional	
3. Good boy/nice girl	Please and help others; concern for maintaining good relationships and earning others' approval; conformity to peer and group norms.
4. Society-maintaining	Respect authority and social rules; maintain the existing social order.
Postconventional	
5. Social contract or legalistic	Obey useful, albeit arbitrary, social rules; appeal to social consensus and majority rule as long as minimal basic rights are safeguarded. The U.S. Constitution is written using this stage of reasoning.
6. Conscience and universal principles	Autonomously recognize universal rules, such as justice and equality, that are rational and logically consistent and reflect a respect for equal human rights and the dignity of each individual.

The so-called *higher* stages come later than the *lower* stages in human development, but this in itself does not prove that the higher stages of moral development are morally better. Cognitive-development psychologists are well aware that we cannot logically draw a conclusion regarding what *ought to be* from what *is*. Higher stages are preferable because people at these stages are more satisfied with their moral decisions. People, in general, *prefer* a solution to a moral problem that uses the highest stage of moral reasoning conceptually available to them.[49]

Kohlberg also points out that *philosophers* believe that the principled reasoning that characterizes the higher stages of moral reasoning is more desirable than the cultural relativism that characterizes the conventional stages and the egoism or ethical subjectivism of the preconventional stages. Most world philosophers have long held that autonomous moral reasoning, universality and impartiality, compassion and a concern for justice, and mutual respect are the hallmarks of sound moral reasoning.

Because each new stage of moral development integrates the components of the previous stage, later stages provide us with better tools for resolving crises. People who operate at a higher stage of moral reasoning are less likely to make moral decisions that they will later come to regret. Our concept of the moral community also becomes more inclusive as we mature, going from the self-centered egoism of the young child to universal respect for all beings.

First, something should be said about the sense in which higher stages are meant to be better. Following Piaget, "better" does not mean a higher stage subject has more raw intelligence (brain power) or higher moral status . . . Rather, higher stages are said to be better conceptual tools for making sense out of the world and deriving guides for decision making. It is the same sense of "better" when we say that being able to do long division is better than only being able to do sums. Having the conceptual tools of long division enables us to solve math problems that would be difficult to do if we did not have those concepts. . . . In summary, who says higher stages are better? Subjects do themselves. As people outgrow old ways of thinking—as they see them as too simplistic and inadequate—they still understand them but don't prefer them.

—JAMES REST, *Moral Development in the Professions: Psychology and Applied Ethics* (1994), pp. 16–17

Most people, to some extent, draw from all stages. Egoists recognize universal moral principles that they at least expect others to follow. And even when we have advanced to the stage where we feel a sense of moral responsibility and compassion for all people, the small family group or friendships continue to form the core of the moral community for most people.

A person will prefer the current stage of moral development until it is, in turn, replaced by a newly comprehended stage. Each stage represents an equilibrium point, so a person will generally remain in that stage until sufficient cognitive or social disequilibrium has occurred. People move beyond their current stage when they encounter a crisis that their current mode of thinking is unable to satisfactorily resolve.

For example, until the age of forty-three, Aung San Suu Kyi had been leading a quiet life in England as a housewife and academic, before she was transformed into a powerful and charismatic leader of the Burmese people. In April 1988 she returned to Rangoon to care for her dying mother. While living in England, she had heard about the political unrest and shooting of demonstrators. She was also knowledgeable about Burmese politics. However, not until Aung San Suu Kyi returned to Burma and came face-to-face with the crisis facing her people was she transformed. "Overnight, Aung San Suu Kyi became the leading representative of the movement for freedom and democracy."[50]

Unlike the accumulation of purely theoretical knowledge, gains made in moral development affect a person's decision-making in new circumstances and their real-life behavior.[51] One's level of moral reasoning is positively correlated with honesty and altruistic behavior—what Piaget called practical morality. A study of eighty-six subjects found that only nine percent of people at stage 2 and thirty-eight percent of people at stage 4 would offer help to someone who appeared to be suffering from drug side effects; yet all of the subjects at stage 6 offered their assistance.[52] Higher stages of moral reasoning are also positively correlated with higher scores on other components of moral behavior and on developmental scales such as ego development, self-esteem, and mental health.

Cross-Cultural Findings

Studies from more than forty Western and non-Western countries support Kohlberg's theory that stages of moral development are universal. The cross-cultural findings also lend support to the theory that some cultures are more prone to promote virtue in their citizens. Kohlberg found, for example, that people who live in the United States, when matched by age and education, score lower in measures of moral development than people from Iceland or Canada but higher than people living in Taiwan. Another study found that certified public accountants (CPAs) who are partners in U.S. business firms tend to reason at the conventional stage of development and are primarily influenced by the need to be affiliated with their business associates and to follow the rules and norms of their firm. Indeed, CPAs who are at a higher stage of moral reasoning are unlikely to be promoted to upper management positions![53] Canadian CPAs, in contrast, are more independent in their moral judgment and better able to handle moral conflicts.

Subcultures and institutions also influence a person's stage of moral reasoning. One of the greatest frustrations of our current prison system is that criminals often come out in worse shape than when they entered prison. In a 1972 study, prisoners were found to interact with the guards primarily in terms of stage 1 behavior—avoiding coercion and punishment. However, with each other, the prisoners were primarily in stage 2, acting out of mutual self-benefit but without any genuine respect for each other. The researchers concluded that prison life tends to mold prisoners into a morality that was lower than their "private best," that is, their moral behavior outside the prison environment.[54]

Some people move through the stages faster than others. Some, including many prison inmates, never get above the second stage. Most high school students and college freshman use primarily stage 3 moral reasoning; as such, they tend to be very conformist and easily influenced by their peer culture. This phenomenon in college students has been dubbed the "freshman personality."[55]

On a more hopeful note, formal education has been found to be an important factor in promoting moral development, probably because it challenges us to analyze our worldviews. The movement from conventional to postconventional moral reasoning involves a paradigm shift or change in our worldview. Educator and philosopher Dwight Boyd refers to the condition in which students have trouble making the transition from conventional to principled moral reasoning as "sophomoritis."[56]

When young people leave their family of origin and enter college, they often experience a crisis. Events that conflict with our cherished worldviews—such as encountering people from different backgrounds and learning new ideas—can precipitate disequilibrium. During the transition from conventional to postconventional moral reasoning, students are often torn between the rejection of moral values as relative and the reluctance to commit to universal moral principles. This conflict can manifest itself in hedonistic disregard for any moral values—either relative or universal.

> Because [college] students generally have not yet internalized the principles necessary to make ethical judgments, they substitute personal and subjective criteria. This makes it appear as though they lack character. A more accurate description is that they are in the process of developing it.[57]
>
> —GREGORY BLIMLING, "Developing Character in College Students" (1990)

Unfortunately, most college students do not complete the transition to postconventional moral reasoning. A college education instead tends to push students into a higher level of *conventional* reasoning. In other words, a traditional college education can make students less reliant on the opinions of their peers; however, the trade-off is that they conform more to wider societal norms rather than becoming more autonomous in their thinking.

Criticisms of Kohlberg's Stages

Kohlberg's stages have been found to hold true transculturally, but his theory, at least as it was initially formulated, has been criticized for inadvertently reflecting the biases of U.S. culture. For example, Kohlberg did not find much change in level of moral development after the age of twenty-five. However, most of his subjects were students; very few were over the age of forty or fifty, a time of life that is revered in many non-Western cultures for its wisdom.

1. The Master said, "At fifteen, I had my mind bent on learning."

2. "At thirty, I stood firm."

3. "At forty, I had no doubts."

4. "At fifty, I knew the decrees of Heaven."

5. "At sixty, my ear was an obedient organ for the reception of truth."

6. "At seventy, I could follow what my heart desired, without transgressing what was right."[58]

—*Confucian Analects*

The adequacy of Kohlberg's description of children's moral reasoning has also been called into question. According to Kohlberg, very young children act morally because of fear of punishment from those in positions of authority over them. This interpretation has not been supported by recent research, however. When children are asked why they share, some will say to avoid punishment or because they want something in return, as Kohlberg predicted they would, but most children share out of a sense of empathy for other people.[59] Similarly, other studies suggest that moral sentiment is more important than principled moral reasoning in women's moral development.[60]

Before the late 1970s, researchers in both medicine and psychology routinely used only male subjects, based on the assumption that men were generic humans and that generalizations about women could legitimately be made from studies done only on men. In keeping with this thinking, the subjects in Kohlberg's initial studies were all male. Adding insult to injury, Kohlberg even drew the conclusion on the basis of his all-male research that men operate at a significantly higher level of moral reasoning than do women, the majority of whom were determined to be at stage 3.

Exercises

1. Do you agree that we have an intrinsic drive toward inner growth? Or do people, as the expression goes, "never change"? Illustrate your answer, using examples from your own life.

2. Has the strategy you use for making moral decisions changed since you were a child? since you started college? If so, how has it changed? Do you think the strategy you use now is better or more effective than your earlier strategies? If so, explain why. Are you satisfied with your current level of moral reasoning? Discuss why or why not.

3. According to Kohlberg, different cultures encourage people to remain at different stages of moral development. Discuss some of the forces in our own culture that discourage people from developing past the conventional stage but encourage us to develop beyond the preconventional stages.

   What changes in U.S. public policy would you suggest that might make this culture more conducive to moral development and virtuous behavior? For those of you who have lived in different cultures, how do other cultures encourage or inhibit moral development? How might some of the positive aspects be integrated into U.S. public policy?

4. Different professions seem to have an impact on moral development. For example, studies have found that, in the United States, professional education in fields such as business and teaching actually tends to inhibit moral development.[61] A liberal arts education, on the other hand, tends to enhance moral development. Why might this be so? How can professional education be changed to encourage moral development?

5. Given that the average criminal is at the same level of moral reasoning as a junior high school student, is it fair that criminals are held responsible for their actions while youths who commit the same crimes get lighter sentences or are excused on the grounds that they are not mature enough to make moral decisions? To what extent should a person's level of moral reasoning be taken into account when holding someone culpable for their antisocial actions?

Carol Gilligan: The Care Perspective

The elusive mystery of women's development lies in its recognition of the continuing importance of attachment in the human life-cycle. Woman's place in man's life-cycle is to protect this recognition while the [masculine] development litany intones the celebration of separation, autonomy, individuation, and natural rights . . . Only when life-cycle theories divide their attention and begin to live with women as they have lived with men will their vision encompass the experience of both sexes and their theories become correspondingly more fertile.
                                        —CAROL GILLIGAN, *In a Different Voice* (1982), p. 23

Women and the Care Perspective

The neglect of both philosophers and psychologists to take the women's perspective into account has created the false impression that women are morally deficient compared to men. Kohlberg's gender-biased research was under-

Carol Gilligan (b. 1936), professor of education at Harvard University. Gilligan argues that Kohlberg's theory of moral development does not offer an adequate explanation of how women make moral decisions. Through her research with women, Gilligan developed a stage model of moral reasoning based on what she called the care *perspective.*

standably unacceptable to many researchers and feminist philosophers. Carol Gilligan, who had studied with Kohlberg, decided that it was time to correct this.

> It is obvious that the values of women differ very often from the values which have
> been made by the other sex . . . [Yet] it is the masculine values that prevail.[62]
>
> —VIRGINIA WOOLF, *A Room of One's Own* (1929)

In her interviews with women and through her study of women in literature, Gilligan concluded that women's moral development tends to follow a different path than men's. Men tend to be duty- and principle-oriented; women are more context-oriented and tend to view the world in a more emotional and personal way. Women's moral judgment, Gilligan found, is characterized by a concern for themselves and others, accepting and maintaining responsibility within relationships, attachment, and self-sacrifice. Gilligan named this the *"Care Perspective,"* in contrast to Kohlberg's "Justice Perspective." In her research with women, Gilligan postulated three stages of moral development (see Table 6.2).

TABLE 6.2 Gilligan's Stages of Moral Reasoning in Women [63]

STAGE	DESCRIPTION	MORAL COMMUNITY
Preconventional	Self-centered	Viewing one's own needs as all that matters.
Conventional	Self-sacrificing	Viewing others' needs as more important.
Postconventional	Mature care ethics	Able to balance one's own needs and the needs of others

Although Gilligan's and Kohlberg's theories emphasize different aspects of moral development, their stages are roughly parallel. Although gender can influence how our moral development unfolds, the basic paradigms or "ground plans" that inform our moral development are the same for both theories. For example, the preconventional stage in both Gilligan's and Kohlberg's theories includes egoists and ethical subjectivists. Similarly, people at the conventional stage are heteronomous cultural relativists who look to their culture for moral guidance.

The different descriptions of the conventional stage are not surprising, given the different ways in which men and women are socialized in our culture. Men, for the most part, are socialized to be the upholders of law and order and to believe that maleness carries certain privileges. Women, on the other hand, are taught that being a good woman involves self-sacrifice and placing the welfare of others before her own.

In both Kohlberg's and Gilligan's theories, the postconventional stage is represented by autonomous moral reasoning: The person looks to transcultural values—whether these are in the form of principles of justice and respect or sentiments such as compassion and empathy. The transition to the postconventional stage for women, according to Gilligan, involves realizing that any individual woman has as much moral value as the next person. Kohlberg emphasized cognitive disequilibrium as playing a key role in pushing people into a higher stage of moral development; Gilligan and many other feminist ethicists place more importance on *social disequilibrium* as the "gate" to moral development. More recent studies also suggest that the effect of "the emotional interactive experience of moral-social conflict" may be more important for men as well as women for facilitating moral development. [64]

Women and Self-Sacrifice

Because of women's inferior social status in most cultures, their socialization generally involves internalizing the message that they should nurture and care for the needs of others. Failure to recognize their own equal worth as humans can be costly for women, however. In situations of famine, for example, women starve to death at a higher rate than men do. When there is not enough for everyone, women will often engage in deliberate self-deprivation, offering men the best food at the expense of their own nutritional needs.[65]

> Put it down in capital letters: SELF-DEVELOPMENT IS A HIGHER DUTY THAN
> SELF-SACRIFICE. The thing which most retards and militates against women's
> self-development is self-sacrifice.[66]
>
> —ELIZABETH CADY STANTON to a reporter

Gilligan claims that U.S. society does not encourage the transition to moral maturity. The current emphasis on individuality over interdependence, rather than nurturing trust, serves to maintain distance between ourselves and others by discouraging the development of relationships built on mutual caring. Thus, our concept of moral community remains stunted along with our own moral development.

The identification of the "good" woman or self-sacrificing wife with deference to others' needs and wishes can be destructive not only to women's self-esteem but to their ability to have a genuine caring relationship. In Amy Tan's novel *The Joy Luck Club,* Rose Hsu Jordan, the American-born daughter of An-Mei Hsu, does everything she can to be the perfect wife to her American husband, Ted Jordan. She sacrifices her own dreams of a career and always defers to her husband's wishes—even when he asks for her opinion—until she is no longer able to make decisions for herself:

> I thought about things, the pros and the cons. But in the end I would be so confused, because I never believed there was ever any one right answer, yet there were many wrong ones. So whenever I said, "You decide," or "I don't care," or "Either way is fine with me," Ted would say in his impatient voice, "No, you decide. You can't have it both ways, none of the responsibility, none of the blame."

Ted, an autonomous moral reasoner, wants a wife who can think for herself. When he asks Rose for a divorce, she is stunned. Her perfect world is shattered, and she experiences severe social dissonance.

Only by going through the agony of the separation and hearing the story of her grandmother An-Mei Hsu's marriage in China to an abusive husband does Rose finally come to realize that she does have choices. By learning to say "no" to her husband and to express her anger at being betrayed, Rose is finally able to make the transition to mature care ethics and, in the end, establish a relationship with Ted that is based on mutual care and respect rather than self-imposed servility.

> There seems to be a line of development missing from current depictions of adult development, a failure to describe the progression of relationships toward a maturity of interdependence.
>
> —CAROL GILLIGAN, *In a Different Voice* (1982), p. 155

Synthesizing the Justice and Care Perspectives

Gilligan has been unfairly criticized as trying to drive a wedge between female and male ways of thinking, thereby promoting a type of biological destiny based on gender. Some studies support Gilligan's theory,[67] but others have found gender differences in moral reasoning to be insignificant.[68] However, Gilligan does not claim that the care perspective is superior to the justice perspective or even that it is more desirable for women to reason from a care perspective.

In later studies, Gilligan and others found that both the justice and care perspectives are present in most people's thinking, although each of us tends to emphasize one perspective over the other. Although women are more likely to prefer the care perspective, Gilligan acknowledges that some women have a strong justice orientation, and some men, including many philosophers, are very empathetic and care-oriented. Philosopher David Hume, for example, believed that moral sentiments are more important than abstract moral principles of justice for producing moral actions. Buddhist ethics likewise emphasizes compassion and community over abstract reason.

> Reason instructs us in the several tendencies of actions, and humanity (sympathy) makes a distinction in favor of those which are useful and beneficial.
>
> —DAVID HUME, *Enquiry Concerning the Principles of Morality* (1751)

Both Gilligan and Kohlberg came to agree in their later work that the most adequate moral orientation is one that takes both the justice and care perspectives into consideration; the two perspectives, rather than being mutually exclusive, complement and enrich each other.[69] The strength inherent in the mature care perspective is that it calls attention to our attachment to each other and to the particular needs and circumstances of individuals. However, by focusing on the individual and on relationships, care ethics also tends to ignore wider issues of equality.

The justice perspective, in contrast, focuses on justice, overcoming oppression, and the ideal of equality for all people. This more detached focus on justice can occur, however, at the expense of attention to individual needs. The most adequate moral orientation, therefore, is one that takes both perspectives into consideration and focuses on the development of both the affective and cognitive aspects of conscience.

Exercises

1. Which of these two approaches, care or justice, do you emphasize in your own moral reasoning? Illustrate your answer with specific examples. What might you do to strengthen whichever of the two perspectives is weaker?

2. Gilligan argues that our "depictions of adult development" tend to discourage moral maturity. In our culture, it is generally believed that people pretty much cease to develop after their early twenties. Aging is consequently associated with deterioration rather than growth. Do our present youth-oriented society, our fear of aging, and degradation of older people discourage moral maturity? How?

*3. If you are doing community service work, how has it helped to strengthen your moral reasoning? Which of the two perspectives, care or justice, has it had the greatest impact upon? Explain, using specific examples from your own experience.

*4. People sometimes justify their failure to confront others who are behaving in a morally immature manner on the grounds that criticism would not make a difference anyway. This attitude fails to take into account that each of us exists only as part of a wider community. Do we have a moral obligation to confront others or share our stories of moral struggle and growth with others, as An-Mei Hsu, Rose's grandmother, did in *The Joy Luck Club*?

   Discuss a time when hearing someone else's story changed your way of thinking and helped you to grow morally—whether this occurred during your community service work, through a personal encounter with a teacher or friend, or even as a result of a movie that you saw or a novel that you read.

James Rest: The Four Components of Moral Behavior

> *There is widespread agreement that there are more components to morality than just moral judgment. The trick, however, is to identify what else there is in morality, and how all these pieces fit together.*
>
> —JAMES REST, *Moral Development in the Professions* (1994), p. 22

Most studies have found that the stages of moral reasoning are positively correlated to moral behavior;[70] other studies have found no correlation.[71] These findings suggest that moral reasoning is not the only determinant or component of moral behavior. Proficiency in making moral judgments does not in itself guarantee that one will act morally: We do not always act in accord with reason, and we are often tempted to put aside our moral principles. We may fail to act morally because of peer pressure or fear, even when we know what is right. Moral behavior, in other words, is a complex phenomenon that cannot be represented as a single variable.

> We all know people who can render very sophisticated judgments but who never follow through on any course of actions; or people who have tremendous follow through and tenacity but whose judgment is single-minded.[72]
>
> —JAMES REST, "Research on Moral Development:
> Implications for Training Counseling Psychologists" (1984)

Psychologist James Rest has identified four components of moral behavior: (1) moral sensitivity, (2) moral judgment or reasoning, (3) moral motivation, and (4) moral character. These components work together to produce moral behavior. A deficiency in any of these components, Rest notes, can result in a failure to act morally.

Moral Sensitivity

Moral sensitivity is the awareness of how our actions affect others. As such, it involves the ability to empathize and imagine ourselves in another person's shoes. Problems such as poverty, social isolation, and homelessness exist, in part, because we simply don't see the problem. There are striking differences in people's sensitivity to the needs and welfare of others. People such as Mother Teresa, for example, are highly sensitive to the suffering of others. People who are morally sensitive are more likely to extend a helping hand and to engage in community service. These people are more in tune with their conscience and more likely to feel guilty when they harm another person or to feel moral indignation in the face of injustice. Morally sensitive people also do better academically and make better roommates in college.[73]

In contrast, people who are deficient in this component of moral behavior are often unable to recognize a moral situation. They may fail to act morally simply because it did not occur to them to do so. Morally insensitive people may make offensive comments, not out of malice, but simply because they are unaware of the effect of their comments on others. Insensitivity to others' suffering can present itself as unrealistic optimism and "minimizing" of other people's distress. Making statements such as "don't worry" or "things always work out for the best" to someone who has suffered a terrible misfortune can add further to their despair and isolation. Morally insensitive people are sometimes even proud that others' bigoted comments or behavior does not bother them and accuse those who do react with resentment or indignation as being "overly sensitive."

Those who are able to see pain, unmoved, will soon learn to inflict it.

— MARY WOLLSTONECRAFT, *A Vindication of the Rights of Women* (1792), p. 256

Gender differences have been found to exist in moral sensitivity, depending on the situation. In discussions following a pressured-for-sex drama, fifty-eight percent of the women recognized the coercion but only twenty-two percent of the men did.[74] During the 1991 U.S. Senate Judiciary Committee hearing regarding Anita Hill's allegations that Supreme Court nominee Clarence Thomas sexually harassed her, many people expressed surprise that the policymakers—the senators—were so poorly informed and morally insensitive regarding the problem of sexual harassment in the workplace. "The insensitivity and lack of comprehension about the complex psychology of sexual harassment displayed by the senators questioning the witnesses in the Clarence Thomas hearing," wrote one lawyer in her commentary on the case, "was, in a word, unbelievable."[75]

The development of moral sensitivity can be enhanced by experiences that provide opportunities to see the world from other people's perspectives.[76] The actual perception of a person in distress can trigger empathy; hearing other people's stories can also contribute to one's consciousness-raising. Abstract classroom discussions of other people's suffering, in contrast, have been found to have little effect on people's actual feelings of empathy for them.[77] Only when we are painfully sensitive to actual suffering can we begin to move toward changing the social conditions that perpetuate injustice and suffering. Indeed, one of the strengths of feminist ethics is its recognition of the importance of cultivating moral sensitivity through consciousness-raising.

Moral Reasoning or Judgment

The prevailing view that reason is the highest attribute of humans has led many Western philosophers to focus on moral reasoning and neglect the other components of moral behavior. Although some philosophers, such as Plato, claim that knowing what is right entails doing what is right, recent studies of moral behavior indicate that moral reasoning is insufficient in itself to bring about moral action. On the other hand, without first engaging in critical judgment, our well-intentioned actions can hurt innocent people and lead to moral tragedies.

Moral judgment that is not tempered with moral sensitivity can lead to behavior that is rigid and unfeeling. Justice untempered with feelings of mercy can lead to taking revenge on the offending party. Loyalty to one's peer group or country, when not balanced by feelings of sympathy for people outside of one's community, can lead to blind obedience, as happened in Nazi Germany, or gang warfare, as in our own cities.

People who are deficient in moral reasoning do not recognize the different moral values and considerations involved in making a moral decision and thus tend to come up with simplistic solutions. Not revealing the name of a fraternity brother who raped a woman is justified in the name of loyalty; lying about an affair is justified on the grounds of sparing another person's feelings. These people often fail to see the full repercussions of their decisions and become easily baffled in situations where they are presented with conflicting values.

People who are competent moral reasoners, in contrast, make more satisfactory moral decisions, from both their own point of view and that of moral philosophers. Proficiency in moral reasoning affects our lives at all levels. Studies show that people whose capacity for moral reasoning is well developed are more fulfilled by their careers, are more likely to pursue further education, are more involved in their communities, and have higher self-esteem.[78]

Real-life exposure to ideas that do not fit in with our earlier, more simplistic ideas seems to be a condition for the development of moral reasoning.[79] Practice in resolving moral dilemmas, the acquisition of proficiency in logic, and the study of ethical theory also contribute to the development of this component. These strategies have been found to be particularly effective when combined with a study of the stages of moral development, such as those put forth by Lawrence Kohlberg and Carol Gilligan.[80]

Moral Motivation

Political philosopher Edmund Burke once wrote that "the only thing necessary for evil to triumph is for good men to do nothing." Many otherwise good people know what is right and are sensitive to the moral issues involved; however, they lack the motivation to put this knowledge into action or praxis. People who fail to act on what they know is right are known as weak-willed.

To see what is right and not to do it is want of courage.

—CONFUCIUS

Moral motivation entails putting moral values above competing non-moral values. People who do not place much importance on moral values are less likely to take moral values into consideration when "resolving" a moral dilemma.[81] Nationalistic and economic values, concerns about our popularity, conformity to cultural or peer group norms all can take precedence over what we clearly recognize to be the morally right action. Dysfunctional families often place a higher value on the appearance of harmony—what others will think—than on the welfare of the individual members of the family.

Some students place a higher value on getting good grades than on honesty. Thirty to sixty-five percent of college students admit to some form of academic dishonesty, including cheating on tests, stealing library books, and destroying other students' lab experiments.[82] Some students justify their dishonesty by stating that morality is relative, but most acknowledge an awareness that what they did was wrong.

The motivation to behave morally is intimately tied in with how we define ourselves. Social reformers such as Martin Luther King, Jr., and Henry David Thoreau were highly motivated morally. Socrates also made it clear, during his trial, that doing the right thing was more important to him than any nonmoral values such as money, reputation, or even life itself. Unlike Socrates, though, most people allow themselves to be defined by others. People who define themselves primarily in terms of their popularity rating with their peers may fail to act morally, even when they know what is right and are sensitive to the suffering of others.

> Men pride themselves that they have a kind heart because they wish that every one might be happy; but merely to wish is not the sign of a kind heart; we are kind-hearted only in so far as we actually contribute to the happiness of others: that alone betokens a kind heart.
>
> —IMMANUEL KANT, *Lectures on Ethics* (1775–1780)

Group mores can also weaken our motivation to do what we know is right, because group behavior is more often motivated by nonmoral values than is individual behavior. Social activist and theologian Reinhold Niebuhr (1892–1971) wrote this about the My Lai massacre during the Vietnam War:

> . . . individual American soldiers murdered non-combatant women and children. They did so, not primarily because their moral judgment that such action was morally right was immature, or because, as individuals, they were "sick" in some sense, but because they participated in what was essentially a group action taken on the basis of group norms. The moral choice made by each individual soldier who

pulled the trigger was embedded in the larger institutional context of the army and its decision-making procedures. The decisions were dependent in large part on a collectively shared definition of the situation and of what should be done about it. In short, the My Lai massacre was more a function of the group "moral atmosphere" that prevailed in that place at that time than of the stage of moral development [reasoning] of the individuals present.[83]

People who are highly motivated morally are more likely to act on their beliefs about what is right. Dentists who score high on a measure of moral motivation, for example, are far more likely than other dentists to treat a patient who has tested positive for HIV and to agree that the profession has a responsibility to treat patients known to be infected with other blood-borne diseases.[84]

Improvement in this component of morality involves knowing how to recognize and critically analyze different types of values—moral and nonmoral. Practice in exercising our moral judgment, through discussions of situations that involve conflicts between moral and nonmoral values, can serve to strengthen moral motivation. Moral motivation can also be enhanced by meeting role models who are happy and successful and concerned about moral issues, as "active moral agents in a wider social world."[85]

Moral Character

The last component of moral behavior is moral character, which is related to integrity. A person of high moral character has managed to integrate the other three components of moral behavior into their personality. Moral character predisposes us to act morally. It includes personality traits such as ego strength, high self-esteem, courage, perseverance, and strength of convictions. Traits such as assertiveness, courage, competence, and the expectation of success also contribute to a person's willingness and ability to take moral action.[86]

When asked about the good person, Tzu-lu replied:

"He cultivates himself and thereby achieves reverence."

"Is that all?"

"He cultivates himself and thereby brings peace and security to his fellow men."

—CONFUCIUS, *The Analects*, Bk. XIV, 42

People who have strong moral character are better at regulating their own behavior and are less likely to be distracted by short-term rewards. They will persevere in accomplishing their goals, even in the face of strong pressures to do otherwise. For example, when reading the biographies of moral reformers such as Gandhi and Lucretia Mott, one cannot help but be impressed by their perseverance in the face of seeming defeat and their calm self-confidence when defending their position in spite of overwhelming opposition. People who are deficient in moral character, on the other hand, are easily distracted and cannot be depended upon, because they lack the courage of their convictions and are liable to back down when the going gets rough.

Moral sensitivity, moral reasoning, moral motivation, and moral character all have an important influence on our moral behavior. The failure to act morally can occur because of a deficiency in any one of these components. In other words, these four components do not work independently of each other. Rather, they "comprise a *logical* analysis of what it takes to behave morally."[87]

Exercises

1. Ethical subjectivisim is a popular moral theory among nonphilosophers. If morality is simply a matter of personal feeling, though, a person who is morally insensitive will have fewer moral obligations to others than a person who is morally sensitive. It would not be morally wrong, for example, for a morally insensitive person to break promises, rape, cheat, or engage in racist activities, because they do not recognize these as moral issues.

   Do you agree that, if a person does not feel bad about harming another person, then it is not wrong for that person and may even be the morally right decision? Is insensitivity a legitimate reason for excusing such behavior? Relate your answer to experiences you have had with people who were lacking in moral sensitivity.

2. People who make offensive comments are sometimes unaware of the effects of their comments on others. Do we have a moral duty to help people become aware of their insensitive behavior? If you agree that we do, then we ourselves must use sensitivity and tact when pointing out that the behavior was morally insensitive. Some people will become angry and defensive when their offensive behavior is pointed out, but others will resolve to become more sensitive in the future.

   Break up into groups and choose one of the following scenarios for role play or discussion. How should you respond? What reasons did you use, or could you have used, when pointing out to the person making the insensitive comments that they should not have done so?

   a. You are at a party when someone makes a joke that is racist (or sexist or homophobic).

   b. A female student in your calculus class is having trouble understanding an assignment. She raises her hand and asks the professor to explain a point regarding the assignment. He replies that she shouldn't worry her pretty little head about such matters but should instead ask one of the men in the class to help her with her homework. The professor, encouraged by the resulting laughter, goes on to suggest, with a wink, that if she can't find someone else to help her, he is available after hours.

3. Moral tragedies occur because people are deficient in at least one of the components of moral behavior. Think of a time when you made a moral decision that you later came to regret. How did a deficiency in one (or more) of the four components contribute to your poor decision?

4. Make a list of values that are important to you. Which of these values are the most important? Which are the least important? Highlight the moral values on your list. Which are more important to you, moral or nonmoral values? Why? How does this affect your moral motivation?

5. Plato argued that, because people are rational by nature, reason is sufficient to motivate a person to do what is good: If a person knows what is good, they will be good. He believed that wrong actions are attributable solely to ignorance about goodness. David Hume and Carol Gilligan, on the other hand, argue that feelings play a more important role than reason in motivating us to act morally.

   What motivates you to act morally? Illustrate your answer with examples from your own experience.

6. Discuss your own moral development in light of the four components of moral behavior. Illustrate each component, using specific examples. Which components are the strongest and which are the weakest? What can you do to strengthen the weaker components?

7. How does your moral hero or role model, as discussed in Chapter 1, exemplify each of these four components of moral behavior?

*8. Has your community service work contributed to the development of any of the four components of moral behavior? How? Illustrate your answer with specific examples from your community service.

Moral Maturity: Moving Beyond Ethical Relativism

One day we will learn that the heart can never be totally right if the head is totally wrong. Only through the bringing together of head and heart—intelligence and goodness—shall man rise to a fulfillment of his true nature . . . The call for intelligence is a call for open-mindedness, sound judgment, and love for truth. It is a call for men to rise above the stagnation of closed-mindedness and the paralysis of gullibility.

—MARTIN LUTHER KING, JR., *The Strength to Love* (1963), p. 45

Why should we be concerned about our moral development? If we are happy the way we are, what is wrong with staying in the conventional stage of moral reasoning for the rest of our lives? After all, the American norms—the "American way of life"—have served most of us well so far.

The problem with being a cultural relativist or conventional moral reasoner is that, when cultural norms change, the cultural relativist—for better or for worse—just changes along with them. Most of us, for example, are convinced that something as horrendous as the Holocaust could never happen here, but Stanley Milgram's studies of obedience tell a different story. His study, described in Chapter 2, exposed the willingness of most adults in the United States to uncritically follow the norms or commands of those in authority, even when they believed that they killed another person:

> Ordinary people, simply doing their jobs, and without any particular hostility on their part, can become agents in a terrible destructive process. Moreover, even when the destructive effects of their work become patently clear, and they are asked to carry out actions incompatible with fundamental standards of morality, relatively few people have the resources needed to resist authority.[88]

One of the most outstanding characteristics of Nazi Adolf Eichmann was his ordinariness. Indeed, what is so frightening is that Eichmann exemplifies the type of moral reasoning espoused by the majority of American adults. He is everyman. He was a good husband and parent. He was well liked and respected by his friends. According to his minister, he was "a man with very positive ideas."[89] Several psychiatrists who examined Eichmann certified him as normal. Eichmann went to considerable lengths during his trial to point out that he was not prejudiced against Jews and had never harbored any negative feelings toward them.

Did his participation in the extermination of millions of Jews bother his conscience? Eichmann's inability to engage in autonomous moral reasoning and his lack of moral sensitivity left him caught in a web of doublethink and fallacious thinking, where his purported feelings toward Jews and his actual behavior were completely at odds. At his trial, Eichmann recalled that "he would have had a bad conscience only if he had not done what he had been ordered to do"[90]—to ship millions of men, women, and children to their deaths with great bureaucratic efficiency.

Our moral development, how we interact with others, and self-actualization are all intimately connected. The higher our level of moral development, the more consistent our behavior will be with our beliefs and our conscience. Morally good people not only sympathize with those who are suffering but take active steps to help alleviate that suffering and to restore justice and a sense of community. These people are willing to speak out on behalf of themselves and others, when they witness an injustice, and will take effective and well-thought-out action to correct that injustice.

Moral maturity involves overcoming resistance and rigidity in one's thinking and one's perception of the world. The ability to be flexible in our thinking involves the recognition that there is more than one way to approach a given problem and also the ability to effectively integrate the various components of moral development.

Exercises

1. Briefly describe your character or personality. Now describe yourself as the person you would like to be. Compare the two descriptions. Which description of you has the stronger moral character? What steps can you take to strengthen your moral character?

2. Has your college experience enhanced your moral development? If so, what experiences at college have had an impact on your moral development? Are there any experiences that worked to inhibit your moral development? If so, what were these experiences? Why did they have a negative effect on your moral development?

*3. During World War II, when the Nazis first cautiously introduced the idea of requiring Jews to wear the yellow star of David, the King of Denmark, a man of very high principles, announced that he would be the first to wear one. The people of Denmark quickly followed suit. Without the cooperation of the Danish people, the Nazis were unable to tell which of the Danes were Jews and which were non-Jews, thus making deportation of Jews impossible. Indeed, it was said that Nazi officials who had lived in Denmark for years were noticeably affected by this experience and thus could no longer be trusted to carry out Nazi policy.

   How do public figures who have reached a higher stage of moral reasoning—such as the King of Denmark, Martin Luther King, Jr., Elizabeth Cady Stanton, and Gandhi—have a positive effect on the moral development of others in their culture? Are there any public figures in this country, or people you have met through your community service work, that you admire as highly moral people? Discuss the influence, if any, these people have had on your own moral development.

Summary

1. *Conscience* provides *knowledge* about right and wrong, *motivates* us to do what is right, and *demands* that we act in accord with it.

2. There are *three main forces* that shape our *conscience:* heredity, learning or environmental factors, and conscious moral direction.

3. *Heredity* or *biological factors* include natural virtues such as sympathy and a sense of justice. The frontal lobes of the brain also appear to play a critical role in conscience.

4. *Learning* or *environmental factors* that shape our conscience include our cultural norms, our family, and our experiences. Cultural relativists, behaviorists, and Freudians maintain that morality is the result of environmental forces.

5. *Conscious moral direction* involves active deliberation and accepting responsibility for our moral decisions. Most philosophers contend that the development of conscious moral direction is necessary for becoming a truly moral person and a person of integrity.

6. Conscience involves both **moral sentiments** and **reason.**

7. The *affective* element of conscience includes moral sentiments or feelings such as sympathy, "helper's high," moral outrage, and guilt.

8. The *cognitive* element of conscience involves making rational moral judgments.

9. The affective and cognitive elements of the conscience work together.

10. *Jean Piaget* noted that children go through distinct stages of moral development. The first stage he labelled the **stage of heteronomy.** The second stage he called the **stage of autonomy.**

11. Jean Piaget also distinguished between practical and theoretical morality. **Theoretical morality** is judgment dissociated from actual action. **Practical morality** involves our actual motivations and sense of obligation.

12. The *cognitive-development approach* to moral development is based on the following assumptions and findings:
    * Certain concepts, such as moral excellence, are fundamental to all humans.
    * Humans have an intrinsic potential and drive to grow from lower to higher stages of moral development.
    * Each stage of moral development involves a structurally different mode, or paradigm, for making moral decisions.
    * Stages of moral development are universal and transcultural.
    * People progress through the stages sequentially; they do not skip stages.
    * Gains made in moral development tend to be retained.
    * People tend to prefer the highest stage of moral development that is conceptually available to them.
    * It is more desirable to reason at a higher stage.

13. *Lawrence Kohlberg* identified three levels of moral development, each having two stages. The *preconventional level* includes punishment and obedience and the egoist stages; the *conventional level* includes the good boy/nice girl and culture-maintaining stages; the *postconventional level* includes social contract reasoning and principled moral reasoning. Only about ten percent of U.S. adults ever reach the postconventional stage of moral reasoning.

14. Although *college* tends to move students into a higher stage of moral reasoning, most college students do not successfully make the transition into the postconventional stage.

15. *Culture and profession* have an impact on one's level of moral reasoning.

16. *Carol Gilligan* argued that women, in general, are more likely to use a *care perspective* and that men are more likely to use a justice perspective in their moral reasoning.

17. Gilligan postulated three stages of moral reasoning: *preconventional* or self-centered, *conventional* or self-sacrificing, and *postconventional* or *mature care ethics.*

18. Gilligan and Kohlberg later came to agree that *moral maturity* involves a synthesis of both care and justice perspectives.

19. *James Rest* identified *four components of moral behavior:*

    - **Moral sensitivity** is the awareness of how our actions affect others.

    - *Moral reasoning or judgment* involves the ability to make critical judgments regarding moral values and various courses of action.

    - *Moral motivation* entails placing moral values above competing nonmoral values.

    - *Moral character* involves having certain personality traits, such as courage, perseverance, and high self-esteem, that predispose us to act morally.

20. Working on our *moral development* is important because, otherwise, we are likely to simply follow cultural norms, even when they are destructive.

Morality as Universal

Most philosophers maintain that moral principles are universally binding on all people regardless of their personal desires, culture, or religion. These philosophers argue that moral principles are discovered, rather than being created by humans.

Individual interests or cultural customs can influence how a particular moral principle is carried out; however, fundamental moral principles are transcultural. For example, the Kabloona Eskimos were expected to assist their elderly parents to die. We do not do this in the United States, but we are expected to provide care for our elderly parents. In both cases, the duty of fidelity (loyalty) to one's parents is being honored. The methods of honoring this duty, however, are different in these two cultures.

This section will begin by looking at ethical egoism. According to ethical egoists, the only moral principle is to do what is in our own best self-interest. Unlike ethical subjectivism, ethical egoism is based on a universally binding moral principle and is not simply a matter of acting on our whims or desires. We *ought* to do what benefits us even when we feel like engaging in self-destructive behavior.

Utilitarianism, in Chapter 8, expands the concept of interest or benefit to include the whole community. The principle of utility requires us to maximize pleasure and minimize pain for the greatest number rather than just seeking our own happiness.

Chapter 9 on deontology focuses on our duty rather than on the consequences of our actions. Duty, or doing what is right for its own sake, is the foundation of morality. Deontologists differ, however, regarding the source of duty (reason or intuition) and also on whether moral duties are absolutely binding.

Chapter 10 covers rights ethics. Natural rights ethicists claim that rights stem from our human nature and exist independently of our duties. Most rights theories, however, do not exist as a separate theory but as part of a broader moral theory such as ethical egoism, utilitarianism, or deontology.

The final chapter covers virtue ethics. Virtue ethics emphasizes right being over right action. Virtue ethics and theories of right action are not alternatives to ethical theories that stress right conduct; rather, they complement each other.

Instead of being mutually exclusive like ethical subjectivism and cultural relativism, universal theories generally focus on one particular aspect of morality rather than providing a comprehensive picture. Most of the moral philosophers included in Section III include aspects of more than one of these theories in their moral philosophy.

CHAPTER 7

Ethical Egoism
Morality Is Acting in Our Best Self-Interest

The achievement of his own happiness is man's highest moral purpose.
—AYN RAND, *The Virtue of Selfishness* (1964)

The individual is most likely to contribute to social betterment by rationally pursuing his own best long-range interests.
—ROBERT G. OLSON, *The Morality of Self-Interest* (1965)

What Is Ethical Egoism?

Gyges' Ring

The story of Gyges' ring in Plato's *Republic* is often used to illustrate **ethical egoism.** In this dialogue, Glaucon tries to convince Socrates that it is better for people to do only that which benefits themselves. "Those who practice justice," Glaucon argues, "do it unwillingly because they lack the power to do injustice." To make his point, Glaucon tells the story of Gyges, who was a shepherd in the service of the ruler of Lydia. Gyges found a gold ring in a chasm, following a violent storm and earthquake. Before long Gyges noticed that, when he turned the setting of the ring so that it faced the inside of his hand, he became invisible to those around him. When Gyges realized his power, he arranged to become a messenger to the king. When he arrived at the king's residence, he seduced the queen, killed the king, and took over the empire.

From this, Glaucon concluded that it is more reasonable to be unjust—if we have the opportunity to do so without getting caught. If a just man and an unjust man both wore the same ring, Glaucon argues, their actions would be no different. Indeed, the clever person, "while doing the greatest injustice, . . . has nevertheless provided himself with the greatest reputation for justice."[1]

Like ethical subjectivism, most versions of egoism are exclusionary: They focus on isolated individuals who, like Gyges, are concerned only with their own interests. Each human is therefore an island unto himself, rather than being interdependent and an integral part of a community or web of life. Ethical egoism differs from ethical subjectivism, however, because it is concerned with *a person's best self-interest.* Our best self-interests, in turn, are identified with those that are rational. Ethical subjectivism, in contrast, asks only what people desire or feel is right for them. The ethical egoist identifies happiness with the pursuit of rational self-interest. Happiness is thus the *purpose* of ethics. Ethics must define for us the means of achieving this happiness, whether those means be direct or indirect.

What we feel is right for us is not always the same as what is in fact in our own self-interest or what will make us happy. Unlike ethical subjectivists, ethical egoists are not recommending that we mindlessly act out our desires but instead rationally calculate which actions would most benefit us. Hanging out in bars, smoking cigarettes, or skipping classes may be things we want to do, but these activities, for the most part, are not in our best self-interest. Sometimes we must forego our immediate desires to fulfill our long-term interests.

Seeking our own interests does not necessarily entail ignoring the interests of others, because our long-term interests might best be served by allowing others to also pursue their interests: Ethical egoists are opposed to putting other people's interests *before* our own. We are justified in considering the interests of others, if it is in our self-interest to do so. If by pursuing our own self-interest, we just happen to benefit someone else, that's fine. Helping others is often in our own self-interest, because they will then be more likely to help us when we need them. In fact, sometimes the best way to get ahead is to do something for someone who is in a position to give us something we value in return.

Elements of ethical egoism are found in many ethical theories, including those of Plato, Aristotle, Herbert Spencer, Jeremy Bentham, John Stuart Mill, and David Hume. Indeed, in Socrates' response to Glaucon, he does acknowledge that it is morally acceptable for people to act in ways that benefit themselves. In fact, Socrates argues that being just benefits a person more than being unjust. However, he also argues that justice is also a good in and of itself, independent of its benefit to the just man. At this point, Socrates deviates from the position of the ethical egoist who claims that self-interest is the only moral reason for choosing one particular course of action. Most philosophers, like Socrates but unlike the ethical egoists, claim that personal happiness is only one of several goods by which to judge the morality of an action.

Egoism Versus Egotism

Before we proceed with a more in-depth look at ethical egoism, we must first understand what ethical egoism is not. *Egoism is not the same as egotism.* An

egotist is a person who is arrogant, boastful, inconsiderate, and self-centered. Egotistical behavior is not necessarily in one's best self-interest, because arrogant and boastful people tend to alienate others and, by doing so, limit their opportunities for happiness. Ethical egoism, in contrast, stems from high self-regard, whereas the egotism of the braggart more often stems from *poor* self-esteem and a need for approval.

The term "egoism" has also been used incorrectly to describe the lonely existence of a solipsist. **Solipsism** is the belief that we cannot prove the existence of anything outside of our own minds or ideas. Using the "method of doubt," René Descartes concluded that all we can know with certainty is our own mind. Consequently, for all practical purposes, I am the only being in the universe. The outside world exists only as an object of my consciousness. If others do not actually exist, I cannot know the good of the Other, and hence there is no point in pursing the common good.

> I am left alone, as the only creature of God in the universe in that forlorn state of Egoism, into which it is said, some of the Disciples of Des Cartes were brought by his philosophy.
>
> —THOMAS REID, *Essays on the Intellectual Powers of Man* (1785)[2]

Unlike the egocentrism of the solipsist, which is grounded in the metaphysical claim that one can know only one's own existence, ethical egoism does not imply that I am the only being in the universe. Instead, ethical egoism claims that, even though others exist, I am the being whose interests are *most* important.

Ethical Egoism	Moral = individual self-interest
Ethical Subjectivism	Moral = individual feelings
Hedonism	Moral = pleasure (individual or societal)

Egoism is also not the same as hedonism. **Hedonism** is a broad philosophical doctrine that considers pleasure to be the *standard* of value. Pleasure is identified with happiness, so whatever gives us pleasure becomes the guide to our actions. Philosophical hedonism takes many forms. The Cyrenaics, a philosophical school founded by Greek philosopher Aristippus of Cyrene (c. 435–c. 360 B.C.E.), taught that pleasure is achieved by the immediate gratification of all our sensual desires. Greek philosopher Epicurus, on the other hand, distinguished between the pleasures of this type of hedonism and ethical egoism. Epicurus argued that the concept of pleasure as the ultimate good is implanted in our mind by nature. As an ethical egoist, however, Epicurus is referring to rational pleasures, not the pleasures of debauchery and sadism.

> When we say that pleasure is the goal we do not mean the pleasures of the dissipated and those which consist in the process of enjoyment . . . but freedom from pain in the body and from disturbance in the mind. For it is not drinking and continuous parties nor sexual pleasure nor enjoyment of fish and other delicacies of a wealthy table which produce the pleasant life, but sober reasoning which searches out the causes of every act of choice and refusal and which banishes the opinions that give rise to the greatest mental confusion.[3]

Hedonism is concerned only with our immediate pleasures; ethical egoism involves caution and taking into consideration both the short-term and the long-term consequences of our actions. Rational or enlightened self-interest of the type that Epicurus supported involves prudence. Ethical egoists would avoid cheating on a test, even though it may help them in the short run, because it is more beneficial in the long run not to rely on cheating.

Exercises

1. Do you agree that there is a difference between an egoist and an egotist? If so, use examples to illustrate your answer. Was Gyges, in Plato's *Republic,* an egoist or an egotist? Support your answer.

2. Is there a distinction between pleasure and happiness? What is the connection, if any, between pleasure and morality and between happiness and morality? Use examples to support your answer.

3. Is prudence the same as morality? An egoist may argue that it is prudent not to cheat, but if you had Gyges' ring, wouldn't it be more prudent to cheat? What if you were prevented from studying for an important final exam because of illness? During the test you notice that you can see the answers of the person in front of you, a straight A student. You are sitting in the back of the room, so no one will see you cheat. The proctor has temporarily left the room. Wouldn't it be in your self-interest to copy some of the answers from the test in front of you? How would an ethical egoist answer this question?

*4. Nathaniel Hawthorne once wrote: "Happiness is as a butterfly which, when pursued, is always beyond our grasp but which, if you sit down quietly, may alight upon you." What is happiness for you? Does happiness come from directly seeking it, or does it come from pursuing other goals? Explain. If you are doing community service, relate your answer to your service.

5. Is happiness sufficient to define what is in our own best self-interest? Are there any other criteria you can use to determine whether an action is in your best interest? Were there times in your life when you did not act in your own

best interest? How did you know what was in your own interest? What is the relationship between your best self-interest and that of others?

6. Most superhero myths—such as that of Superman, Wonder Woman, and Batman—entail a "normal" person becoming invisible and being replaced with the persona of a superperson. Glaucon claimed that, if we could disguise our identity under a cloak and mask, we would use our superpowers for unjust ends rather than in the service of humanity. Do you agree? What would you do if you could become invisible, such as Gyges did, or mask your identity, like the superheroes can?

Psychological Egoism

For every man by natural necessity desires that which is good for him.
—THOMAS HOBBES, *Philosophical Rudiments, English Works* (1839–1845), vol. 2, p. 25

There are two main types of egoism: ethical egoism and psychological egoism. Ethical egoism is a normative theory about how things *ought* to be. We ought to act in the way that is in our own best self-interest. *Psychological egoism,* in contrast, is a descriptive theory about how things *are.*

Thomas Hobbes (1588–1679) was the first major philosopher, except for Machiavelli, to present a completely individualistic picture of human nature. Thomas Hobbes was born in England when the Protestant Reformation was in full swing. The Reformation brought with it wars and major shifts in political and ecclesiastical power. Hobbes claimed that he was born prematurely, because his mother took fright when she heard about the approaching Spanish Armada. The turbulent political atmosphere of Hobbes' early years convinced him that people form into societies only from fear of death and the need for security to pursue their interests.

Hobbes regarded people as basically egoists. Although it may appear that people care about the good of others, according to Hobbes, they are basically selfish, aggressive, and quarrelsome. Without society, he said, we would all live in a "state of nature" in which life would be "solitary, poor, nasty, brutish and short."[4] People do live within a society and agree to obey certain rules, but this does not mean that we are no longer egoists by nature. Like Glaucon, Hobbes believed that we agree to abide by the rules of society, or to live under a "social contract," only because it benefits us.

Hobbes also denied that there is anything noble about the so-called moral sentiments. We feel pity or sympathy for another person, he claimed, only because their misfortune is a reminder that the same thing could happen to us. Because we identify with people who are good, we feel much greater pity when a good person suffers misfortune than we do when an evil person suffers. Even great acts of charity and altruism, according to Hobbes, are

Thomas Hobbes (1588–1679), English political philosopher. Hobbes believed that humans are egoists by nature. Without societal rules to control our natural selfishness, life, Hobbes claimed, would be "solitary, poor, nasty, brutish and short."

performed only because we delight in demonstrating our powers and superiority by showing the world that we are more capable than those we serve.

According to sociobiologists such as E. O. Wilson, we humans, like other animals, are genetically programmed to act in ways that further our own self-interest. In his book *On Human Nature,* Wilson claims that altruism is fundamentally selfish, because it actually increases our chances of passing on our genes to future generations. Studies by sociobiologists have found that people prefer partners who are altruistic; thus, altruistic concern for others actually benefits us by enhancing our desirability as mates.

> Can the cultural evolution of higher ethical values gain a direction and momentum of its own and completely replace genetic evolution? I think not. The genes hold culture on a leash . . . Human behavior—like the deepest capacities for emotional response which drive and guide it—is the circuitous technique by which human genetic material has been and will be kept intact. Morality has no other demonstrable ultimate function.

Psychological Egoism Explained

But what of people who take drugs, smoke cigarettes, and act in ways that undermine their relationships and their career? A psychological egoist who is not so concerned with the perpetuation of the species may reply that taking drugs or smoking or being a jerk may have brought that particular person

Rescuing victims of a car bombing in Beruit, Lebanon, 1986. Some people will go to the rescue of others despite considerable risk to their own lives. According to sociobiologist E. O. Wilson, altruistic behavior, such as going to the rescue of people in distress, is genetically programmed into humans and serves to increase our chances of passing on our genes to future generations.

more happiness than *not* engaging in these seemingly destructive actions. After all, drugs get us high, smoking is relaxing, and sabotaging relationships and careers gets us off the hook, thus freeing us up for other pursuits.

> We say that pleasure is the starting-point and the end of living blissfully. For we recognize pleasure as a good which is primary and innate. We begin every act of choice and avoidance from pleasure, and it is to pleasure that we return using our experience of pleasure as the criterion of every good thing.
>
> —EPICURUS, "Letter to Menoeceus"

Other psychological egoists respond by using a weaker version of the theory. They argue that, although people may not always *act* in their own self-interest, they are always *motivated* to act in their own best interest. People sometimes fail to act in ways that benefit them. Epicurus argues that this happens, not from lack of motivation, but because of error and ignorance. For example, a person who has been abused since childhood may not realize that abuse is not a normal part of an intimate relationship. Or a person may underestimate the pain that can accompany their actions. Most smokers, for example, started smoking as children, when they were not fully cognizant of the consequences of their actions.

Indeed, no matter what example we produce, the psychological egoist can always reply that the person must have acted as they did because it brought him or her more pleasure than pain. A person who commits suicide brings a painful existence to an end. For a woman remaining in an abusive relationship, the economic and emotional security must outweigh the pain of the abuse. And so on.

The Limitations of Psychological Egoism

On the surface it may appear that psychological egoism is an airtight theory, but the problem is that psychological egoists will not allow any explanations that do not fit into their theory. No matter what happens, they explain it as an example of egoism: "People are always motivated by self-interest; therefore, whatever people do must have been motivated by self-interest." Such circular reasoning, or begging the question, adds nothing to our explanation of human motivation.

One of the requirements of any good scientific theory is that it must be **falsifiable**.[5] This means that there must be some type of evidence or argument that could count against it. For example, the theory that the Earth was flat could be, and was, disproved by explorers who sailed around the world and by observing the shape of the Earth's shadow on the moon during an eclipse. Psychological egoists, on the other hand, cannot devise any hypothetical situations that might disprove their theory.

Another problem with psychological egoism is that it is very difficult to know for certain what actually motivates people. Our motives for performing an action and the consequences of that action are not always the same. People like Mother Teresa may derive great satisfaction from their altruistic actions, but this is not necessarily what motivated such people to help others in the first place. It is even difficult to figure out our own motives sometimes! Consider how often you have replied, when asked why you did something, "I don't know."

Dan Stock, a 38-year-old policy analyst, was relaxing on a beach in southern New England. He looked up and saw an older man and a child caught in a strong current. Without a second thought (or so he reports), Stock ran into the water, followed by his Labrador retriever, Angus. Together they swam out and saved the drowning swimmers. As a result of Stock's heroic action, he became a sort of local hero, a recognition that he greatly enjoyed. Why did he risk his life? He did not risk his life to pass on his genes; the swimmers were complete strangers. When he was asked why he swam

Dan Stock and his Labrador retriever, Angus. On July 9th, 1995, Stock and his loyal dog saved two people from drowning at a Rhode Island beach.

out into a dangerous current to save two drowning people, Stock replied that he didn't give it a second thought. He simply acted on impulse; it seemed to be the only right thing to do.

In cases such as this one, psychological egoists claim that the real motive, even though it is unconscious, is self-benefit. In the case of a martyr who gives his or her life to save others, the motive is either lasting recognition after death or ensuring a place in Heaven. But how do we know this was Stock's motive? He is not religious. And what is the point of recognition after our death, if we are no longer around to enjoy it?

Also, sometimes we do struggle because our self-interest (or at least what appears to be in our self-interest) conflicts with what we believe to be the right thing to do. For example, you may be tempted to keep a wallet that you find—especially if it contains a lot of cash and you are a poor college student! But instead, with a sigh, you turn it in to the lost and found. No one sees you do this except the anonymous person at the counter. You receive no praise for your actions. One alternative explanation for returning the wallet might be that you are motivated by a sense of duty rather than pure self-interest.

Egoism as a Prescriptive Theory

Asking why we behave as we *do* and asking how we *ought* to behave are two distinct questions. Unlike psychological egoism, which is a description of human behavior and motivation, ethical egoism is a prescriptive theory about what we ought to do. Even if we agree that humans have a tendency to behave selfishly, this is *not* the same as saying that they ought to behave selfishly. To draw this conclusion is to commit the fallacy of irrelevant conclusion. Ethical egoists, on the other hand, argue that, although we may not always act out of self-interest, we *ought* to do so.

Although both Hobbes and Epicurus were psychological egoists, ethical egoists do not necessarily accept psychological egoism. Indeed, if we always acted in our own self-interest, there would be no need for moral theory because there would be no such thing as immoral behavior! It seems rather redundant to tell people that they ought to do what they are going to do anyway.

Ethical egoists are not just saying that it is morally justifiable to pursue our own self-interest: They maintain that we ought to pursue our own self-interest *exclusively*. Not only are we justified in behaving selfishly; we *ought* to do so.

Exercises

1. Think back to times when you acted in ways that did not increase your happiness or were not in your own self-interest. Were the reasons simply ignorance or error? Why else might people act in ways that might not bring about the greatest pleasure for themselves?

2. Do you agree with E. O. Wilson that all our actions, including those such as doing community service and helping others, have as their ultimate function the perpetuation of the species? Can you think of an action, any action, that could not be explained as an example of psychological egoism?

*3. Do you agree with Hobbes that all acts of charity are done simply to make us feel better than the people we are "helping"? Is your community service work motivated by a desire to feel superior? If so, how?

4. Glaucon, in his story about Gyges' ring, claims that, if we could become invisible, we would most likely act in ways that benefited us. Do you agree? If you were invisible, would you act only in ways that benefited you? If not, why not? Illustrate your answer with examples.

   In the scenario about finding a wallet full of money when no one is around, wouldn't we benefit most if we either kept the money or made a big show of returning the wallet? How might Glaucon have responded to the person who returned the wallet?

Ayn Rand (1905–82), Russian-born American novelist, screenwriter, and philosopher. Rand advocated ethical egoism and laissez-faire capitalism. She believed that the United States is the only moral country in the world.

Ayn Rand: "Objectivist Ethics" and Rational Egoism

> *For centuries, the battle of morality was fought between those who claimed that your life belongs to God and those who claimed that it belongs to your neighbors . . . no one came to say that your life belongs to you and that the good is to live it.*
>
> —AYN RAND, *Atlas Shrugged* (1957)

The current popularity of ethical egoism has been fueled by the work of American novelist, screenwriter, and philosopher Ayn Rand (1905–82). Rand defends a version of ethical egoism that she called "objectivist ethics."

Rand was born in St. Petersburg (Leningrad), Russia, in 1905. In 1931, she immigrated to the United States. Her philosophy is in part an outgrowth of her experience living under both the Soviet and the U.S. systems of government. Rand became disillusioned with the demoralizing effects of collectivism and Soviet Communism, and she concluded that ethical egoism, as exemplified by laissez-faire capitalism, is the only philosophy compatible with respect for the integrity and the reality of the individual human. To Rand, the United States was the "noblest, and, in its original founding principles, the *only* moral country in the history of the world."[6] Rand believed that we can best create an atmosphere where each individual can pursue their own interests by protecting peoples' individual liberty rights.

According to Rand, there is no other source of values than objective reality—hence, her term "**objectivist ethics.**" Right and wrong, according to Rand, are natural rather than metaphysical concepts. Like Hobbes and E. O. Wilson, Rand maintained that we value that which helps us to survive, and what helps us to survive is what is in our own self-interest.

> Ethics is an *objective, metaphysical necessity of man's survival*—not by grace of the supernatural nor of your neighbors nor of your whims, but by the grace of reality and the nature of life.

Rand adopted what first appears to be an Aristotelian view of human nature; she argued that reason sets us apart from all other species. According to both Rand and Aristotle, other animals act automatically, but reason is essential for our survival as humans. Since reason *is* necessary for survival, reason has moral value for humans. Therefore, we *ought* to act in a rational manner. Therefore, to behave irrationally is to behave immorally.

> Man cannot survive as anything but man. He *can* abandon his means of survival, his mind, he *can* turn himself into a subhuman creation and he *can* turn his life into a brief span of agony—just as his body can exist for a while in the process of disintegration by disease. But he *cannot* succeed, as a subhuman, in achieving anything but the subhuman—as the ugly horror of the antirational periods of mankind's history demonstrate. Man has to be man by choice—and it is the task of ethics to teach him how to live like man.

When Rand talks of survival, she is not talking merely about biological survival, but rather "that which is required for the survival of man *qua* man." Like Aristotle, Rand boldly declares: "Accept, as your moral ideal, the task of becoming a man."[7] However, at this point, Rand and Aristotle part ways. For Aristotle, humans are fundamentally social beings. Through our membership in a polis, our lives derive moral value, and through this we can fulfill our nature as humans. "He who is unable to live in society, or who has no need because he is sufficient for himself," writes Aristotle in his *Politics,* "must be either a beast or a God."[8]

Rand, in contrast, regards humans as fundamentally solitary individuals, each pursuing his or her own personal self-interest. Unlike Aristotle, who views the state, rather than the individual, as a self-sufficient whole, Rand argues that "there is no such entity as 'society,' . . . only individual men."[9] Her ideal society, or more accurately "collection of individual men," is an atomistic society where each of us must live and work only for ourselves and never for others. This type of society, she claims, is the objectively real world—the only world in which we can prove our value and find rational happiness.

Rand's rational virtues, consequently, all involve the cultivation of individuality rather than social virtues. Her concept of rationality admonishes us to

1. Be *independent* (live by the work of our own mind).
2. Have *integrity* (don't sacrifice our convictions to the opinions of others).
3. Be *honest* (don't fake reality).
4. Be *just* (neither seek nor give that which is unearned or undeserved).

Rand assumes that any rational person would accept her list of virtues and what she calls the supreme value of productive work.

In Rand's novel *The Fountainhead,* Howard Roark is presented as her ideal of the moral person. Roark, a successful architect, lives his life entirely for himself. He asks nothing of other people and feels no obligation to help others. "Nothing is given to man on earth," he declares in a speech before a jury. "Everything he needs has to be produced. And here man faces his basic alternative; he can survive in only one of two ways—by the independent work of his own mind or as a parasite fed by the minds of others . . ."[10]

Rationally self-interested people help others only if, by doing so, they will get something in return. Rand refers to voluntary cooperation as the *principle of trade* or justice. Doing something for someone else is morally justified *only* when we can expect to get something of similar value in exchange. Altruism, on the other hand, involves self-sacrifice or giving without expectation of return; therefore, altruism is immoral.

> As a basic step of self-esteem learn to treat as the mark of a cannibal any man's *demand* for your help. To demand it is to claim that your life is his property . . .
>
> —AYN RAND, *Atlas Shrugged* (1957)

Christian ethics teaches us that selfishness and pride are the original sins and that altruism is a virtue. Rand turns this equation upside down. She maintains that centuries of being taught that we must live for others has eroded our sense of self-esteem and left us feeling guilty and full of self-hatred. For her, altruism is the equivalent of the Christian original sin and selfishness is the greatest virtue. Rand refers to an altruist who, in her view, attempts to cultivate a pseudo-self-esteem by pleasing others as a "*second-hander.*" Altruism and compassion are vices, she argues, because all altruism is based on self-sacrifice and demands by others to give them something that they have neither earned nor deserve. Altruists are willing to sacrifice their lives and interests to benefit others. This attitude not only turns the giver into an object; it also turns the receiver into a parasite. "The only good which men can do to one another," exhorts Howard Roark, "and the only statement of their proper relationships is—Hands off!"[11]

> Altruism is the theory of ethics that motivates the hostility toward capitalism and
> egoism. According to altruism, a morally good action is one that places others
> above self; as such, altruism commands self-sacrifice. It does not mean kindness or
> gentleness, but the act of giving up a higher value for the sake of a lower value or
> non-value.
>
> —JERRY KIRKPATRICK, *In Defense of Advertising: Arguments from Reason,*
> *Ethical Egoism and Laissez-Faire Capitalism* (1994), p. 18

Rand was not merely claiming, as Gyges did, that acting in our own self-interest is good only for those individuals who practice her philosophy. On the other hand, neither is she claiming that pursuing our rational self-interest is synonymous with promoting the common good. What Rand believes is that people in general would be happier if we, as individuals, pursued our own self-interest instead of trying to help others.

Exercises

1. Is Rand's depiction of the "rational virtues"—those that are in our own self-interest—any better than the version of egoism presented to us by Gyges? Why should we be independent and honest if we could advance our self-interest by stealing someone else's ideas or property? Why should we be just if we can get away with being unjust? Why should we work if we can spend our days lying out in the sun?

2. Rand assumes that, if we lived in a perfectly laissez-faire society, always following our own self-interest and not hindering others from doing the same, conflicts between one person's self-interest and another's would not arise. Do you agree with her? Support your answer with examples.

*3. Discuss how your life would be affected if all your interactions with other people were based on "trade." How would acting on this principle affect your community service work? Do you agree with Rand that the "principle of trade" is the same as "justice"? Discuss this in light of your own understanding of the moral principle of justice.

*4. Do you agree with Rand that the only good that people can do for each other is "hands off"? What effect would this principle have on people who now depend on others, such as social service and government agencies, for certain services? Would these people be better off, as Rand claims, if we stopped giving them "hand-outs"?

Ethical Egoism and Laissez-Faire Capitalism

Productive work is the central purpose *of rational man's life.*
   —AYN RAND, *The Virtue of Selfishness: A New Concept of Egoism* (1964), p. 27

Ayn Rand regarded the individual as the fundamental unit of economic activity. She also believed that the law of supply and demand is natural to human activity. From these two assumptions, she drew the conclusion that laissez-faire capitalism is the natural, and hence the best, economic system for human beings. **Laissez-faire capitalism** is an economic system based on individual freedom, the pursuit of rational and prudent self-interest, and minimal government interference.

Scottish economist and moral philosopher Adam Smith (1723–90) laid out the foundations of laissez-faire capitalism in his book *Wealth of Nations*. The best society, he argued, is one where everyone is allowed the freedom to pursue their own self-interest in the marketplace. Smith's book was published in 1776—the same year that the American colonies declared their independence—and it had a profound effect on the founding fathers of the United States.

> As every individual . . . endeavors as much as he can both to employ his capital in the support of domestic industry, and so to direct that industry that its produce may be of the greatest value; every individual necessarily labours to render the annual revenue of the society as great as he can. He generally, indeed, neither intends to promote the public interest, nor knows how much he is promoting it . . . he intends only his own gain, and he is in this, as in many other cases, led by an invisible hand to promote an end which was no part of his intention . . . By pursuing his own interest he frequently promotes that of the society more than when he really intends to promote it. I have never known much good done by those who affected to trade for the public good. It is an affectation, indeed, not very common among merchants, and very few words need be employed in dissuading them from it.

Individual freedom, as the primary economic value, was also affirmed by the 1789 *Declaration of the Rights of Man and Citizen* that heralded the beginning of the French Revolution. The declaration stated: "Every man is free to use his physical strength, his industry, and his capital as shall seem to himself to be good and useful. He may produce what he pleases, and produce it as he sees fit."

Laissez-Faire Capitalism

Laissez-faire capitalists view human nature as basically prudent and rationally self-interested. Because only laissez-faire capitalism permits the freedom to engage in trade, it is "the only social system consonant with man's rational nature."[12] The theory contends that, if everyone were allowed to pursue their own self-interest, the result would be the most efficient use of resources. In a free-market economy, consumers are free to spend their money in whatever manner brings them the greatest satisfaction. The capitalists, in turn, create jobs for workers by investing their money and energy in the production of goods that bring the greatest happiness to the consumer, thereby maximizing their own profits in the process. By acting selfishly, in other words, each person is actually benefiting others!

Of course, Rand and the laissez-faire capitalists do not claim that we always act in a prudent and rationally self-interested manner. Ignorance and error, as Epicurus pointed out, can cloud our reasoning. Sometimes workers stay in jobs that don't make the best use of their talents, and consumers do not always spend their money in the most prudent manner.

Marketing professor and ethical egoist Jerry Kirkpatrick argues that advertising is one of the most effective means of combating ignorance and error. "Nothing, as far as I am concerned," Kirkpatrick writes, "could be more benevolent than advertising, beacon of free society."[13] According to Kirkpatrick, advertising provides us with important knowledge and guides us toward continuous economic progress.

> Considering that advertising appeals to consumers to give up a lower value—namely, money—for the sake of a higher value—goods and services, and that producers use advertising to help them give up a lower value—the goods and services—for the sake of a higher value—the money, altruism can never grant moral value to advertising.

The failure and eventual collapse of the Communist economy in the former Soviet Union has further confirmed for many people the superiority of capitalism and individualism over economic systems based on Marxist principles. There is no doubt that capitalism, as an economic system, has produced massive wealth and technological advancement. However, because capitalism is successful in raising the overall wealth and productivity, does that mean it is moral? Both Marxist and liberation ethicists argue that it is possible to have a successful economic system that raises the gross national product and productivity but that is nevertheless unjust.

Some of the most outspoken critics of capitalism and ethical egoism are Marxists. Karl Marx did agree with the capitalists that people can find fulfillment in productive work; however, he also believed, like Aristotle, that we are primarily *socially* productive beings. The egoism of capitalism, therefore, was to Marx one of its greatest evils. Marxists claim that, rather than promoting the interests of the majority, capitalism benefits only a few at the expense of the many. Ethical egoism, therefore, is not a philosophy of "humans qua humans," as Rand claimed, but is instead a philosophy of the elite.

Marx predicted that, with capitalism, the chasm between the rich and the poor would continue to grow, a trend that has actually been occurring in the United States since 1970.[14] Between 1977 and 1992, the most prosperous fifth of the U.S. population gained twenty-eight percent in their real income after taxes. For the richest one percent of the population, the gain in real income was ninety-one percent. The middle class, on the other hand, just barely managed to hold its own, while the poorest fifth lost seventeen percent in their real income.[15] The trend toward economic inequality, rather than being a phenomenon of the 1980s as economists had speculated, has actually accelerated in the 1990s.[16] To keep a stranglehold on the means of production, according to Marx, the wealthy would have to use not rational but irrational means such as force—police, military, and legal force—to keep the poor from revolting.

Ethical egoists seem to assume that everyone is in a position to be a trader. They do not question the assumption that certain people deserve to control the wealth because of their socioeconomic status. Marxists, on the other hand, point out that people's talents and their ability to trade skills and goods in a free-market economy vary enormously. Poverty, lack of access to resources, poor health, and social discrimination are only a few of the factors that place certain people at a distinct disadvantage. Women, in particular, have suffered in a capitalist system, because much of women's labor, especially that which is based on caring and communal values, is unremunerated and undervalued. Patriarchal social structures also limit women's opportunities and access to resources and high-paying jobs.

> The poor, the wretched of the earth . . . are calling into question first of all the economic, social, and political order that oppresses and marginalizes them, and of course the ideology that is brought to justify this domination.
>
> —GUSTAVO GUTIERREZ, *The Power of the Poor in History* (1979), p. 191

Since World War II, with the expansion of the international marketplace, the ethical egoism that underlies capitalism has been used more and more to justify multinational corporations' use of the cheap labor and resources in Third World nations. Liberation ethicists have become especially adamant in their denouncement of capitalism as immoral, exploitative, and a form of institutional violence: "The functioning of the [multinational] capitalist economy," writes liberation ethicist Gustavo Gutierrez, "leads simultaneously to the creation of greater wealth for the few and greater poverty for many."[17] The assurances of the ethical egoists that the wealth generated—in terms of industry, jobs, and education—will benefit the indigenous people by "trickling down" to them, until they too will eventually be able to compete in the world market, has not been borne out, according to Gutierrez.

Savage Inequalities

A history of colonization has also placed many people in the world at a great disadvantage "trading" in an international market. Where the colonizers come in and take over valuable resources and large tracts of land, the indigenous population is left with either impoverished land or no land at all. Meanwhile, technology and wealth remain concentrated in the hands of a few wealthy nations, such as Japan and the United States, while the people living in poorer areas of the world are becoming poorer and poorer.

Even in the United States, the optimistic assumption that opportunities are equally available to everyone who is willing to take advantage of them is clearly incorrect. Beginning early in childhood, certain groups of people are at a disadvantage when competing in the marketplace. Jonathan Kozol notes in his book *Savage Inequalities* that, although there is no evidence of deliberate racism, those who allocate resources to school districts at the state level make decisions that penalize the poorer districts. For example, in New York City, "the poorest districts in the city get approximately 90 cents per pupil from these legislative grants, while the richest districts have been given $14 for each pupil."[18]

Liberation ethicists argue that the ethical egoism inherent in laissez-faire capitalism does not take seriously the dignity and integrity of each individual human, because the moral community includes only those humans ("traders") who have the ability and the opportunity to act in ways that promote their own self-interest. But what can a starving child trade with a capitalist in exchange for food and shelter? Is it really more degrading for a starving person to be fed and nurtured back to health by a caring community of people than to die of starvation? To respond to the plight of people who are starving by telling them to act in ways that promote their own self-interest is nothing but a meaningless gesture.

Rand argues that altruism is parasitic and degrading to the recipient, yet both liberation ethicists and Marxists claim that it is the demands that the capitalists place on the workers that are cannibalistic, rather than the demands of the world's poor for a fair share of the wealth. The capitalists, Marxists argue, did not get where they are by themselves but by using the labors of others for their own gain. Because the capitalists own the means of production, the workers are reduced to chattels. In other words, capitalism turns labor into a commodity—thereby reducing the workers to objects who must sell their labor to the capitalist to survive. Thus, workers become dispirited and alienated from the product of their labor. Their labor is not based on "voluntary cooperation," nor are they receiving an equal share in the products of their labor. Instead, most of the money goes to the capitalists and wealthy shareholders.

Caribbean psychiatrist and political theorist Frantz Fanon (1925–61) likewise denounces the competitive individualism of ethical egoism as a tool of the oppressor. Like Marx, Fanon regards capitalism as a means of keeping the workers oppressed. Because many workers do not have "goods" to trade on the economic market, they remain at a perpetual disadvantage, falling further and further behind. The workers, in turn, are blamed for their failure to compete on an even footing with those who oppress them. Furthermore, Fanon argues, ethical egoism's harsh indictment of altruism and communal self-interest prevents people who are oppressed from coming together and working as a group to overthrow their oppressors.

> Individualism is the first to disappear. The native intellectual had learnt from his masters that the individual ought to express himself fully. The colonialist bourgeoisie had hammered into the natives' mind the idea of a society of individuals where each person shuts himself up in his own subjectivity, and whose only wealth is individual thought. Now the native who has the opportunity to return to the people during the struggle for freedom will discover the falseness of this theory. The very forms of organization of the struggle will suggest to him a different vocabulary. Brother, sister, friend—these are words outlawed by the colonialist bourgeoisie, because for them my brother is my purse, my friend is part of my scheme for getting on . . .[19]

Fanon, instead of embracing the ethical egoists' motto "Look out for yourself," urges people to adopt a community-based ethics where "the interests of one will be the interests of all, for in concrete fact everyone will be discovered by the troops, everyone will be massacred—or everyone will be saved."

With our increasing focus on individual material wealth and the decline of communitarian values, ethical egoism continues to be used as a moral justification for the lifestyle of the new socioeconomic elite. The only moral solution to the oppression of the poor, Marxists and liberation ethicists argue, is to renounce the egoist ideology that underlies capitalism. It is unjust for people's share of societal goods to be directly dependent on their ability to compete in the capitalist marketplace. A more moral economic system, according to them, is one where people care for each other as a community. This philosophy is summed up in the Marxist slogan "From each according to his ability, to each according to his needs."

Individual Versus Social Responsibility

Rand dismisses the Marxist critique of capitalism as an unrealistic longing for "a society in which man's existence will be automatically guaranteed to him—that is, in which man will not have to bear responsibility for his own survival."[20] One of the requirements for survival as a human is to grow. Rand argues that capitalism, by its very nature, creates optimal conditions for progress and growth by challenging people to do their best to further their lives. A socialist society, where rewards are not tied to our achievements, Rand maintains, will lead to stagnation rather than creating conditions for growth.

Both Rand's theory of ethical egoism and the critics of capitalism offer important insights. Rand emphasizes the importance of individual responsibility; Marxists and liberation ethicists remind us of the importance of social responsibility. However, an adequate moral theory must consider and integrate both the individual and social aspects of morality. Although capitalists are not necessarily greedy or exploitative, an egoist ethics offers no reason or incentive for people not to pursue their own ends at the expense of others. On the other hand, an ethical theory like Marxism, which for the most part ignores the individual, can just as surely create a sense of alienation by swallowing up individual interests and goals into the concept of the good of the community.

Exercises

1. Do you agree with laissez-faire capitalists that people are essentially rational and prudent? What might keep people from being rational and prudent? Are people behaving immorally when they do not act in a prudent and rationally self-interested manner? Use examples from your own life to illustrate your answers.

2. In economics, the trickle-down theory is based on the assumption that the benefits of a policy that helps the capitalists will trickle down to the poorest of the poor; if the rich have more money to spend they will presumably invest more in business, create more jobs, and sell more goods, to maximize their profits. Has this policy worked? Why or why not?

3. Do you agree with Kirkpatrick that advertising is an important source of knowledge in our culture? Does advertising also give us wisdom? Relate your answer to the discussion in Chapter 2 on logic and moral reasoning.

4. Marxist philosopher Herbert Marcuse argues that advertising does not respond to people's actual needs and desires but creates an artificial demand for sometimes worthless and even destructive products. Meanwhile, people's real needs, such as low-cost housing, better medical care, and nutritious food, go unmet. How might Kirkpatrick respond to Marcuse's accusation? Who do you think has the stronger argument? Why?

5. Is the Marxist analysis fair to Ayn Rand's position? How does it fail to acknowledge the importance that Rand places on the protection of people's

liberty rights and the freedom to pursue their own interests? Would Rand approve of what the multinational corporations are doing in poorer nations? Why or why not? What solution might she suggest for dealing with the problems of starvation and the plight of poorer nations in the world economy?

6. J. D. Sethi, an economic planner and writer from New Delhi, India, points out that capitalist economics fails to take into consideration the basic human rights of all people. There are a "large number of Third World Nations" where the "people have been brutally exploited and denied minimum basic economic subsistence." He writes that "the development strategies of the last two decades have failed to give benefits of development to the poor people." As part of the solution to this problem, he suggests that all people be "guaranteed certain basic economic needs," including education, primary health care, nutrition, family planning, and road and housing development," as well as jobs for "all people who are seeking jobs."[21]

   Do you agree with Sethi? Do all people have basic rights that are independent of having to earn these rights? Why or why not? Do people have rights to receive certain societal goods in addition to their rights to pursue their self-interest? How might Ayn Rand respond to Sethi?

7. The oppression of women and minorities in this country has resulted in more limited access to the free market system than that enjoyed by white males. Government intervention in the form of affirmative action programs is intended to correct this inequality. However, is affirmative action a morally acceptable solution? Ethicist Lisa Newton maintains that the "reverse discrimination" that she claims is associated with affirmative action is wrong because it turns people into "petitioners for favors."[22] Do you agree with her? Why or why not?

   How would an ethical egoist approach affirmative action and the problems of racism and sexism in our culture?

Ethical Egoism and the Moral Community

Many words have been granted me, and some are wise, and some are false, but only three are holy; "I will it!" Whatever road I take, the guiding star is within me; the guiding star and the lodestone which point the way. They point in but one direction. They point to me.

—AYN RAND, *The Anthem* (1938), p. 109

The Ego and Self-Esteem

According to developmental psychologists, most children are egoists: Their actions are, for the most part, motivated by self-interest. The egoism of the child provides the groundwork for building self-esteem and, as such, should be nurtured. Without first developing self-love, we cannot truly care for others. "To love is to value," Rand writes. "Only a rationally selfish man, a man of *self-esteem,* is capable of love . . . The man who does not value himself, cannot value anything or anyone."[23]

By pointing out the importance of self-love, Rand provides an important corrective to moral ideologies that glorify self-sacrifice and putting the needs of others first. However, by universalizing egoism as a moral principle—rather than seeing it as a stage in our moral development—we remain forever stunted at the level of a young child or prisoner. Indeed, like a typical prisoner, most egoists are trapped in their own self-interest—shut away from the richness of the wider moral community.

Egoism and concern for our own well-being become integrated into the higher stages of moral development, rather than being discarded when we move on to later stages. Egoism, in other words, is not the goal of morality, as Rand would have it; it is the seed from which our moral community grows to become more and more inclusive.

The moral community of ethical egoists is limited to themselves and those who can benefit them. Thus, the ethical egoists' moral community will vary depending on their needs and who can benefit them the most. Ethical egoism, rather than reaffirming the dignity of the human being, sees other people, not as people with intrinsic worth, but as objects for one's own gratification and benefit.

Egoism has recently come under attack from several philosophical camps. Philosopher James Rachels maintains that ethical egoism fails as a moral theory because it contains a logical contradiction in its definition of the moral community.[24] Ethical egoism claims to be the only moral theory that is compatible with respect for the integrity of individual humans, but, in practice, it divides the world into two groups: myself and the others. My interests count more than those of other people. I am in the moral community, and others are outside of it unless they have something they can "trade" with me.

However, Rachels asks, how can I justify placing my interests above those of others if everyone has equal moral worth? There is little doubt that by habitually putting others' needs before our own, as servile people do, we deny our own worth and consequently the principle of the dignity of all people. But by claiming that one person's interests (my own) are more important than those of others, ethical egoism is no better than racism or sexism or nationalism; each places the interests of certain groups of people above the interests of other groups. Thus, ethical egoism condones the very attitude it claims to oppose by requiring me to act as though my interests were more important than those of other people, thereby elevating one person (myself) over others. How can ethical egoists argue that all human life is of ultimate value, while also saying that I ought to give preferential treatment to my own life? If we cannot justify our own preferential treatment, Rachels concludes, then ethical egoism is "unacceptably arbitrary."

Communitarianism

American philosopher Hazel Barnes (b. 1915) also charges that egoism evades the "vision" of what it really means to be fully human, a concept that must include responsibility—our response to others qua persons, beings with moral value rather than objects that are merely means to our ends. By denying this, egoism deprives us of vast areas of human experience and growth.

> Any ethics, sooner or later makes some sort of appeal to the need and desirability of the expanded self . . . I rejected [Rand's ethical egoism], not because it is self-centered or because it seeks self-aggrandizement. I criticize it for being selfish in the pejorative sense of restricting the horizons of the Self so as to leave the self-center, not enriched but impoverished, not blown up but withered and blighted. The Self of the Objectivists runs the risk of the only child—it is not unloved, but it is likely to be spoiled, ailing, and fretful, due to overprotection and the too close attention which prevents the growth of responsible freedom.

The primary challenge to ethical egoism in this country and the go-it-alone liberalism that it supports comes from a new postliberal U.S. philosophy known as *communitarianism*. Strands of communitarianism are found in many traditional moral philosophies, such as those of Aristotle and Confucius, but modern communitarianism developed primarily as a response to the individualism of American liberalism. Communitarians regard the democratic community as the basis of ethics. The human community—which encompasses community decisions, social conventions, and historic and religious traditions—rather than the individual, defines the moral community.

United States sociologist and leader of the new communitarian movement Amitai Etzioni maintains that there is considerable social consensus in the United States regarding the importance of traditional family values, moral instruction in the schools, and fighting crime by restricting individual rights. By tossing out the primacy of the individual and advocating community as an end in itself, communitarians, however, run the risk of slipping into cultural relativism. As one critic writes, ". . . one person's fond wish for community leads to another's fear of repression. Americans felt a strong sense of community when they put Japanese-Americans in concentration camps in the 1940's and persecuted suspected Communists in the 1950's."[25] Communitarian values based on consensus can also be used to support abortion, just as these values could have been used 150 years ago to justify slavery and the oppression of women. Community consensus (popular appeal) is irrelevant to the morality of abortion, slavery, or equal rights for women.

Substituting a sense of community for individual rights does not guarantee that everyone will be part of the moral community or even that those who are will be treated with equal respect. However, neither does ignoring community and defining the moral community purely in individualist terms assure that all people will be treated with respect.

Exercises

1. To what extent do you define your moral community in terms of how others can benefit you? Has your concept of the moral community changed since the beginning of the semester? If so, how?

2. Does self-love require that you put your needs before those of others? Explain why or why not. What is the relationship, if any, between your feelings regarding your own self-worth at any particular time and your consideration of the needs of others? What types of activities make you feel happiest and most positive about yourself?

3. Is communitarianism a viable alternative to ethical egoism? Do shared community values provide a better basis than individual rights for defining the moral community? Why or why not?

Self-Interest and Happiness

> *The task of ethics is to define man's proper code and values and thus to give him the means of achieving happiness.*   —AYN RAND, *The Virtue of Selfishness* (1964), p. 33

Ayn Rand claims that her moral theory is based on objective, discoverable facts about human nature and what makes humans happy. She also maintains that "the achievement of happiness is man's highest moral purpose."[26]

> Good is neither an attribute of "things in themselves" nor of man's emotional states, but an evaluation of the facts of reality by man's consciousness according to a rational standard of value. (Rational, in this context, means: derived from the facts of reality and validated by a process of reason.) The objective theory holds that the *good is an aspect of reality in relation to man*—and that it must be discovered, not invented, by man.

Even if we do accept Rand's premise that happiness is the goal of human existence, a moral theory based on the assumption that humans have a certain type of disposition or nature that humans, in general, do *not* have is an unacceptable theory. Ethical egoism assumes that human nature is such that we find happiness by pursuing our own self-interest. In other words, if a life spent pursuing our personal self-interest does *not* lead to or maximize our happiness, then ethical egoism is a false theory. If ethical egoism is correct, on the other hand, self-interested people—that is, people who value independent lifestyles, productive labor, and rationality—should be, in general, happier people. Altruistic and caring people, in contrast, should be unhappier about their lives.

Despite Rand's concern with objective reality, she never made a study of what sorts of pursuits make people happier! In fact, studies do not confirm Rand's apparently "objective" observations of what makes people happy. In the early 1980s, Dutch sociologist Ruut Veenhoven carried out an extensive study of 245 other studies on happiness from all around the world.[27] "Happiness," for the purpose of his study, was defined as "the overall appreciation of life-as-a-whole." To his surprise, Veenhoven found that many commonly accepted ideas about happiness are not verified by actual studies.

Rand's moral philosophy, for example, assumes that people who value independence and rationality and who live a productive and autonomous lifestyle are, on the whole, happier. Veenhoven found that, in the Western world, hard work and productive labor are often believed to be one of the most important contributing factors to happiness; however, this belief was not verified by the studies. "Recent studies in western nations," he reports, "found no great differences in happiness between employed and unemployed people." Nor are people who work harder happier.

People who are happier place a greater value on happiness, but these people do not, for the most part, achieve happiness through the pursuit of their own self-interest. Rand's view that those who place a greater value on directly pursuing what Veenhoven calls "self-actualization values" are happier people was not borne out by the studies. Happiness levels are actually *relatively low* among people who place a high value on rationality or "*intellectual values* ('wisdom,' 'logic,' 'understanding')." The level of happiness "was also slightly lower among those who stressed *independence of others* ('individualism,' 'inner directedness,' 'freedom') and *self-control*. These negative correlations were most pronounced among males."[28]

On the other hand, a person's happiness with their life as a whole was "relatively high among the ones who gave a high ranking to "social values ('love,' 'sympathy,' 'friendship,' 'forgiveness,' 'tolerance,' 'group participation')." Happiness was also closely related to participation in volunteer organizations.[29]

These findings are directly contrary to the claims made by ethical egoists regarding human nature. As such, these studies suggest that ethical egoism is an unacceptable theory, because its basic premise regarding human nature appears to be incorrect.

Exercises

*1. Referring to your answer to Question 2 in the previous section, relate Veenhoven's findings regarding happiness to your own life. Does doing community service work make you feel happier? Why?

2. In Leo Tolstoy's novel *The Death of Ivan Ilych,* Ivan Ilych has lived a comfortable and prosperous life. After completing law school, "Ivan Ilych soon arranged as easy and agreeable a position for himself as he had at the School of Law. He performed his official tasks, made his career, and at the same time amused himself pleasantly and decorously . . . The pleasure connected with his work were pleasures of ambition; his social pleasures were those of vanity . . ."[30] His relations with his family likewise were based on trade-offs and the self-interest of each member.

In the end, his good life spent pursuing his own self-interest leads only to despair in the face of his impending death. As he lay in his bed dying, "the question suddenly occurred to him: 'What if my whole life has really been wrong?'. . . He lay on his back and began to pass his life in review in quite a new way. In the morning when he saw first his footman, then his wife, then his daughter, and then the doctor, their every word and movement confirmed to him the awful truth that had been revealed to him during the night. In them he saw himself—all that for which he had lived—and saw clearly that it was not real at all, but a terrible and huge deception which had hidden both life and death."[31]

Do you agree with Tolstoy that a life spent pursuing one's own self-interest may be pleasant at the time but is not a life well spent—a life of true happiness? How would you feel about your life if you found out today that you had only a few months to live? What would you do differently if you had your life to live over?

The Strengths and Limitations of Ethical Egoism

Ethical egoism contains two important truths: (1) we all want to be happy, and (2) feeling good about ourselves and taking our interests seriously is important to our happiness. These truths have been mostly ignored in moral systems emphasizing self-sacrifice and altruism as the highest moral duties.

One of the strengths of ethical egoism is that it inspires us to stand up for ourselves and not to let other people take advantage of us. It also demands that we take responsibility for our actions and our lives. However, the simplicity of ethical egoism, appealing as it may be, is also one of its weaknesses. Are there really only two alternatives: selfishness or self-sacrifice? Is pursuit of our rational self-interest the only or even the best path to happiness? Scientific studies suggest that it is neither. And even if pursuing our rational self-interest were the best means to individual happiness, does this, on its own, justify ethical egoism?

By having individual happiness as its only goal, ethical egoism becomes self-defeating. This phenomenon is known as the "hedonist paradox." If we try to pursue only our own happiness, we are often left feeling frustrated and alienated. Individual happiness seems to be more often the by-product of other activities than a goal in itself. Indeed, as Veenhoven's study suggests, if we seek other goals in life—such as helping others, having relationships, or achieving wisdom—these activities often make us happy, even though we were not motivated by self-interest.

Rand's assumption that there would be no clashes if people pursued their own rational self-interest and did not interfere with other people's right to pursue their self-interest is certainly questionable. In a world of limited resources and opportunities, people's rational self-interests sometimes come into conflict. When this happens, ethical egoism is unable to provide any guidelines for resolving the conflict. Ethical egoism, if universalized, becomes disruptive of the social order, rather than providing a universal principle.

British philosopher Mary Midgley criticizes Rand's philosophy as promoting an "extreme egoist individualism." She claims that Rand's philosophy, which is so popular among students today, is a rehashing of social Darwinism with its glorification of commercial freedom and elitism as "survival of the fittest." Midgley also argues that Rand's version of ethical egoism isolates the individual in a "fragmented, non-listening world" where morality is reduced to the private morality of subjectivism and that, like ethical subjectivism, ethical egoism gives the powerful permission to thrive and pursue their lifestyles at the expense of the weak.

Ethical egoism fails to take into account that we human beings exist as part of a wider community. Protecting people's liberty rights—what Rand perceived to be the government's primary task—is insufficient to guarantee that everyone will, in fact, have the liberty to pursue their own rational self-interest. We do not exist as isolated individuals who can act independently of social constraints. Sometimes, as the liberation ethicists point out, exploitation of certain groups of people is built right into the fabric of a society. On the other hand, if we were to substitute communitarianism for ethical egoism, we would be throwing out the proverbial baby with the bathwater, because basing morality on community well-being and consensus can also lead to the exclusion of certain groups of "socially unacceptable" people from the moral community.

Rand believed that capitalism would encourage people to be their moral best. However, studies have shown that this is not the case. A business education in the United States and the socialization process within U.S. business firms actually tends to inhibit and even decrease a person's level of moral reasoning, rather than attracting people of high moral integrity.[32] People who use higher levels of moral reasoning have a poor chance of rising to upper management positions in U.S. business firms.

Ethical egoism, and the system of laissez-faire capitalism that it extols, may be attractive to those who are rich and have the power to pursue their own self-interest. The devastating effects of this ideology on the people and nations who are not in positions of economic power, however, is becoming more and more evident with the increasing accumulation of wealth and social goods in the hands of fewer and fewer people and the destruction of the environment in the name of economic progress.

Although Rand was vehemently opposed to cultural relativism, the high value she placed on productive work and rugged individualism as the keys to happiness seems to be based on Western capitalist norms rather than on a transcultural description of human nature. Rand claimed to base her ethics on empirical observations of human nature, but she never bothered to do a study of her own or consult other studies on what makes people happy. In fact, studies show that being involved in productive paid labor is not related to happiness. By extolling productiveness as one of the highest virtues, Rand appears to be promoting the values of American civil religion rather than a universal moral philosophy.

In many Eastern philosophies, the moral life is not identified with denying the individual self or ego nor with pursuing rational self-interest or productive labor. Many schools of Eastern ethics, in particular, emphasize *overcoming* egoism and self-interest as a virtue and the path to true happiness. Moral maturity is viewed in terms of beyond the self—the diffusing of *the one* or individual ego into *the One,* the I am into the I AM. According to these philosophies, we are all part of the same web of life—the same great "self"—rather than separate, isolated beings.

Abandoning all desires, what

　Man moves free from longing,

Without self-interest and egotism,

　He goes to Peace.

This is the fixation that if Brahmanic, son of Prtha;

　Having attained it he is not (again) confused.

Abiding in it even at the time of death,

　He goes to Brahman-nirvana.

—*Bhagavad Gita*, Ch. II, 71–72[33]

In Confucian ethics, virtue is associated with the interests and well-being of the community rather than individual self-interest. Perfect virtue, as that of the Master, involves becoming free of egoism.[34] By this, Confucian ethics does not mean a life of self-sacrifice. There are times when self-denial may be called for, such as saving a drowning child without first negotiating to see what is in it for us. And it may sometimes be right to pursue our own self-interest. But, in general, the right path consists of choosing the medium between these two extremes. The association of the moral life and happiness with seeking the mean is also found in Aristotle's philosophy. The idea that morality does not require putting our interests aside but balancing our needs with those of others is also a central theme in Carol Gilligan's theory regarding moral reasoning and moral maturity. Ethical egoism, in contrast, rejects any sort of compromise. Altruism and our own self-interest are seen as diametrically opposed: "There are two sides to every issue," writes Rand. "One is right and the other is wrong, but the middle path is always evil."[35]

The principle of the philosopher Yang was—"Each one for himself." Though he might have benefited the whole kingdom by plucking out a single hair, he would not have done it.

The philosopher Mo loves all equally. If by rubbing smooth his whole body from the crown to the heel, he could have benefited the kingdom, he would have done it.

Tsze-mo holds a medium between these. By holding that medium, he is nearer the right. But by holding it without leaving room for the exigency of circumstances, it becomes like their holding one point.

—*The Works of Mencius*[36]

English poet Samuel Coleridge (1772–1834) sees modern Western history primarily as a regression in egoism and anarchic separation that leaves the "individual in a self-centered predicament." This, he regards, not as a fulfillment of the human will as Rand does, but as an intentional abandonment of the human will. Like the Eastern philosophers, he urges us not to deny the self but to go beyond our self-centeredness.[37]

The task of ethics may take us beyond our self-centeredness, yet Rand's ethical egoism is an important reminder that the journey begins in the self. Only by first respecting ourselves and expecting the same from others can we eventually move beyond self-centeredness to genuine respect for others.

Exercises

*1. Do you agree with Mencius that moral action in general involves striking a midpoint between self-interest and self-denial? Or do you agree with Rand that there is no halfway point between the two? Illustrate your answer with examples, including ones from your community service work.

2. Norwegian dramatist Henrik Ibsen wrote: "There is no way you can bene-fit society more than by coining the metal you know is yourself."[38] What do you think he meant by this? Relate your answer to Question 2, page 260, on *The Death of Ivan Ilych.*

3. Do you agree with Mary Midgley's argument that Rand's ethical egoism is simply a reworking of Spencer's theory of social Darwinism? Relate your an-swer to the spread of multinational corporations into non-Western nations.

4. What do you think Coleridge meant when he said that modern people, with their stress on atomistic individualism, are abandoning the human will? How would Ayn Rand most likely respond to Coleridge? Relate the Eastern con-cept of Oneness and Coleridge's concept of the "whole one Self" to that of moral community.

Summary

1. *Egoism* is concerned with what is in a person's rational *self-interest.* Ethical subjectivism is concerned with what people *desire or feel* is right for them.

2. An **egotist** is a person who is arrogant, inconsiderate, and boastful. An **ego-ist** is a person who pursues his or her own self-interest. **Solipsists** are people who believe that they cannot prove the existence of anyone but themselves.

3. **Hedonism** is the theory that happiness or pleasure is the *standard* for mea-suring the value of our actions. **Ethical egoism** is the theory that happiness is the *purpose* of ethics.

4. *Psychological egoism* is a descriptive theory. There are two versions of psycho-logical egoism: The first states that humans always *act* to further their own self-interest. The second version states that humans are always *motivated* to act in their own self-interest. *Glaucon* in Plato's *Republic* and the philosophers *Epicurus* and *Thomas Hobbes* all argued that humans are basically psychologi-cal egoists.

5. Because psychological egoism will not admit any evidence against it, it fails the test of **falsifiability** and, therefore, is a pseudo-theory rather than a real theory.

6. Ethical egoism is a *normative theory* that states that we always *ought* to act in our own rational self-interest.

7. Many philosophers, including *Aristotle,* believe that *happiness* is an important value. However, they disagree with ethical egoists that it (a) is the only moral value and (b) can best be achieved through pursuing individual self-interest.

8. *Ayn Rand's* version of ethical egoism is known as **objectivist ethics.** Objec-tivist ethics is based on the claim that right and wrong are naturalistic con-

cepts based on objective reality and survival. Rand argues that humans are fundamentally solitary creatures, each pursuing our own *rational self-interest.* *Productive work* is the central interest of the rational person's life. The only proper relationship for people is that of *traders,* where each party benefits from the transaction.

9. The ethical egoist regards *altruism* as immoral, because it involves self-sacrifice.

10. Ethical egoism supports an economy based on **laissez-faire capitalism.** Laissez-faire capitalism, as explained by *Adam Smith,* emphasizes the pursuit of rational and prudent self-interest, individual freedom, and minimal government interference.

11. *Karl Marx* and liberation philosophers such as *Gustavo Gutierrez* and *Frantz Fanon* all denounced laissez-faire capitalism as the unjust morality of the oppressor.

12. Ethical egoism reduces the moral community to the individual self.

13. *Ruut Veenhoven,* in his study of factors that contribute to *happiness,* found that people who valued rationality and independence were relatively unhappy; people who engaged in volunteer work and gave a high rating to social values were relatively happy. These findings are in direct contrast to the ethical egoist's description of what contributes to human happiness.

14. According to developmental psychologists, egoism is a normal stage in a person's *moral development.* Most people move beyond egoism in their teens.

15. Most philosophers reject the ethical egoist's dichotomy between self-denial and self-interest. Confucian philosopher *Mencius* writes that what is right is generally found in the *medium* between these two extremes. Some philosophers suggest that the path to true happiness entails going beyond *egoism* and realizing the interconnectedness of us all (the One).

CHAPTER 8

Utilitarianism
The Greatest Happiness Principle

*Nature has placed mankind under the governance of two sover-
eign masters,* pain *and* pleasure. *It is for them alone to point
out what we ought to do . . .*
— JEREMY BENTHAM, *Principles of Morals and Legislation*
(1789)[1]

*It is the business of the benevolent man to try to promote what is
beneficial to the world and to eliminate what is harmful.*
— MO TZU, *Universal Love,* Pt. III, Sect. 16

*I regard utility as the ultimate appeal on all ethical questions;
but it must be utility in the largest sense, grounded on the permanent interests of a man as a progressive being.*
— JOHN STUART MILL, "On Liberty" (1859)[2]

Utilitarianism and the Principle of Utility

The Principles of Utilitarianism

Utilitarian ethics has had a profound influence during the past two centuries upon social reform and the shaping of public policy. Although there
are various versions of utilitarianism, there are certain fundamental ideas
common to all utilitarian theories. Most importantly, utilitarian theories are
future-looking or **consequentialist.** Actions themselves are neither intrinsically right nor wrong. Instead, the rightness or wrongness of an action is
determined solely by its consequences. In other words, "the ends justify the
means." Utilitarianism is also **teleological** because it is oriented toward a particular goal: the greatest net happiness for all.

According to utilitarians, the desire for happiness is universal, and humans intuitively recognize it as the greatest good. Because utilitarian theory is
concerned with the happiness of society, rather than just the individual, this
theory is sometimes referred to as "social hedonism." However, psychological

egoists and hedonists maintain that people are concerned only with their own interests or pleasures. Most utilitarians, on the other hand, believe that people are naturally sympathetic and concerned with promoting the happiness of others as well. This feeling of unity with our fellow creatures—what Chinese utilitarian Mo Tzu called "universal love"—is deeply rooted in our character. According to John Stuart Mill, the concern for universal happiness is so basic to the human character that a person

> . . . may be unable to conceive of the possibility of happiness to himself, consistently with conduct opposed to the general good . . . [A] direct impulse to promote the general good may be in every individual one of the habitual motives of action, and the sentiments connected therewith may fill a large and prominent place in every human being's sentient existence.[3]

Because humans desire unity with each other, ethical egoism is incorrect not only as a prescriptive theory but even in its description of how to best achieve our own happiness. According to utilitarians, what counts is not just our happiness but the happiness of the whole community of **sentient beings**—that is, beings who are capable of feeling pleasure and pain.

> The utilitarian standard of what is right in conduct is not the agent's own happiness, but that of all concerned. As between his own happiness and that of others utilitarianism requires him to be strictly impartial as a disinterested and benevolent spectator. In the golden rule of Jesus of Nazareth, we read the complete spirit of the ethics of utility.
>
> —JOHN STUART MILL, *Utilitarianism* (1863)[4]

To the question "What is it that makes people happy?" utilitarians respond that *pleasure* makes humans and other sentient beings happy. *Pain* and privation of pleasure, on the other hand, cause unhappiness. Actions that produce the most pleasure or happiness are good; those that promote pain are bad. The only intrinsic good, in other words, is pleasure; the only intrinsic evil is pain.

Happiness, however, cannot be implied simply from preferences or a majority vote, because people's choices are not always well-informed. The majority, either because of ignorance about the nuances of an issue or because of irrational traditions and cultural norms, can be mistaken about the best action or the best social policy in terms of utility. Nor can sentiment alone provide a sufficient foundation for morality. The great British utilitarian Jeremy Bentham referred to unreflective sympathy as the "principle of caprice."[5]

Sentiments such as sympathy are often based merely on subjective feelings of approval and disapproval without any rational grounds to support those feelings.

What we need instead, utilitarians maintain, is a rational principle to guide people's moral choices. This principle is the *principle of utility* or the **Greatest Happiness Principle.** It states that

> actions are right in proportion as they tend to promote happiness, wrong as they tend to produce the reverse of happiness.[6]

Rather than simply relying upon our feelings of sympathy or benevolence, utilitarians recommend that each person "test his particular feelings by reference to this general principle, and not the general principle by reference to his particular feeling."[7] If an action conforms to the principle of utility, it is morally right; if not, it is morally wrong. The principle of utility also requires that we be impartial; each person who will be affected by our decision should get equal consideration.

Most philosophers believe that intentions are important when judging the morality of an action, but for utilitarians the sole criterion is the action's consequences. For example, in the case of Kitty Genovese, it would not have mattered whether someone called the police because the noise of her screaming was keeping them awake or whether their motive stemmed from a sense of duty to help those in distress. What counts is that, by making the phone call, they would probably have saved her from further pain.

The utilitarian emphasis on the consequences of our actions (or lack of action), grounds it in reality rather than on abstract principles or subjective intentions. As such, utilitarian theory is an important corrective to the often-expressed excuses such as "I didn't intend any harm" or "Don't blame me; I'm not the one who did it."

Utilitarians, on the other hand, do not deny that intentions and moral character are important. They realize that people with good intentions and a virtuous character are more likely to act in ways that benefit others. Utilitarians such as Mill wrote of the importance of cultivating our natural "feeling of unity with our fellow creatures,"[8] what Australian utilitarian J. J. C. Smart refers to as an attitude of "generalized benevolence."

Rule-Utilitarianism and Act-Utilitarianism

Utilitarian theory is sometimes broken down into act-utilitarianism and rule-utilitarianism. This distinction is the creation of modern philosophers, not one recognized by either Bentham or Mill. *Rule-utilitarians* are concerned with the morality of particular classes of actions, such as stealing and keeping promises. According to these people, we should, in any particular situation, follow the rule that in general brings about the greatest happiness for the greatest number.

Act-utilitarians are more concerned with the morality of particular actions. No actions, including stealing, torture, killing, and breaking promises, are considered to be inherently immoral. Universalizing moral rules against these actions fails to take into account that there may be situations, albeit rare, where lying, stealing, torturing, or killing may be the best means to maximize happiness. Rather than following general rules, the morality of each action should be judged on the basis of its utility, rather than on the basis of general rules. Rule-utilitarians, in contrast, insist that we should follow a rule even when it is clear that, by doing so in a particular case, we will cause more pain than pleasure.

Because obedience to rules is more important than utility, rule-utilitarians are not considered true utilitarians by some modern philosophers. Instead, they are regarded as, to use the words of J. J. C. Smart, "rule worshippers." In response, rule utilitarians acknowledge that adopting a policy of always following the rules may not maximize utility in a particular case, but in the long run it is the best way to achieve the goals of utilitarianism.

Most utilitarians accept a position somewhere between the two extremes of act- and rule-utilitarianism. They are aware that there is not always time, nor the foreknowledge and skill, to calculate all the possible consequences of an action. They also realize that much of our moral knowledge is passed down in the form of general moral rules about the tendencies of certain classes of action to produce pleasure or pain. Therefore, following general rules can be expedient when we do not have time to calculate the resulting pain and pleasure of a particular action.

> [I]t would be unworthy of an intelligent agent not to be consciously aware that the action is of a class which, if practised generally, would be generally injurious, and that this is the ground of the obligation to abstain from it.
>
> —John Stuart Mill, *Utilitarianism* (1863)[9]

The utilitarian's concern for the happiness of all sentient beings—regardless of their abilities, gender, social status, or even species—reflects the moral ideal of equality that was so important during the late eighteenth century. This ideal gave rise to both the American and French revolutions. The utilitarians hoped that this moral ideal would someday be extended to all sentient beings—both human and nonhuman. The following famous passage was penned by Bentham in 1789, the first year of the French Revolution and shortly after the French had outlawed slavery:

The day may come when the rest of the animal creation may acquire those rights which never could have been withholden from them but by the hand of tyranny.

The French have already discovered that the blackness of the skin is no reason why a human being should be abandoned without redress to the caprice of a tormentor. It may one day come to be recognized that the number of legs, the villosity of the skin, or the termination of the *os sacrum* are reasons equally insufficient for abandoning a sensitive being to the same fate. What else is it that should trace the insuperable line? Is it the faculty of reason, or perhaps the faculty of discourse? But a full-grown horse or dog is beyond comparison a more rational, as well as a more conversable animal than an infant of a day or a week or even a month old. But suppose they were otherwise, what would it avail? The question is not, Can they *reason?* nor, Can they *talk?* but, Can they *suffer?*[10]

The principle of utility or Greatest Happiness Principle, utilitarians maintain, is fundamental not only to human nature but to all moral theories throughout the world. The utilitarian philosophy of Mo Tzu, for example, developed as a challenge to Confucianism and Taoism. Buddhist ethics, although it places much more emphasis on character or virtue ethics, also contains a strong element of utilitarianism. In Buddhist ethics **ahimsa**, or non-hurting, is regarded as an unchanging eternal law. Buddha asks: "And what, monks, is Right View? It is, monks, the knowledge of suffering, the knowledge of the origin of suffering, the knowledge of the cessation of suffering, and the knowledge of the way of practice leading to the cessation of suffering. This is called Right View."[11]

Although nonutilitarians may regard other moral concerns as more fundamental than the principle of utility, deontologist John Rawls writes that "all ethical doctrines worth our attention take consequences into account in judging rightness. One which did not would simply be irrational, crazy."[12]

Exercises

1. Utilitarian theory is frequently used to formulate social policies around issues like AIDS testing and distribution of social goods such as scholarships and medical benefits. Find some examples of utilitarian thinking in some of our current government policies or policies at your college. Explain why these policies illustrate utilitarian thinking.

*2. Do you agree with utilitarians such as John Stuart Mill that concern for our own happiness cannot be separated from a concern for the common good? How might Ayn Rand respond to Mill? Do you have a direct impulse to promote the common good? Or do you only promote the common good when it is in your best self-interest to do so? Relate your answer to your community service work.

Mo Tzu: Utilitarianism as Universal Love

He should work to promote what is beneficial to the world, both directly and indirectly, and avoid what is of no benefit. Such is the way of the superior man.

—MO TZU, *Against Confucians,* Pt. I, Sect. 39 [13]

Mo Tzu, also known as Mo Ti, lived in China during the period of the "hundred philosophers" (the late sixth to the early third century B.C.E.). This remarkably fertile period in Eastern thought was paralleled by the golden age of Greek philosophy in the West. *Mo Tzu* was born about 470 B.C.E., the same year that Socrates was born and nine years after the death of Confucius. Little is known of Mo Tzu's family, but it is believed that he was the son of a slave.

Confucianism and Taoism, then both relatively new philosophies, were the prevailing philosophies at the time. Mo Tzu despised Confucians and regarded them as uptight, pretentious, and characterized by mindless devotion to meaningless rituals. Mo Tzu advocated utilitarianism as an alternative to what he regarded as the passivity of Confucianism and Taoism. Both Confucianism and Taoism stress virtuous character over action. In Confucianism, virtue is associated with honoring tradition. The virtue ethics of Taoism, which emphasizes letting go and allowing virtue to flow naturally out of the Tao (the way the universe operates), is even more passive than Confucianism. Mo Tzu was as committed to peace and harmony as Confucianists and Taoists, but he did not believe that harmony came about from simply the unfolding of the natural order of things (the Tao) or from following tradition.

Despite Mo Tzu's contempt for Confucianism, he accepted a version of the Confucian principle of "*jen,*" or love, as the overriding moral principle. However, unlike Confucius, Mo Tzu believed that this principle should be applied equally and universally to all people.

Like Western utilitarians, Mo Tzu viewed morality pragmatically. The good society could best be achieved not through passivity but by actively seeking and promoting the good of the many. Unlike other Chinese philosophers, however, Mo Tzu was not content to simply condemn harmful acts. He believed that we also have a moral obligation to promote the happiness of others. Mo Tzu taught that hate is the primary cause of pain in the world, universal love, the source of happiness and what is beneficial.

Mo Tzu was concerned primarily with social and political reform. He was convinced that the ways of the people could be changed with the proper leadership, by rulers who take delight in universal love and mutual benefit and strive to put these principles into practice. By using the standard of utility or universality, Mo Tzu believed, we can achieve a world of peace and harmony.

As Confucius emphasized filial loyalty, Mo Tzu argued that our obligation to promote the happiness of others is universal rather than based on our particular affiliations. Therefore, it is wrong to count the happiness of our family and friends as more important. According to Mo Tzu, we should give equal consideration to the happiness of all who will be affected by our actions, no matter what their social standing or relationship to us:

> [T]he Confucians corrupt men with their elaborate and showy rites and music . . .
> They propound fatalism, ignore poverty, and behave with the greatest arrogance.
> They turn their backs on what is important, abandon their tasks, and find contentment in idleness and pride. They are greedy for food and drink and too lazy to work.

Mo Tzu especially denounced the Chinese aristocrats and feudal lords whose luxurious lifestyles and wasteful spending on dances, elaborate funerals, and other rituals added nothing to the material welfare of the nation or the common people. China's social order at that time was very hierarchical, so Mo Tzu's insistence on equality and distributing benefits in a manner that maximized the happiness of the greatest number were radical ideas that frequently met with ridicule.

Although Mo Tzu realized that people often act in harmful ways, he was also an optimist who believed that reform is possible. On a practical level, he argued, it is not enough to simply criticize people or practices; there is an element of chaos and selfishness in society and in humans that must first be overcome in order to achieve the good society. Therefore, he argued, we have a moral obligation to offer practical alternatives and to actively work for a better society. Any idea or principle that cannot be put into action is useless.

> Now if we seek to benefit the world by taking universality as our standard, those with sharp ears and clear eyes will see and hear for others, those with sturdy limbs will work for others, and those with a knowledge of the Way will endeavor to teach others . . . When all these benefits may be secured merely by taking universality as our standard, I cannot understand how the men of the world can hear about this doctrine of universality and still criticize it!

Mo Tzu, like his contemporary Socrates, had a reputation for being confrontational when trying to get his message across. Mo Tzu was said to be as eccentric in his dress and manners as in his style of philosophizing; he spent his life moving from feudal court to feudal court. During his travels, he would engage rulers and other people he met along the way in philosophical discussion, all the time trying to convince them to live by seeking the good of the many. This did not sit well with those who benefited from the hierarchical ethics of Confucianism.

Not surprisingly, Mo Tzu's philosophy of equality irritated those in power, who eventually refused to listen to him. Mo Tzu responded by founding his own school to train people for the public life. During his life, he was popular with the common people and had about three hundred followers or disciples. Mo Tzu died in 391 B.C., and the Moism school of philosophy died out soon after his death. However, Mo Tzu's philosophy continues to exert an influence on Chinese thought to this day.

Exercises

*1. What do you think Mo Tzu meant when he said that hate is the primary cause of harm in the world? How does universal love contrast with hate? Is universal love a realistic goal? Relate your answers to your community service work.

2. Mo Tzu emphasized the importance of actively working toward reform and a better society, rather than just talking about theory. Can focusing too much on moral theory become a means of resisting action? Discuss a time when you were guilty of passivity regarding a social issue. How might you become a more active moral agent?

3. Confucius taught that our love should be strongest for our relatives and friends and less so for those who are not as closely affiliated with us. Mo Tzu, in contrast, taught that universal love should not be partial or play favorites. Discuss these two competing concepts of moral obligation. Do we have as strong a moral obligation to benefit people we do not know as we do to our own friends and family? Support your answer using examples from your own life.

4. Unlike the philosophy of Mo Tzu, ethical egoism teaches that we should be more concerned for our own happiness than the happiness of others. Imagine a dialogue between Ayn Rand and Mo Tzu. How would each of them most likely respond to the other's teachings?

Jeremy Bentham: Utilitarianism and Social Reform

The interest of the community is one of the most general expressions that can occur in the phraseology of morals.

—JEREMY BENTHAM, *Principles of Morals and Legislation* (1789), Ch. 1

English jurist, philosopher, and social reformer Jeremy Bentham (1748–1832) was born more than a millennium after Mo Tzu. Like Mo Tzu, though, Bentham promoted utilitarianism primarily as a tool of social reform. The industrial revolution, coupled with the widespread political unrest that culminated in the American and French revolutions, brought about tremendous changes in Western society during the late eighteenth and early nineteenth century. Before 1700, ninety percent of Europeans made their living off the land. The early 1700s saw the growth of home-based manufacturing and commerce.

Jeremy Bentham (1748–1832), English jurist, philosopher, and social reformer. Bentham developed his utilitarian theory primarily for legislation and social reform. Bentham's body is shown here in a glass case at the University of London. The head on his shoulders is a wax head; his real head is shown at his feet in this photo. Bentham bequeathed his estate to the university on the condition that his body be present at all the board meetings.

The sudden surge in population growth in Europe during the late eighteenth century and the rise of the factory system in the mid-nineteenth century precipitated a shift from an agricultural and commercial society to a modern industrial society. People from the countryside flocked into the new industrial centers in search of jobs and a better life. The introduction of new technologies and large-scale machinery led to increased specialization; together with mechanization of the means of production, this made the workers increasingly dependent upon their employers. The increasing dependence of the workers, in turn, led to the advent of child labor, widespread poverty among the working class, and the creation of vast urban slums.

Bentham's Utilitarian Theory

Bentham developed his utilitarian theory in response to the flagrant injustices of his time and the desperate needs of the poor and exploited workers. Bentham was born in London in 1748, and his life spanned a period of remarkable political and economic change. He lived through both the American and French revolutions and the Napoleonic Wars. He also witnessed the rise of the parliamentary system in England and the passing of the Reform Bill—a bill that extended the vote to all middle-class citizens.

Bentham's moral theory was inspired primarily by the theories of Epicurus (341 B.C.E.–270 B.C.E.) and David Hume (1711–76). Hume and Epicurus claimed that certain traits are virtues because of their utility, or usefulness. Bentham took Hume's ethics one step further by arguing that utility provides the only source of political obligation for the state. He believed that the principle of utility alone provides the test of what a law ought to be and which laws ought to be obeyed.

> It appears to be matter of fact, that the circumstance of utility, in all subjects, is a source of praise and approbation: that it is constantly appealed to in all moral decisions concerning the merit and demerit of actions: . . . and, in a word, that it is a foundation of the chief part of morals, which has a reference to mankind and our fellow-creatures.
>
> —DAVID HUME, *An Enquiry Concerning the Principles of Morals* (1751), p. 231

Bentham, unlike most moral philosophers, was concerned not particularly with the moral education of the individual but with social reform. His objective was to devise a more practical moral theory that could form a secure, scientific foundation for developing social policy and legislation and for critiquing the existing legal system. Many of the moral values espoused by the philosophers of that time he found to be too abstract to have much practical application for social reform.

Bentham graduated from Oxford in 1763 and continued on to study law. He was called to the bar at the young age of nineteen. Although Bentham never actually practiced law, he remained interested in jurisprudence and legal reform throughout his life. His disgust with the British government convinced him that democracy was the best political system. Besides his book *The Principles of Morals and Legislation,* published in 1789, Bentham wrote several pamphlets exposing government abuses and urging reform. Like the ideology underlying the French and American revolutions, Bentham's philosophy was deeply imbued with the ideals of equality and democracy. In particular, he called into question the old "moral values" that favored the status quo and justified inequality as part of God's natural order.

Bentham was convinced that only superstition and tradition prevented people from behaving rationally. He was especially skeptical of the church and institutional Christianity; he regarded the Christian virtues of submissiveness, humility, and self-sacrifice—which were advocated (but rarely practiced) by those in power—as standing in the way of morality and social reform. Behaving in a certain way because of fear of "punishment at the hands of a splenetic and revengeful Deity," Bentham argued, is the "offspring of superstitious fancy." [14]

Bentham's theory differs from traditional morality and the top-down approach that was used by the English government to formulate social policy. Utilitarian theory instead adopts a practical "bottom-up" approach—that is, it begins with the happiness of the people rather than imposing morality and social ideals upon them from above.

> [T]he happiness of the individuals, of whom a community is composed, that is their pleasures and their security, is the end and the sole end which the legislator ought to have in view.
>
> —JEREMY BENTHAM, *Principles of Morals and Legislation* (1789), Ch. 3.1

The Utilitarian Calculus

Bentham believed that the purpose of ethics is not only to tell us what our duties are, but to provide us with a test or criterion so that we can know these duties. To this end, he developed the utilitarian calculus (also known as the "calculus of pleasures" or the "hedonic calculus") as a means of scientifically determining which action, or policy, is morally preferable. He pointed out that this process need not be carried out before every moral judgment or legislative decision, but it should always be kept in mind.

Using the utilitarian calculus, each unit of pleasure counts as one **hedon.** Each unit of pain receives a negative value. Bentham came up with a list of seven factors that he believed should be considered when measuring the total amount of pleasure and pain caused by any action.

1. Intensity involves the strength of the pain or pleasure. The greater the intensity of the pleasure, the higher the positive value we assign to it. Conversely, the greater the intensity of the pain, the greater the negative value we give it. All else being equal, the act that produces the most pleasure is morally preferable.

2. Duration refers to the length of time that the pleasure or pain lasts. A pleasure of long duration is preferable to one of short duration. A pain of short duration is better than one of longer duration. For example, the hour or so of pain we get from having a cavity filled by a dentist outweighs both the intensity and duration of pain we would have to suffer if we let the cavity go untreated.

3. Certainty refers to the probability that the pleasure or pain will occur. Physicians might choose a time-honored treatment over a new experimental treatment for a medical condition, simply because they believe it is more likely that the old treatment will relieve the symptoms.

4. Propinquity, or nearness in time, is related to certainty. Generally, we can be more certain of immediate pleasures. Deferred pleasures, on the other hand, may be greater, if realized, but may never actually come to fruition.

5. Fecundity means that the pleasure is productive of more pleasure, rather like a stone thrown in the water and producing ripples. For example, a college education is, in general, more fecund than spending four years beachcombing.

6. Purity entails pleasure that does not cause pain at the same time. The less pain we cause in bringing about a pleasurable consequence, the better the action. If there will be a lot of pain, the dentist ought to use pain-killers when drilling our teeth, even though she could achieve the same long-term results by drilling without novocaine.

7. Extent refers to the number of sentient beings affected by the action. In general, the more beings that experience pleasure or the fewer that experience pain as a consequence of the action, the higher the utility of the action.

The total happiness of the community is simply "the sum of the interests of the several members who compose it." Each of these seven factors should be given equal weight when making a decision. To determine the best social policy, we simply add up all the hedons. The higher the total pleasure, the greater the positive value. If the proposed policy has a higher positive than negative value, then it is a good policy. For example, imposing a mandatory curfew on campus may be inconvenient or cause pain to some people. But if it makes the campus more secure and increases the overall sense of well-being on campus, then it is morally justified.

Although utilitarian calculus looks relatively straightforward and works well in some cases, it can be quite confusing. For example, how much pleasure should count as one unit or hedon? Can all pleasures and pains even be quantified? Although some pleasures—such as economic security and graduation rates—can be quantified, how do we assign a value to the pleasure of being in a relationship? or of overcoming a neurosis or phobia? or the pleasure of enjoying good music? People also respond very differently to pain and pleasure. Should the pain of a hypochondriac, for example, count more than the pain of a stoic? In addition, it seems arbitrary to assign each of the seven factors equal weight. For example, if the pleasure of the community is so important, then why does extent make up only one-seventh of the final total in the utilitarian calculus? Are there other factors, such as the quality of the pleasure, that should also be included in our calculations? Despite these problems and its lack of scientific accuracy, the utilitarian calculus is still very useful as a guideline.

Bentham was especially interested in applying his utilitarian calculus to the reform of the criminal justice system. He was opposed to the concept of retributive justice ("an eye for an eye, a tooth for a tooth"). Because punishment involves harming people without any increase in happiness as a result, he argued that "all punishment is mischief; all punishment in itself is evil." As an alternative, Bentham proposed a prison system based on reform and rehabilitation. His plan for a model prison, the Panopticon, was sanctioned by an act of Parliament in 1791. A site was selected and money allocated for its construction; however, the prison was never built.

The failure of the English government to carry through the plan for a new prison further persuaded Bentham that the government did not have the welfare of the common people at heart but was more concerned with its own advantage. Despite this setback, Bentham's ideas on prison reform have had a major impact on our current criminal justice system. Although modern prisons often fail to live up to their name as "correctional facilities," they are far more humane than the prisons of two hundred years ago.

Bentham's utilitarian theory, with its concerns for equality and impartiality in the application of the principle of utility, has also had a major influence on policymaking in the United States. As such, utilitarianism helps to compensate for the hierarchical definition of moral community that has plagued our Western concept of justice. For example, studies show that our criminal justice system tends to be more sympathetic and lenient toward people who are closer to the center of the moral community, as defined by our culture. For example, seventy-five percent of those convicted under the federal Drug Kingpin Act have been white. However, ninety percent of those who have faced capital punishment under this law are members of a minority. Similarly, women in the United States face harsher penalties for killing a man, even if in self-defense, than a man does for killing a woman.[15]

Bentham, ever true to his principle of utility and his genuine concern for the well-being of the community, left his body for dissection to the Webb Street School of Anatomy—the first person ever to do so. His stuffed remains are still on display at University College in London.

Exercises

1. How do superstition and tradition interfere with maximizing pleasure for the greatest number in our society? in your school? What might a utilitarian suggest for overcoming superstitions and tradition?

2. Do you agree with Bentham that punishment is an evil? If not, on what grounds can punishment, including capital punishment, be morally justi-

fied? Does punishment of criminals actually decrease the overall happiness of society, as Bentham maintains? What policy would a utilitarian most likely propose for dealing with criminals?

3. Does social ethics require a different strategy than personal ethics? If so, how do the two strategies differ? On what grounds can you justify the differences?

4. At one time, there were not enough kidney dialysis machines for everyone who needed them. One hospital in Seattle, Washington, used the utilitarian calculus to decide who would get dialysis. Age, health, involvement in community activities, the importance of a person's job to the community, and the number of dependents were just some of the factors taken into consideration in making a decision. The group of people making the decisions was dubbed the "God Committee," because most of the patients who were denied kidney dialysis died as a consequence. Was this utilitarian solution the best way, from a moral point of view, for allocating kidney dialysis machines? Would the "God Committee" have approved giving Joe DiMaggio preferential treatment for a transplant, just because he was a celebrity? Support your positions.

5. Because of Bentham's radical concern for equality and his belief that the quantity, not quality, of pleasure is important, his philosophy has been referred to by some philosophers as "pig philosophy." Do you agree with Bentham that the pleasure of a pig or dog or cat is as important as that of a human? If not, why not? If so, how would or should this affect your treatment of other animals? Should this affect public policy regarding practices— animal farming and experimentation on nonhuman animals—that cause great suffering to other animals but bring pleasure to humans?

6. Discuss the following case studies, using the utilitarian calculus:

   a. A group of women at Brown University were frustrated because they felt that the administration and the city police were not doing enough to prevent date rape on campus, so they decided to take the matter into their own hands. They wrote the names of men who had allegedly raped them on the wall of one of the ladies' rooms in a prominent building on campus. Use the utilitarian calculus to determine whether their action was morally justified. What other action, if any, would have produced a higher value?

   b. School-related stress among college students is a major source of unhappiness. Although a moderate level of stress can actually enhance our capacity to learn, both high and low levels of stress have been found to be damaging to the learning process and to students' general sense of well-being. Excessive stress—distress—can lead to panic, depression, and dropping out of school as the students attempt to distance themselves from the source of the stress.[16]

   Using the utilitarian calculus, draw up a proposal for your university or even for your class that would optimize stress levels, thereby maximizing students' learning and sense of well-being. Before applying the utilitarian calculus, you will probably first need to do some fact-finding and make a realistic assessment of the alternatives that might be acceptable to those who have the power to implement policy. Present your proposal to someone in authority. How does this person respond? If necessary, modify your proposal to maximize its utility—utility, of course, includes having your proposal, or at least parts of it, implemented!

c. Bruce, a senior accounting major and university basketball star, injured his knee in a game a few weeks before the end of the season. Bruce can play the last few games of the season if he is given a painkiller. If Bruce doesn't play, however, it is almost certain that the team will not win the final play-offs. On the other hand, if Bruce does play, he will probably cause permanent injury to his knee and walk with a limp for the rest of his life. Losing the play-offs may be costly to the university, which is already in serious financial trouble because of the state budget deficit; the opposing team's school is not in financial trouble. Bruce says he would rather not take the chance of permanently injuring his knee. Using the utilitarian calculus, decide whether Bruce has a moral obligation to play basketball.

*7. Using the utilitarian calculus, discuss whether community service should be mandated, either as part of the school curriculum or as part of a compulsory national service program.

John Stuart Mill: Reformulation of Utilitarianism

It is quite compatible with the principle of utility to recognize the fact that some kinds of pleasure are more desirable and more valuable than others. It would be absurd that while, in estimating all other things, quality is considered as well as quantity, the estimation of pleasures should be supposed to depend on quantity alone.

—JOHN STUART MILL, "Utilitarianism" (1863), Ch. 2

The influence of Bentham on the philosophy of John Stuart Mill (1806–73) can hardly be overestimated. Bentham's close friendship with the Mill family was a source of both intellectual inspiration and companionship. Mill was born in London in 1806, the eldest child of Harriet Burrow Mill and philosopher and journalist James Mill. Mill was educated at home, where he began learning Greek at age three. Bentham, who never married nor had any children of his own, became absorbed in the education of John Stuart, who was two at the time Bentham met the family. The Mill family moved to London to live near Bentham and also spent six months of each year with Bentham at Ford Abbey in Somerset.

Before the age of fourteen, Mill never associated with children his own age—only with his family and his father's utilitarian friends, including Jeremy Bentham, who helped educate him to carry on the utilitarian tradi-

John Stuart Mill (1806–73), English philosopher and member of Parliament. Mill was educated by his father, James Mill, and Jeremy Bentham to carry on the utilitarian tradition. After going through an emotional crisis in his early twenties, Mill began to question and reformulate some of the basic assumptions of Bentham's utilitarian philosophy.

tion. Although Mill apparently enjoyed Bentham's company and had great respect for him, he hated the rigorous program of education, but was too afraid of his father, a cold and arrogant man, to object. John Stuart Mill later wrote that "mine was not an education of love but of fear." [17]

In 1823, Mill began working as a clerk for the East India Company, where his father was a high official. At the age of twenty, Mill had an emotional breakdown and sank into a deep depression that lasted for two years. He blamed the depression partially on the habit of analysis, which, he said, had a tendency to wear away at one's feelings. This depression helped to free him from the hold that his father had on him.

Around 1830, Mill met and became a lifelong friend of Harriet Taylor, a liberal and highly educated woman. Although she was married at the time and their friendship became the source of much gossip, they became very close friends. They married in 1851 after the death of her husband. Although Taylor never published under her own name, she had a tremendous influence on Mill's thinking and on his radical reformulation of Bentham's utilitarian theory. Mill wrote that he consulted her opinion on all of his works; Mill claimed that his well-known book *On Liberty* (1859) was a joint production.

When the East India Company went out of business in 1858, Mill accepted an invitation to run for Parliament. He remained in Parliament as a member for Westminster until 1868. Mill was already in poor health due to tuberculosis; he died suddenly in 1873 after contracting a local fever.

Where Mill and Bentham Concurred

Although Mill held Bentham in great esteem, he came to recognize the inadequacies of Bentham's theory. Mill was also aware that Bentham was often criticized for failing to do what he had never set out to accomplish in the first place. Bentham's contributions to social ethics and legal reform were enormous. These contributions, Mill wrote in his biography of Bentham, should not be overlooked in our zeal to point out the deficiencies in his theory:

> . . . there is hardly anything positive in Bentham's philosophy which is not true . . . when his practical conclusions are erroneous, which in our opinion they are very often, it is not because the considerations which he urges are not rational and valid in themselves, but because some more important principle, which he did not perceive, supersedes those considerations, and turns the scales.[18]

Like Bentham, Mill was greatly interested in political matters and social reform. Mill was an advocate of free trade, parliamentary reform, secret voting, equality for women and universal suffrage, annual elections, trade unions, and reform of land tenure.

Mill agreed with Bentham that superstition and tradition were serious impediments to the smooth, rational operation of society. For example, in Mill's book *The Subjection of Women* (1869), he argues that traditional attitudes that oppress women prevent them from being as happy as they might otherwise be and also get in the way of women fully using their talents. "If there is anything vitally important to the happiness of human beings," Mill wrote, "it is that they should relish their habitual pursuit. This requisite of an enjoyable life is very imperfectly granted, or altogether denied to a large part of mankind."[19]

Like Bentham, Mill believed that education is an important tool for overcoming ignorance, one of the main causes of unhappiness. The primary role of education is to help men and women become more rational and autonomous. Mill was, however, opposed to compulsory state schooling as a means of educating the public. "A general State education," he maintained, "is a mere contrivance for moulding people to be exactly like one another: and as the mould in which it casts them is that which pleases the predominant power in the government."[20] On the other hand, Mill believed that the state should enforce universal education, whether that education be carried out at home, in a school, or in the workplace.

Where Mill and Bentham Diverged

Despite Mill's admiration for Bentham, they disagreed on several counts. Bentham was a strong advocate of equality; Mill disagreed that all pleasures are equal. According to Bentham, equality is not a description of actual equality of ability. It is instead a moral ideal or prescription of how we ought to treat sentient beings. The happiness of any one individual is no more or less important than that of another. What is important, according to Bentham, is the quantity of pleasure, not the quality of a pleasure. The pleasure of playing darts is no different from the pleasure derived from writing a poem or listening to Beethoven. The pleasures of a pig should count no more or less than those of a human.

Mill, in contrast, argued that some pleasures are more desirable than others. Mill maintained that human life is *qualitatively* better than the life of non-human animals. Like Aristotle, he believed that the intellectual pleasures, which engage the mind, are superior to those of the body. Thus, the rational pleasures, even though they are less intense at times, are morally preferable to the simple pleasures of a pig. Just as the pleasures of the human are "higher" than the pleasures of other animals, so too are the pleasures of the cultured person higher than those of the uneducated person or the fool. The pleasure of drinking beer or watching television all evening, for example, is of a lower quality than that of spending the evening listening to a Beethoven concert or reading the poems of Elizabeth Barrett Browning. Mill supported this hierarchy of pleasures by claiming that people who had an opportunity to experience both the higher and the lower pleasures would prefer the higher (rational) pleasures. People persist in engaging in lower pleasures, he argued, only because of ignorance and superstition.

It is better to be a human being dissatisfied than a pig satisfied; better to be a Socrates dissatisfied than a fool satisfied. And if the fool, or the pig, is of a different opinion, it is because they only know their own side of the question.

—John Stuart Mill, "Utilitarianism" (1863), Ch. 2[21]

Mill also argued that to pursue happiness as our only goal is self-defeating. Pleasure itself is not the only criterion for judging the morality of an action. Instead, the aspect of human life that philosophers associate with human dignity or integrity is set up as morally good independent of the quantity of pleasure. By introducing the concept of the quality of pleasure and criteria other than pleasure, Mill moved away from being a strict utilitarian like his mentor, Jeremy Bentham.

> Those only are happy who have their minds fixed on some object other than their own happiness . . . Ask yourself whether you are happy, and you cease to be so . . . Treat not happiness, but some end external to it, as the purpose of your life . . . and if otherwise fortunately circumstanced you will inhale happiness with the air you breathe.[22]

Mill believed that the primary means of ensuring happiness is to respect the dignity and personal autonomy of others. The freedom to make our own decisions, Mill argues, is basic to human happiness. Therefore, a society that protects people's liberty and autonomy provides the best conditions for happiness to flourish. As a liberal and a strong advocate of liberty rights,[23] Mill rejected Bentham's concept of justice as impartiality being a first-order good. Impartiality demands that no one's happiness counts any more than the happiness of anyone else. Therefore, justice as impartiality can be used to defend the use of one person or a group of beings to maximize happiness for others. For example, justice as impartiality might permit the execution of an innocent person in order to restore harmony to a community disrupted by a particularly heinous crime. Instead of justice as impartiality, Mill advocated a concept of justice that focuses primarily on autonomy or self-determination. Justice as impartiality is good only if it first satisfies the needs of autonomy. The justice system in the United States, with its concern for protecting the rights of the accused, is closer to Mill's concept of justice.

The principle of **non-maleficence,** or what Mill calls the *"no harm principle,"* was more important to Mill than the duty to directly maximize the overall happiness of the community. The "no harm principle" prohibits individuals or the government from interfering with another's actions except to prevent actions that will have harmful consequences. Mill writes: "As soon as any part of a person's conduct affects prejudicially the interest of others, society has jurisdiction over it, and the question whether the general welfare will or will not be promoted by interfering with it, becomes open to discussion."[24]

By "harm," Mill did not simply mean feeling offended or inconvenienced by someone else's actions. What Mill meant by "harm" was actually causing physical injury to others, unjustly encroaching on someone else's legitimate rights, the use of duplicity in dealing with others, taking unfair advantage of others, or selfishly failing to protect others from injury. Condemning or placing obstacles in the way of someone's pursuit of a particular lifestyle cannot be justified solely on the grounds that most people in that society find the lifestyle offensive. For example, Mill's "no harm principle" was used by the committee in England whose 1957 Wolfenden Report led to the legalization of homosexual acts between consenting adults.

Mill was also opposed to censorship because of the human tendency to want to censure opinions that are at variance with those of the majority. Like Bentham, Mill hoped that his ideas would be useful as guidelines for legislation and for the creation of a more tolerant society. Indeed, Mill's views on censorship continue to play a key role in the current debates over censorship of pornography and restrictions upon freedom of speech.

Exercises

1. Mill once said of his childhood: "I never was a boy; never played at cricket; it is better to let Nature have her way."[25] But if Nature had had her way with Mill, would he have become such an influential philosopher and social reformer? To what extent do parents have the right, or the moral obligation, to oversee and direct their children's lives—even if it means restricting their freedoms and choices—if by doing so they can bring about greater utility for society and, hence, happiness for everyone concerned?

2. Mill's distrust of state-run education is not without foundation. Studies have shown that a public school education, rather than counteracting superstition and tradition, actually reinforces prejudices such as racism and sexism and other attitudes associated with the current patriarchal status quo.[26] One study concluded that schools, rather than being the proverbial melting pot or "great equalizer of the conditions of man," actually close off some children's futures by perpetuating existing social inequalities.[27]

   Reflecting back upon your own schooling and your college education, how, if at all, has it served to limit the development of your talents and your pursuit of happiness as a member of this society? Discuss how a utilitarian might restructure our current education system to make it more rational, progressive, and less society-maintaining.

3. Do you agree with Mill that human pleasures have greater moral value than the pleasures of animals? How would adopting either Bentham's or Mill's position influence public policy regarding the use of animals to benefit humans?

4. Mill assumed that people who have experienced both higher and lower pleasures will prefer the former. However, is this true? Poor-quality novels sell more copies than the literary classics, despite children's exposure to the classics in school. And soap operas are a lot more popular than documentaries on public television. Discuss examples from your own life where, despite exposure to both higher and lower pleasures, you still preferred the lower pleasures. Why does this happen? How might Mill respond to this phenomenon?

*5. Mill's reformulation of utilitarianism, like social Darwinism, has been used to morally justify a policy of cultural imperialism, where more educated Westerners could impose their "pleasures" and values on more primitive cultures, under the guise of benefiting the people living in these cultures. Do you think this conclusion follows from Mill's idea that the quality of some pleasures is greater than others? To what extent does this attitude lead to the neglect of the interests of certain groups of people in our own culture? Relate your answer to your community service work.

6. Acquired immunodeficiency syndrome (AIDS) has reached global epidemic proportions. In the first ten years since its initial diagnosis in 1981,

12.9 million people have tested positive for HIV, the virus that causes AIDS. Of those who have developed AIDS, ninety-five percent have died.[28] In the United States, AIDS is spreading most rapidly among teenagers and young adults and is now one of the leading causes of death of adults in their thirties. Unlike most other contagious diseases, HIV remains dormant for several years (generally nine to fifteen years), during which time the infected person can unwittingly pass the infection on to others.

Imagine that the administration of your college has requested your input in the formulation of a policy designed to stem the spread of AIDS on campus. Under consideration are policies involving mandatory AIDS testing for all incoming students, voluntary AIDS testing, the distribution of free condoms and hypodermic needles, and education about the nature of AIDS. Using the principle of utility, devise a policy that would provide the maximum utility. Are you satisfied with this policy? Why or why not? Would Mill approve of your policy? Why or why not? What type of policy would Bentham most likely suggest?

7. A 1976 film entitled "Sociobiology: Doing What Comes Naturally," which focuses on the genetic differences between men and women and on aggressive behavior, was distributed to high schools and colleges. One critic wrote, regarding the film:

> One horrifying segment [of the film] shows American planes bombing Vietnamese villages while the sound track suggests that war is the process by which the better genes win out in the struggle for survival and that the pillage and rape that accompany conquest have biological roots—the conquerors are trying to spread their genes. This film is so objectionable that the sociobiologists who are interviewed in the film disavow any connection with it.[29]

Should this film be banned? Could its ban be justified by using Mill's "no harm" principle? Why or why not?

Utilitarianism and the Moral Community

[No] truth appears to me more evident, that beasts are endow'd with thought and reason as well as man. —DAVID HUME, *A Treatise of Human Nature* (1730), p. 176

It is an implication of this principle of equality that our concern for others and our readiness to consider their interests ought not to depend on what they are or what abilities they possess. —PETER SINGER, *Animal Liberation* (1990)

Utilitarian ethics calls into question the Western anthropocentric view of the moral community. Like most Eastern philosophies, utilitarianism extends the moral community to encompass all sentient beings. Because of their concern for equality, autonomy, and the happiness of all sentient beings, utilitarians have historically been in the forefront of movements for human equality and the welfare of nonhuman animals. Although in the last century we have come to accept (more or less) the ideal of human equality, the notion of equality among all sentient beings still seems absurd and counterintuitive to many Westerners. However, Mill points out that "intuitive perception is of principles of morality and not of the details."[30] J. J. C. Smart likewise notes that many of our "intuitive" moral concepts may be, in fact, nothing more than cultural norms or prejudices:

> Admittedly utilitarianism does have consequences which are incompatible with the common moral consciousness, but I tended to take the view "so much the worse for the common sense moral consciousness." That is, I was inclined to reject the common methodology of testing general ethical principles by seeing how they square with our feelings in particular instances.

Australian utilitarian Peter Singer maintains that not to grant the same consideration to a nonhuman animal who has the same cognitive ability as a human is to engage in speciesism. Like racism and sexism, **speciesism** is a prejudice or bias against certain beings simply because of their membership in a particular group.

> Racists violate the principle of equality by giving greater weight to the interests of members of their own race when there is a clash between their interests and the interests of those of another race. Sexists violate the principle of equality by favoring the interests of their own sex. Similarly speciesists allow the interests of their own species to override the greater interests of members of other species. The pattern is identical in each case.
>
> —Peter Singer, *Animal Liberation* (1990), p. 9

Our inclination to disregard the moral worth of animals besides ourselves must be examined in light of the principle of utility and the ideal of equality, rather than our particular cultural prejudices. Once we do so, most utilitarians maintain, we will find that these prejudices cannot be rationally justified but are merely the outgrowth of ignorance and tradition.

Not long ago, the concept of human equality seemed equally foolish to many people—including most philosophers. Slavery was regarded as morally acceptable for many centuries. The inferiority of women was also long accepted as beyond question. When Mary Wollstonecraft published her *Vindication of the Rights of Woman* in 1792, her views were received by most people with ridicule. One critic, Thomas Taylor, wrote in response to her tract that, if equality should apply to women, then why should it not be applied also to dogs, cats, horses, and other "brutes"? Since this, he suggested, was patently absurd, it would be ludicrous to extend equal rights to women. Taylor's response may seem absurd to us today, but at the time it seemed to make good sense to most people.

The inclusion of the pleasure and pain of other animals in our utilitarian calculations, however, does not entail that nonhumans must be treated the same as humans. This conclusion would be as absurd as Taylor's argument that women should not be given the right to vote because, if so, the right to vote would have to be extended to all animals. Morally, there is no point in extending the right to vote or to attend public school to dogs and cats and horses, because they have no interest in and would derive no pleasure from these activities. What gives a human pleasure and what gives a cat pleasure can be very different things. Children also have somewhat different preferences than adults. Similarly, it would be nonsensical to argue that, if women ought to be given free prenatal care, this right should also be extended to men. In other words, Taylor's argument against granting equal rights to women, because the same rights would then have to be extended to all animals, is based on a mistaken concept of equality as sameness. Following is another excerpt from Singer's *Animal Liberation*:

> . . . concern for the well-being of children growing up in America would require that we teach them to read; concern for the well-beings of pigs may require no more than that we leave them with other pigs in a place where there is adequate food and room to run freely. But the basic element—the taking into account of the interests of the being, whatever those interests may be—must according to the principle of equality, be extended to all beings, black or white, masculine or feminine, human or nonhuman.

Although respecting the interests of other species does not entail treating them the same as humans, certain conclusions do follow if we accept the utilitarians' claim that the principle of utility should be extended to all sentient animals. Singer concludes that, just as it is wrong for us to eat other humans, it is wrong to eat other animals, since a vegetarian diet is equally nutritious and perhaps even more so for humans. He contends that it is particularly immoral to eat animals who are raised on farms where modern confinement techniques not only cause tremendous suffering to the animals but also frustrate their natural desires and instincts. Similarly, most medical experiments using sentient animals are immoral. Humans may benefit from this practice, but Singer argues that this does not in itself justify the suffering and death of an estimated 70 to 120 million laboratory animals every year.[31]

The use of nonhuman animals to benefit humans is often justified on the grounds that humans have a greater mental capacity. But not even Mill, who ranked human pleasure above those of other animals, would say that this

In the 1980s, pictures such as this one of a primate restrained in a pain research experiment were brought to public attention by People for the Ethical Treatment of Animals. Due to public outcry, many research laboratories reformed their animal-testing practices. However, the U.S. Congressional Office of Technical Assessment reports that the number of animals used in experimentation in the United States each year ranges from 10 to 100 million.

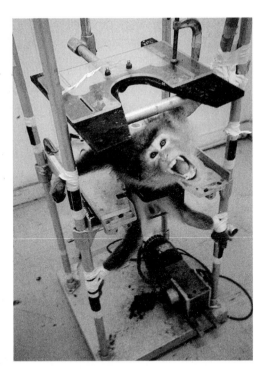

alone justified the suffering of laboratory animals and the restriction of their liberty. If our concern is to benefit humans, then it could even be argued that it would be preferable to use brain-damaged humans rather than nonhuman animals, because the results would be more accurate. Indeed, the use of certain "nonproductive" groups of humans, such as elderly people and children who are mentally retarded, has been justified by researchers on utilitarian grounds.

> Whenever experimenters claim that their experiments are important enough to justify the use of animals, we should ask them whether they would be prepared to use a brain-damaged human being at a similar mental level to the animals they are planning to use.
>
> —PETER SINGER, *Animal Liberation* (1990), pp. 82–83

Singer argues for the inclusion of sentient nonhuman animals in our moral community, yet he cautions us not to interpret this as implying that all lives have equal worth. Like Mill, Singer believes that certain qualities, such as self-awareness and the capacity for abstract thought, are higher pleasures and should be given greater consideration. This, however, does not justify speciesism; nor does it justify the degradation of humans that lack these capabilities, because sentience, or the capacity for pain and pleasure, is still the foundational criterion for inclusion in the moral community.

The principle of utility demands that people do not take refuge in religious and cultural traditions but instead examine their actions and decisions in light of the actual consequences. This entails educating us to overcome our ignorance regarding the extent to which our lifestyle is built upon the suffering of other people or animals and the gradual destruction of the environment. It means that we need to reexamine our cultural and economic values. Does economic progress lead to greater happiness for society in general? Or does it increase the happiness of the few at the expense of the many—including the millions of other species that share this planet with humans? Utilitarian theory also requires that we consider both the short-term and long-term consequences of our actions on the environment, not only for humans but for all sentient beings.

Exercises

1. Do you agree with Singer that "most humans are speciesists"? If you are a "speciesist," on what grounds do you morally justify it?

2. Although we no longer capture and put humans from other cultures on display, it is still considered morally acceptable to place nonhuman animals in zoos for educational purposes. Can this practice be morally justified? If so, does this justification also allow us to hold humans from other parts of the world captive for the purpose of public education?

3. Do you believe that lack of malicious intentions can be used to morally justify actions that indirectly harm other animals? Why or why not? Do you ever cite your intentions, including lack of malicious intentions, to excuse behavior that may bring pain and suffering to others?

4. How does your lifestyle contribute to the suffering of other human and nonhuman sentient beings, as well as the destruction of the environment? What steps can you take to make your lifestyle less destructive to the happiness of others and more in accord with the requirements of the principle of utility?

Euthanasia and the Principle of Utility:
Is Death Always a Harm?

Planned death is a rational system that honors self-determination and extracts from a purposeful, unavoidable death the maximum benefit for the subject, the subject's next of kin, and for all of humanity.

—JACK KEVORKIAN, "Medicide: The Goodness of Planned Death,"
Free Inquiry (Fall 1991), p. 15

One of the issues currently facing us is the formulation of a social policy regarding the moral permissibility of actively bringing about one's own death or that of another sentient being. Utilitarians do not believe in the sanctity or intrinsic worth of life. The worth of a particular life depends only upon the degree to which the pleasures of that life outweigh the pain of continued existence.

Many people regard it as morally acceptable, and perhaps even obligatory, to euthanize an animal companion who is old and in pain; some of the same people think that it is wrong to do the same for their ailing parents or grandparents. They may support this discrepancy by arguing that the killing of a nonhuman animal—as long as it is done in a quick and painless manner—is not as immoral as killing a human, because humans have aspirations for the future which other animals do not. Religious ethicists also argue that the taking of human life, which is created in the divine image, is a sin against God. Singer argues:

> What we need is some middle position that would avoid speciesism but would not make the lives of the retarded and senile as cheap as the lives of pigs and dogs now are, or make the lives of pigs and dogs so sacrosanct that we think it wrong to put them out of hopeless misery . . . At the same time, once we realize that the fact that a being is a member of our own species is not in itself enough to make it always wrong to kill that being, we may come to reconsider our policy of preserving human lives at all cost, even when there is no prospect of a meaningful life or of existence without terrible pain.

In David Hume's essay "Of Suicide," he supports the moral permissibility of suicide on the grounds of utility and autonomy. Thus, Hume would support voluntary euthanasia, especially when the pain in a person's life outweighs the pleasure that he or she derives from living. Hume rejects the unproven assumption that God wills that we never take our own life no matter how miserable we are. He also rejects the anthropocentric view that human life has a special sacred value that the lives of other beings lack. "The life of man," Hume writes, "is of no greater importance to the universe than that of an oyster."[32] A time may come when we are no longer productive members of society, and our life no longer brings us any happiness. The removal of misery, Hume contends, is a good consequence even if suicide is an unfortunate means to that end:

> All our obligations to do good to society seem to imply something reciprocal. I receive the benefits of society, and therefore ought to promote its interests; but when I withdraw myself altogether from society, can I be bound any longer? . . . I am not obliged to do a small good to society at the expense of a great harm to myself: when then should I prolong a miserable existence, because of some frivolous advantage which the public may perhaps receive from me?[33]

Some ethicists oppose the deliberate ending of human life on the grounds that, unlike killing animals who lack a concept of the future, suicide thwarts humans' future aspirations. However, this argument does not make sense to a utilitarian, because death marks the end of sentient existence. At the point of death, there no longer exists a being who can suffer from the pain of having had his or her aspirations thwarted. Also, some people, such as those who are suffering from terminal illnesses, have no future aspirations except to be relieved of their suffering through death. Death represents the fulfillment, rather than the thwarting, of future aspirations in these cases. In some situations, where there is great suffering and the person desires death, death may be less of an evil than that person's continued existence. When this is the case, killing oneself or another person may, in fact, be the most beneficent act.

But what about the pain to those left behind? The distress brought on by the loss of a loved one (human or nonhuman), however, is only relevant when the deceased person is a member of a family or community who would be pained by his or her loss. Indeed, if the harm to a person's family and community is increased by the continued existence of a person, that person may even have a moral obligation to commit suicide, as in the case of the elderly Eskimos.

On the other hand, not all utilitarians support euthanasia as a blanket public policy. Most humans have an understanding of and fear their impending death. Simply the awareness that they, too, may be put to death when they are no longer "useful" to society could be a cause of great suffering and anxiety. Among the Kabloona Eskimos, the elderly father had a say not only about the timing of his death but also about the manner in which he would die. According to John Stuart Mill, security and a safe environment are "the most indispensable of all necessaries after physical nutriment . . ."[34] For this reason, utility would require a social policy that protects human lives, even though these lives may not be valued by others. Feeling safe and secure entails that a person's autonomy be respected in issues of life and death: People should have some choice in the time and manner of their death.

Exercises

1. Is it morally acceptable to euthanize people who have terminal illnesses and who want to end their lives? Why or why not?

   Is it morally acceptable to euthanize patients with burdensome illness, such as people in comas or with severe brain damage, who are unable or unwilling to give their consent to the procedure? Support your position.

2. Dr. Jack Kevorkian believes that death can be a benefit to a person under certain circumstances. Since 1990, Dr. Kevorkian has assisted in more than forty suicides. Most, but not all, of his patients suffered from terminal illnesses. Judith Curren, a 42-year-old mother of two young children whom Kevorkian assisted to commit suicide in March 1996, did not have a terminal illness. She was suffering from obesity, depression, alleged spousal abuse, and possibly chronic fatigue syndrome as well. Is suicide justified in cases where a person does not have a terminal illness but just finds life burdensome and devoid of pleasure? Why or why not? How would a utilitarian respond to this question?

The Strengths and Limitations of Utilitarianism

The utilitarian insistence on equality and impartiality is both one of its greatest strengths and one of its weaknesses. Justice as impartiality presumes that people living in a community share a common conception of the good. Deontologist John Rawls criticizes classical utilitarian theory for its failure "to take seriously the distinction between persons."[35] Different people, he notes, have different needs and different projects or goals. The capitalist's idea of happiness, for example, is not the same as that of the religious contemplative. What gives one person great pleasure—such as improving the schools, setting aside public playgrounds and park lands, or building a new bowling alley—may not bring another person pleasure at all. Most people also agree that there are other good things besides pleasure. Friendship and aesthetic enjoyment, for example, also bring us happiness.

Justice, according to Rawls, demands not simply impartiality but also that we treat people fairly and in proportion to both their needs and their merits; a person who has worked hard, he argues, deserves a raise or promotion simply because they have done a good job. Utilitarians, on the other hand, are not concerned with what a person deserves, but whether giving rewards on the basis of merit produces the most utility.

In their concern for maximizing the happiness of the greatest number, utilitarians fail to give sufficient attention to the integrity of the individual. Integrity and personal responsibility need to be taken into consideration when determining the rightness or wrongness of an action. Utilitarianism sometimes requires us to act in ways that violate our integrity and our conscience. Actions do not just happen as part of a wider context of the general good: Each of us is responsible for what we do as individuals. For example, requiring someone to kill an innocent person simply to bring about peace in a community involves using people simply as a means to a greater social good. If someone is pressured into killing an innocent person to prevent the deaths of others, the assassin will feel bad about what he or she did, even though (according to the utilitarian calculus) the action greatly increased the general good.

> The essential defect of the "ideal utilitarian" theory is that it ignores, or at least does not do full justice to, the highly personal character of duty.
>
> —W. D. Ross, *The Right and the Good* (1930)

According to utilitarians such as Jeremy Bentham, feelings such as guilt or regret are morally relevant only if they are based on certain characteristics of the situation that tend to promote pleasure and diminish pain. On the other hand, most people believe that moral sentiments do matter. Utilitarianism, by telling us to ignore or try to overcome feelings of moral repugnance toward certain actions, alienates us not only from personal responsibility for our actions but also from our moral sentiments and conscience. Conscience is more than a calculator of the common good. If someone refuses to kill an innocent person, even to preserve social order, it still seems incorrect to say that he or she is responsible for the deaths that may result.

Utilitarianism imposes an impossible standard by requiring that we act in ways that maximize happiness. Although we may agree that it is good to act in ways that promote happiness and to avoid acting in ways that cause pain to others, to expect people to *always* act in ways that maximize happiness for the greatest number imposes too great a burden on people. If we took the principle of utility seriously, some critics claim, we would be obliged to spend all of our spare time benefiting the community by performing community service, caring for poor children, and helping others. This would leave us no time to pursue our own plans or to do things we enjoy such as watching television, playing with our happy and well-fed children, or taking a nice bubble bath.

Mill responds that this criticism is based on a misinterpretation of utilitarian theory. The purpose of utilitarian ethics, he points out, is the "multiplication of happiness," rather than the maximization of happiness in all cases. To expect people to always act to maximize happiness for the greatest number is simply unrealistic. Mill writes:

It is a misapprehension of the utilitarian mode of thought, to conceive it as implying that people should fix their minds upon so wide a generality as the world, or society at large. The great majority of good actions are intended not for the benefit of the world, but for that of individuals, of which the good of the world is made up; and the thoughts of the most virtuous man need not on these occasions travel beyond the particular persons concerned, except so far as is necessary to assure himself that in benefiting them he is not violating the rights, that is, the legitimate and authorized expectations of any one else.[36]

Since people do not have intrinsic moral value, they can be used as a means only. Most philosophers, however, believe that it is wrong to use a person only as a means, regardless of the beneficial consequences for the community. One of the weaknesses of Bentham's strict utilitarianism is that, if the sole goal of morality is to maximize the total utility of the community, there are times when the happiness of society can be increased by scapegoating or punishing an innocent person. However, doing this involves ignoring a person's liberty rights in order to maximize utility—a conclusion that Mill, in his reformulation of Bentham's theory, found objectionable.

Strict utilitarians respond to this criticism by pointing out that, in almost all cases, scapegoating is wrong because, in real life, lies are often found out. When this happens, it does great damage to people's sense of security and trust. Also, our faith in the criminal justice system will be undermined if it is discovered that the criminal justice system is punishing people who are known to be innocent. Despite these disclaimers, strict utilitarian theory allows us to treat people as a means to an end if, by doing so, we will likely increase the happiness of all concerned.

Utilitarianism has also been criticized for defining the good with a physical or psychological quality like pleasure. By doing this, according to G. E. Moore, utilitarians commit the **naturalistic fallacy.** Moore claimed that the "good" is not based on any observations about the world but is instead intuitively known or self-evident. Goodness is a nonnatural, intuitive quality or entity that is unanalyzable and indefinable. Therefore, Moore argues, we cannot go from an observation about what *is* (we seek pleasure and avoid pain) to a statement about what *ought to be* (we ought to maximize pleasure and minimize pain).

Moore's criticism is based, in part, on a misinterpretation of Hume's defense of utility in moral theory. Hume agreed that it is indeed impossible to produce a valid, logical moral conclusion from empirical premises alone. However, Hume also pointed out that this does not imply that what *is* is not important for discerning what *ought to be.* Nevertheless, Moore's allegation that utilitarian theory is flawed because it is based on the naturalistic fallacy became one of the primary reasons that utilitarianism fell into disfavor with modern philosophers.

Some more recent thinkers—including Ayn Rand, E. O. Wilson, and Mary Warnock—have begun to question Moore's criticism of utilitarian theory.

Like Hume, they argue that what *is* must be taken into account when formulating a moral theory.

> For is it not a fact that some types of behaviour tend to do good, and others do harm? And how in the end, if not on the basis of this fact, can we make sense of discriminating some actions as right in morals, and others as wrong?
>
> —MARY WARNOCK, ed., *Utilitarianism* (1962), p. 31

Despite its limitations, utilitarian theory offers some powerful insights into the nature of morality and provides helpful guidelines for applied ethics. Utilitarian theory is a reminder that any moral theory that does not take happiness and consequences into account as a goal of morality should be regarded with suspicion. The purpose of morality is not to make our lives more tedious or to make us feel more guilt-ridden, but to improve the quality of our lives by promoting ideals and behavior that provide optimal conditions for us to flourish both as individuals and as a community.

> Whether happiness be or be not the end to which morality should be referred—that it be referred to as an end of some sort, and not left in the dominion of vague feeling or inexplicable internal convictions, that it be made a matter of reason and calculation, and not merely sentiment, is essential to the very idea of moral philosophy.
>
> —JOHN STUART MILL, "Bentham" (1838)

Utilitarian theory also serves as a reminder that we should be ready to provide good reasons for our moral decisions. It is not enough to simply fall back on ethical subjectivism or mere opinion. Among the reasons we need to consider are the consequences of our decisions. Even, G. E. Moore, who, as we noted earlier, turned out to be one of the most celebrated critics of utilitarian theory, wholeheartedly agreed with the utilitarians that consequences must be taken into consideration:

All moral laws, I wish to shew, are merely statements that certain kinds of actions will have good effects. The very opposite of this view has been generally prevalent in Ethics . . . It has been characteristic of certain schools of moralists, as of moral common sense, to declare that the end will never justify the means. What I wish first to point out is that "right" does and can mean nothing but "cause of a good result," and is thus identical with "useful": when it follows that the end always will justify the means, and that no action which is not justified by its results can be right.

The primary weakness of utilitarianism is not its claim that consequences are important in morality but its claim that *only* consequences matter. It is not that utilitarian theory is wrong but that it is incomplete. The appealing *simplicity* of utilitarianism, which is one of its most attractive features, is also one of its weaknesses.

One of the greatest strengths of utilitarian theory, on the other hand, is that it challenges us to rethink our traditional notions about moral community, in particular our anthropocentrism. It reminds us that tradition alone cannot serve as a foundation for morality. By questioning our common sense or traditional philosophical notions of morality, utilitarian theory demands that we analyze these concepts and either justify them or discard them.

Exercises

1. Tying rewards to individual merit puts tremendous pressure on people to achieve, often at the expense of others. Is our emphasis on individual merit as one of the primary criteria for giving out rewards—such as income, grades, and social recognition—simply a bias of our capitalist system, where people are expected to compete with each other for a share of social goods? Is there another system that might be preferable in terms of maximizing the overall happiness of the community? Support your answer.

2. Using Bentham's concept of justice as impartiality, discuss how students' work should be evaluated and graded in college. Support your answer in light of the principle of utility.

3. Have you ever had to choose between your personal integrity and utility? If so, explain how you made your decision, regarding the most moral course of action. How would a utilitarian most likely regard the morality of your solution? Were you satisfied with your decision? Why or why not?

Summary

1. Utilitarianism is a **consequentialist** theory. An action is right or wrong depending on the consequences of that action.

2. Utilitarianism is a **teleological** theory. The happiness of the community is the proper goal of our actions.

3. The *principle of utility,* also known as the **Greatest Happiness Principle,** states that "actions are right in proportion as they tend to promote happiness, wrong as they tend to produce the reverse of happiness."

4. Happiness is identified with *pleasure,* unhappiness, with *pain.* The only intrinsic good, therefore, is pleasure.

5. The principle of utility applies to all **sentient beings,** not just humans. Sentient beings are those capable of experiencing pleasure and pain.

6. Chinese philosopher *Mo Tzu* promoted utilitarianism as an alternative to Confucianism and Taoism. He taught that hate is the primary cause of harm in the world and universal love the source of happiness.

7. British philosopher *Jeremy Bentham* advocated utilitarianism primarily as a tool of *social reform.* Bentham argued that all pleasures are equal.

8. Bentham came up with a *utilitarian calculus,* which included seven factors that he said should be taken into account in calculating the total amount of pleasure and pain produced by an action. These seven factors are *intensity, duration, certainty, propinquity, fecundity, purity,* and *extent.*

9. *John Stuart Mill* disagreed with Bentham that all pleasures are equal. He claimed that the pleasures of being a human are of a superior *quality* to the pleasures of being a nonhuman animal, because the pleasures of the intellect are superior to the pleasures of the body.

10. Mill believed that protecting people's autonomy or **liberty rights** is the best way of maximizing happiness in a society.

11. Mill's "no harm principle," also known as the principle of **non-maleficence,** prohibits individuals and governments from interfering with someone's actions except to prevent harm.

12. *Rule-utilitarianism* states that we should follow the rule that, in general, brings about the greatest happiness for the greatest number. *Act-utilitarianism* states that the morality of each action should be judged upon its utility.

13. Utilitarians include all sentient beings in their moral community. Australian utilitarian *Peter Singer* argues that not granting the same consideration to a nonhuman animal that we would to a human with the same cognitive ability is to engage in **speciesism.**

14. Because human life does not have intrinsic worth, *death* is not always a harm. When the suffering of a life outweighs its pleasure, death may be morally permissible.

15. The utilitarian concept of justice as *impartiality* fails to take into account the importance of individual integrity and personal responsibility.

16. British philosopher G. E. Moore argues that utilitarianism is flawed because it commits the **naturalistic fallacy** by going from about what *is* (pleasure and pain) to a statement about what *ought to be* (principle of utility).

17. Utilitarianism, with its emphasis on the importance of consequences and happiness, is a useful and powerful moral theory. It is currently making a comeback among philosophers and social policymakers.

CHAPTER 9

Deontology
The Ethics of Duty

Two things fill the mind with ever new and increasing admira-
tion and awe, the oftener and more steadily we reflect on them:
the starry heavens above and the moral law within.
  —IMMANUEL KANT, *Critique of Practical Reason*[1]

Look to your own duty; do not tremble before it . . .
  —*Bhagavad Gita*[2]

Deontology and Duty

Deontology is one of the most popular approaches in ethics. Deontological theories regard duty as the basis of morality. The word **deontology** comes from the Greek word *deon*, meaning duty or that which is obligatory. Moral duties are not the same as legal duties or cultural norms. Moral duties, according to deontologists, are transcultural and universally binding. If a cultural norm or law conflicts with a moral duty, then the moral duty should take precedence over the legal duty.

There are strong strands of deontological ethics in both Confucian and Hindu ethics and in many Western ethical theories. The high standards of moral excellence put forth by deontologists have also inspired psychologists, such as Lawrence Kohlberg, to study moral development and to map the transition to postconventional moral reasoning, as exemplified in deontological ethics.

For deontologists, the moral law is not defined in terms of consequences or whether it promotes some goal, as it is in ethical egoism and utilitarian theory. Instead, the moral law is an end in itself. Moral duty requires the recognition of and submission to moral laws or rules. This involves having the right intentions. Kant taught that we should act purely out of good will, not because of rewards or punishment or other consequences. Hindu ethics, in the *Bhagavad Gita*, also teaches that righteous living (*dharma*) requires discipline and acting out of a sense of duty rather than out of concern for the consequences of our actions:

> Be intent on action, not on the fruits of action;
> Avoid attraction to the fruits
> and attachment to inaction!
>
> Perform actions, firm in discipline,
> relinquishing attachment;
> be impartial to failure and success—
> this equanimity is called discipline.

With the exception of Kant, who believed that morality involves following absolute rules, most deontologists regard moral duties as *prima facie*. An **absolute duty** is one that is always morally binding regardless of the circumstances. There are no exceptions. For example, Kant regarded the duty not to lie as an absolute duty. A **prima facie duty,** on the other hand, is morally binding unless it conflicts with a more pressing moral duty. The duty not to lie, for example, may conflict with the duty to prevent someone's death. In this case, a prima facie deontologist may decide that the duty to prevent someone's death overrides the duty not to lie.

Duties can also be positive or negative. A *positive duty* entails actively doing something, such as extending a helping hand or returning a favor. A *negative duty,* on the other hand, requires us to restrain ourselves from doing something, such as stealing, cheating on a test, or beating up a motorist who has dented our fender or cut us off in traffic. Most general duties have both negative and positive elements. The duty of non-maleficence or "do no harm," for example, is usually a negative duty. We should not harm others, even when we feel a desire to do so. Non-maleficence, however, can also be a positive duty, when it requires us to actively do something to stop or remove a harm, such as calling the police when we see someone being assaulted. Non-maleficence as a positive duty also involves taking action to prevent future harms from occurring, such as warning employees about risks in the workplace or strapping young children into car seats.

Although deontologists agree that duty is the basis of morality, they differ in their views regarding the source of moral duty. Kant maintained that moral duty can only be grounded in reason. Sir W. David Ross, on the other hand, claims that moral duties are self-evident: We know what they are through intuition. However, Ross in his book *The Right and the Good* also acknowledged the importance of reason in the application of our duties:

> the moral order . . . is as much part of the fundamental nature of the universe as is the spatial or numerical structure expressed in the axioms of geometry or arithmetics. In both cases we are dealing with propositions that cannot be proved, but that just as certainly need no proof . . .

> We have no more direct way of access to the facts about rightness and goodness and about what things are right or good, than by thinking about them; the moral convictions of thoughtful and well-educated people are the data of ethics just as sense-perceptions are the data of a natural science . . . The verdicts of the moral consciousness of the best people are the foundation on which we must build.

Deontology is often presented as diametrically opposed to utilitarian theory, but this is misleading. Utilitarians also regard duty as important. "It is part of the notion of Duty in every one of its forms," wrote John Stuart Mill, "that a person may rightfully be compelled to fulfill it."[3] Utilitarianism, however, is more limited in scope than is deontology. For a utilitarian, our only duties are to maximize happiness (duty of beneficence) and to minimize pain (duty of non-maleficence) for the greatest number. Deontologists, on the other hand, emphasize duty for duty's sake rather than because of its consequences.

[H]edonistic utilitarianism in its turn needs a correction. On reflection it seems clear that pleasure is not the only thing in life that we think good in itself, that for instance we think the possession of a good character, or an intelligent understanding of the world, as good or better. A great advance is made by the substitution of "productive of the greatest good" for "productive of the greatest pleasure."

—W. D. Ross, *The Right and the Good* (1930)

Deontologists have been accused of being nothing more than rule utilitarians, yet deontology is not the same as rule utilitarianism. Rule utilitarians and deontologists both believe that rules should be universal; however, the reasoning behind the formulation of the rules is different. The rule utilitarian asks which rules in general bring about the best consequences in terms of utility or the "greatest happiness." Deontologists, in contrast, ask whether a rule, such as "do not lie," is logically consistent. In other words, would a rational person wish that this rule be made a universal moral law? Mill argues that asking this question necessarily requires that we consider the consequences of adopting a particular rule. However, deontologists go beyond the consequences of an action.

Deontologists take into consideration more than just happiness when deciding which rules should be universalized. Kant, for example, acknowledges that we have a duty to assure our own happiness since "discontent with one's state, in a press of cares and amidst unsatisfied want, might easily become a great temptation to the transgression of duty." However, unlike the utilitarians, Kant and other deontologists consider the pursuit of happiness an indirect duty because we already have in us "the strongest and deepest inclination towards happiness."[4]

Exercises

1. When making moral decisions, do you act purely from a sense of duty? Discuss other considerations, such as consequences, fear of punishment, or peer pressure, that motivate you to behave morally. Which of these motives, if any, would still cause you to do the right thing, even if all the other motives were absent?

2. Are a person's intentions relevant to doing good? Is being virtuous and acting out of a sense of duty more important than doing good because of the consequences?

3. In light of the concept of positive and negative duties, discuss the following ruling by the District Court judges who presided over Adolf Eichmann's trial. Eichmann had never himself killed or even given an order to kill a Jew or any other human being. The thought of killing someone was repugnant to him. Although he had been fully informed about the mass killings of Jews, his response was that this had nothing to do with his job. Nevertheless, the court found him guilty, ruling that "the legal and moral responsibility of him who delivers the victim to his death is, in our opinion no smaller and may even be greater than the liability of him who does the victim to death."[5]

   Scientists and others, such as laborers or secretaries, work in industries that harm others or the environment or that create products that cause harm or death to others. Should these people be held morally responsible for the harm? What about our negative duties, as consumers, to avoid products created by these industries?

4. Name some moral duties other than those aimed at producing good consequences or avoiding pain. Give specific examples of these duties, and explain why you consider them to be moral duties.

Confucius: Duty and the Community

The cultivation of the person depends upon setting the mind in the right.

—CONFUCIUS, in *The Commentary of Tseng*[6]

Confucian moral philosophy is a blend of deontology and virtue ethics. Kung-fu-tzu, known in Western writings as Confucius (the Latinized version of his name), was born in the feudal state of Lu in China in 551 B.C.E. As a young man, Confucius sought employment in the service of a prince, working as a keeper of the granary and a supervisor of flocks. However, he had

Confucius (551 B.C.E.–479 B.C.E.), Chinese philosopher. Confucius, one of the most revered philosophers in China, lived during the period of the "hundred philosophers" (the late sixth to the early third centuries B.C.E.). This period in Eastern philosophy was paralleled by the golden age in Greek philosophy.

trouble holding onto a position because he was too outspoken about the proper conduct of the rulers. So, he had to give up his dream of becoming a government official and settled for being a teacher.

Confucius was mostly self-educated. He is said to be the first professional teacher in China, and he began what would become a tradition of wandering scholars in China. As a teacher, he was a deeply principled conservative. Between the ages of fifty-six and sixty-eight, he traveled from province to province with his pupils, teaching and trying to influence the rulers. Confucius became the most revered philosopher in China and radically changed Chinese philosophy by focusing on our duties to humanity rather than on spiritual concerns. Confucius died about 479 B.C.E. at the age of eighty.

Like Bentham and Mo Tzu, Confucius was interested in promoting a moral system that could be used to formulate public policy and to provide people with a stable and harmonious social order. Unlike the utilitarians, though, Confucius believed that the only way to put society back on the right path was to instill in people a respect for duty as set forth in the tradition of the ancient sages. Mo Tzu, on the other hand, objected to reverting to tradition to achieve this goal rather than looking to future consequences.

Although Confucius looked to tradition for moral guidance, he was not a cultural relativist. He believed that the duties prescribed by the ancient sages were universal and binding upon all people. He also believed, like Kant, that these duties could be known through the use of reason.

In Confucianism, *yi,* or righteousness, demands that we do what is right simply because it is our moral duty. Moral knowledge—knowledge of our duties—is possible because our minds are united with the universe. To do our moral duty is to act in accord with the universal principle—the *Tao,* also known as *The Way.* The Way, writes neo-Confucian philosopher Chi Hsi (1130–1200), is "the principle that nourishes and develops all things."[7] The Way is part of our nature, just as Kant regarded moral law as being within each of us: We cannot be separated from it.

The Way, like Kant's fundamental moral principle, provides a general principle. "What is this principle?" Tzu-kung asks Confucius:

> "Is there a single word which can be a guide to conduct throughout one's life?"
> The Master said, "It is perhaps the word 'shu.' Do not impose on others what you yourself do not desire."[8]

Western deontologists tend to focus on the individual; Confucian deontology emphasizes communitarian values over individual autonomy. And unlike with ethical egoism, in Confucianism our duties to our family and community are always more important than the pursuit of our individual interests. There are five duties of universal obligation; these include the duty between ruler and citizen as well as duties between different members of the family. According to Confucius, the moral qualities or virtues by which these duties are "carried out are three . . . Wisdom, compassion and courage. These are the three universally recognized moral qualities of man."[9]

When asked about being filial the Master answered: "Never fail to comply . . .
When your parents are alive, comply with the rites in serving them; when they die, comply with the rites in burying them."

—CONFUCIUS, *The Analects,* Bk. II, 5

This emphasis on communitarian duties, however, does not entail ignoring our own moral development. The duty of self-cultivation is an important duty in Confucian philosophy, primarily because it makes us better citizens and members of the community. Self-cultivation involves developing our reasoning and mental abilities; it also includes avoiding activities, such as drunkenness and debauchery, that cloud our reason.

Self-cultivation and social duty are not considered to be at odds, as they often are in Western philosophy. They are simply different aspects of the whole or the Tao. Because duty is associated with The Way, or Tao, by doing our duty we can achieve inner harmony and inner peace as well as world peace. Duty, however, is not something that is imposed on us from the outside. According to Confucius, only by cultivating a sense of duty and harmony within ourselves can we hope to achieve peace in our family, in our society, and in the world at large:

> When things are investigated, then true knowledge is achieved; when true knowledge is achieved, then the will becomes sincere; when the will is sincere, then the heart is set right (or then the mind sees right); when the heart is set right, then the personal life is cultivated; when the personal life is cultivated, then the family life is regulated; when the family life is regulated, then the national life is orderly; and when the national life is orderly, then there is peace in this world.

According to Confucians, people who neglect self-cultivation will not have a mind that is in harmony and equilibrium. People who lack inner harmony are more likely to make mistakes in their viewpoints, and this can lead to harm and disruption of the harmony of the community.[10] Only those who honor the duty of fidelity and maintain harmony within their families are suitable to be leaders of the state.

Exercises

1. Confucius believed that communitarian duties were more important than pursuing our individual self-interest. Ayn Rand, in contrast, thought that the best way to achieve a stable society and individual happiness was by putting our self-interest above communitarian values. Using examples from your own experience, discuss which argument is the strongest.

2. The divisions between inner and outer peace are not as definite in most Eastern philosophies as they are in Western philosophies. Both the Confucian and the Buddhist approaches to world peace require self-awareness and social awareness in equal measure.[11] Do you agree that inner and outer harmony go together? Why or why not? Can people who are not at peace with themselves, their family, and their community still effectively promote world peace? Why or why not? Does world peace begin with self-cultivation? Or does self-cultivation, in your experience, require putting your needs above those of the wider community? Support your answer.

3. The duty of filial piety is also found in the Western tradition in the biblical commandment requiring us to honor our parents. What does this mean? Does the duty of filial piety entail mindlessly doing everything our parents tell us to do? How should we respond to abusive parents or to parents whose "plans" for our future conflict with our own? Relate your answer to the Confucian duty of self-cultivation that involves the development of reason.

Immanuel Kant: The Categorical Imperative

Act only on that maxim through which you can at the same time will that it should become a universal law.

—IMMANUEL KANT, *Fundamental Principles of the Metaphysics of Morals* (1785), p. 421

Duty and the moral "ought" emerged as a dominant theme during the seventeenth and eighteenth centuries in Western philosophy. This period of Western intellectual history, known as the *Period of Enlightenment,* was equaled only by the fifth and fourth centuries B.C.E., which witnessed not only the golden age of ancient Greek philosophy but the birth of Confucianism and Moism in China and Buddhism in India.

The Enlightenment gave rise to some of the most influential philosophy in Western history, including the deontology of Immanuel Kant (1724–1804) and the rights ethics of John Locke (1632–1704) and Thomas Jefferson (1743–1826). The rise of science and technology during this period reinforced the ancient Greek belief in the fundamental rational nature of humans and the potential of reason to solve all our problems. The concern with the public sphere that was so central to the philosophy of Plato and Aristotle was gradually replaced with an emphasis on autonomy and the dignity of the individual. The individual life, independent of the community, became a value in and of itself.

The Life of Immanuel Kant

Immanuel Kant was perhaps the greatest and most influential of the Enlightenment ethicists. Kant was born in 1724 in Königsberg, Prussia, the son of a saddler. His mother, an uneducated German woman who was a devout Pietist (a Lutheran sect), was remarkable for her good character and natural intelligence and had a great influence upon her son's development. Kant was the fourth of nine children and the oldest surviving child. Kant himself was born with a deformed chest and was barely five feet tall as an adult. Outwardly, he lived a very simple life. He never married. He admired the French Revolution from afar but avoided getting involved in any political controversies. Because of his poor health, he maintained a strict regimen that was so regular that people could set their watches by the time he walked past their house.

In 1755, Kant got a job as privatdozent at the University of Königsberg; this licensed him to give lectures. However, he was paid not by the university, but by the students. Kant would lecture for as many as twenty hours per week on subjects ranging from fireworks and physical geography to metaphysics. As a lecturer he was playful, witty, humorous, and entertaining. To his many friends, he was a role model and an inspiration. Yet, despite his popularity as a teacher, Kant remained poor for many years. Though he never traveled, he

Immanuel Kant (1724–1804), German philosopher. Kant (seated second from the left) is shown enjoying dinner with his friends. One of the leading Western philosophers, Kant was said to be witty and entertaining as well as a role model and inspiration to his many friends.

enjoyed the company of other people. Kant's most notable trait, it was said, was his sincerity and his devotion to the concept of moral duty.

In 1770, after many years of trying to procure a permanent teaching position, Kant was finally appointed Professor of Logic and Metaphysics. Kant's first great work in philosophy, *Critique of Pure Reason,* was not published until 1781, when Kant was in his late fifties. It was followed, however, by several other great works.

During his later years, Kant gained fame as a sort of oracle and Königsberg became a shrine of philosophy. People would come from all around to consult Kant on all sorts of issues, including the lawfulness of vaccinations. In 1790, Kant's health began to decline, and he died in 1804, having spent his entire life in Königsberg.

The "Ought" Quality of Morality

In his early writings, Kant acknowledged the role of a natural moral sense or feeling of concern for others. However, as Kant became more involved in the critical, analytical philosophy that dominated Continental Enlightenment philosophy, he moved away from his earlier position to draw a sharp distinction between reason and feelings.

Kant's concern went beyond the analytical aspect of ethics, however. He also insisted on the necessity of an empirical component in moral knowledge.

Kant believed that most people already *knew* right from wrong. In fact, like Aristotle, he used the everyday experience of morality, along with the tentative presumption that our ordinary knowledge of morality is legitimate, as the starting point of his method. In doing so, Kant took care not to confuse morality with cultural relativism, which he strongly opposed. What interested him about our ordinary knowledge of morality were the very general moral principles that transcend cultural particulars.

Kant believed that the problem most people have is not in *knowing* what is morally right, but in *doing* it. His primary concern as a moral philosopher was not to produce a list of duties but to establish a metaphysical groundwork or foundation for ethics that would explain, once and for all, why we *ought* to behave morally. To accomplish this, he first asked: What gives morality its imperative or "ought" quality? What is the supreme principle of morality that provides a solid foundation for moral judgment? Kant believed that empirical data and feelings, though not irrelevant, are insufficient to provide the foundation for moral law.

Only reason, Kant concluded, can provide a sound foundation for the universality of morality. Kant wanted to keep morality free from the taint of self-interest and external considerations (heteronomy). If there is a moral law and if it is to be morally binding, Kant insisted, then it must be logically compelling. As a rational being, I can only will what is not logically contradictory; this includes not making an exception of myself. If a particular action is right or wrong, it must always be so. Otherwise, we are being logically inconsistent.

Because the formulation of general moral principles cannot be derived from empirical experience, he concluded that moral knowledge must be a priori. An *a priori* proposition is one that we can know to be true prior to or without reference to actual experience. Kant refers to the a priori aspect of morality as the metaphysical foundation of morality.

> Duty is the need to act out of respect for the law.
>
> —IMMANUEL KANT, *Fundamental Principles of the Metaphysics of Morals* (1785)

Kant's Categorical Imperative

Carrying this line of thinking one step further, Kant argued that reason requires not only that moral duties be universal but also that they be *absolutely* binding. There can be no exceptions. For example, we should *never* lie, even in a situation where lying might have beneficial consequences, such as lying to a murderer in order to save someone's life. Unlike **hypothetical imperatives,** which tell us we ought do something *if* we desire to achieve a certain result—

such as telling a lie to save a life—moral obligations are categorical, or unconditionally binding upon us. A **categorical imperative** states that we ought to do something regardless of the consequences.

The categorical imperative is also a formal principle—that is, it lacks a specific content. It has been compared to the Tao, or The Way, in Eastern philosophy. Kant came up with two formulations of the categorical imperative. The first formulation states:

> Act only on that maxim through which you can at the same time will that it should become a universal law.

Kant believed that all rational beings would agree with this formulation of the categorical imperative, even though there may be disagreement about the particular details of moral behavior. To illustrate what he meant by this, he drew an analogy between ethics and mathematics. To someone unskilled in mathematics, the three triangles below all look different, just as at first glance different ethical systems can appear to be unrelated.

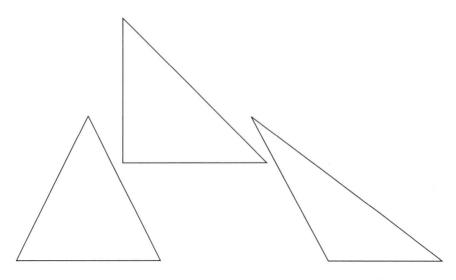

However, through the application of reason, we can discover formal principles that govern all triangles. Similarly, by the use of reason, he claimed, we would all come up with the categorical imperative as the foundation of morality.

As a formal principle, the categorical imperative provides a framework for deriving moral maxims or laws, such as "do not lie" or "honor your parents," that can be applied in specific situations. When deciding whether a particular rule or maxim is moral, we need only ask ourselves whether what we are proposing has the formal character of law—that is, would we as a rational person will that it be a universal law? To illustrate his point, Kant considers a maxim that would allow us to make "lying promises," promises that we do not intend to keep. In answer to the question "Does a lying promise accord with duty?" Kant writes:

> I have then to ask myself "Should I really be content that my maxim (the maxim of getting out of a difficulty by a false promise) should hold as a universal law (one valid both for myself and others)? And could I really say to myself that every one may make a false promise if he finds himself in a difficulty from which he can extricate himself in no other way?" I then become aware at once that I can indeed will to lie, but I can by no means will a universal law of lying; for by such a law there could properly be no promises at all . . . and consequently my maxim, as soon as it was made a universal law, would be bound to annul itself.[12]

Reason as the Foundation of Morality

Because reason, according to Kant, provides the foundation of morality, morality would not exist in the world without rationality. This makes humans, and other rational beings, very special beings in Kant's mind. Whereas rational beings have free will, everything else in nature operates according to physical laws. Because autonomy is essential for dignity, only rational beings have intrinsic moral worth. As beings with intrinsic worth, rational beings can never be treated as expendable but must be respected with dignity as ends in themselves. This society of all rational beings, according to Kant, constitutes the "*Kingdom of Ends.*" This ideal is summed up in the second formulation of the categorical imperative:

> So act as to treat humanity, whether in thine own person or in that of any other, in every case as an end in itself, never as a means only.

We have a duty to always respect people as ends in themselves; Kant was not implying by this that we could *never* treat another person as a means, however. Obviously, this would be impossible. We use our teachers as a means of furthering our education; we use bus drivers as a means of getting to school or to work; we use doctors as a means of healing our bodies. Kant was saying that we cannot treat a person *only* as a means. In other words, we cannot discard our teachers once the semester is over; nor can we simply dispose of a bus driver or a doctor once we no longer need their services in the way we discard a pen or a tongue depressor once it is no longer of use to us. Even though we may no longer have any use for these people, we still have a moral obligation to continue to treat them with respect and dignity.

Our moral duty to "be honest," for example, must be consistent with the second formulation of the categorical imperative. Honesty requires not just raw truth, but also stating the truth in a way that respects the dignity of people as ends in themselves. Telling someone who asks you how she looks that she is ugly shows a lack of respect for her as a person. On the other hand, people deserve an honest answer. A person who has lied, Kant claims, no matter how well-intentioned ("I didn't want to hurt his feelings"), has failed in their duty to the other person, because the lie restricts their autonomy. To lie to another rational being to spare their feelings is to offer them a profound insult regarding their ability to make decisions about their own life or their ability to handle the truth.

Kantian philosophy has shaped the way we as Americans define the moral community perhaps more than any other modern philosophy. Deontology, with its emphasis on the intrinsic worth of rational beings, has traditionally been regarded as an important corrective to strict utilitarian theory where an individual may be sacrificed for the greater good of the community. On the other hand, Kant defined the moral community more narrowly than utilitarians. Utilitarians include all sentient beings, whereas Kant insisted that only rational beings are worthy of moral respect.

> So far as animals are concerned we have no direct duties. Animals are not self-conscious and are there merely as a means to an end. That end is man.
>
> —IMMANUEL KANT, "Duties Towards Animals and Spirits" (1779)

Even though nonhuman animals lack intrinsic worth, according to Kant, he still argued that cruelty to nonhuman animals is morally wrong except when such cruelty directly benefits humans, such as in science experiments; however, cruelty to nonhuman animals is not considered wrong because animals have any rights that we as rational beings are bound to respect. Instead, cruelty to nonhuman animals is wrong because it often spills over into an attitude of meanness and hardness in our dealings with other humans.

Exercises

1. Do you agree with Kant that reason provides the foundation of morality? Why or why not? Would all rational people agree with the categorical imperative? Is it logically necessary, as Kant claims, that all moral imperatives be categorical? Support your answer.

2. In the summer of 1995, the French navy arrested the crew and passengers of two Greenpeace ships who were protesting the resumption of nuclear testing in the South Pacific off the coast of Tahiti, an island under French rule. Those arrested included a U.S. congressional delegate and the leader of a Polynesian

independence movement. There were also massive anti-French demonstrations in Japan against the proposed French nuclear testing. Australian prime minister Dave Keating asked France to call off the tests. "They have no moral right," Keating said, "to conduct these tests. It is an expression of contempt to the people they wish to call their neighbors."[13]

What do you think Keating meant by this statement? Discuss your answer in light of Kant's categorical imperative. Would Kant agree with Keating? Why or why not?

Do you agree with Prime Minister Keating that the French had no "moral right" to conduct nuclear testing in the South Pacific? How would a cultural relativist reply to this? a utilitarian? Which response do you think is best, from a moral point of view? Explain why.

3. Apply the categorical imperative to the following scenarios:

   a. Your roommate Beth has been depressed lately. She's been drinking a lot, not keeping up with her studies, and has even talked about committing suicide. One evening she agrees to go to a party with you. As you're ready to leave the apartment, she asks you how she looks. In fact, she looks pretty awful. Her mascara is smeared, her hair is unkempt, and her clothes are dirty and unsuitable for the occasion. How do you answer her question?

   b. Your best friend Grace just got engaged to marry Bob. Grace can only say how wonderful Bob is and how well he treats her, but you have reason to believe otherwise. Every so often, she turns up in class with a black eye. When you ask what happened, she says she fell. Recently, you learned from a sorority sister that Bob had dated before he met Grace that Bob physically abused her, and, in fact, she had to be hospitalized after one particularly brutal attack. Grace asks you to be her maid of honor at her wedding. What do you say?

4. Compare Kant's description of the categorical imperative to the Eastern notion of The Way. How are the two concepts similar? How do they differ? Discuss the strengths and weaknesses of each approach.

5. One of the arguments against the "insanity plea" is that it is degrading and implies that the defendant has no autonomy or control over his or her own life. Do you think the "insanity plea" should be eliminated? Support your answer.

6. Are you satisfied with Kant's definition of personhood and moral community? Using Kant's definition of personhood, is it morally permissible to treat humans who are nonrational, such as infants and brain-damaged humans, as means to an end? Why or why not?

   What criteria could we use to determine whether another being (say, an alien from another planet) is rational or has self-consciousness?

The "Good Will" and Proper Self-Esteem

We cannot think of anything in the world or outside of it that could be purely good—something that is good in itself, without qualification—except a good will.
—IMMANUEL KANT, *Fundamental Principles of the Metaphysics of Morals* (1785), p. 393

Kant's Concept of the Good Will

The duty to improve ourselves as moral people is important in virtually every ethical system. In both Confucian and Buddhist ethics, continuous self-improvement through right living and right thinking is the only way to reach moral excellence. For Kant, the development of the good will, and with it proper self-esteem, is the only way to ensure that we will consistently do our duty.

According to Kant, reason, rather than emotion, directs the will. As autonomous and rational beings, we have the ability to use our reason to discern what is right and wrong without needing to rely on outside authorities. A person of **good will**, unlike a heteronomous moral agent, always acts out of a sense of duty and a reverence for the moral law without regard for consequences or immediate inclinations. The good will, Kant wrote, "is already present in a sound understanding and requires not so much to be taught as merely to be clarified." [14] As autonomous beings, people of good will are free from external pressures. They are lawgivers unto themselves; that is, they impose the moral law upon themselves. Kant, however, was not suggesting that morality is relative or subjective. Instead, he believed that all rational beings would arrive at the same conclusions regarding what is right and wrong.

> If you love those who love you, what credit is that to you? Even sinners love those who love them. If you do good to those who do good to you, what credit is that to you? For even sinners do the same. And if you lend to those from whom you hope to receive, what credit is that to you? Even sinners lend to sinners, to receive as much again. But love your enemies, and do good, and lend, expecting nothing in return.
>
> —Luke 6:32–35

A person of good will can be depended upon to do what is right, even when other motives are absent. An action that is done out of sympathy or because one enjoys helping others, rather than out of a sense of duty, may be praiseworthy; however, according to Kant, such an action has no moral worth. It is easy to help others who may someday return the favor or to feel compassion for those who are like us. Acting out of duty and the good will, however, involves the intention to do what is right, regardless of our feelings or any rewards: "It is doubtless in this sense that we should understand too the passages from Scripture in which we are commanded to love our neighbor and even our enemy," Kant writes. "For love out of inclination cannot be commanded; but kindness done from duty—although no inclination impels us . . . it is this practical love alone which can be an object of command." [15]

The term "duty," unfortunately, has acquired a somewhat negative connotation in the minds of many people. Indeed, Kant has often been interpreted as promoting a sort of joyless duty. However, Kant was not suggesting that we ought not to feel sympathy for others or receive joy from helping others or from personal friendships. Kant believed that friendship is important as a means of connecting with others. Friendship also contributes to the development of our moral character by inspiring virtues such as compassion, wisdom, generosity, and happiness—virtues that make it easier for us to act in accordance with the good will. Indeed, from what we know about Kant, instead of being like the emotionless and humorless Mr. Spock of "Star Trek," as he is sometimes assumed to be, Kant was described by his friends and students as a man of great feeling and compassion. "How often he moved us to tears," wrote one of his friends,

> how often he agitated our hearts, how often he lifted our minds and feelings from the fetters of selfish eudaemonism [inner happiness] to the higher consciousness of freedom, to unconditional obedience to the law of reason, to the exaltation of unselfish duty! [16]

Virtues like compassion may make it easier for us to do our duty and, for this reason, are important to cultivate; for Kant, however, the good will alone *motivates* us to do our duty. The sentiments that might accompany a moral action are not what make the action moral, because we have a moral duty to help others even when we do not feel sympathy for them or when we get no joy out of helping them. If we separate our motivations, it is the motive of duty, rather than immediate inclination, that gives an action its moral worth. However, Kant did not believe that we should not act unless our motives are pure. It is partly by forming friendships and exhibiting respect for others that we nurture the good will.

Cultivating the Good Will

Community service can help to develop the good will. For example, an ethics student chose to do community service work with Habitat for Humanity (a nonprofit organization that builds homes for low-income families), not out of good will, but primarily out of self-interest. "I chose to do this work," he wrote in the introduction to his journal, "because I very much enjoy working outdoors and also enjoy framing houses." At the beginning of the semester, this student was at the lower level of conventional reasoning. By the end of the semester, though, he had entered the postconvention level that exemplifies Kant's principled reasoning. As expected, his motivation for volunteering changed as he progressed in his moral development. At the conclusion of his journal, he wrote:

> It seems to be pure caring which fuels the desire to give to others, and it seems to be a very moral thing to do . . . I initially began this volunteer work because it was required for this class; but I noticed that the people [who worked on the project with him] did not need a class to make them come out and build this house.[17]

By caring for others as beings with intrinsic moral value (what the student calls "pure caring," as opposed to sentimental caring) the student volunteer strengthened his own good will. By the end of the semester, he was more autonomous. He continued to help even after the semester was over, because it was the right thing to do, rather than because of extrinsic incentives.

Cultivating the good will and a sense of duty is an important corrective to our "feel good" approach to morality. If duty ("pure caring") is our sole motive, then we do not need to make excuses for not acting morally. For most of us, Kant pointed out, obstacles and subjective limitations, such as self-interest and pleasure, can at times take priority over the good will.

A perfectly good will such as the Will of God, on the other hand, has no obstacles to overcome; it acts purely out of the good will. For the perfectly good will, Kant writes, "there are no imperatives. 'I ought' is here out of place, because 'I will' is already of itself necessarily in harmony with the law."[18] Here, there is no distinction between reason and inclination. The perfectly good will always acts in accordance with the "ought." The concepts of duty and moral obligation are irrelevant, because these come into play only when reason and inclination are in conflict. The moral life of the imperfect being, in contrast, is one of continual struggle between moral duty (reason) and desire.

The Moral Philosophy of Dr. Seuss

Children's author Ted Geisel (better known as Dr. Seuss) is one of the great champions of Kantian deontology, although he never labels it as such. His story *Horton Hatches the Egg* (1940) exemplifies what Kant meant by the good will. This story also illustrates that the Kantian concept of the good will does not imply ignoring particular relationships or our sentiments.

In this delightful children's story, Mayzie, the lazy bird, tricks her friend Horton into sitting on her egg so she can take a "brief" vacation. Horton, who is a kind and compassionate (if somewhat gullible) elephant, agrees. Now Lazy Mayzie, as it turns out, is a weak-willed bird; when there is a conflict between her moral duty and her self-interest, she simply follows her immediate inclinations. She breaks promises when it is inconvenient for her to keep them and is even remiss in her filial duty to her own child, the egg. Horton, on the other hand, is an autonomous moral agent—an elephant of good will—who puts duty above both immediate inclinations and sentiments. He continues to sit on Lazy Mayzie's nest out of a sense of duty—he *promised* he would:

> I meant what I said and I said what I meant . . . An elephant's faithful 100%.

In the end, Horton's sense of duty sustains him through the mockery of others (the pull of heteronomy), the freezing cold of the winter, and capture (self-interest), and even mutual care ethics (as opposed to "pure caring"), because it soon becomes clear that Lazy Mayzie no longer has any intention of returning. Nor does Horton back out, as many of us would do, because Mayzie does not live up to her end of the bargain. Instead, like a person of good will, Horton continues to do his duty even under the most adverse circumstances. Horton, in the end, is recognized as a hero. He also stands up for himself and wins custody, over Mayzie's protests, of the baby he nurtured through "egghood."

The Duty of Self-Improvement

The cultivation of a good will involves the recognition that we have a duty to treat people as beings of infinite value. As rational beings, we have just as much moral value as anyone else. For deontologists, such as Kant and Confucius, the duty of self-improvement is one of our most important duties. We have a duty to treat ourselves with respect, just as we have a moral duty to treat others with respect and dignity.

> The greatest love I can have for another is to love him as myself. I cannot love another more than I love myself . . . Our duties towards ourselves [therefore] constitute the supreme condition and the principle of all morality . . . He who transgresses against himself loses his manliness and becomes incapable of doing his duty toward his fellows.
>
> —IMMANUEL KANT, "Duties to Oneself"[19]

Kant, in particular, was highly critical of moral philosophies that teach that a person "should give a thought to himself only after he has completely fulfilled his duty towards others."[20] He believed that our primary moral duty was self-respect and the development of proper self-esteem.

No one can demand of me that I should humiliate myself and value myself less than others; but we all have the right to demand of a man that he should not think himself superior. Moral self-esteem, however, which is grounded in the worth of humanity, should not be derived from comparison with others, but from comparison with the moral law.[21]

By this, Kant was not advocating ethical egoism, though. Self-respect is not the same as pride or putting our own interests first, but neither does a person with self-respect value themselves less than others. Instead, self-respect stems from our sense of moral duty and, as such, is the basis of our respect for others.

The importance of proper self-esteem in our moral development has been verified by psychological studies. Studies of well-being show a high correlation between positive self-esteem and high esteem for others. Young people with high self-esteem also "have more friends, are more apt to resist harmful peer pressure, are less sensitive to criticism or to what people think, have higher IQs, and are better informed, more physically coordinated, less shy and subject to stage fright, and are more apt to be assertive and get their needs met. High self-esteem is considered by some to be the essential core, the basic foundation, of positive mental health."[22]

Proper self-respect, besides being related to respect for others, also makes one less dependent upon the opinions and reactions of others. People who have high self-esteem receive more respect from others and are less vulnerable to being exploited by others.[23] People with low self-esteem, on the other hand, "are especially vulnerable to developing stress disorders [such as] underachievement at school, depression, irritability, anxiety, fatigue, nightmares, hyperactivity, aggressive behavior, withdrawal from others, nervous laughter, body aches and emotional tension."[24] A survey of four thousand Kansas schoolchildren in kindergarten through third grade found that forty-two percent of the children experienced these negative symptoms.[25]

When one is doubtful about one's worth, it is easy to use another's actions and reactions to define oneself.

—VIRGINIA SATIR, *The New Peoplemaking* (1988)

Deontologists maintain that self-esteem is a meaningless concept unless it is grounded in the cultivation of good will. Promoting self-esteem as an end in itself has recently become a driving force in parenting and education. In order to "build" self-esteem, children are routinely praised and encouraged to praise themselves with such phrases as "you're terrific," "you're the best," "you're the smartest," "you're the prettiest," and "you are exactly what God intends you to be." In psychotherapy, clients are told to simply repeat these clichés to themselves rather than sorting out their priorities and changing their lives accordingly. According to educational psychologist William Damon, this current emphasis on self-esteem as an end in itself, independently of a person's character or actions, does not develop self-esteem but instead engenders distrust of adults and a false self-image:

> Even though these white lies are intended to help rather than to deceive, children can and do see through them. If repeated often enough, these deceptions will undermine the child's trust in the adult's veracity. Even more dangerous, perhaps, children may actually internalize these empty phrases and dissociate their feelings of self-worth from any conduct that they are personally responsible for.

Self-esteem that is not founded upon the development of moral character and good will encourages self-deception, egoism, and narcissism, rather than genuine moral growth. In 1993, eight students from Lakewood High School in California were taken into custody for raping and molesting girls as young as ten years old. The boys, it turned out, belonged to a gang in which they won points through sexual conquest. Their activities were well-known around the school and were even accepted as normal by some school authorities and members of the community: "Boys will be boys." When the boys were interviewed on a talk show, they responded with pride: "I'm definitely comfortable with myself and my self-esteem," one of the boys said to Maury Povich on "Dateline." When asked if he liked himself, one of the other boys answered, "Yeah, why wouldn't I? I mean, what's not to like about me."[26]

Unlike egotism, proper self-esteem is not the result of empty praise or membership in a gang. According to Kant, we have a duty to use our freedom responsibly. People who rely on the flattery of others to inflate their self-esteem are not free; true self-respect does not depend on outward achievements or the praise of others but comes from having a good will and living a principled life, no matter how terrible our life situation may seem to be. Like happiness, proper self-esteem cannot be pursued as an end in itself. It is developed by seeking and living the good life.

The development of proper self-esteem or self-respect is critical to our growth as autonomous moral reasoners. In Carol Gilligan's scheme of moral development, for example, in order to make the transition from the conventional stage of moral development (where others' needs come before our own) to the postconventional stage (where we are able to balance our needs with those of others), we must first realize that we have equal moral worth. Only by saying "no" to exploitation and subservience and "yes" to the spirit of the categorical imperative that allows no one to treat a person (including ourselves) as only a means to an end can we fulfill our moral duty to ourselves and to others.

Exercises

*1. What motivates you to engage in good actions? What happens when you lack the inclination to do good? Illustrate your answers with examples from your life. If you are doing community service work relate your answer to your work.

*2. Many people who do community service work do it for extrinsic motives. It may be a class requirement, or they might be doing it because they enjoy it. Kant would say, in these cases, that community service is not a moral action on their part. This is different, however, from saying they ought not to do it. On the other hand, it does raise the question of whether students should be required to engage in service learning even though they feel no sense of moral duty toward those they are working with. Are teachers and students using the people of the community *only* as a means—that is, as a means to promote their own moral development?

3. Read about the life of a moral reformer or examine the life of your own moral hero. What motivated this person to continue even when the cause seemed hopeless? Was it reason or sentiment—or both? Explain.

4. Do you agree with the deontologists that we have a duty to develop proper self-esteem? Do you treat yourself with self-respect? Explain. How does self-respect, or the lack of it, affect your treatment of other people?

Sissela Bok: Is the Duty Not to Lie Absolute?

> *To be truthful (honest) in all deliberations, therefore, is a sacred and absolutely commanding decree of reason, limited by no expediency.*
> —IMMANUEL KANT, *Critique of Practical Reason* (1788)

> *Kant holds that "a conflict of duties and obligation is inconceivable," that if one does one's duty, one will turn out to have had no conflicting obligation. It is this refusal to consider conflicts of duty which drives Kant into such inflexible positions.*
> *Most have held the contrary view—that there are times when truthfulness causes or fails to avert such a great harm that a lie is clearly justified.*
> —SISSELA BOK, *Lying* (1978), p. 41

A person of good will, according to Kant, always does their duty no matter what the consequences. Kant assumed that moral maxims regarding our duties, such as "keep your promises" and "do not lie," would never conflict with one another because they are based on reason. He used the following example to illustrate his point that moral duties are absolute:

> After you have honestly answered the murderer's question as to whether his intended victim is at home, it may be that he has slipped out so that he does not come

in the way of the murderer, and thus that the murder may not be committed. But if you had lied and said he was not at home when he had really gone out without your knowing it, and if the murderer had then met him as he went away and murdered him, you might justly be accused as the cause of his death. For if you had told the truth as far as you knew it, perhaps the murderer might have been apprehended by the neighbors while he searched that house and thus the deed might have been prevented. Therefore, whoever tells a lie, however well intentioned he might be, must answer for the consequences, however unforeseeable they were, and pay the penalty for them.[27]

According to Kant, not even the most altruistic intentions justify neglecting our duty not to lie, even a lie to save someone's life. He claims that, if the murderer had found and killed his victim because of your honesty, you are not responsible for the death of the victim. Your only moral duty in this case was not to lie. The murderer bears full responsibility for his actions.

However, what about cases where it is almost certain that a lie will save many lives? Deontologist Sissela Bok, in her book *Lying,* suggests that, although lying is generally wrong, there may be isolated cases where the duty to lie conflicts with the more important duty to protect innocent human life. She defines a *lie* as "any intentionally deceptive message which is stated"[28] to distinguish lying as a moral action from unintentionally misleading someone because of ignorance of the truth or withholding the truth.

Bok discusses the case of vessels used to smuggle Jewish refugees out of Nazi-occupied areas as an example of a situation when lying might be morally required. A patrolling Nazi boat that happened to pass these vessels would call out and ask the captain of the vessel whether there were any Jews on board. If the captain responded "no," the Nazis would let the vessel go on its way. If the captain said "yes" or refused to answer, the Nazis would board the vessel and shoot the Jews. Would it still be moral, in this case, to tell the truth?

Kant would say "yes." However, Bok asks, is not preventing murder more important than telling the truth? By telling the truth don't we bear at least some of the responsibility for the resulting deaths? "[I]t is a very narrow view of responsibility which does not also take some blame for a disaster one could easily have averted," Bok writes regarding Kant's position, "no matter how much others are also to blame. A world where it is improper even to tell a lie to a murderer pursuing an innocent victim is not a world that many would find safe to inhabit."[29] Although lying may be morally regrettable, Bok concludes in some circumstances lying may be the only way to avert danger. In these cases, lying may be morally justified.

When else is a lie morally justifiable? Bok is well aware that most people lie too much and far too easily. As a deontologist, she acknowledges that we have a duty not to lie. On the other hand, unlike Kant, she also recognizes the importance of looking at consequences. Bok rejects utilitarianism as too simplistic, however, to deal with complex situations where the outcome of one's actions is uncertain. She argues that we ought not to lie even if, by doing so,

Sissela Bok (b. 1934), Swedish-born American philosopher, writer, and educator. The daughter of two Nobel prize winners—Alva and Gunnar Myrdal— Bok is primarily interested in the application of moral theory to real-life issues such as lying, euthanasia, and war and peace.

the net benefit will be the same as that brought about by not lying, because lying restricts the autonomy of the person who is the target of our lie. By lying, the liar gains power over the person they have duped. Bok maintains that deception may well outrank force as a means of getting people to acquiesce.

Because we have a duty not to lie we need to justify those times when we do lie. In Bok's examination of the excuses we use, she notes that paternalism is one of the most common: the claim by the liar that they are benefiting the person they are duping. Parents, doctors, politicians, and other people in positions of power may be tempted to use this excuse to justify their lies, but in almost all cases, Bok notes, this claim stems from a failure to respect the dignity and intrinsic worth of other people whom liars regard as "lower" than themselves.

Another common excuse is that the lie is being told in the name of a "higher good," as in the Milgram study. In this study, subjects were led to believe that they were delivering actual shocks to the learner. This, however, involved treating a person as a means in the name of the higher good—in this case, increasing our knowledge about human behavior.

People may also justify their lies on the grounds that the other person lied to them first. However, this in no way justifies lowering ourselves to lie to them. To do so is a violation of our own dignity as well as that of the other person. Bok also rejects the excuse that it is okay to lie to someone simply because he or she is our enemy. Lying to an enemy in wartime incurs the risk of increasing their hostility. It also damages the trust of one's compatriots, because lying to the enemy necessarily involves deceiving the general public. Even during wartime, lies are not justified except in situations of clear crisis.

Although Bok admits that lying is only rarely justified, unlike Kant, she allows lying when the duty not to lie conflicts with more pressing moral duties. When deciding whether lying is morally justified in a particular case, Bok suggests that we use the following criteria: First, we should *look for another alternative to deception*. For example, will telling the truth work? If so, we ought to tell the truth. Secondly, we should *ask ourselves whether the lie can pass the test of publicity* by examining the lie from the viewpoint of others. Moral justification must be capable of being made public and accepted by "reasonable persons." Finally, we should *engage in personal soul-searching*. Would we like to be lied to in this situation? If we would not like to be the person being duped, then we ought not to do it to someone else.

Kant believed that, for moral duties to be universal, they had to be absolute; however, does this necessarily follow? Bok, like other deontologists, agrees with Kant that moral rules such as "do not lie" should be universal rather than relative to an individual or a culture. Everything being equal, we expect everyone to abide by this rule. If there were no rule against lying, society as we know it would soon come to a grinding halt. But would we also want to make the rule "do not lie" absolute—that is, binding in *every* case? Like Bok, most deontologists say "no." They disagree with Kant that accepting a moral rule as universally valid entails going the extra step to claim that it must also be absolutely binding—that there can never be any exceptions. By doing this, critics claim, Kant has committed the fallacy of accident.

Exercises

1. In the Dr. Seuss story *Horton Hatches the Egg,* what if the hunters had told Horton they would shoot all the other animals in the jungle if Horton did not get off the egg or if he did not tell them where Lazy Mayzie had gone? Should Horton have continued sitting on the egg, even though he could have prevented the death of others by breaking his promise to Mayzie?

2. Using Bok's list of criteria, discuss whether the deception in each of the following case studies is morally justified.

   a. It is said that what matters most in Japan is not that everything is always perfect, but that everything always appears to be perfect. Well-attended funerals and weddings, for instance, are important to a family's honor, and some people are willing to pay "convenience agencies" anywhere between $200 and $1500 for fake "friends," "family," and "colleagues." The "guests" are briefed about what to say to bolster the image of the family, thus saving the family from the shame and social stigma that would result if others should find out the truth about them or their family background.

Young men who want to impress a woman friend with their bravery might also hire a "punk" to hassle them, so they can step in and challenge the "punk," who then runs away. In Tokyo, one of the most densely populated places on earth, these deceptions are rarely discovered. Is this type of deception, undertaken to avoid shame or social stigma, morally justified?

b. The majority of parents in the United States believe that it is morally acceptable, even praiseworthy, to tell their young children that Santa Claus is a real, physical person. Is it right to tell children this, even though it is a lie?

c. A 1989 study at a major hospital revealed that the majority of doctors were willing to use deception in certain circumstances. For example, three-quarters of them said that they would not report a case of gonorrhea to the health department, even though they were required to do so by law, if the infected husband was worried that his wife would leave him when she learned he had been unfaithful. About two-thirds stated that, if questioned by the wife, they would back up the husband's story that he was taking the antibiotics for another problem. Even more disturbing was the finding that forty percent of doctors would engage in deception if they accidentally killed a patient by giving them an overdose of medicine.[30] Are these lies morally justified? How would Bok, Kant, Mill, Bentham, and Rand each respond to this question?

d. According to former abortion rights advocate and abortion clinic director Dr. Bernard Nathanson, the number of maternal deaths due to illegal abortions was intentionally exaggerated to gain public support for the legalization of abortion. "I confess that I knew the figures were totally false," he later wrote. "But in the 'morality' of our revolution, it was a useful figure, widely accepted."[31] Are lies like these justified, if they are for the "greater good"?

e. Police sometimes use entrapment to catch criminals and gangsters. In Atlantic City, New Jersey, the mugging of tourists returning from the casinos has become such a problem that the police have established an anti-mugging decoy squad. A police officer pretending to be a drunk and disorderly tourist is dropped off in a neighborhood where there have been recent muggings. As a result of the efforts of this decoy squad, muggings have dropped by sixteen percent. Is the deception justified? Why or why not?

W. D. Ross: Prima Facie Deontology

. . . no act is ever, in virtue of falling under some general description, necessarily right . . . [because] moral acts often (as every one knows) and indeed always (on reflection we must admit) have different characteristics that tend to make them at the same time prima facie right and prima facie wrong; there is probably no act, for instance, which does good to anyone without doing harm to someone else, and vice versa.

—W. D. Ross, *The Right and the Good* (1930), Ch. 2

Scottish deontologist W. D. Ross (1877–1971) argues that, by insisting that a rule such as "do not lie" be an absolutely binding moral rule, the rule destroys itself, because there are times when lying may be the right course of action.[32] Kant was in the difficult position of formulating moral rules so that there are never any exceptions to the rule. Kant thought it would be possible to derive absolute moral maxims from his categorical imperative, but in fact, the application of the categorical imperative is not as easy as it first appears to be.

One of the weaknesses of Kant's ethical theory is that it does not give us any actual guidelines about how to word moral maxims. Instead of "do not lie," how about "do not lie except to save someone's life"? However, this wording is still too narrow; there may be other situations where lying is morally justified. To list all of these situations would be tedious, if not impossible. Furthermore, in the vast majority of situations, the maxim "do not lie" is a good moral rule.

Most deontologists overcome this difficulty by saying that moral duties, while universal, are prima facie—a term popularized among moral philosophers by Scottish philosopher W. D. Ross. Prima facie duties are moral duties that may on occasion be overridden by stronger moral claims. Kant argued that duties are absolute because they are derived from reason, and it is logically inconceivable for duties to conflict. Ross turned Kant's argument around. From a logical point of view, duties cannot be absolute because there are particular situations where they come into conflict. Because duties are context-bound, the particular circumstances and possible consequences will affect which moral duties are most important in any given situation.

Kant reduces morality to abstract duties or the "ought." Ross, however, points out that there are times when the "ought" or good and what is right are not the same. In other words, we may acknowledge that we *ought* not to lie, but situations may occur where it is *right* to lie. If lying seems the only way to save someone's life, then, even though in principle we ought not to lie, in this case it would be the right thing to do. Recognizing the "ought" as having universal validity does not necessarily entail that these principles are absolute or always the right ones to follow in every situation.

Although Ross agreed with the utilitarians that consequences matter when applying moral principles, like Bok he rejected the most basic assumption of utilitarian theory that only pleasure has intrinsic value. Ross argued instead that "no amount of pleasure equals the smallest amount of virtue." Utilitarian theory, Ross claimed, does not do full justice to the highly personal character of duty that Kant captured in his concept of the good will. Ross also found utilitarian theory inadequate because, by focusing only on future consequences, it neglects the past as well as ongoing duties:

> The theory of ideal "utilitarianism" . . . seems to simplify unduly our relations to
> our fellows. It says, in effect, that the only morally significant relation in which my

TABLE 9.1 W. D. Ross' Seven Prima Facie Duties

Future-Looking Duties
 Beneficence (the duty to do good acts and to promote happiness)
 Non-maleficence (the duty to do no harm and to prevent harm)

Duties Based on Past Obligations
 Fidelity (duties arising from past commitments and promises)
 Reparation (duties that stem from past harms we caused others)
 Gratitude (duties based on past favors and unearned services)

Ongoing Duties
 Self-improvement (the duty to improve our knowledge and virtue)
 Justice (the duty to give each person equal consideration)

---

neighbors stand to me is that of being possible beneficiaries by my actions. They do stand in this relation to me, and this relation is morally significant. But they may also stand to me in the relation of promisee to promiser, of creditor to debtor, of wife to husband, of child to parent, of friend to friend . . . and the like.

Ross identified seven prima facie duties, which he claimed that we intuitively know (see Table 9.1). These include the future-looking utilitarian duties of non-maleficence (minimize pain) and beneficence (increase happiness). By "duties" Ross does not mean motivation but a duty to perform a certain action. We do not have a duty to feel grateful or to regret past harms that we have caused. Our duty is to perform certain actions—such as keeping promises and repaying favors—irrespective of our motives.

Besides the two future-looking duties that stem from the principle of utility, Ross also recognized two ongoing prima facie duties and three that stem from past commitments.

Self-Improvement

Self-improvement is the first of Ross' ongoing prima facie duties. By self-improvement, deontologists do not mean getting a new wardrobe and a makeover or job training. Self-improvement as a moral duty entails constantly striving to improve our knowledge (wisdom) and our virtue. The duty of self-improvement is important in virtually every ethical system. For both Confucius and Kant, self-improvement and the development of proper self-esteem is absolutely essential to the cultivation of the good will. The Hindu and Buddhist concept of Karma likewise involves the duty to cultivate within ourselves "peacefulness, self-control, austerity, purity, tolerance, honesty, knowledge, wisdom and religiousness." In Buddhist ethics, continuous self-improvement through right living and right thinking is the only way to reach moral excellence and enlightenment. Moral self-improvement does not end in this lifetime. Buddhists believe that we are repeatedly reincarnated until we reach moral enlightenment. Even the utilitarians believe that self-improvement, although not a direct duty, is important, because a person with a benevolent and virtuous disposition is more likely to act in ways that benefit others.

Justice

The ongoing duty of **justice,** like self-improvement, is recognized by just about every moral system. A sense of justice emerges in children, regardless of their culture, at a very young age. Because duty is regarded by many philosophers as the most important duty of all, it will be discussed in greater detail in the following section.

Duties based on past obligations are not recognized by utilitarians except to the extent that they can be subsumed under the future-looking duties of non-maleficence and beneficence. For example, a utilitarian may urge us to keep a promise, not because we made a past commitment to someone, but because by not keeping our promise we may damage future trust. Deontologists, on the other hand, believe that past actions do create moral obligations independently of any possible future consequences.

It is plain, I think, that in our normal thought we consider that the fact that we have made a promise is in itself sufficient to create a duty of keeping it, the sense of duty resting on remembrance of the past promise and not on thoughts of the future consequences of its fulfillment.

—W. D. Ross, *The Right and the Good* (1930)

Fidelity

Fidelity, the first of the three duties based on past obligations, stems from past commitments we have made. We keep promises, for example, not because we are thinking of beneficial future consequences, but because of our past action in making the promise and because it is our duty to keep our promises. Like promises, some commitments are voluntary—for example, wedding vows or commitments to our friends, college, or career. For instance, a firefighter has a duty to attempt to save someone caught in a burning building, whereas we do not because we have not made a commitment to that profession.

The duty of fidelity can also stem from involuntary commitments. The duty of filial piety, for example, is very important in Confucian deontology. Yet, most of us did not have a choice about who our parents would be or what country we would live in. Nevertheless, we still have a commitment to care for our elderly parents and to be loyal to our country (within the limits of moral decency).

When people do not keep their commitments, we may feel resentment and a sense of betrayal. Those who have a strong sense of fidelity to their past commitments, like Horton in Dr. Seuss' story, are people whom we can trust to keep their word. They remain loyal even when they are tempted to stray or to divulge secrets.

Morality, on the other hand, cannot be reduced to one duty. Moral duties can come into conflict. In these situations, we must use reason to decide which duty or duties are most important. Fidelity that is not grounded in reason can lead us astray. People like Adolf Eichmann were willing to participate in the murder of thousands of Jews in the name of fidelity to their country. Gang members steal, maim, and kill, all in the name of loyalty to their gang. Because blind loyalty can be such a powerful sentiment, very few individuals will engage in whistle-blowing by informing on coworkers or others in their social group who are engaged in immoral activities. Those who do blow the whistle often do so at considerable personal risk, including the risk of being ostracized by their coworkers and friends.

Reparation

The duty of **reparation** is also based on past actions. Reparation requires that we make up for past harms that we have caused others. These harms may have been direct or indirect, individual or collective, intentional or unintentional. Reparation involves respecting the dignity and intrinsic worth of the person we have harmed. It also requires acknowledging our wrongdoing and taking action to compensate the person we have harmed. Unlike retribution, which requires punishment for past wrongdoing, reparation serves to re-establish balance between people by having the wrongdoer make some sort of restitution to the harmed party.

The extent of reparation owed depends on the magnitude of the harm and the degree of our active and willing participation in bringing about the harm. For a relatively small harm, a simple apology will generally suffice. Greater harms, such as causing someone grave bodily or mental injury or centuries of oppression visited upon a certain class of people, demand more extensive restitution, such as offering large sums of money or taking action to improve the condition of the people who have suffered from past injustices. Automobile insurance companies, for example, act as our agents in making reparation to other people we have harmed by our careless driving. Some judges sentence minor offenders to do community service as a way of repaying the community for the harm they have caused to the people of the community.

Gratitude

Gratitude is the third duty that is based on past actions. Our sense of gratitude is evoked when we receive gifts or unearned favors and services from others. Like reparation, gratitude is linked to the duty of justice. The demand for fair exchange or expressing gratitude for favors done is one of the first ways a child learns the duty of justice.

Gratitude is regarded as morally admirable in virtually every culture. Many psychologists and sociologists regard gratitude as an inborn emotional response. Sociologist Georg Simmel maintained that gratitude is the fundamental bond that forms and holds societies together.[33] The Roman statesman and philosopher Cicero called gratitude "the mother of all virtue." Not to show gratitude or to return a favor begrudgingly is seen as a great insult and an indication of a mean personality. The Omaha Indians of North America said of the ungrateful person: "He does not appreciate the gift. He has no manners."

Most Western deontologists claim that we have duties only to other rational beings, but some philosophers see gratitude as having more global implications. Ecologist and environmental philosopher Thomas Berry wrote in his book *The Dream of Earth:*

> If the earth does grow inhospitable toward human presence, it is primarily because we have lost our sense of courtesy toward the earth and its inhabitants, our sense of gratitude, our willingness to recognize the sacred character of habitat, our capacity for the awesome, for the numinous quality of every earthly reality.[34]

Gratitude stems from a natural impulse to maintain proper balance and equality. W. D. Ross maintained that gratitude is not merely a matter of sentiment but requires the use of our reason to know when it is morally appropriate. When the giver and the receiver are of equal status, the receiver is in a position to express gratitude in a way that recreates and affirms the importance of balance in the relationship. It also serves to deepen the commitment to a relationship. The exchange of gifts as a means of strengthening relationships is probably most obvious among family, lovers, and close friends.

Give as much as you receive and all is for the best.

—Maori (New Zealand) proverb

However, giving to another person who has less power and who is not able to return the favor can also be a means of dehumanizing and gaining power over the weaker person by creating in that person an ongoing sense of gratitude and obligation. Indeed, the charge of ingratitude is one of the most frequent accusations made by the rich against the poor.

Gifts make slaves just as whips make dogs.

—Eskimo proverb

Conflicting Duties

Any of these duties can come into conflict with each other or with any of the ongoing or future-looking duties. Because moral duties are prima facie, at least according to most deontologists, whenever we have a conflict or moral dilemma, we must carefully weigh each duty, decide which are the most compelling in that particular situation, and try to arrive at a resolution that honors as many of the duties as possible.

Although Ross admits that his list of prima facie duties may be incomplete, he also believed that all reflective, rational people would agree that these are moral duties. "There is nothing arbitrary about these prima facie duties," he wrote. "Each rests on a definite circumstance which cannot seriously be held to be without moral significance."[35]

Because moral duties are prima facie, they can come into conflict in a particular situation. We may promise a friend not to tell anyone that she has AIDS. However, this promise can conflict with the duty of non-maleficence if we later discover that she is being sexually promiscuous and is lying to her partners about her condition. When faced with a moral dilemma, we have to decide which of the competing moral duties is the most compelling under those particular circumstances.

According to W. D. Ross, there is no set formula for determining which action we should take in a moral dilemma. The general duties themselves may be self-evident, but judgments about our duties in a particular case are not. Instead, we need to use reason and creativity to make judgments about our duty in that situation. Ross believed that this lack of clarity is due to the nature of moral decision-making, which, he claims, is more like creating a work of art than solving a mathematical problem: The finished paintings might look very different, but we are all painting from the same palette. Universal moral principles, like the artist's palette, provide the form rather than the specific content of our final decision. Ross believed that, to demand ethicists to provide us with predetermined moral decisions is as unreasonable as it would be for artists to demand their mentors to tell them exactly how their finished pictures should look.

There is no computer program that can provide us with preset formulas for solving our real-life moral dilemmas. Like any creative undertaking, moral decision-making requires the proper tools and expertise in reasoning, but it also demands that we personally enter into the process. The sort of moral decisions we make says as much about the kind of people we are as it does about the universal moral principles themselves.

Exercises

1. Discuss whether moral duties are prima facie or absolute. Does the concept of duties as prima facie weaken the moral law, as Kant feared it would? Support your answer.

2. Select one of the case studies from Question 3 at the end of the previous section. When deciding if lying was morally justified in this case, were there other morally relevant considerations besides the consequences of the actions? If so, what were these considerations? Were they based on past or present duties? Which of the duties conflicted? How did you resolve the conflict? Was your solution the same as that of other people in the class? If not, were some of the solutions better than others? Support your answer.

3. Do you agree with W. D. Ross that all rational people would agree with his list of prima facie duties? Are there any other duties you would add to his list or any that you would remove? Support your answer.

*4. In Edward Westermarck's book *The Origin and Development of the Moral Ideas* (vol. 2: 158), he argues that gratitude is only for equals. Those with less power do not owe the duty of gratitude to those who have much more than they do. Do you agree with Westermarck that those without power or with little power do not owe gratitude to those in power who are helping them? Do people being served by social service agencies owe gratitude to those that support these services through their taxes, charitable donations, or volunteer work? Think of an example from your own life where someone who had significantly more power than you did performed a favor or service for you. Did this create a duty of gratitude on your part? If not, why not? If it did, how did you carry out the duty of gratitude?

5. Using the steps outlined in Chapter 2, pages 72–73, for resolving moral dilemmas, try to resolve the following moral dilemmas or one of the dilemmas listed at the end of that section, taking into consideration the different prima facie moral duties.

   a. Rose and Joe have been living together in a monogamous relationship for the past two years—since the beginning of their sophomore year at college. They both agreed, at the time they moved in together, that either could leave the relationship at any time. However, Rose unexpectedly became pregnant. Because she is opposed to abortion, she has resigned herself to having the baby. When Rose is six months pregnant, Joe decides to leave. He leaves a short note saying, "It was fun while it lasted, but it's time for me to move on." What should Rose do?

b. You are a rookie police officer. You have been asked to serve as an undercover agent to catch drug dealers on campus. This involves posing as a college student. Should you accept the assignment?

The Duty of Justice

Justice is the first virtue of social institutions, as truth is of systems of thought.
—JOHN RAWLS, *A Theory of Justice* (1971), p. 3

If then the unjust is the unequal, the just is the equal; everyone accepts this conclusion without demanding a reason for it.

. . . distributive justice can be stated as a proportion, and the unjust in this sense is a violation of proportion. What is unjust, therefore, is what is either too much or too little.
—ARISTOTLE, *Nicomachean Ethics*, Bk. 5, Ch. 3

The duty of justice is regarded by many philosophers as our most important duty as members of our community. The ongoing duty of justice requires that we give each person equal consideration. Because laws and social institutions are generally the agencies for balancing conflicting interests, the issue of justice is closely tied in with that of the good society; however, legal justice is not always consistent with moral justice. Not all laws are just, nor are all demands for justice addressed by laws. The duty of justice is generally subdivided by philosophers into two types: distributive and retributive justice.

Distributive Justice

Distributive justice refers to the fair distribution of benefits and burdens in a society. Benefits include education, highways, housing, economic opportunities, and police and fire protection. Taxes, jury duty, and military conscription are examples of shared burdens. Distributive justice presupposes that (1) there are conflicts of interest and (2) people have competing claims for certain limited or scarce societal goods.

Having enough air to breathe is not, or at least not yet, an issue of justice, because there is enough air for everyone. On the other hand, there are not enough well-paying jobs, college scholarships, or affordable housing. Therefore, the distribution of these latter goods is an issue of justice. Because there is a limited amount of money available for college scholarships, if you get a scholarship someone else will be denied one. When there is not enough of something to satisfy everyone, how should the goods be distributed?

Distributive justice requires impartiality: treating equals equally and unequals in proportion to their individual differences. Circumstances are rarely equal, however, so disagreements frequently arise in the actual application of this principle. Simply giving everyone an equal share is not necessarily just, because not everyone shares the same concept of the good life nor does everyone have the same needs. If we gave everyone a small scholarship to go to college, for example, that would be unjust to those who want to go to college but need more than a small scholarship and a waste of money for those who have no desire to go to college.

Marxist philosophers emphasize need as the key criterion in distributive justice. They claim that the economic arrangements of the capitalist system are unjust because many people's basic needs go unmet while the capitalists and their families continue to control more and more of the society's resources, including college degrees.

Aristotle, on the other hand, maintained that justice does not necessarily entail that everyone should get the same amount of society's resources. He was opposed to democracy, preferring instead an oligarchy or an elitist political system based on merit (meritocracy). Those who have contributed most to the community, he argued, deserve the most in return.[36]

Most philosophers believe that both need and merit should be taken into consideration. The issue of merit or achievement in distributive justice is particularly relevant for the distribution of goods such as scholarships, rewards for achievement, and skilled jobs. People who have worked hard deserve a raise or a promotion simply because they have done a good job, regardless of their need for additional income.

Awarding high-paying jobs and college scholarships solely on the basis of merit, on the other hand, is considered unjust by some philosophers because not all of us have the same opportunities to achieve educational and professional goals. These philosophers reject Aristotle's elitist concept of justice, pointing out that past injustices and economic disadvantages have limited the opportunities of marginalized groups of people. Justice based on a meritocracy also tends to further increase the gap between the haves and the have-nots. In the United States during the past thirty years, for example, the wealth has become more and more concentrated in the hands of a small percentage of people. In 1963, twenty-five percent of the population owned thirty-five percent of the wealth. By 1983, twenty-five percent of the wealth was concentrated in the hands of only one-half percent of the population!

In a just society, we all deserve a fair opportunity to pursue our goals. To create fair opportunities, affirmative action programs have been established to compensate formerly disadvantaged people for past deprivations. Some philosophers, however, are opposed to affirmative action; they claim that it can create resentment among white men, lower the quality of work, and turn minorities and women into "petitioners for favors."[37] These philosophers contend that true justice requires changing the system that first led to the injustice.

Deontologist John Rawls (b. 1921) addresses some of these problems in his book *A Theory of Justice*. Justice, he argues, demands not only impartiality but treating people fairly and in proportion to their needs as well as their merits. There are inequalities of birth and natural endowment (what Rawls calls the "*natural lottery*") and historic circumstances that are undeserved but that create disadvantages for certain people. People who have lower than average intelligence, or who are not born into wealth, are systematically excluded from enjoying the opportunities that others take for granted. Simply redistributing the wealth through welfare and charity does not solve the root problem, as long as the underlying conditions that disadvantage certain people still exist. What is needed, Rawls argues, is a change in the social system, so that it does not permit these injustices to occur in the first place.

> Although we may be entirely within our rights, according to the laws of the land and the rules of our social structure, we may nevertheless be participating in general injustice, and in giving to an unfortunate man we do not give him a gratuity but only help to return to him that of which the general injustice of our system has deprived him.
>
> —IMMANUEL KANT, *Lectures on Ethics,* "Duties Toward Others" (c. 1779)

Rawls' solution to this problem is to found justice upon a social contract. To establish a social contract that is unbiased and based on impartiality, Rawls suggests using a conceptual device that he terms the "veil of ignorance." Under the **"veil of ignorance,"** each person is ignorant of the advantages and disadvantages—including, for example, economic standing, gender, intelligence, health, place of birth—that he or she will receive in this life. This prevents people from promoting principles of justice that are biased in their favor.

Under these conditions of impartiality, Rawls argues that all rational people would agree upon the following *two principles of justice*:

> *First:* Each person is to have an equal right to the most extensive basic liberty compatible with a similar liberty for others.
>
> *Second:* Social and economic inequalities are to be arranged so that they are both (a) reasonably expected to be to everyone's advantage, and (b) attached to positions and offices open to all.[38]

Using these two principles of justice, Rawls suggests that the primary social goods be distributed equally. **Primary social goods** include social goods, such as housing, food, police protection, and education, that are necessary

John Rawls (b. 1921), Harvard University philosopher and political theorist. In his book A Theory of Justice *Rawls offers a theory of justice based on social contract theory—a concept that has its roots in classical Greek philosophy.*

to pursue our liberty rights and our concept of the good life. Nonessential goods, on the other hand, do not need to be distributed equally as long as the inequalities are still consistent with the rights of others to pursue their liberty and enjoy fair opportunity.

One of the problems with Rawls' theory is determining what constitutes a natural disadvantage: Aren't almost all of our abilities and disabilities, at least to some extent, a result of the "natural lottery"? For example, it has been documented that taller people and more attractive people have an advantage in the job market. Also, some people are more extroverted, a quality rewarded in our society. Studies also show that the oldest child and only children tend to be more highly motivated as adults and make better leaders. Almost every president of the United States has been either an oldest or an only child. Should shortness, birth order, or introversion be considered undeserved disadvantages that create a right to some form of public assistance or affirmative action in hiring?

Rawls' assumption that all rational people would, under the "veil of ignorance," agree upon these two principles has also been called into question. Some people might be willing to take greater risks, and others might prefer a less egalitarian distribution of social goods. Despite these criticisms, Rawls' theory of justice has provided a powerful tool for reforming social institutions and has been used to develop policy in areas such as health care reform, education, and the economy.

Retributive Justice

Retributive justice, the second type of justice, involves punishment for wrongdoing. Punishment for a crime, according to most deontologists, is our duty because the moral order requires that the guilty should suffer in proportion to the magnitude of their crime. W. D. Ross writes: "The offender, by violating the life, liberty, or property of another, has lost his own right to have his life, liberty or property respected."[39] Retributive justice, according to Kant, belongs to the judicial or penal system, rather than private judgment. Retributive justice is not the same as revenge, which is based on sentiment rather than reason:

> The penal law [retributive justice] is a categorical imperative; and woe to him who creeps through the serpent-windings of utilitarianism to discover some advantage that may discharge him from the justice of punishment . . .
>
> It is the principle of equality, by which the pointer of the scale of justice is made to incline no more to the one side than the other. It may be rendered by saying that the undeserved evil which any one commits on another, is to be regarded as perpetrated on himself. Hence it may be said: "If you slander another, you slander yourself . . . if you strike another, you strike yourself; if you kill another, you kill yourself." This is the right of retaliation (jus talionis); and properly understood, it is the only principle which in regulating a public court, as distinguished from mere private judgment, can definitely assign both the quality and quantity of a just penalty.

Some philosophers regard retributive justice as neither rational nor self-evident. The utilitarians were opposed to retribution because it involved the deliberate infliction of pain and deprivation. Punishment can only be morally justified, according to utilitarians, on the grounds of the future-looking duties of beneficence and non-maleficence. Thus punishment should be used only when the beneficial effects of it outweigh the evil of inflicting pain on a sentient being. The impersonal demands of retributive justice can also come into conflict with care ethics and the moral principle of ahimsa (nonviolence). A justice system based on punishment has also been criticized for simply increasing violence in the world and in the heart of the wrongdoer, rather than restoring justice. Jesus in particular speaks out against retributive justice (*lex talionis*) (Matthew 5:38–39):

> You have heard that it was said "An eye for an eye and a tooth for a tooth." But I say to you, Do not resist one who is evil. But if anyone strikes you on the right cheek, turn to him the other also.

Retributive justice remains one of the most controversial of the moral duties. Kant's notion of harming another person as a means of showing respect for that person seems odd to some people. Most people feel guilty when they do wrong, yet guilt does not entail an expectation of punishment. Indeed, fear of punishment will more often lead to deception regarding our wrongdoing rather than accepting blame. Also, the negative response of most wrongdoers to punishment, including increased resentment and lowered self-esteem, should cause us to reexamine the belief that retributive justice is our moral duty.

Exercises

1. Do you agree with Kant and W. D. Ross that retributive justice is a moral duty? Why or why not? Does retributive justice justify capital punishment, or should there be limits on retribution? Support your answer.

2. Linking rewards to merit puts tremendous pressure upon people to achieve, often at the expense of others. Is our emphasis on merit as the primary criterion for giving out rewards such as income, grades, and social recognition simply a bias of our capitalist system where people are expected to compete with each other for their share of social goods? Is there another system that might be preferable? Support your answer.

3. How should income be distributed? Is it fair that people who have been working at a job the longest, yet no longer have dependent children and have accumulated savings over the years, get paid far more than younger workers who usually have greater needs—such as a family to support and a mortgage to pay? How should we balance merit and need in distributing economic resources?

4. Rawls considers disabilities as part of the "natural lottery." But, aren't our talents and abilities also part of the natural lottery? Is it really fair that people who are more intelligent, innately more gifted, or naturally more competitive get paid more and get a greater share of societal goods? How, if at all, should these factors be taken into consideration in distributing societal goods?

5. Certain people and also certain nations have natural advantages over others. The United States and Canada, for example, are both countries rich in natural and technical resources. Does such a natural advantage create in wealthy nations a duty of justice to share their wealth with nations that are at a natural disadvantage? Support your answer.

6. Certain groups of people, such as Native Americans and African Americans in the United States, have been severely disadvantaged in the past by social institutions that discriminated against them. To what extent does society have a moral duty to compensate these groups or to redistribute social goods to groups of people whose ancestors have been gravely disadvantaged in the past?

7. To what extent is it morally permissible for a society to use coercion to force people to share the societal burdens? As taxpayers, should we be held responsible for supplying the needs of others who are not working or who cannot support themselves?

The Strengths and Limitations of Deontology

Western deontologists have been accused of promoting an abstract moral philosophy that sacrifices community in the name of individual autonomy. Kant's description of the moral community as a collection of autonomous units has especially come under fire. In Kantian deontology, the private life replaces the public life as the sphere of our moral actions. German philosopher Georg Hegel (1770–1831) questioned Kant's belief that individual autonomy and rationality are possible prior to membership in an ethical community. Kant's assumption that people are basically autonomous, private units who are free to carry out the moral law fails to take into consideration that we are all part of a wider social network of relationships.

Hegel argued that our sense of self cannot exist outside of personal interaction and community; we are woven together in a common web. Like Confucius, Hegel believed that the unhappiness of one is the unhappiness of us all. Hegel drew an analogy between modern society and a zoo filled with animals, each in its own cage with no community spirit. Indeed, Kant's emphasis on individualism has been suggested as a contributing factor to our modern-day sense of alienation and the creation of a society where many of us live isolated lives in fear of crime and violence.

The deontologists' concern with justice and abstract principles of duty, rather than with community, has also been criticized by feminist care ethicists such as Carol Gilligan and Nel Noddings as a distinctively male approach that ignores caring relationships. Although studies have shown that deontology is not a distinctly male approach, nor is care as distinctly female as Gilligan first thought, feminist care ethicists nevertheless raise an important point. Practical morality, they argue, is constructed dialectically through interaction with others, not merely by an autonomous examination of the dictates of our reason. By reducing morality to one component—moral judgment—deontology fails to take into account the influence of relationships and the role of moral sensitivity in informing our moral values. Knowing what is right on the level of reason does not necessarily mean that we will do what is right. Reason alone, without the ability to sympathize with others, seems unable to produce the categorical imperative or to inspire us to respect others. Abstract rational principles, care ethicists argue, are insufficient to motivate us or provide us with concrete guides to action. History has, time and again, shown how easy it is for us to set aside these abstract formal principles and slip back into dogmatism, violence, and intolerance.

Nietzsche likewise accused Kant's moral rationalism of being hostile to life by its rejection of the natural passions and instincts of life.[40] Nietzsche argued that true morality is dominated by an instinct for life, not abstract reason. Thus, moral judgments that are impersonal and universal should not be taken seriously.

> [Virtue] must be our own invention, our most necessary self-expression . . . The fundamental laws of self-preservation and growth demand the opposite—that everyone invent his own virtue, his own categorical imperative. A people perishes when it confuses its duty with duty in general.

Nietzsche's criticism of deontology is partly based on a misperception of the concept of duty. Kant and other deontologists such as Confucius and W. D. Ross do not believe that doing one's duty is antithetical to personal growth and relationships nor to the expression of our natural passions and instincts. They are aware that the love of mankind in general is not a good substitute for particular friendships and relationships. There is no logical contradiction involved, for example, in universalizing a maxim that states: "In life-threatening situations we should first, all other things being equal, try to save ourselves and those who are members of our immediate family." In fact, rational people would hardly be willing to universalize a maxim that states: "I ought to do, or be willing to do, for anyone what I do for my family and friends." In other words, a justice-based ethics, as Gilligan refers to deontology, and a care-based ethics are not necessarily incompatible with each other.

Most deontologists believe that consequences, though not as important as duty, should be taken into consideration. Therefore, Kant's denial that consequences are morally relevant has also been criticized by utilitarians and other deontologists. John Stuart Mill points out that the categorical imperative, by its very nature, requires that we take consequences into account when adopting moral rules. According to Mill, rational people would not universalize a moral rule that would harm, rather than benefit, the moral community:

> When Kant propounds as the fundamental principle of morals, "So act, that the rule of conduct might be adopted as a law by all rational beings," he virtually acknowledges that the interest of mankind collectively . . . must be in the mind of the agent when conscientiously deciding on the morality of the act. Otherwise he uses words without a meaning; . . . To give any meaning to Kant's principle, the sense put upon it must be, that we ought to shape our conduct by a rule which all rational beings might adopt with benefit to their collective interests.

Despite these shortcomings, the strengths and richness of deontology far outshine its weaknesses. In any case, it would be a mistake to consider any philosophical theory, or even any scientific theory, as a finished or complete statement about a particular phenomenon. One of the characteristics of a good theory is that it is open-ended and generates further thought. In this respect, deontology has made important contributions to the study of ethics.

Although Kant's moral philosophy, because of its formal character and lack of specificity, suffered a serious decline in popularity among philosophers during the first half of the twentieth century, it is now making a comeback. Few philosophers accept Kant's moral philosophy in its entirety; still, Kantian deontology is one of the most, if not *the* most, influential and fertile moral philosophies in modern history. Kant's thinking has had a major influence on modern European and American moral philosophers such as Sissela Bok, John Rawls, and W. D. Ross; it has also left its mark on philosophers around the world.[41] Deontology, with its emphasis on the dignity of the individual, has also had a major influence on the development of rights ethics in both Western and non-Western philosophies.

Exercises

1. Read the following quote from André Gide's novel *The Immoralist:*

   "If there's one thing I detest it's a man of principles," [Michel said].
   "You're right," Menalque answered, laughing, "he is the most detestable kind of person in the world. You can't expect any kind of sincerity from him, for he only does what his principles have ordered him to do, or else he considers what he does as a transgression."

   Are people of principle detestable, as Michel and Menalque claim? Or are they the best and most sincere of people, as Kant claims?

2. Nietzsche claims that Kant's approach to moral education, with its emphasis on duty, promotes a boring herd morality. Nietzsche writes: " 'What is the task of all higher education?' To turn men into machines. 'What are the means?' Man must learn to be bored. 'How is that accomplished?' By means of the concept of duty . . . 'Who is the perfect man?' The civil servant. 'Which philosophy offers the highest formula for the civil servant?' Kant's."

   Do you agree with Nietzsche that a deontological approach to moral education turns people into machines? Support your answer.

Summary

1. **Deontology** is a popular approach to ethics in world philosophies and religions.
2. According to deontologists, for an action to have moral worth it must be done from a sense of *duty.*
3. Since all rights have a corresponding duty, **rights ethics** is sometimes regarded as a branch of deontology.
4. Deontologists disagree about the ultimate source of moral duties—whether it is reason or intuition.
5. The difference between utilitarianism and deontology is, in part, one of emphasis; utilitarians regard consequences, rather than duty, as most important for morality.

6. *Confucian* moral philosophy is a blend of deontology and virtue ethics. Confucianism emphasizes community responsibility over individual autonomy.

7. Duty and the "ought" were important themes in seventeenth- and eighteenth-century European *Enlightenment* ethics.

8. *Immanuel Kant* is the most influential Western deontologist. Kant wanted to establish *a groundwork or foundation for morality* that would explain why we ought to behave morally. He claimed that reason provides the foundation of morality.

9. A **hypothetical imperative** tells us that we ought to do something if we want to achieve a certain result. A **categorical imperative** states that we ought to do something regardless of the consequences.

10. Kant's categorical imperative states that we should be willing to *universalize moral maxims* and that we should *never treat a person only as a means to an end.*

11. Kant's categorical imperative is a **formal principle**—that is, it lacks specific content.

12. According to Kant only *rational beings* are able to act freely or autonomously. Therefore, only rational beings such as humans have intrinsic moral worth. Nonhuman animals are not part of the moral community or *kingdom-of-ends.*

13. A person of **good will** acts out of an autonomous sense of duty. This sense of duty, according to Kant, stems from reason.

14. One of our primary moral duties is the development of *self respect* or *proper self-esteem.*

15. Kant claimed that moral duties are **absolute duties** and that there are no exceptions to this rule.

16. *Sissela Bok* and *W. D. Ross* claim that moral duties are prima facie. A **prima facie duty** is a moral duty that may be overridden on occasion by stronger moral claims.

17. Bok argues that it may be permissible, under certain circumstances, to break a moral rule such as "do not lie."

18. Ross lists seven prima facie duties: *Beneficence* and **non-maleficence** are future-oriented duties; **fidelity, reparation,** and **gratitude** are duties based on past actions; *self-improvement* and *justice* are ongoing duties.

19. There are two types of justice: retributive justice and distributive justice. **Retributive justice** requires punishment for wrongdoing. **Distributive justice** is concerned with the fair distribution of social goods.

20. *John Rawls* maintains that distributive justice should be based on *impartiality* and *fairness.*

21. *Georg Hegel* rejects Kantian deontology as focusing too much on individual autonomy and ignoring the importance of community.

22. *Feminist care ethicists* criticize moral theories such as deontology that privilege reason.

CHAPTER 10

Rights Ethics
The Other Side of Deontology

. . . all acts and duties which follow from the rights of others are
the most important of the duties we have towards others . . .
There is nothing in the world so sacred, as the rights of others.
  —IMMANUEL KANT, "Duties Dictated by Justice"[1]

We hold these truths to be self-evident, that all men are created equal,
that they are endowed by their Creator with certain inalienable Rights,
that among these are Life, Liberty and the Pursuit of Happiness.
  —United States Declaration of Independence, July 4, 1776

To one man's natural right there corresponds a duty in other persons: the
duty, namely, of acknowledging and respecting the right in question.
  —POPE JOHN XXIII, "Pacem in terris" (1963)

The Emergence of Rights Ethics in Modern Society

Issues involving rights are one of the primary topics of moral debate today. Human rights is not a new concept, however, the articulation of human rights by philosophers is a relatively recent development. With the exception of natural rights ethics, rights ethics does not exist as a separate theory but as part of broader moral theories such as deontology, utilitarianism, and natural law ethics. Even where rights have not been explicitly discussed in traditional writings, such as in Buddhist philosophy, the assumption of rights is embedded in the concepts of duty and respect for the dignity of people.

The Divine Right to Rule

Before the eighteenth century, the focus of moral theory was primarily on duty—duty to the king, to God, to the state, to the church, and to the moral law. The language of rights in Western philosophy emerged mainly in the context of the growing confrontation with the principle of absolute sovereignty. Kings had previously claimed to have the divine right to rule. Now, their subjects were claiming that they also had rights that the sovereigns were bound to respect. This dissatisfaction culminated in the West in 1789 with the French Declaration of the Rights of Man and Citizen and the American Bill of Rights.

---

1. Men are born and remain free and equal in rights; social distinctions may be based only on general usefulness.

2. The aim of every political association is the preservation of the natural and in-alienable rights of man: these rights are liberty, property, security, and resistance to oppression.

3. The source of all sovereignty resides essentially in the nation; no group, no individual may exercise authority not emanating expressly therefrom.

4. Liberty consists of the power to do whatever is not injurious to others; thus the enjoyment of the natural rights of every man has for its limits only those that assure other members of society the enjoyment of those same rights; such limits may be determined by law.

—The French Declaration of the Rights of Man and Citizen (1789)

Cultural relativists claim that the moral rights outlined in these documents did not exist before the acceptance of these documents by their respective societies. Rights ethicists disagree; they claim that these documents did not create rights that did not previously exist. Instead, the writers of these documents were demanding that rights that were formerly denied now be recognized.

In theory, these documents recognized the equal rights of all humans, but this was not the case in actual practice. In the United States the existence of slavery and the denial of certain basic rights to women, such as the right to vote and the right of married women to own property, precipitated a second rights movement.

The Women's Rights Movement

Many of the people who were involved in the abolitionist movement, such as Elizabeth Cady Stanton and Frederick Douglass, were also involved in the women's rights movement. Elizabeth Cady Stanton was born in 1815 into an affluent family in Johnstown, New York. Her parents had wanted boys and were openly disappointed by the birth of their daughters. As a child, Eliza-

Signing of the Declaration of Independence, 1776. The American Declaration of Independence was based, in part, on Locke's theory of natural rights and the belief that there are certain in-alienable rights that all people are bound to respect.

beth imitated her brother's academic achievements and even managed to convince her parents to send her to Troy Female Seminary in New York, one of the first women's academies to offer women a quality education. There, she studied logic, physiology, and natural law ethics. In 1840, she and her new husband, journalist Henry Stanton—also an abolitionist and women's rights activist—attended a global antislavery conference in London. However, she was excluded from participation in the conference because of her gender. At this conference she met Lucretia Mott. Together, they began making plans for the first women's rights convention, which was held in Seneca Falls, New York, in 1848. In 1851, Stanton also joined forces with feminist Susan B. Anthony.

Elizabeth Cady Stanton and Lucretia Mott were the driving forces behind the writing of the "Declaration of Sentiments and Resolutions of the First Woman's Rights Convention."[2] In her address to the First Woman's Rights Convention, Elizabeth Cady Stanton referred to the principles and guaranteed rights that were put forth in the U.S. Declaration of Independence and Bill of Rights.

> [W]e are assembled to protest against a form of government existing without the consent of the governed—to declare our right to be free as man is free . . . The

Elizabeth Cady Stanton (1815–1902) with Susan B. Anthony (1820–1906). Stanton and Anthony were two of the leading forces in the fight for women's rights in the United States.

world has never yet seen a truly great and virtuous nation, because in the degradation of woman the very fountains of life are poisoned at their source.

Stanton believed that suffrage (the right to vote) was part of a greater problem. She was a brilliant orator and writer; she protested the sexual abuse of women and championed coeducational education and the concept of men and women taking equal responsibility for the care of their children. Stanton served as president of the National Woman's Suffrage Association from 1869 to 1890. The NWSA opposed the fourth amendment to the U.S. Constitution, which granted the vote to all "male citizens aged twenty-one years of age" and older, because of its exclusion of women.

Stanton also believed that organized religion promoted superstition and hostility against women. Her *Woman's Bible,* a study of sexism in the Old Testament, stirred up a storm of outrage when it was published in 1895. Stanton died in 1902. It was not until 1920, long after the deaths of Stanton and Susan B. Anthony, that women were given the right to vote in the United States.

The Second World War

A third event giving rise to a renewed interest in rights ethics was World War II. The atrocities of the Holocaust led people to reflect upon fundamental moral questions. The events of the war also brought to light the weaknesses and dangers of cultural relativism—in this case, the cultural relativism that had tried to justify the horrors of the Nazi regime. If rights are the creation of society, as cultural relativists claim, then rights can be removed by societal laws, as happened in the 1936 German supreme court ruling that deprived Jews of most of their rights.

> It is a preconception of the Universal Declaration of Human Rights that in spite of the diversity in cultures and differences in existential conditions in the world, a common standard of rights can be established for all people and nations.
>
> —MANSOUR FARHANG, Iranian ambassador to the United Nations[3]

Human Rights

In 1948, the United Nations issued the Universal Declaration of Human Rights. According to this declaration, human rights are not simply a Western creation but belong to all people everywhere. The Universal Declaration was followed by the push for decolonization in Asia and Africa and the challenge for Westerners to overcome Eurocentric thinking both at home and abroad. International pressure from government groups and organizations such as Amnesty International has also been put on countries that engage in gross human rights violations, such as torture and genocide.

> Men are equal. For, though they are not of the same age, same height, the same skin and the same intellect, these inequalities are temporary and superficial, the soul that is hidden beneath this early crust is one and the same for all men and women belonging to all climes . . . The word "inequality" has a bad odour to it, and it has led to arrogance and inhumanities, both in East and West.
>
> —MOHANDAS K. GANDHI, *None High, None Low* (1975), p. 2

In India, under Gandhi's leadership, rights ethics (which was strongly influenced by Buddhist ethics), emerged as a direct challenge to the unequal privileges of the caste system. With the strong emphasis of Buddhist ethics on the dignity of all beings, Buddhist ethicists have become some of the leading advocates of rights ethics, promoting not only human rights but also the rights of nonhuman animals and the environment.

Moral Versus Legal Rights

Because humans exercise their rights within a social structure, there is considerable overlap between the content of moral rights and that of legal rights. Much of the current debate over rights in the United States focuses on constitutional rights; however, moral and legal rights can conflict. Because the U.S. Constitution and our laws are not the source of fundamental moral rights, it is possible to have a legal or constitutional right that violates a moral right. The fact that women did not have the legal right to vote in this country until 1920 did not mean that there was no moral basis for the demand that women be given voting rights; the fact that women now have the legal right to abortion, likewise, does not necessarily mean that the right to abortion is a moral right.

> The legal rights of which [a person] is deprived, may be rights which *ought* not to
>
> have belonged to him; in other words, the law which confers these rights, may be a
>
> bad law.
>
> —JOHN STUART MILL, *Utilitarianism* (1863), Ch. 5

We also have certain legal rights, such as the right to operate a motor vehicle, that are not moral rights nor do they violate any moral rights. Similarly, not all moral rights are legal rights. We have a moral right, but not a legal right, to fidelity from our spouses or significant others. We also have a moral, but not a legal, right not to be deceived.

Cultural relativists maintain that these distinctions between moral and legal rights do not exist. They insist that there are no moral rights independent of legal rights. In the U.S. Supreme Court Dred Scott v. Sanford decision of 1856, the court ruled that "the right of property in a slave is distinctly and expressly affirmed in the Constitution . . ." If moral rights were the same as legal rights, this ruling should have settled the slavery issue once and for all. However, the claim that slavery violated the rights of African Americans continued to be presented by abolitionists despite this court ruling. Other public protests that occur when certain rights—such as freedom of speech or the right to a fair trial—are withdrawn or violated by the government also suggest that our legal rights are based on independent, nonlegal rights.

Also, some cultures deny certain groups of people the same rights that are enjoyed by those in power, but this does not mean that these cultures do not accept, at least in theory, a moral standard of human equality. Rights ethicists John Locke and Thomas Jefferson recognized, in theory, the moral equality of all humans. Yet at the time "equal rights" were legally extended only to white male landowners. (Indeed, Jefferson himself was a slaveholder.) Moral rights, in other words, rather than being derived from legal rights and cultural norms, can even run contrary to them. Even cultures that torture and deny basic rights to certain groups of people still generally recognize the basic moral standard of human equality. In response to the cultural relativists' claim that the concept of human rights is a Western cultural norm, it is interesting that the powerful Western nations, not the non-Western nations, were the most reluctant to endorse the U.N. Universal Declaration of Human Rights.

Exercises

1. Bring in newspaper or magazine articles that pertain to rights. In each of the examples, discuss the nature of the particular rights that are in question.

2. What is the relationship between moral and legal rights? Was Stanton's claim that women lacked equal rights justified? If so, why do you think Americans were, and to some extent still are, so resistant to granting women equal rights? Are any groups of people nowadays being denied the same rights that other people enjoy? Discuss your answer in light of the various human rights documents.

3. Should moral rights always be backed up by laws or rules? Most people believe that we do not have a moral right to use racist and sexist terms or to engage in activities that demean other people. However, even if we agree that we do not have a moral right to demean others through our words and actions, does this imply that derogatory language and activities should also be illegal? For example, should the Ku Klux Klan be legally forbidden to use inflammatory and racist language or to burn crosses on their own property or to march in public areas? How about professors who use language that demeans certain students in the class? Should universities have rules that ban the use of such language? Support your answer.

*4. Does the issue of rights ever arise in the course of your community service work? If so, what are these rights? Are the people who claim that they have, or should have, these rights able to exercise them? If not, why not?

John Locke: Natural Rights Ethics

The state of nature has a law of nature to govern it, . . . that being all equal and independent, no one ought to harm another in his life, health, liberty, or possession . . . And that all men may be restrained from invading others' rights . . .

—JOHN LOCKE, *Second Treatise on Civil Government* (1690), Ch. II, Sect. 6–7

Rights are generally seen as either (1) derived from duties or (2) natural and existing independently. If rights are derived from duty, there are no rights apart from duties. If a person has a right, then we have a duty or obligation to honor that right.

The philosophical doctrine of natural rights first appeared in Western philosophy in the seventeenth century as a demand for equality for all people. This represented a complete break from the feudalistic and aristocratic notions of human rights that were based on social privilege. Natural rights ethicists argue that all humans have rights apart from their membership in a civil society or political state. According to these ethicists, rights are self-evident and God-given. As such, rights exist independently of and prior to any duties we may have: These rights stem from our human nature. We have certain rights simply because we are human. We do not have to qualify to have rights, nor do we earn them. Humans alone have rights because of our special creation in the image of God. The claim of equality, for example, is not something we "invent" or determine by law; it is self-evident, even though humans are obviously unequal in terms of physical, mental, and social characteristics. These rights are *inalienable;* they cannot be taken away. Because only humans have rights, according to most natural rights ethicists, the term "natural rights" is often used synonymously with the term "human rights."

John Locke and Thomas Hobbes

John Locke and *Thomas Hobbes* were two of the most prominent natural rights ethicists. According to them, the primary purpose of government is to protect humans in the exercise of their equal rights. Although we might possess perfect freedom in the state of nature, our enjoyment of it is very uncertain. The **state of nature** is the condition in which people lived before the formation of the state of government. Since all societies have at least a rudimentary form of government, it is uncertain whether people ever actually lived in a state of nature. Nevertheless, Hobbes argued that, in this state of nature (whether real or hypothetical), there would be "continual fear, and danger of violent death; and the life of man, solitary, poor, nasty, brutish, and short." In the state of nature, people are egoists, each asserting their rights without concern for others. Therefore, people enter into a social contract so that everyone might better preserve their own rights. Hobbes limited our most fundamental natural right to self-preservation. He believed that subjects have no natural rights against the sovereign except self-preservation. Locke, on the other hand, expanded the concept of natural rights to include the rights to life, liberty, and property.

John Locke (1632–1704) was born in Somerset, England, and raised in a liberal Puritan family. He remained a deeply religious man throughout his life. His family was also involved in political activism. His father, a country

John Locke (1632–1704), English philosopher. A natural rights ethicist, Locke believed that rights stem from human nature and exist independently of duties. Thomas Jefferson, author of the American Declaration of Independence, was greatly influenced by Locke's rights ethics.

attorney, had fought on the parliamentary side in the first rebellion against Charles I.

Locke lectured in Greek and Latin at Oxford until he was appointed Reader in Censor of Moral Philosophy in 1664. His father's death in 1661 left him with a small inheritance; because he was unhappy with scholastic philosophy and found it too obscure and useless, he used this opportunity to broaden his studies. In 1665 Locke entered the diplomatic service, and in 1672 he was appointed Lord Chancellor by the Earl of Shaftesbury. In 1670 Locke went to France, where he remained for five years. When he returned to England, Shaftesbury was involved in a plot against King James II and was forced to flee to Holland. Locke, worried about his own safety, also took refuge in Holland, living there under an assumed name. He did not return to England until shortly after the revolution of 1688, when the Dutchman William of Orange was placed upon the throne of England. Back in England, Locke continued his writing. His treatises on civil government, education, and religion were immensely popular. Locke was a man of the people; he dressed in plain English clothes of sober grey cloth and wrote at a level that was understandable to non-scholars. He died in 1704. "His death," a friend wrote, "was like his life, truly pious, yet natural, easy and unaffected."[4]

Thomas Hobbes was horrified by the idea of citizens rebelling against their sovereign, but Locke thought that we should resist a government that misuses its power to deny our natural rights. Because government arises from a social contract among people and because people have equal rights, Locke believed that the best form of government for protecting our natural rights is a democracy. In his *Two Treatises of Civil Government,* published in 1690, Locke attacked the idea of the divine right of kings, thus justifying the revolution of 1688 in which William of Orange took over the English throne.

Locke was especially concerned that government respect what he believed to be our natural right to own property. The right to own property, according to Locke, is conditional upon our use and enjoyment of the property. By mixing our labor with the land and using the fruits of our labor, it becomes our property. Locke believed that this stipulation on private ownership would assure that there was enough land for everyone. According to Locke, God gave the world to humans as a resource; the vast wilderness of the earth was created by God for humans to subdue and turn into provisions to support human life. Locke's religious views were reinforced by the Enlightenment concept of nature that depicted the world as a giant machine without any life or value of its own. The world has only instrumental value defined in terms of human desires. Land that was left in or allowed to revert to its natural uncultivated state was, in Locke's mind, "spoilage" or "waste land." Only by being mixed with human labor and human industry do natural resources acquire value. Locke was particularly contemptuous of the "several nations of the [Native] Americans" who did nothing to "improve" the land. "A king of a large and fruitful territory there," Locke wrote, "feeds, lodges, and is clad worse than a day-labourer in England."[5]

Locke was convinced that, even if every man had as much property as he could make use of and even if the population of the earth was doubled, there would still be more than enough land for everyone. For those who could not find sufficient land in England or Europe, he suggested "let him plant in some in-land, vacant places of America."[6] Because the Native Americans did not cultivate their land but left it in a wasteful state of wilderness, the European settlers, according to Locke, could rightfully take possession of it.

Locke was aware that some people might try to take possession of more property than they could use, thus letting some of the property go to waste. Because the law of nature is unwritten and indeterminate, it is easy for people in the state of nature to misapply it when there is no established judge. Therefore, Locke believed that civil laws were needed to determine and to protect property rights:

> [T]he supreme power cannot take from any man part of his property without his own consent; for the preservation of property being the end of government, and that for which men enter into society, if necessarily supposes and requires, that the people should have property; without which they must be supposed to lose that, by entering into society, which was the end for which they entered into it . . .

Locke's political theory was formulated at a time when there was already considerable political unrest. Locke's doctrine of natural rights, with its belief that there are certain inalienable human rights that all societies and people are bound to respect, found expression in both the French and American revolutions. The doctrine had a profound influence on the thinking of Thomas Jefferson, who was only twenty-six when he wrote the first draft of the Declaration of Independence. The influence of natural rights ethics in the United States is especially evident by the way that rights are usually discussed without any reference to duty.

Ayn Rand

Ayn Rand is one of the foremost contemporary defenders of natural rights ethics. According to her, the doctrine of natural rights created the possibility of free societies. The United States has the honor of being the first free society founded upon natural rights ethics. Only through capitalism, Rand argued, can individual rights and a free society be sustained. "Those who advocate laissez-faire capitalism," she wrote, "are the only advocates of man's rights." Only in a capitalist society does the right to life and property belong to the individual rather than to the government. In a capitalist society, the sole purpose of government is the protection of our individual rights. Our ability to choose how to use our property and our choice of a career and of where to shop or where to sell our goods or labor are regarded as intimately related to our freedom to pursue the good life. Inadequate resources may limit our freedom and our ability to achieve our concept of the good life, but according to Rand, this cannot be used as a general objection to free enterprise.

> The most profoundly revolutionary achievement of the United States of America was *the subordination* of society to *moral law.*
>
> The principle of man's individual rights represented the extension of morality into the social system—as a limitation on the power of the state, as man's protection against the brute force of the collective, as the subordination of *might* to *right.* The United States was the first *moral* society in history.

According to Rand, moral rights define and protect our freedoms without imposing obligations on anyone else. For example, the right to property does not entail an obligation to provide people with property; the right to life does not entail an obligation to provide people with the necessities of life. Rand believed that the people who use violence to deprive others of their rights are only a small minority. The harm that these criminals have done in our free society is infinitesimal, she contended, compared to the horrors perpetuated by governments who believe they have the right to restrict people's liberties in the name of the social good.

The doctrine of natural rights has received considerable criticism. One of the greatest weaknesses of natural rights ethics is its lack of grounding in reason and social experience. Locke believed that "natural reason" [and] "revelation" [alike] "give us an account of those grants God made of the world to Adam and to Noah."[7] However, there is considerable disagreement over exactly what these natural rights are, and there is no way of resolving the disagreement. Just as kings claimed that they had a divine right to rule, the dogmatic claim that rights are natural or self-evident leaves us no room for a rational justification for these rights. Also, because natural rights exist independently of and prior to duty, natural rights ethics has been accused of promoting ethical egoism rather than containing it.

Annette Baier

Annette Baier argues that the liberalism supported by natural rights ethics does not take into account the limitations placed upon marginalized groups by traditional societal roles. Although voluntary agreement is the paradigm of moral obligation in liberal morality, women and children are excluded from entering into voluntary trade agreements, if they accept their traditional roles.

> Contract is a device for traders, entrepreneurs, and capitalists, not for children, servants, indentured wives, and slaves. They were the traded, not the traders.
>
> —ANNETTE BAIER, *Ethics* (1986), p. 247

This situation creates what Baier calls an internal contradiction in liberals' moral beliefs regarding equal human rights. This contradiction, she notes, does not "vanish once women have equal legal rights with men, as long as they are still expected to take responsibility for any child they conceive voluntarily or nonvoluntarily, either to abort or to bear and either care for or arrange for others to care for."[8] This failure to acknowledge and take into account the limitations that society places on certain groups of people is one of the major weaknesses of natural rights ethics.

Exercises

1. Are moral rights self-evident? If so, make a list of the rights that you regard as self-evident. Share your list with other students in the class. If there is disagreement, how might you resolve this disagreement? Is the use of theology—the claim that God endowed humans with special rights—adequate as a foundation for our moral rights, as natural law ethicists claim? If not, what justifications do you use to claim that there are certain moral rights?

2. Some Americans believe that our current government is not protecting their equal rights, as affirmed by the U.S. Constitution. Do people have the right, or even a duty, to rebel against a government that does not uphold people's

rights? Does this justify violent revolution, as occurred in the American and French revolutions, or acts of terrorism? Compare and contrast the solution proposed by natural rights ethicists and the natural law ethicists' use of civil disobedience.

*3. Does the belief in rights as natural, rather than derived from duty, work to the benefit of those who have the least power in our society? Or does it merely further empower those who are already privileged? Discuss. Relate your answer to your community service work.

4. The capitalist market system was, to a large extent, influenced by John Locke's writings on property. However, Locke was writing at a time when the human population of the world was one-tenth of what it is now. Would John Locke agree that our current system of ownership is consistent with natural moral rights? Explain.

    If our legal rights regarding property ownership are inconsistent with certain moral rights, should the laws regulating property ownership in this country be changed? If so, what changes would you make? What changes, if any, might Locke make? Support your answer.

5. Do we have a right to own property and homes that we are not inhabiting while others go homeless? How might Locke, if he were alive today, respond to the homeless situation? Are you satisfied with his response? Explain why or why not.

6. Do we have a moral right to property and inheritance that were acquired through someone else's forced labor, such as slave labor and the exploitation of people living under conditions of poverty? Explain.

7. According to Locke, Native Americans had no claim on the land, with the exception of the land that they were cultivating at the time. Do you agree? Why or why not?

8. To what extent has Locke's attitude toward property influenced our attitude toward the wilderness and land use in the United States and other capitalist economies? Do you agree with his view of the wilderness and of the role of humankind in the world? Support your answer.

9. Do you agree with Ayn Rand that capitalism is the only system that can protect our individual freedoms? Support your answer. How would Locke most likely respond to Rand's position? Create a dialogue between Rand and Locke.

The Marxist Critique of Natural Rights Ethics

[The] political liberators reduce citizenship, the political community, to a mere means for preserving these so-called rights of man; and consequently, that the citizen is declared to be the servant of egoistic "man," . . . and finally it is man as a bourgeois and not man as a citizen, who is considered the true and authentic man.

—KARL MARX, "On the Jewish Question" (1843)

The Life of Karl Marx

Karl Marx (1818–83) was one of the most influential critics of natural rights ethics. Marx was born in Prussia (now part of Germany). When he was six years old, his father, Heinrich Marx, converted from Judaism to Lutheranism, baptizing himself and his children as Protestants. As a young man, Marx studied law, his father's profession, in Berlin and in Bonn. But he soon decided that he was more interested in philosophy; he completed a Ph.D. in philosophy in 1841 at the age of twenty-three. Marx was opposed to the more traditional theoretical approach to philosophy. The role of the philosopher, he believed, is not simply to interpret the world but to change it. Marx initially intended to become a university teacher but abandoned the idea to become the editor of a radical newspaper.

In 1843 Marx married his childhood friend Jenny von Westphalen, the daughter of a high government official. Later that year, the couple moved to Paris and Marx joined the Communist League. In Paris, Marx began his lifelong friendship with Friedrich Engels, the son of a wealthy German textile manufacturer. In 1844, Marx was accused of high treason by the Prussian government, and the following year he renounced his Prussian citizenship under pressure from the government. In 1848, he and Engels published the *Communist Manifesto*. Because of Marx's radical ideas, he found himself unwelcome on the Continent. So, in 1849, he and his family settled permanently in London, where he lived in poverty, choosing to devote his energies to fighting for the rights of the downtrodden working class (proletariat).

Marx as the Champion of the Proletariat

Marx believed that the plight of the workers was due, in part, to the general acceptance of natural rights ethics. On the surface, natural rights ethics is an abstract philosophical theory. In reality, Marx argued, the list of so-called natural rights is historically conceived to justify certain economic and political systems. For example, Locke's "natural right to own property" (including slaves) serves to protect the holdings of those in power—the landowning bourgeois—rather than the majority of people who cannot afford to exercise their "natural" right to own property. The right to own property, in turn, justifies free-market capitalism and ethical egoism, by legitimating the increasing accumulation of property in the hands of the few, independently of any duties toward or consideration of those who are unable to exercise this right.

Marx regarded political revolutions such as the American and French revolutions, which were grounded in the doctrine of the natural rights of isolated individuals, to be destructive of community and the interests of those who lacked the power to assert these so-called natural rights. Rights, Marx argued, do not exist as an abstraction, but as part of our membership in a community. A right that can only be exercised if we have the power to assert

Karl Marx (1818–83), German philosopher, labor leader, and socialist. Marx was a critic of the individualistic natural rights theory underlying capitalism. He argued instead that rights exist as part of our membership in a community.

ourselves, he contended, is a "meaningless mockery" to those who lack social and political power. Rights are not based on self-assertion, Marx maintained; rather, rights are demands that create duties for society to provide its members with certain social goods.

> The political revolution [based on natural rights] therefore abolished the political character of civil society. It dissolved civil society into its basic elements, on the one hand individuals, and on the other hand, the material and cultural elements which formed the life experience and the civil situation of these individuals . . .
> A specific activity and situation in life no longer had any but an individual significance. They no longer constituted the general relation between the individual and the state as a whole.
>
> —KARL MARX, "On the Jewish Question" (1843)[9]

Natural rights ethicists believe that government exists to protect our rights. However, because we must first be in a position to assert these rights, in a capitalist society government exists to protect the individual rights of landowners at the expense of the majority who do not own property. For

Marxists, real freedom means liberation from this egoistic bourgeois system of morals. Marx, instead, had a social concept of liberty. Humans, he believed, are naturally cooperative, but the institution of private property and the class system created thereby prevent humans from being free to exercise their potential.

Marx argued that our rights are not just based on our ability to assert them, but also on our interests and needs as members of a community. Our right to property, in other words, does not mean merely that we have an abstract right to own property, but also that the community should provide us with property. To use another example, if a person has a right to an education, then the state has a corresponding duty to provide this education. Indeed, one of the ten points of Marx's 1883 *Communist Manifesto* was the establishment of "free education for all children in public schools." In contrast, according to the self-assertion model adopted by natural rights ethicists, only those who could assert their rights by having the means to pay for property or an education would be entitled to own property or to receive an education.

True equality and freedom, according to Marx, entails communal ownership of property rather than individual ownership. Marx was not suggesting the type of Communism in the old Soviet Union, where the government merely took over the role of oppressor. Instead, Marx had in mind a society where the people were truly in charge and where the government was merely a bureaucracy for ensuring the fair distribution of social goods. Whether or not this sort of "utopia" is possible, given the realities of human nature, is still under debate.

A complete victory of society will always produce some sort of "communist fiction," whose outstanding political characteristic is that it is indeed ruled by an "invisible hand," namely, by nobody. What we traditionally call state and government give place here to pure administration—a state of affairs Marx rightly predicted as the "withering away of the state," though he was wrong when he believed that this victory of society would mean the eventual emergence of the "realm of freedom."

—HANNAH ARENDT, *The Human Condition* (1958), pp. 44–45

Marx was considered a prophet of socialism. However, Marxism was never intended to be the formal ideology of a political party but a manifesto for the working class (proletariat). Indeed, both Marx and Engels were opposed to the formation of a separate Communist party. Although Marx was not opposed to violent revolution to overthrow the capitalist economy, he envisioned the possibility of a nonviolent revolution in more democratic countries such as the United States and Britain. Marx died of a lung tumor in 1883. After Marx's death Engels continued Marx's work by editing his notes and manuscripts for publication. Two of Marx's daughters, Laura and Eleanor also continued their father's work through their participation in the movement to help the working class.

Gustavo Gutierrez

Many contemporary rights movements, such as that led by Peruvian **liberation ethicist** and social activist Gustavo Gutierrez, accept Marx's criticism of natural rights ethics. Gutierrez was born in Lima, Peru, in 1928. A mestizo (part Quechuan Indian), Gutierrez was born among the oppressed rather than the privileged in his country. As a boy, Gutierrez contracted a serious case of osteomyelitis that forced him to be bedridden for six years during his adolescence. The disease also left him with a permanent limp. During these years, Gutierrez developed a fascination for the medical profession. After considering a career in medicine, Gutierrez found his real interest in the priesthood. He was an excellent student; the church sent him to Europe to study, where, in 1955, he completed a master's degree in philosophy and psychology at Catholic University in Louvain, Belgium. He also studied theology in France and Rome.

After almost a decade, Gutierrez returned to Peru and found that his first-rate theological education did not fit with the social reality of poverty in Latin America. He began to formulate his own theology, based on his involvement with the people of Rimac, a slum in Lima. Between 1960 and 1968, Gutierrez grew increasingly dissatisfied with the official position of the church in Latin America. He believed that the church should rethink its position on contraception, the ordination of women, the economic structure in Latin America, and the Gospel's understanding of violence. Gutierrez was a pacifist, and as such, he was instrumental in organizing a group of radical priests to work together to shape a new vision for the church. Gutierrez is also a world-renowned writer, teacher, public speaker, and social activist. Despite his fame, he still prefers to remain among the poor in the slums of Lima, where he works and lives six days each week.

Gutierrez is critical of laissez-faire capitalism, with its focus on liberty rights and its presumption that setting up a democracy will ensure human rights. Systems of democracy based on liberalism, Gutierrez maintains, do not protect the rights of the poor. Instead, the right to private ownership has been granted at the expense of the rights of the poor. Liberal democracy claims to promote equal rights but "is only for the middle class and actually only enhances the flexibility with which the prevailing system exercises its domination over the popular masses." [10]

Gustavo Gutierrez (b. 1928), Peruvian liberation ethicist and social reformer. Gutierrez opposes capitalism as unjust and oppressive to the poor. He believes that the right to liberty, rather than the right to own property, is one of the most fundamental rights.

Natural rights ethicists claim that capitalism is a natural economic system; Gutierrez, like Marx, argues instead that any attempt to separate the ideology of natural rights ethics—and the capitalist system that it supports—from its historic roots is to ignore historical reality. Gutierrez points out that the landowning bourgeoisie rose out of the dying feudal world. The political power of the kings was eventually replaced by that of the bourgeoisie; like the aristocracy they replaced, they claimed to have an absolute and inalienable right to control the economy—a private economy that Gutierrez describes as "based on private enterprise—and on the vicious exploitation of workers (in Europe) and the poor (in colonial and neocolonial lands)."[11]

Although Gutierrez accepts the Marxist critique of capitalism, he envisions a society founded upon a theology of liberation. Natural rights ethics is based on self-assertion. Gutierrez turns this upside down. A society where the rights and dignity of everyone are respected, he argues, must start from the "underside of history" by defending the rights of those who have been oppressed and plundered by the world. True democracy, according to Gutierrez, cannot be imposed upon a culture but must instead be preceded by the development of a just economic system:

> Defending human rights means above all defending the rights of the poor. It is a prophetic theme, and one deeply rooted in the tradition of the church. And it must be kept in mind in order to avoid falling into the liberal focus with regard to human rights. The liberal approach presupposes, for example, a social equality that simply does not exist in Latin American societies.

Unlike natural rights ethics, the Marxists' and liberation ethicists' concept of rights is firmly embedded in the historical process. The natural rights emphasis on abstract concepts of equality and democracy in the West gave rise to the mistaken belief that everyone shares a common concept of the good life; however, this cannot be assumed. Insensitivity to the historical and social contexts in which moral rights are exercised can lead to misunderstandings or even the belief that people from other cultures are morally stunted. This assumption, Gutierrez points out, has often been used to justify imposing Western notions of moral rights on other nations.

> This alternative language [of "rights of the poor"] represents a critical approach to the laissez-faire liberal doctrine to the effect that our society enjoys an equality that in fact does not exist. This new formulation likewise seeks constantly to remind us of what is really at stake in the defense of human rights: the misery and spoliation of the poorest of the poor, the conflictive character of Latin American life and society, and the biblical roots of the defense of the poor.
>
> —GUSTAVO GUTIERREZ, *The Power of the Poor in History* (1979), p. 87

Respect for Cultural Diversity

Chinese president Jiang Zemin criticized the United States' interference in Chinese–Taiwanese politics in a speech given at the United Nations on October 19, 1995. He objected to "certain big powers" [who] were meddling in Chinese affairs 'under the cover of freedom, democracy and human rights.'" According to Zemin, China has its own cultural destiny and issues that require it to "determine its own path" on human rights.[12]

Respecting cultural diversity, however, does not imply that we must fall back into ethical relativism or refrain from ever criticizing other cultures. In fact, Marxists and liberation ethicists are highly critical of cultures where the rights of the poor and powerless are not taken seriously. As Marx warned, we must take care not to simply accept the interpretations of those in power.

Exercises

1. Do you agree with Marx that the concept of natural rights is a political weapon for justifying the privileges of the economic and political elite, thus limiting the freedom of the majority? Support your answer. How might Ayn Rand respond to Marx's criticisms of natural rights ethics?

2. Marx believed that, if property were communally owned, criminals would disappear. Under true communism, he argued, there would be no need for the powerful military and police forces that are typical in capitalist societies. Rand, on the other hand, believed that putting control of property in the hands of the government would do more damage than that done by criminals. Discuss their respective positions.

3. Are laissez-faire capitalism and communism the only alternative systems for protecting human rights? Discuss what type of society might be best for optimizing human freedom while nurturing community and interdependence. What concept of moral rights did you use to come up with your ideal society? Is it compatible with the concept of natural rights as put forth by Locke and Rand, or with Marx's views of rights as community based? If not, how does it differ?

4. In Gutierrez's book *The Power of the Poor in History*, he argues that a prophetic interpretation of the Bible, rather than Locke's individualistic interpretation, provides the best foundation for a rights ethics that is consistent with justice and respect for human dignity. Do you agree? How might Locke and Marx respond to Gutierrez? Support your answer.

Rights and Duties

> The right of every man to life is correlative with the duty to preserve it; his right to a decent standard of living, with the duty of living it becomingly; and his right to investigate the truth freely, with the duty of pursuing it even more completely and profoundly.
>
> —POPE JOHN XXIII, "Pacem in terris" (1963)

Like the Marxists, most philosophers maintain that moral rights do not stand on their own but are derived from duty. Utilitarianism, deontological theories, natural law ethics, and Buddhist ethics all base rights on duty. Although moral rights imply a corresponding duty, not all duties have a corresponding right, however. Because moral duty is a broader concept, rights ethics is sometimes included as a branch of deontology.

According to duty-based rights ethics, rights are not granted but are rather something to which we are entitled. Others have a duty to honor our rights. In contrast, natural rights ethicists such as Locke and Rand argue that our possession of a right does not imply that someone else has a duty to honor that right. In other words, according to natural rights ethicists, all rational beings have rights, but these rights exist only in theory. Being able to actually claim these rights sometimes boils down to having the power—generally political power—to successfully assert ourselves.

Philosophical concepts and the paradigms they support, as we noted earlier, do not exist in a vacuum but have real-life consequences. Basing rights on the power to assert ourselves or the presence of an effective agent who will act on our behalf allows us to disregard not only the rights of nonhuman animals but also the rights of those groups of humans who lack the political power or force of law to exercise their moral claims. For example, the United States courts have ruled that Native Americans, in accordance with treaties, have a right to certain lands; however, they have no legal means for regaining that land. So, practically speaking, this natural right is useless. If the social contract makes no provision for the assertion of a particular right, then there is no duty on anyone's part to respect that right—as in the case of the Native Americans' right to certain lands.

On the other hand, if rights are derived from duty, then we are placed under an obligation to make sure that rights are honored. Our failure to discharge this obligation or duty becomes a violation of a person's right. If I have a duty not to lie to you, then you have a right to the truth or at least not to be lied to. If you have a duty of reparation, then I have a right to restitution from you. If we both have a right to a minimal standard of living, then the community has a moral duty to provide us with certain necessary goods. If you have the right not to be harmed, society has a duty to provide security in the form of police protection. Natural rights, however, because they are "self-evident," lack this grounding in duty, depending instead on our ability to assert these rights.

Rights as Derived from Duties

Jeremy Bentham attacked the notion of natural rights as "simply nonsense: natural and imprescriptible rights, rhetorical nonsense—nonsense upon stilts." Rights, according to Bentham, are neither natural nor inalienable. Instead, rights are derived from the principle of utility and are therefore calculable and changing, depending on the interests and needs of those involved. The government and the legislators, not individuals, must determine what rights are appropriate for producing the greatest happiness of the greatest number. Although Bentham agreed with Hobbes that people are naturally egoists, he did not accept egoistic striving as the basis of rights. Without government to curtail selfishness, he argued, any talk of rights makes no sense. All rights stem from the laws of society and, therefore, cannot be inalienable. "There is no right," Bentham argues, "that, when the abolition of it is advantageous to society, should not be abolished."[13]

John Stuart Mill likewise believed that rights exist only within a social context and are derived from the principle of utility: We have a right to walk the streets without fear of being molested or robbed, because society has a duty of non-maleficence to protect us from harm:

> When we call anything a person's rights, we mean that he has a valid claim on society to protect him in the possession of it, either by the force of law, or by that of education and opinion . . .

> To have a right, then, is, I conceive, to have something which society ought to defend me in the possession of. If the objector goes on to ask, why it ought? I can give him no other reason than general utility.

Unlike Bentham, who argued that there are no absolute and inalienable rights, Mill believed that the right of individual liberty is absolutely binding on society and that the only time our liberty can be curtailed is when we are using it to interfere with another person's liberty rights. Mill argued that people have a right to their own bodies and should be free to pursue their own plans as long as they do not harm anyone else.

One of the difficulties with using the principle of utility as the sole basis of rights is that there is no right to life—what many consider to be the most basic right—independent of utility. If it would benefit society to deprive certain people of their lives—bombing cities or killing handicapped children—then, according to the principle of utility, we ought to do so. Individual rights, in other words, cannot be reduced to utility. The greatest good for the greatest number is not necessarily good for the individual.

Immanuel Kant also argued that rights stem from duties. "Respect for the rights of others," Kant wrote, "is rooted in principle." According to Kant, the basis of rights is not the principle of utility but the categorical imperative. Because the categorical imperative requires that we treat other persons with dignity, one of our chief duties is respect for the rights of others. Rights protect our status as people. The categorical imperative does not create any specific rights but rather the formal right to be treated with respect. Our equal right to be treated with dignity is the strongest claim we can assert; it does not need to be justified. According to Kant,

> It is our duty to regard [others] as sacred and to respect and maintain them as such . . . Woe unto him who trespasses upon the right of another and tramples it underfoot! His right should be his security; it should be stronger than any shield or fortress.

Kant argued that, as beings with intrinsic worth, we all have an equal right to share in the goods provided us by nature. God has provided the bounty of nature, but the dividing up of the goods has been left to humans. Therefore, the duty of justice requires each of us to make sure that others receive an equal share and that we each restrict our own consumption. Those of us who have a greater share of the world's wealth, Kant says, have a duty to be charitable and to share our wealth with those who are poor.

When people begin to ignore human dignity, it will not be long before they begin to ignore human rights.

—G. K. CHESTERTON, *All Is Grist* (1932)

In both Judaism and Christian liberation ethics, the right to own land is limited by the landowners' duty to share with the poor. The Torah requires landowners to leave portions of their fields and vineyards for the poor, so they will not go hungry (Leviticus 14:9–10; Deuteronomy 24:19–20). In a similar manner, a person has a right to food stamps because the state has a duty of distributive justice to ensure that citizens have certain social goods that are essential to a life of dignity. The connection of duty to rights is particularly strong in modern Christian liberation ethics, as is the demand for equal rights for those who are currently being oppressed.

The Catholic Concept of Human Nature

The Roman Catholic theory of human rights is based in natural law theory, which is, in turn, based upon the concepts that (1) humans are rational and, therefore, have free will and (2) our human nature is the source of our rights and duties. Although Catholics ground rights in human nature and a theological worldview, as in natural rights ethics, the notion of rights is also strongly linked with the concept of duty. The belief in our duty to respect the intrinsic worth and rights of all humans—even those who are not rational or sentient—has made Catholic natural law ethicists adamant in their opposition to abortion and euthanasia—particularly involuntary euthanasia.

> Any human society, if it is to be well-ordered and productive, must lay down as a foundation this principle, namely, that every human being is a person, that is, his nature is endowed with intelligence and free will. By virtue of this, he has rights and duties, flowing directly and simultaneously from his very nature. These rights are therefore universal, inviolable and inalienable.
>
> —POPE JOHN XXIII, "Pacem in terris" (1963), para. 9

The classic expression of the Roman Catholic doctrine on human rights is contained in Pope John XXIII's 1963 encyclical "Pacem in terris," which affirms the equality of all humans "by reason of their natural dignity." Furthermore, the rights that stem from natural law should be protected by human law and special programs to ensure the rights of "the less fortunate members of the community [who are] less able to defend their rights."[14]

The Catholic Church is still in the process of assimilating human rights theory. Although the church has been a powerful force in the international fight for equal human rights, it has been accused of ignoring the human rights doctrine within its own Canon of Law by excluding women from ordained ministry and from most positions of power within the church and by forbidding men who are ordained the right to marry and restricting their right to freedom of inquiry and expression. The church has responded to these accusations by stating that "the principles which rightly apply to human societies in general do not apply to the church because of its divine institution, its supernatural end, its specific objectives and practice, and its dependence on Scripture for its basic norms and structure."[15] However, this raises the question of whether God would require immoral means—in this case, the denial of basic rights—to achieve a divine end. Some Catholic ethicists argue that the denial of these rights is inconsistent with natural law theory.

> Are we to suppose that human development proceeds along radically different lines once we enter the ecclesial sphere—and that the innermost truth about humanity is at odds with the development of human personality and human rights?
>
> —JOHN LANGAN (Jesuit priest), "Human Rights in Roman Catholicism" (1982)

Prima Facie Rights and Duties

The concept of moral duties is generally considered to be broader than that of rights. Moral rights imply a corresponding duty, but not all duties have a corresponding right. The duty of beneficence, which entails doing good merely for the sake of good, does not imply that others have a right to our kindness and services. Community service is generally based on the duty of beneficence; however, once you make a commitment to perform community service, such as serving at a soup kitchen on a particular day, the people you are working with now have a right, based on your duty of fidelity, to expect your services on that day.

Like duties, most rights are prima facie rather than absolute and can be overridden in a particular case by a more compelling right or duty. For example, we do not have an absolute right to freedom of speech or to own property. The duty of non-maleficence, to use another example, is more compelling than the freedom to yell "fire" in a crowded theater. Our right to own property is limited by the duty of justice. On the other hand, the extent to which our right to own property is limited will vary from culture to culture. As we pointed out earlier, the principles underlying moral duties and rights are very general; consequently, their application in a particular context and the relative importance of each of these prima facie rights and duties can vary tremendously.

When Cultures Clash

Divergent interpretations and ordering of rights and duties can lead to conflict when two cultures come together. In the West, we regard liberty rights as more compelling than duties of fidelity stemming from our membership in a community. Confucian deontologists, on the other hand, regard parents' rights to filial loyalty from their children to be more important than the children's individual liberty rights.

This clash between the Western emphasis on individual rights and the Eastern emphasis on communal rights is evident in the following example. During the mid-nineteenth century, a group of Brahmins (the priestly caste in India) came before the British magistrate with the complaint that the outcasts, who had traditionally pulled their car, had refused to do so since becoming Christians. Without the outcasts pulling the car, the religious feast could not be held. It was the duty of the outcasts to provide physical labor for the rest of the community; hence, the Brahmins had a right to expect the outcasts to perform this duty. After a careful study of the case, the British magistrate decided not to take action against the outcasts, because he believed that by becoming Christians they had assumed new duties and rights. In coming to this decision, the magistrate placed individual liberty rights above the rights of the community. In the mind of the British magistrate, to force the outcasts to pull the cart would have been a violation of their right to religious freedom.[16]

The diversity among cultures has led some people to conclude that the concept of rights is culturally relative and a Western invention. Cultural relativists point out that many non-Western nations have cultural customs which do not respect the rights of women, children, and certain groups. These are their values and, repulsive though they may seem to us, we should not interfere with them. A case in point is the custom of female circumcision, which is practiced in more than 20 African countries and some parts of Asia. Many Western nations find this practice barbaric and oppressive to women, yet a majority of the women in these cultures see it as a rite of passage into womanhood. Most ethicists disagree with the cultural relativists, however. They argue that the duty to respect the dignity of all humans may require us to interfere when the rights that affirm that dignity are being seriously violated.

In 1994, for example, the United Nations created a tribunal to investigate human rights violations against women in Rwanda. Human rights advocate M. Cherif Bassiouni supported the United Nation's efforts to prosecute war crimes against women in Rwanda. "[Rape]," she says, "is a great way to destroy a person. It destroys dignity and self-esteem. It weakens you to your core."[17] Although some people protested the creation of this tribunal as Western nations "forcing" their moral standards on other cultures, other groups, particularly international women's groups, applauded the attention the world has finally given to gender-related acts of violence such as rape.

Respecting human rights on an international level also involves respecting cultural diversity and national self-determination. On the other hand, respect for the equal rights of all people also involves a duty to protest cultural practices that trample upon the most basic human rights of certain groups of people, thereby depriving them of their dignity.

Exercises

1. Are the various "natural human rights"—such as the right of self-preservation and the right to life, liberty, property, and happiness—always consistent with the duty to respect human dignity? Support your answer.

2. In the United States, religious freedom is curtailed when it interferes with the collection of taxes. Pacifists and conscientious objectors are compelled, despite their objections, to pay taxes to support the military. If pacifists refuse to pay their federal income taxes, their salary can be garnished and their property seized. How would Locke, Marx, and Mill each respond to this limitation placed on the right to religious freedom and freedom of conscience by our duty to share in the financial burden of our society?

3. Like duties, most rights are prima facie. Do we have a *moral* right to own handguns? (Do not confuse moral right with legal or constitutional right, when discussing this issue.) Does the alleged right to own a handgun conflict with any other moral rights or duties? If so, what are these other rights and duties? Are they more compelling than the right to own a handgun? Support your answer.

4. A U.N. International Criminal Tribunal was formed in 1993 to investigate reports of atrocities and human rights violations in Bosnia. Dusko Tadic, a "simple" café owner who looks like an "ordinary Joe," is being charged with participating with fellow Bosnian Serbs in "murders, rapes, assaults, and tortures in mid-1992, primarily at the notorious Omarska prison camp where thousands of Muslims and Croats were held."[18]

   Either as individuals or as a nation or as members of the United Nations, do we have a duty to interfere in other nations' affairs when we perceive apparent human rights violations, such as in Bosnia and the Middle East? If so, what does honoring this duty require? Is the use of violence acceptable? If so, to what extent?

Buddhist Rights Ethics

[R]espect for the individual and the recognition of rights is not a static but a dynamic fact which makes it imperative that as we affirm our own individual rights we must also be willing to give up ourselves in order to affirm the rights of others.

—TAITETSU UNNO, "Personal Rights and Contemporary Buddhism" (1988), p. 140

Although Western philosophers have done an admirable job by calling our attention to human rights, they did not discover human rights. Buddhists, in particular, have been very active in many of the contemporary rights movements. The principle of human rights can be found in Buddha's teachings on the "Holy Community" (*Aryasamgha*). Unlike natural law ethics and natural rights ethics, Buddhist ethics is not founded upon a theological world-view that places humans below God but above nonhuman animals. Instead, the reality of human interdependence with all other beings is at the heart of contemporary Buddhist rights ethics: The world shares in the sufferings and joys of all. Buddhism, therefore, stresses the importance of cultivating universal awareness, including harmony with nature. Our most important duty is not to harm living beings (ahimsa). Given the principle that all living beings, not just humans, have a correlative right not to be harmed, then, the right to be treated with respect extends not just to humans but to all of nature.

Buddhist rights ethics affirms the absolute worth of the individual being; at the same time, it also regards the individual as subservient to the good of the many— not in a hierarchical but in a relational sense. Rights do not exist as some abstract and inalienable list of individual claims, but instead are grounded in experience and our participation in the universal whole. The concepts of equality and moral rights are meaningful only to the extent that they belong to the greater holistic realm of existence. When applied to a single individual, rights are meaningless, because the concept of one being existing independently of its context—nature as well as society—is incomprehensible to Buddhists.

Events originate in relationship. Consequently, we have a duty to affirm and respect the rights and dignity of others. To see ourselves as isolated individuals is to fragment or truncate ourselves. To be true to the self is to extend beyond oneself. Each event in our lives—each life process—is "virtually dependent on or related to all the elements present within the surroundings . . . In other words, each individual is responsible for maintaining an extensive concern for everything that lies in his or her path of experience."[19]

> What is necessary is a new understanding of reality, a new vision of the ideal community, based on the interdependence and interconnectedness of life, such that each reality becomes simultaneously master and servant to others. When this is realized on an elemental level, there is no room for any form of ego or self-assertion—one claiming superiority over all others—for that goes against the true nature of reality and spells self-destruction.
>
> —TAITETSU UNNO, "Personal Rights and Contemporary Buddhism" (1988), p. 145[20]

To achieve self-actualization, we need to break out of the shell of individualism and "to appreciate the greater extensive realm of existence in which we basically live and thrive."[21] Because morality demands that we continually expand our moral community and realm of existence, it does not make sense in Buddhist ethics to speak of rights from a strictly human point of view. Relationship involves not just other human beings but all living beings and all of nature. Western natural rights ethics, in contrast, allows and even encourages us to regard nature purely objectively and to continue to exploit it, which devalues both humans and nonhumans.

> When non-self is manifested, when each reality reveals itself in suchness, one realizes the interdependence and interconnectedness of all life, the true form of existence more real and elemental than anything conceivable by human consciousness alone. In this understanding human beings are not the center of the universe . . . Such an understanding inevitably leads to the realization that what we call "rights" inheres not only in people but equally in all sentient beings, as well as in nature itself.
>
> —TAITETSU UNNO, "Personal Rights and Contemporary Buddhism"[22]

Contemporary Buddhist ethicists regard the egoism of natural rights ethicists, and their contention that rights belong only to those who have the power to assert these rights, as destructive to individual self-realization and to community. They argue that we cannot solve worldwide problems of human misery and environmental destruction while permitting a pluralism based on individualism that allows people the right to freely pursue their own concept of the good life at the expense of other human and nonhuman beings.

> *Samma ajiva* stands for the perfect purity of livelihood, devoted entirely to the pursuit of the ideal of sainthood . . . *samma ajiva* draws attention to the necessity of adopting a morally acceptable means of livelihood and avoiding occupations that might be materially productive but morally reprehensible. These occupations include trading in weapons, living beings, flesh, intoxicants or drugs and poisons.
>
> —P. DON PREMASIRI, "The Relevance of the Eightfold Path" (1991), pp. 138–139

The Buddhist concept of right livelihood involves, above all, avoiding occupations that harm others. Our Western economy, based on an individualistic concept of natural human rights, where there is no correlative duty to act compassionately and avoid harming others, has created a world where danger and misery abound. P. Don Premasiri, a philosopher at the University of Peradeniya in Sri Lanka, writes: "Commercial interests associated with excessive greed hinder responsible people from taking effective measures to prevent the miseries resulting from these social menaces." He suggests that Buddhist ethics offers an alternative communal vision of rights that may have even greater relevance for today's world than it did in Buddha's time.

Exercises

1. Examine your college major and your future career plans in light of the Buddhist concept of right livelihood and in light of the libertarian concept of laissez-faire capitalism. Which approach do you think is most consistent with the demands of Kant's categorical imperative? Explain.

2. Buddhist ethicists see rights not in individualistic terms, but in relation to our membership in the global community. How should we, as members of a wealthy nation, balance our rights with the rights of survival of people in poorer nations? How might a Buddhist ethicist answer this question? Discuss your answer in light of your own lifestyle and our national policy.

3. Discuss what changes, if any, the adoption of Buddhist rights ethics as the foundation of our economy would have on our lifestyle in the United States. How might Locke, Marx, and Gustavo Gutierrez, respectively, respond to these changes?

Liberty Rights and Welfare Rights

Each person is to have an equal right to the most extensive liberty compatible with a similar liberty for others.   —JOHN RAWLS, *A Theory of Justice* (1971), p. 60

No one can compel me to be happy in accordance with his conception of the welfare of others, for each may seek his happiness in whatever way he sees fit, so long as he does not infringe upon the freedom of others to pursue a similar end which can be reconciled with the freedom of everyone else within a workable general law—i.e. he must accord to others the same right as he enjoys himself.

—IMMANUEL KANT, "On the Relationship of Theory to Practice in Political Right" (1792)

Just as there are different categories of duties, rights can also be divided into different types. Moral rights are generally divided into liberty rights and welfare rights. **Welfare rights** entail the right to receive certain social goods such as adequate nutrition, housing, education, and police and fire protection. **Liberty rights** entail the right to be left alone to pursue our legitimate interests without interference from the government or other people. Our **legitimate interests** are those that do not violate other people's similar and equal interests. A murderer, for example, may have an interest in being found not guilty in a court of law, but she does not have the right to an innocent verdict. A misogynist may have an interest in keeping women out of the workplace, but this does not give him the right to discriminate in hiring, because that would violate women's right to equal opportunity. Parents may have an interest in having a night on the town with a friend, but they do not have the right to do so if this violates their young children's right to security and reliable supervision.

Legitimate Interests

According to libertarians, respect for other people entails allowing them the freedom to develop and exercise the capacities that are necessary for them to pursue their own concept of the good. This includes freedom of speech, religion, and privacy, as well as freedom from coercive interference from the government. Consequently, most libertarians—such as Locke, Rand, and Mill—believe in minimal government. The freedom to choose or to discover the life that is best for oneself is basic to the exercise of autonomy. This freedom is limited only by an appeal to one's sense of reason and fairness.

> Individuals have rights and there are things no person or group may do to them (without violating their rights). So strong and far-reaching are these rights that they raise the question of what, if anything, the state and its officials may do . . . Our main conclusions about the state are that a minimal state, limited to the narrow functions of protection against force, theft, fraud, enforcement of contracts, and so on, is justified; that any more extensive state will violate a person's rights not to be forced to do certain things, and is unjustified.
>
> —ROBERT NOZICK, *Anarchy, State and Utopia* (1974), p. ix

Buddhist ethics, on the other hand, interprets legitimate interests in a more communal fashion. Our economic freedoms, including our choice of a career, are subject to restrictions imposed upon us by right livelihood. Rather than simply considering the interests of the individual, the restrictions entailed by the concept of right livelihood serve to protect the integrity of the entire moral community.

Liberty Rights

According to utilitarians, liberty rights stem from the principle of utility. Our legitimate interests include anything that tends to increase (or at least not to decrease) pleasure for the greatest number. For a Kantian deontologist, however, our legitimate interests are circumscribed by the categorical imperative, which prohibits us from treating another person only as a means no matter how many other people will benefit. Consider the example of a Peeping Tom on campus who gets great pleasure from secretly watching coeds undress in their dormitory rooms. Deontologists would argue that this sort of pleasurable "peeping" at someone without their permission is not a legitimate interest. It is wrong for a Peeping Tom to use these women only as a means *even if* the women do not know what was happening and even if neither their happiness nor their freedom is affected by the action of the Peeping Tom. The women's liberty rights place limitations on how we may treat another person *independently* of the consequences. In other words, would-be Peeping Toms have a duty to respect the privacy rights of women, independently of the consequences of doing so.

Because we are humans, we also have a moral duty to respect ourselves. Our liberty rights, in other words, are limited by our duty to treat ourselves and others with respect. We do not have the right to do anything that could infringe upon our own legitimate interests. According to Kant, as humans, our primary interest is the exercise of our rationality and autonomy. Thus, suicide is an abomination because it involves the misuse of freedom of action to destroy oneself and one's freedom: ". . . if I kill myself," Kant wrote, "I use my powers to deprive myself of the faculty of using them. That freedom, the principle of the highest order of life, should annul itself and abrogate the use of itself conflicts with the fullest use of freedom."[23]

> When . . . disappointments and hopeless misery have quite taken away the taste for life; when a wretched man, strong in soul and more angered at his fate than faint-hearted or cast down, longs for death and still preserves his life without loving it—not from inclination or fear but from duty; then indeed his maxim has a moral content.[24]

My life may seem worthless to me or I may be a burden to others, but this is not a sufficient reason for me to bring about my demise.

As a liberal democracy, in the United States we tend to place more importance on liberty rights than on welfare rights. Ayn Rand's rational egoism represents the extreme **libertarian** position, where liberty rights are the only type of rights we are bound to respect. Our choice of a career and how to use our property, including when to buy and sell it, are carefully protected rights in many Western societies. Our emphasis on liberty rights at the expense of welfare rights, however, tends to seriously handicap those who are unable to assert their liberty rights either because of natural disadvantages or because of

traditional roles that limit their options. Simply granting access to certain social goods, such as jobs and education, will not ensure that people will actually be able to purchase or acquire the goods that they need to pursue their
legitimate interests.

Welfare Rights

Gustavo Gutierrez believes that, when working toward the liberation of the
poor, it is far more important to focus on welfare rights than on liberty rights.
When people finally have these welfare rights, he argues, the other liberty
rights will follow. Welfare rights are important, because without a minimal
standard of living, we cannot pursue our legitimate interests. Because we cannot pursue these legitimate interests without certain social goods such as
housing, food, and education, society has a duty to provide and protect these
conditions. In socialist countries, for example, health care is regarded as a
welfare right, and society has a duty to provide its citizens with adequate
health care. In the United States, on the other hand, health care is a privilege.
The only duty the government has in this regard is to protect citizens' liberty
to seek or purchase health care; the government does not have a duty to provide universal health care. Nor does the government have a duty to provide
jobs and housing. The American belief is that, when people are free, then we
can acquire these goods on our own. After all, no one is preventing the jobless
from looking for a job or the homeless from finding a place to live. Libertarians, in particular, object to anything more than a very limited concept of welfare rights, because welfare rights require that someone else, whether another
individual or the government, supply us with social goods. Jobs, schools,
subsidized housing, and medical technology do not occur naturally but are
goods and services produced either directly or through taxation.

> If some men are entitled by right to the products of the work of others, it means
> that those others are deprived of rights and condemned to slave labor.
>
> Any alleged "right" of one man, which necessitates the violation of the rights of
> another, is not and cannot be a right.
>
> —AYN RAND, "Man's Rights" (1963)[25]

John Rawls, like Locke and Rand, believes that the best society places a
premium on noninterference and freedoms such as freedom of speech, freedom of the press, and the freedom to pursue one's concept of the good. However, Rawls departs from a strict libertarian model in regard to claims over

property and other social goods that are necessary for a person to pursue their own interests or their concept of the good. As you may recall from the previous chapter, Rawls states that differences in wealth are permissible only if they serve to benefit the least well-off in society. Justice requires that those who fared poorly in the "natural lottery" are entitled to the same as those who fared well.

To achieve this end, Rawls devised a means whereby society could distribute social goods taking into consideration people's equal interest without interfering with their individual rights—especially those of the people who produce these social goods. He concluded that our right to the products of our labor are arbitrary rather than absolute. We do not have an absolute right to goods that others desperately need, but are merely a surplus for us. Rawls' attempt to resolve the apparent conflict between our liberty rights and the demands of those who are disadvantaged for the products of our labor has been tremendously fruitful and has since been used in formulating policies regarding both political and economic rights. For example, Rawls' model was used to generate a health care policy for the United States to provide state-funded medical care for those who could not afford it and yet allow others the liberty to purchase the best medical care they could afford.

> We see then that the difference principle represents, in effect, an agreement to regard the distribution of natural talents as a common asset.
>
> —JOHN RAWLS, *A Theory of Justice* (1971), p. 101

One of the problems in formulating public policies regarding the distribution of social goods is defining what counts as welfare rights. Do we have a right to free medical care? If so, do we have a welfare right only to minimal medical care or to the best medical care available? Do we also have a right to a college education? Does this mean that we have a right to free tuition if we cannot afford to pay for it ourselves? Do we have a right to a happy childhood?

The extent and limits of our liberty rights can be just as ambiguous. Do we have a right to work in an obscenity-free environment? Or does freedom of speech entail that our coworkers have a right to use obscene language in the workplace? Does freedom of the press extend to publishing racist and sexist material? Do people have a right to smoke cigarettes in public buildings such as restaurants?

Former United Nations ambassador Jeane Kirkpatrick believes that the rhetoric of rights has gotten out of hand. She compares our current practice of issuing endless declarations of human rights to writing "a letter to Santa

Claus." People now have "rights" to such things as "full development of personality," to "peace," to a "new economic order." The assumption that rights are natural and do not have to be justified has contributed to this problem. The list of rights, Kirkpatrick writes, "can multiply indefinitely because no clear standard informs them, and no great reflection produced them." She points out that, when people lack the ability to assert these ideal rights or to fulfill their life goals, they complain that someone or some government must be depriving them of their rights. Kirkpatrick argues that having an interest in achieving a goal is not the same as having a right to that goal and that what is needed instead is a discussion of liberty and welfare rights within a realistic social setting instead of a utopian context.

Exercises

1. Which is most important—liberty rights or welfare rights? Make a list of the rights that you think are most important and another list of those that you consider least important. Which type of rights, liberty or welfare, occurs most in each list? Discuss.

2. Libertarians believe that the power of the government should be limited. In which of the following cases would it be morally acceptable for the government to limit our liberty? Support your answers.

   a. mandatory schooling laws

   b. forcing the homeless into shelters when the temperature drops well below freezing

   c. mandatory steroid and drug testing for athletes

   d. mandatory AIDS testing for medical workers

   e. prohibiting people under twenty-one from purchasing alcohol

3. The line between a liberty right, such as freedom of speech and freedom of the press, and pursuing activities that infringe upon someone else's rights is not always easy to discern. In his book *On Liberty,* John Stuart Mill argued that "liberty of the press [was] one of the securities against corrupt tyrannical government," including the "tyranny of the majority" in democratic countries. Should freedom of the press extend to the publication of inflammatory statements by anti-American militia members? Why or why not? Should freedom of the press include the right to publish pornography? Why or why not?

4. In February 1991, a student was expelled from Brown University for shouting racist, homophobic, and anti-Semitic epithets outside a campus dormitory. The student was drunk at the time. This was the second time the student had been found guilty of violating school rules against engaging in "abusive, threatening or demeaning actions based on race, religion, gender, handicap, ethnicity, national origin, or sexual orientation." President Vartan

Gregorian of Brown University assured the press that Brown University never has and never would expel anyone for exercising freedom of speech. However, Gregorian defended the university's action in this case by arguing that, although the university's code of conduct does not limit free *speech,* it does prohibit *actions* that show "flagrant disregard for the well-being of others."

Do you agree with Gregorian? When, if ever, does speech become action? Discuss how you would have handled the situation if you had been president of Brown University.

5. Lawyer Alan Dershowitz argues that the current trend toward "political correctness" on college campuses is a serious threat to intellectual freedom and promotes intolerance. He notes that the P.C. movement contains two contradictory tenets: "(1) the demand for 'greater diversity' among students and faculty members; and (2) the need for 'speech codes,' so that racist, sexist and homophobic ideas, attitudes and language do not 'offend' sensitive students." Do you agree with Dershowitz that the P.C. movement is a serious threat? How would Mill most likely respond to Dershowitz's argument? How would Gregorian (see previous question) most likely respond?

6. Some people claim that we have a "right not to know." However, as philosophers such as Socrates have pointed out, ignorance can be a vice as well as a means of resistance. Do we have a "right not to know"? If so, when do we have this right? For example, do people living in a democracy have a right to remain ignorant about public policy and issues? Or do they have a duty to become informed?

7. In the United States, where liberty rights generally take precedence over welfare rights, people have a "right not to know" about their AIDS status, even though AIDS can potentially harm themselves and others.

On the other hand, in many states, prisoners can be tested for AIDS without their permission; however, they may still retain the right for others not to know about their status. In some states, convicted rapists and child molesters who are HIV positive or who have another sexually transmitted disease have a legal right to privacy regarding their status. Is their right to privacy, in this case, a moral right as well? If so, should this right override the victims' welfare right to information about potential threats to their health? Do people have a welfare right to know whether a potential partner is infected with the HIV virus? If so, would this justify mandatory AIDS testing?

8. To what extent do people have the right to live in an area that is potentially dangerous? If they have a liberty right to build their homes where they please, do they also have a welfare right to be protected from that danger or to be compensated if they are harmed? Does the government have a duty to compensate victims of natural disasters such as floods and hurricanes who knowingly build (and even rebuild) their homes in areas that are prone to natural disasters? Does the government have a duty to protect people's homes from natural disasters by building hurricane barriers, dams, or other barriers to divert mudslides and floods? Or should the government forbid

people to build homes in high-risk areas that are subject to repeated natural disasters?

9. Do you agree with Jeane Kirkpatrick's criticism of the current proliferation of rights declarations? How can we determine when the claim to a particular right is a "reasonable expectation" and when it is more like writing a "letter to Santa Claus"?

Rights and the Moral Community

Rights arise, and can be intelligibly defended, only among beings who actually do, or can, make moral claims against one another.　　　　　　　—CARL COHEN (1986)[26]

The possession of rights has been interpreted as stemming from either (a) the power of self-assertion or (b) the interests of beings who may or may not be moral agents. These two models are based on two different paradigms that often come into conflict in discussions over who has what rights and what it means to be the bearer of certain rights.

Traditional natural rights ethics supports a model of rights based on self-assertion. According to the self-assertion model, the only beings who have rights are those who can make and defend moral claims. Humans, as beings created in the image of God, have a capacity for rationality and autonomy. Nonhuman animals lack this capacity for moral choice and self-assertion. Therefore, only humans are members of the moral community.

The Self-Assertion Model of Rights

Mary Anne Warren, in her essay "On the Moral and Legal Status of Abortion," supports the self-assertion model of rights. She uses the following list of criteria to determine who is a person and, as such, has rights that we are bound to respect. Warren defines "person" as someone who possesses at least some of the following attributes:

1. Consciousness and . . . the capacity to feel pain;
2. Reason (the developed capacity to solve new and relatively complex problems);
3. Self-motivated activity . . . ;
4. The capacity to communicate . . . on indefinitely many possible topics;
5. The presence of self-concepts and self-awareness . . .[27]

According to Warren, some humans, such as fetuses, newborns, the comatose, and those who are severely mentally retarded, are not persons and, therefore, are not the bearer of rights—except indirectly. An infant may have rights but only indirectly because of the rights of the parents; however, an unwanted infant has no right to life, because the right to life in the case of a nonperson is indirect and dependent upon the child being wanted by a person. In a similar manner, animal companions such as dogs and cats may have indirect rights that other nonhuman animals lack, because their humans have property rights regarding them that we are bound to respect:

> . . . it follows from my argument that when an unwanted or defective infant is born into a society which cannot afford and/or is not willing to care for it, then its destruction is permissible.

One of the problems with this concept of moral community is that it not only excludes fetuses and nonhuman animals but all infants and small children as well as humans with severe brain damage. Yet, we generally recognize and protect the rights of small children and humans with severe brain damage, despite the fact that they are not generally recognized as being capable of free moral judgment and, in some cases, have no potential for rationality.

Another problem with this self-assertion model is its assumption that self-assertion of rights depends on rational thought. Many nonhuman animals, as well as infants, respond with indignation when their interests or needs are ignored or thwarted. They certainly seem to recognize moral claims and respond to them at some level, even though they may lack the power to actually make others acknowledge their rights.

Also, the use of the possession of reason as a necessary criterion to be a bearer of rights not only excludes many humans from the moral community—it also does not succeed in creating a clear line between humans and other animals. Indeed if other animals were incapable of relatively complex reason and of making decisions based on their reasoning, however, there would be no point in using nonhuman animals in learning experiments. On the other hand, the suggestion put forth by philosophers such as Kant and Warren that other animals lack free will and self-consciousness because we cannot prove that they have these faculties is based on the fallacy of ignorance for the most part, rather than any actual proof.

The Interests Model of Rights

An alternative model regarding rights and the moral community is one based upon the principle of equal consideration of interests rather than on self-assertion. The existence of interests is based on our capacity for suffering and pleasure and our concept of the good life. Infants have a right to a secure and safe environment because it is in their interests. The interests model starts with the presumption of moral equality. The principle of equality among humans, as we have already noted, is not based on an empirical description of the actual equality of humans but upon a moral ideal of equal concern for others. This principle of equal respect applies to all humans, regardless of their social and political power or their particular abilities.

The self-assertion model, in contrast, limits "equal" respect to only those humans who have the power to demand respect from others. By doing so, the self-assertion model sets up a contradiction between the principle of equal respect and its claim that rights are based on self-assertion. To make equality of rights based on the possession of rationality and the power of self-assertion is a denial of equal human rights.

> They talk about this thing in the head; what do they call it? ["Intellect," whispered someone nearby.] That's it. What's that got to do with women's rights or Negroe's rights? If my cup won't hold but a pint and yours holds a quart, wouldn't you be mean not to let me have my little half-measure full?
>
> —SOJOURNER TRUTH (1850s)[28]

Pros and Cons of the Two Models

Both the self-assertion model and the interests model have problems in their application. The self-assertion model fails to take into account the social context in which people assert their rights. With the self-assertion model, those with social and political power are able to assert their rights at the expense of those who are weak. The inability of certain groups of people to assert their rights leads to their further degradation, because moral value is measured in terms of ability to assert rights. The interests model, on the other hand, allows the weak and those unwilling to assert themselves to fulfill their interests at the expense of those who work hard.

We believe that people who work hard should be rewarded for their effort, but most of us also believe that those who, through no fault of their own, are unable to pursue their interests have a right to some help. Much of public policy consists in determining what constitutes a legitimate interest and just when this interest becomes a claim upon others.

Discussions of equality and rights in traditional Western moral philosophy have generally been limited to questions of human equality. The impassioned battle for equal rights for all groups of humans during the various civil rights movements fueled a demand for respect for the rights of nonhuman animals as well. Many people who were engaged in the movements for equal rights for humans, such as Mohandas Gandhi, Mary Wollstonecraft, Lord Shaftesbury, Susan B. Anthony, Elizabeth Cady Stanton, Lucy Stone, and Horace Greeley, to name only a few, later became involved in the animal rights movement. Animal liberationist Peter Singer points out that not only humans have legitimate interests:

> Racists violate the principle of equality by giving greater weight to the interests of members of their own race when there is a clash between their interests and the interests of those of another race. Sexists violate the principle of equality by favoring

the interests of their own sex. Similarly, speciesists allow the interests of their own species to override the greater interests of members of other species. The pattern is identical in each case.

If we are to take the concept of "equal interests" seriously, then it must be extended not just to humans but to all sentient beings.

The moral equality of all sentient beings, however, does not entail that humans and nonhuman animals both have the same rights. Different species of nonhuman animals have different interests. There are distinctly human rights, such as the right to religious freedom and the right to a formal education, that other animals lack, because they have no interest in either organized religion or formal schooling. Different people also have different interests. For example, men do not have a right to a mammogram. Able-bodied humans do not have a right to disability insurance. People living in a culture where formal education is necessary to pursue one's interests have a right to an education, but in a society of hunters and gatherers, there is no right to a formal education.

However, all sentient animals—including humans, cats, mice, and birds—have an interest in not being tortured, not because they are capable of rational thought but because they have the capacity to feel pain. The right of nonhuman animals to have enough space in which to pursue their interests is recognized and minimally respected in the Animal Welfare Act and its amendments, regulating minimum space requirements for "laboratory animals." The Animal Welfare Act also expects experimenters to respect animals' interests in health care, proper nutrition, and a clean living space; however, the act does not recognize their liberty rights or their right to life.

> While it is generally acknowledged by philosophers that liberty and freedom from coercion are essential if we humans are to develop and lead the types of lives where we can exercise our powers as rational agents, it is also true that liberty is necessary for many non-human animals if they are to live the sorts of lives, and thrive, in ways that are natural to them.
>
> —JAMES RACHELS, "Why Animals Have a Right to Liberty"[29]

Buddhist rights ethics extends the concept of rights, especially the right not to be harmed, not only to all living beings but to the environment as well. Like the Buddhists, Gandhi's moral philosophy centered on the interconnectedness of all life and the importance of extending moral respect to all living beings if we are ever to have a peaceful world. Gandhi, like the Buddhists, was adamantly opposed to the exploitation of nonhuman animals.

Because we are all interconnected, in Buddhism there is a strong emphasis on welfare rights and the correlative duty to provide care for everyone. Nagarjuna, in the "Friendly Epistle and Jewel Rosary of Royal Advice," for example, recommends not only the total care of all citizens and travelers passing through but also that "a special custodian be appointed to provide food, water, sugar and piles of grain to all anthills, caring also for dogs and birds."[30]

Philosopher Tom Regan, in his book *The Case for Animal Rights,* likewise argues that it is not merely an act of kindness to treat animals with respect. Animals who have desires and interests, an emotional life, and a psychophysical identity over time are what Regan calls "subjects-of-life." Subjects-of-life can be either moral agents or moral patients. Moral agents include those who can be held morally accountable. Moral patients include human infants, people who are mentally handicapped, and most mammals. Both moral agents and moral patients, as beings that are subjects-of-life, have inherent value and a right to respectful treatment. We humans can defend ourselves against other animals that pose innocent threats, such as those that are carriers of diseases harmful to humans, however, we cannot override other animals' rights simply for our own pleasure or to make a profit. The goal of wildlife management, he argues, is to defend animals' rights by providing them with the opportunity to live their own lives free of human predation and exploitation.

The idea of extending equal treatment to all beings runs contrary to the beliefs of philosophers such as Locke, who based his natural rights ethics on the belief that humans are a special and unique creation of God. To base rights on equal consideration of the interests of all living beings, rather than on the so-called special nature of humans, is to deny the "natural" order of creation. This anthropocentric, theologically based worldview of humans not only disallows the possibility of nonhuman beings having rights but grants humans the inalienable right to exploit nonhuman animals and the environment with impunity.

John Rawls points out that our current discussions of justice are limited, because they fail to "embrace all moral relationships . . . and [they] leave out of account how we are to conduct ourselves toward animals and the rest of nature."[31] He suggests that, to devise a correct description of our relations to animals and the environment, metaphysicians will have to "work out a world view that is suited for this purpose."[32]

Exercises

*1. Which model regarding the possession of rights—the self-assertion model or the interests model—is most prevalent in our society? Use examples, including those from your community service work, to support your answer.

2. Discussions of welfare and health care reform bring in the self-assertion model and the interests model. To what extent does our interest in a minimum standard of living or in good health constitute a claim on society to provide these? Does society have an obligation only to make it easier for us to assert these rights? Do children have rights? What about children who are unable to assert these rights?

3. Using John Rawls' two principles of justice, discussed in Chapter 9, page 333, devise a policy regarding the establishment of a "right" to an affordable college education. Discuss how a philosopher who supported the self-assertion model would most likely respond to this policy. Discuss how a philosopher who supported the interests model would most likely respond.

4. Tom Regan argues that other animals have a right not to be eaten by us, used in experiments, or caged in zoos. Discuss his position, in light of the self-assertion model and the interests model of rights. If we accept the self-assertion model, which states that only moral agents have rights, would this justify the use of infants and brain-damaged adults in medical experiments? Defend your position.

5. John Rawls suggests that we need a worldview (interpretation of our experience) that provides better guidance for deciding our moral relationship to other animals and to the environment. Using the three-tier model of reasoning from Chapter 2, page 37, analyze Locke's, Mary Anne Warren's, Buddha's, and Tom Regan's worldviews regarding the proper place of humans in the natural order. Which interpretation is consistent with your experience? How does this worldview affect your thinking on the rights of nonrational humans and nonhuman animals? Explain.

The Strengths and Limitations of Rights Ethics

Rights are an important component of any moral philosophy. Although few philosophers deny that rights are meaningful, the origin and nature of rights have been the focus of considerable debate. Natural rights ethics, which has had a tremendous influence on modern Western culture, has been criticized on several counts. The theological basis of natural rights ethics, which privileges humans as a special creation, is difficult, if not impossible, to justify on either philosophical or empirical grounds.

The belief of natural rights ethicists that rights are self-evident is also problematic. In fact, there is a great deal of disagreement on this issue. Marxists, in particular, have called into question the inalienable right to own property; they argue that rights are historically conceived and often work to protect those in power. The doctrine that rights are self-evident and do not need to be justified has also led to a proliferation of demands for certain rights. Without any criteria for justifying rights, there is no way to decide which of these rights should be taken seriously and which are frivolous. For this reason, most philosophers argue that rights are derived from duties and, in particular, from the fundamental duty of respect for the dignity of others.

The reduction of nonhuman animals and the environment, by natural rights ethicists, to the status of resources for humans has had devastating effects on our environment. Furthermore, the claim of natural rights ethicists that rights are based upon the principle of equality has also led animal rights advocates, such as Tom Regan, to question why this principle should not be extended also to nonhuman animals. Buddhist ethics goes even further and extends rights to all of nature.

Most rights ethicists distinguish between liberty and welfare rights; however, the separation between liberty and welfare rights is not clear-cut. The libertarian assertion that liberty rights do not involve imposing upon the rights of others to the products of their labor, as do welfare rights, ignores the need for the legal and social structures—including the police, the military, and the courts—that are necessary to protect these so-called liberty rights. Liberty rights to own property and businesses, for example, are protected by tax monies, much of which is forcibly taken from people who are too poor to own property. Thus, the self-assertion model favored by libertarians actually depends upon the backing of an extensive and expensive legal and police system.

The philosophical belief that all people are created equal has too often been treated as a description rather than as a moral ideal. Not all people are equally capable of asserting their rights. Basing rights on self-assertion therefore favors those who have access to political and social power at the expense of those who lack this power. The interests model, on the other hand, tends to favor those who are weak—whether because of the natural lottery, restrictive social roles, or just plain laziness—at the expense of those who show initiative.

Rights ethics is problematic if it is used as a complete explanation of ethics, but it is an important component of an ethics theory. Rights are not the same as duties. Rights protect our dignity as persons. The concept of rights focuses our attention on the claim that others must be treated with respect in a way that talk of duties alone does not. If we do not have rights, then all our claims to be treated with respect simply amount to requests for favors and privileges. If there are no rights to freedom and equal opportunity, then we need to make a case for having our freedom or enjoying the same opportunities that others in our society enjoy. The extension of the concept of rights to all humans and even to nonhumans has been a difficult endeavor, but one that has been very fruitful in calling our attention to the dignity of those who are somehow different from us.

Summary

1. The articulation of rights ethics in Western philosophy emerged during the *Period of Enlightenment* as a protest against the concept of *absolute sovereignty*. This dissatisfaction culminated in 1789 with the French *Declaration of the Rights of Man* and the U.S. *Bill of Rights*.

2. *Thomas Hobbes* and *John Locke* were two of the leading rights ethicists of the Enlightenment. *Thomas Jefferson* was especially influenced by the philosophy of John Locke.

3. Slavery and the denial of certain basic rights to women led to a renewed interest in rights ethics in the United States in the mid-1800s. Elizabeth Cady Stanton was active in the abolitionist and the women's rights movements.

4. Interest in human rights was once again aroused following World War II and the *Holocaust*. In 1948 the *United Nations* issued the *Universal Declaration of Human Rights*, which is based on a natural law theory interpretation of human rights.

5. *Moral rights* are not the same as *legal rights*.

6. According to *natural rights ethicists*, such as Hobbes, Locke, and Jefferson, rights are inalienable and exist independently of and prior to duty. These rights are self-evident. They stem from our human nature, which is created in the image of God. All and only humans have rights. The world was created for human use. For this reason, natural rights ethics is often referred to as *human rights ethics*.

7. According to natural rights ethicists, all humans are created equal. This is known as the *principle of equality*.

8. Hobbes and John Locke maintained that people lived in an unpleasant **state of nature** before the formation of government. The primary purpose of *government* is to protect people's equal rights.

9. Locke stated that we have a *natural right to own property*. By mixing our labor with the land, it becomes our property. Locke believed that this stipulation on private ownership would assure that there was enough land for everyone.

10. *Ayn Rand* argued that a **laissez-faire capitalist** society is the only type that can protect people's natural rights.

11. Both Locke and Rand were libertarians. A **libertarian** places more value on liberty rights. A strict libertarian is opposed to placing any social or political restraints upon individual freedom.

12. *Karl Marx* was opposed to any conception of rights that existed independently of the duty of justice. He argued that the list of so-called natural rights was historically conceived to justify certain economic and political systems and to protect the landowning *bourgeoisie*.

13. **Liberation ethicist** *Gustavo Gutierrez* is also critical of laissez-faire capitalism and its focus on liberty rights. Like Marx, he argues that the right to private ownership has been won at the expense of the rights of the poor.

14. Both Marx and Gutierrez argue that rights must be considered within a *historical context.* Westerners cannot impose their democratic notions of rights on non-Western nations.

15. Most philosophers maintain that *rights are derived from duty.* Each right has a corresponding duty.

16. *Jeremy Bentham* thought that any talk of natural rights existing independently of the laws of society was nonsense.

17. *John Stuart Mill* argued that moral rights exist only within a social context and are derived from the principle of utility. Mill also believed that liberty rights were more important than welfare rights.

18. According to *Immanuel Kant,* rights stem from the categorical imperative and from our duty to respect the dignity of all people.

19. *Natural law ethicists,* like natural rights ethicists, maintain that our rights stem from our human nature. However, they also believe that rights and duties cannot be separated and that duties are more fundamental. The Roman Catholic doctrine on human rights can be found in Pope John XXIII's 1963 encyclical **"Pacem in terris."**

20. Most philosophers consider rights to be **prima facie** rather than absolute.

21. *Buddhist rights ethics* is based on our interdependence with all living beings and our duty not to harm other living beings (**ahimsa**). In contrast to the libertarians, for the Buddhists, *right livelihood* involves respecting the rights of others and, above all, avoiding occupations that harm others.

22. There are two basic types of moral rights: **Liberty rights** entail the right to be left alone to pursue our **legitimate interests** (interests that do not violate others' similar and equal interests). **Welfare rights** entail the right to receive our proper share of certain goods.

23. *John Rawls* attempts to resolve the conflict between liberty rights and welfare rights through the application of his principles of justice.

24. Only those in the moral community possess rights. The possession of rights has been interpreted as stemming from either (a) the power of *self-assertion* or (b) the *interests* of beings. Most natural rights ethicists believe that rights are based on self-assertion.

25. *Mary Anne Warren* supports the self-assertion model of rights. The only beings who have rights are those who meet certain criteria which include consciousness, reason, self-motivation, the ability to communicate, and self-awareness.

26. The interests model is based on the principle of equality. *Tom Regan* argues that the principle of equality also applies to nonhuman beings who are the subject-of-life with their own desires and interests.

CHAPTER 11

Virtue Ethics and the Good Life

Ethics is sometimes described as the theory of virtue . . . A man
who complies with coercive laws is not necessarily virtuous.
To be virtuous man must, to be sure, respect the law and be
punctilious in his observance of human rights; but virtue goes
beyond this, to the disposition from which the action . . . arises.
—IMMANUEL KANT, "Introductory Observations,"
Lectures on Ethics

The rule of virtue can be compared to the Pole Star which
commands the homage of the multitude of Stars without leaving
its place.
—CONFUCIUS, *The Analects*[1]

The epithets sociable, good-natured, humane, merciful,
grateful, friendly, generous, beneficent, *or their equivalents,*
are known in all languages, and universally express the highest
merit, which human nature *is capable of attaining.*
—DAVID HUME, *An Enquiry Concerning the Principles*
of Morals[2]

As wealth enriches the house, so virtue enriches the person;
[for with virtue] the mind will be magnanimous and the body
relaxed.
—TSENG TZU[3]

Virtue Ethics and Character

Virtue ethics emphasizes *right being* over *right action*. The sort of person we are constitutes the heart of our moral life. More important than the rules or principles we follow is our character. Virtue ethics, however, is not an alternative to ethical theories that stress right conduct, such as utilitarianism and

385

deontological theories. Rather, virtue ethics and theories of right action complement each other.

Buddhism, Taoism, feminist care ethics, and the moral philosophies of David Hume, Aristotle, and Jesus of Nazareth are often classified as virtue ethics. Confucian ethics has strong traditions of both virtue ethics and deontology. The ancient Greek ethicists, like most Eastern ethicists, focused almost entirely on virtue and character, rather than on duty and principles.

> . . . we are not concerned to know what goodness is, but how we are to become good men, for this alone gives the study [of ethics] its practical value.
>
> —ARISTOTLE, *Nicomachean Ethics*, Bk. 2, Ch. 2

What Is a Virtue?

A virtue is more than just a feeling. A **virtue** is an admirable character trait or disposition to habitually act in a manner that benefits oneself and others. The actions of virtuous people stem from a respect and concern for the well-being of themselves and others. Compassion, courage, generosity, loyalty, and honesty are all examples of virtues. However, virtue is more than simply a collection of disparate personality traits. We often speak of virtue in terms of individual traits, yet it is more correctly defined as an overarching quality of goodness that gives unity and integrity to a person's character. The virtue of *jen* in Confucianism, for example, is translated as benevolence, love, affection, compassion, altruism, or perfect virtue.

A **vice,** in contrast, is a character trait or disposition to act in a manner that harms oneself and others. Vices stand in our way of achieving happiness and the good life. Ill will and anger, uncontrolled sexual desire, sloth and torpor, restlessness and worry, and doubt, for example, are considered in Buddhist ethics to be vices or undesirable character traits. These traits stand in the way of enlightenment and moral perfection.

Not all beneficial traits are virtues. Traits such as health and intelligence are beneficial, but they are not necessarily what we would consider virtues. What distinguishes virtues from other beneficial characteristics, according to most philosophers, is the will—the faculty that allows us to make rational choices. We do not decide to be intelligent or healthy, in the same sense that we choose to be courageous or generous. "If the will be set on virtue," Confucius taught, "there will be no practice of wickedness."[4]

Aristotle divided the virtues into two broad categories: intellectual virtues and moral virtues. The intellectual virtues, he claimed, are based on excellence in reasoning skill and include wisdom and prudence. The moral virtues include courage, temperance, liberality, generosity, magnificence, proper pride, gentleness, truthfulness, justice, patience, friendliness, modesty, and wittiness. According to Aristotle, the intellectual virtues are cultivated through growth and experience, and the moral virtues are cultivated through habit. Wisdom is the most important virtue, because it is the one that makes all other virtues (intellectual and moral) possible. However, knowledge or wisdom alone is not sufficient for moral virtue; practice is also necessary:

> [T]he moral virtues we do acquire by first exercising them. The same is true of the arts and crafts in general. The craftsman has to learn how to make things, but he learns in the process of making them . . . By a similar process we become just by performing just actions, temperate by performing temperate actions, brave by performing brave actions.

Aristotle also distinguished between moral virtues and natural virtues. Traits such as gentleness, friendliness, courage, and loyalty in a cat or a dog, or even in a child, are natural virtues rather than moral virtues because they presumably do not involve the will. In other words, Aristotle would say that Angus, my friend Dan's dog who helped to rescue some drowning swimmers, was simply doing what came naturally to him as a Labrador retriever. In contrast, Aristotle would probably argue that Dan's courageous actions, even though they may have seemed spontaneous, were the outcome of years of cultivating the virtue of courage until it became a habitual response to seeing others in danger.

Deontologist W. D. Ross likewise lists "self-improvement," or the development of a virtuous character, as one of his seven prima facie duties. Indeed, Ross is often considered an Aristotelian in his approach to ethics.[5]

One of the trademarks of virtuous people is that they not only act on principle, but they give us an example to follow: They are our heroes. Persons of character such as Harriet Tubman, Buddha, Jesus of Nazareth, Elizabeth Cady Stanton, Socrates, and Martin Luther King, Jr., do not merely give us principles to follow. More importantly, they give us an example to follow by acting as role models. Virtuous people can be counted on to act in a manner that benefits others. They also show a willingness to perform supererogatory actions—going beyond what is required by everyday morality. Vicious people, on the other hand, only perform "beneficial" actions when it benefits them.

Because people tend to emulate those who are at a higher stage of moral development, a highly virtuous person in a leadership role can have a morally uplifting effect upon the whole community. In the French village of Le Chambon, for example, 3,500 villagers rescued more than 6,000 Jews, mostly children, from the Nazis. The leader of the community was André Trocme, a local pastor who advocated nonviolent resistance to the Nazis and universal love and compassion for all people.

Virtue Ethics Explained

Virtue ethics is based upon certain assumptions about human nature, our purpose, and our potential to achieve good. Most virtue ethicists believe that virtue is important for achieving not only moral well-being, but also happiness and inner harmony. Aristotle referred to this sense of psychological well-being as **eudaemonia.** Eudaemonia is not the same as what utilitarians or egoists mean by happiness. Rather, it is the good that humans seek by nature and which arises from the fulfillment of our function as humans. Eudaemonia is similar to Eastern and modern Western concepts such as enlightenment, Nirvana, self-actualization, and proper self-esteem.[6]

People who are virtuous enjoy being so, according to Aristotle and Confucian philosopher Mencius: "What must a man be before he can be content?" the student asks Mencius. Mencius replies, "If he reveres virtues and delights in rightness, he can be content." By being virtuous, we are most true to ourselves. Therefore, virtue is essential to inner harmony and contentment. "There is no greater joy for me," Mencius continues, "than to find, on self-examination, that I am true to myself. Try your best to treat others as you would wish to be treated yourself, and you will find that this is the shortest way to benevolence."[7] Westerners will recognize this as the Golden Rule in Chinese ethics. It is known as the principle of reciprocity.

In modern Western philosophy, with our emphasis on disembodied reason, we tend to lose sight of the connection between virtue and happiness. However, there is support from social scientists for the claim that there is an intimate connection between happiness and leading a virtuous life. In a review of studies throughout the world on factors that contribute to happiness, Runt Veenhoven found that happiness levels are highest among people who value inner peace, love, sympathy, friendship, forgiveness, tolerance, and group participation—all traits that most philosophers consider virtues. Low happiness ratings were correlated with nonmoral values such as independence (especially in college-age men), freedom, and economic success.[8]

Just as virtue ethicists acknowledge the importance of action, most (if not all) moral philosophies that stress right action also recognize the role of virtue in bringing about right actions. A courageous and compassionate person is more likely to come to someone else's rescue. An honest and loyal person is more likely to carry out the duty of fidelity; a generous person is more likely to act justly than someone who is stingy; and a compassionate person is more likely to refrain from harming others. However, although virtue involves right action, it is not reducible to actions.

> There is nothing which makes [the virtuous person] so much a blessing to [other members of society] as the cultivation of disinterested love of virtue. And consequently, . . . [utilitarianism] enjoins and requires the cultivation of the love of virtue up to the greatest strength possible, as being above all things important to the general happiness.
>
> —JOHN STUART MILL, "On Liberty" (1859)

The Role of Intention

An action may be morally good because it has a certain quality, such as being beneficial; however, this in itself does not make it a virtuous act. "[N]o known ethical standard decides an action to be good or bad because it is done by an amiable, a brave, or a benevolent man, or the contrary," John Stuart Mill writes. "These considerations are relevant, not to the estimation of actions, but of persons."[9]

For example, a wealthy person may give a million dollars to a charity simply because she wants the tax deduction or a building named after her. Although the act itself is good in terms of its consequences, we would probably hesitate to say that she is virtuous for doing it. The actions of a virtuous person, on the other hand, stem from an underlying disposition of concern for the well-being of others and themselves. A poor widow may give her last coin to the needy out of compassion. Although the consequences of her action are not nearly as far-reaching as those of the wealthy patroness, most people would agree that the widow is the more virtuous of the two.

Utilitarians claim that the disposition of a person is irrelevant to the goodness of an action, but they nevertheless recognize the importance of virtue. Mill, for example, was well aware that a virtuous person is more likely to perform good actions and abstain from harming others. Being virtuous not only brings the virtuous person pleasure but also contributes to the happiness of others. For this reason, Mill argued, we ought to cultivate a virtuous and benevolent disposition. According to Mill, it is through the cultivation of our natural feelings of benevolence that we generate the "most passionate love of virtue, and the sternest self-control . . . A person whose desires and impulses are his own—are the expression of his own nature, as it has been developed and modified by his own culture—is said to have character. One whose desires and impulses are not his own, has no character, no more than a steam engine has character:[10]

> Now it is palpable that [people] do desire things which, in common language, are decidedly distinguished from happiness. They desire, for example, virtue and the absence of vice, no less really than pleasure and the absence of pain. The desire of virtue is not as universal, but it is as authentic a fact, as the desire of happiness . . . But does the utilitarian doctrine deny that people desire virtue, or maintain that virtue is not a thing to be desired? The very reverse. It maintains not only that virtue is to be desired, but that it is to be desired disinterestedly.

Cultivating the Good Will

Simply refraining from harming others or from committing injustices is not enough to make us a morally good person. It is also necessary to cultivate a good will. Through the cultivation of virtuous character, Mill claims, society does its duty and protects its interests. Performing morally good actions, in turn, strengthens a virtuous disposition. Action and practice are the means by which our natural predisposition and energies are developed into virtues. According to Mill, reflection, which includes moral analysis, provides the bridge that connects action and the cultivation of a virtuous disposition. Our actions test our old habits and call upon us to reflect on our past actions and to reevaluate ourselves and our alternatives. Reflection, which is grounded in moral values, in turn generates a habitual virtuous moral response.

> A man who, although he has learned to abstain from overt immoral acts, still persists in nursing ill-will harms himself by throwing dirt over himself, like an elephant after his bath . . . With his malevolent mind a man will be burned up. Therefore you should strive to think of all that lives with friendliness and compassion and not will ill-will and a desire to hurt.
>
> —Buddhist Scriptures[11]

In our scholarly impulse to sort everyone's philosophies into neat categories, Immanuel Kant's contribution to virtue ethics is often overlooked. Although Kant's moral philosophy focuses primarily on duty, a virtuous character, as embodied in the good will, was very important to Kant. Indeed, his *Groundwork of the Metaphysics of Morals* opens with a statement, not about duty, but about the importance of good will: "It is impossible to conceive anything at all in the world, or even out of it, which can be taken as good without qualification, except a good will."[12] Even, despite the utmost effort, if the good will is still unable to accomplish anything, it is still good for its own sake.

A person of good will, according to Kant, has good intentions. They are motivated to act for the sake of duty. A virtuous disposition, according to Kant, helps us in our struggle against unruly impulses and obstacles that stand in the way of doing our duty. The more virtuous the person, the easier this struggle will be. Although it is important to develop a virtuous character, what is important in the end is that we act from a sense of duty.

Exercises

1. What is your greatest virtue? If you cannot think of any virtues that you possess, ask your friends, family, or classmates who know you what your virtues are.

2. In Chapter 1, page 7, Question 2, you identified and described your hero. To what extent did you describe your hero in terms of his or her virtues? in terms of actions performed? Which was most important, virtues or actions, in your description? How are this person's virtues and actions related?

3. What is happiness? Do you agree that virtuous people, such as your hero, are happier than vicious people? Are you happier when you are being virtuous? How does being vicious affect you? Relate your answer to the concept of conscience discussed in Chapter 6 and to Gyges' claim in Chapter 7, that the unjust person is happiest.

4. Do you agree with Mill that most people desire virtue and the absence of vice? Answer this question in light of your own moral development and aspirations. Even if we do desire virtue, do we also have a moral duty to cultivate a virtuous character? Support your answer.

   Discuss ways, if any, in which you strive to become a more virtuous person and your motivation for trying to become more virtuous.

*5. Community service in conjunction with an opportunity to reflect on the service provides an excellent opportunity, according to developmental psychologists, to develop virtue and moral character. Discuss ways in which your community service has made you a more virtuous person.

Aristotle: Reason and Virtue

In the moral make-up of the [virtuous man] there is nothing which is at variance with
reason.   —ARISTOTLE, *Nicomachean Ethics*, Bk. 1, Ch. 13

The Importance of Reason for Aristotle

Western philosophy has long considered reason to be more important that
the sentiments or emotions. "Moral" sentiments such as sympathy have often
been dismissed as residual instincts belonging to our lower or animal nature.
Aristotle, for example, taught that the human soul is divided into the rational
and nonrational parts. He regarded humans as basically rational beings who
must strive to control our nonrational nature. Aristotle argued that the nonrational part "from which spring the appetites and desires" participates in reason in a subordinate role.

Aristotle believed that all life has a function that is peculiar to its particular life form. The function peculiar to human life, he claimed, is the exercise
of reason. The function of the excellent man, therefore, "is to exert such activity well."[13] Virtue involves living according to reason and is intimately connected to our proper function as humans. According to Aristotle, virtue is
essential if we are to achieve the good life. When all three elements of the soul
are in harmony, with reason occupying the top position, virtue and happiness
(eudaemonia) are possible (see the figure below). Happiness, Aristotle wrote,
is "an activity of the soul in conformity with perfect goodness."[14] Only by living in accord with reason, which is our human function, can we achieve happiness and inner harmony.

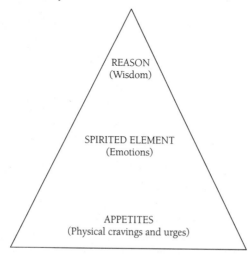

In his later writing, Aristotle equated perfect happiness with a life of contemplation, because, he argued, contemplation is the activity of the gods and,
therefore, blessed above all other activities; however, human nature is not

equal to a life of pure contemplation. Unlike the gods, we have to pursue external goods like food and companionship. For humans to be happy, therefore, we must also live a life of virtue. Buddhist ethicists also emphasize the role of contemplation in the virtuous life, but not because it is an activity of the gods. Contemplation is seen instead as an essential part of the path to achieving virtue and happiness in this life.

> [Among] human activities that which is most akin to God's will bring us the greatest happiness . . . The life of the gods is altogether happy, that of man is happy so far as it includes something that resembles the divine activity.
>
> —ARISTOTLE, *Nicomachean Ethics*, Bk. 10, Ch. 8

According to Aristotle, immorality results from a disordered psyche that is not performing its proper function, to reason well. Virtue serves as a correction to our passions by helping us to resist our impulses and by preventing our passions from interfering with us living the life of reason: the good life. For example, the virtue of courage is a corrective to the emotion of fear. Temperance is the corrective to the temptation to overindulge or to seek immediate pleasure. Aristotle, however, did not want to see passion eliminated; he recognized that emotion is an important component of moral goodness. Although our emotions and passions should always be subject to the control of reason, this is not the same as saying that emotions are bad and should be eliminated. Rather, Aristotle was saying that emotions such as fear or boldness and anger or pity are appropriate at times, but only when they are under the corrective control of reason.

Reason in Moral Philosophy

Thomas Aquinas, who was heavily influenced by Aristotle, also saw virtue as a corrective to our passions or the "animal" side of our nature. Like Aristotle, Aquinas regarded reason as the primary purpose of human life. Aquinas, however, added a new dimension to Aristotelian ethics—that of human sinfulness. In keeping with the Christian concept of human nature as corrupted by the fall, Aquinas argued that reason alone is not enough to keep humans on the right path. Without God's help, we will naturally succumb to weakness and temptation. For Aquinas, supreme happiness and virtue come from knowing God and through communication with God. Therefore, faith in God was the most important virtue to Aquinas, and pride the greatest vice:

> It is impossible for man's happiness to consist in a created good, for happiness is the perfect good which wholly brings desire to rest . . . nothing can bring the will

of man to rest except the universal good. This is not found in any created thing but only in God, for all creatures have good by participation. Hence only God can satisfy the will of man . . . Therefore, man's happiness consists in God alone . . . Ultimate and perfect happiness can only be in the vision of the divine essence.

Hindu ethics, as taught in the *Bhagavad Gita,* likewise holds that enlightenment and moral perfection are achieved by the use of reason. The good life is lived according to the dictates of the mind. The desires are part of our "lower nature," and when these are not under the control of the mind, they can lead us astray:

Even a mind that knows the path
Can be dragged from the path;
The senses are so unruly,
But he who controls the senses
And recollects the mind
And fixes it on me.
I call him illumined.[15]

According to Krishna, the supreme God of the Hindus, the enlightened person refrains from hurting himself and others and seeks through reason to cultivate a virtuous character. The perfect person

feels hatred for no contingent being . . . is friendly, . . . content and ever integrated . . . fearless and pure in heart, steadfast in the exercise of wisdom, openhanded and restrained . . . none hurting, truthful, from anger free . . . at peace, averse to calumny, compassionate to all beings, free from nagging greed, gentle, modest, never fickle, ardent, patient, enduring, pure, not treacherous nor arrogant,—such is the man who is born to inherit a godly destiny.[16]

Exercises

1. Do you agree with Aristotle that having reason control our sentiments is essential for a virtuous character? Support your answer.

2. Aristotle regarded the godly life of pure contemplation as one of pure happiness. In Buddhist ethics, in contrast, contemplation is seen as an essential ingredient on the path to both happiness and the life of virtue. What does the term "contemplation" mean to you? What role, if any, does it play in your moral life?

3. Discuss the following quotes in light of Aquinas' belief that humans are sinful by nature and Mencius' belief that humans are good by nature.
   a. "Scratch a saint, a villain bleeds; beneath each white man, Jim Crow dwells; behind every gentile, an anti-Semite lurks."[17]
   b. "All men have a mind which cannot bear to see the sufferings of others."[18]

*4. The emphasis that Aquinas and other natural law ethicists place on faith as the highest virtue has had a profound influence on both the Catholic and the Protestant concept of service and the good person. Do you consider faith a virtue? If so, in what sense is it a virtue? Discuss the following quote from Mother Teresa, in the context of your community service work.

> The fruit of SILENCE is Prayer
> The fruit of PRAYER is Faith
> The fruit of FAITH is Love
> The fruit of LOVE is Service
> The fruit of SERVICE is Peace

Confucius and Aristotle: The Doctrine of the Mean

We may now define virtue as a disposition of the soul in which, when it has to choose among actions and feelings, it observes the mean relative to us, this being determined by such a rule or principle as would take shape in the mind of a man of sense or practical wisdom. We call it a mean condition as lying between two forms of badness, one being excess and the other deficiency. —ARISTOTLE, *Nicomachean Ethics*, Bk. 2, Ch. 6

Perfect is the virtue that accords with the Constant Mean! —CONFUCIUS, *The Analects*

The doctrine of the mean is found in both Eastern and Western philosophies. According to this doctrine, virtues generally entail moderation or seeking the middle path. Buddhist ethics, for example, denounces the extremes of excessive indulgence and self-mortification or self-denial. For Buddha, the path of liberation—the life of virtue and inner tranquility—entailed taking the Middle Path, also known as the Noble Path. The most thorough explanations of the doctrine of the mean, however, are found in the philosophies of Aristotle and Confucius.

Most virtues entail finding the mean between excess and deficiency. Some character traits or dispositions, however, are good or evil in themselves. According to both Confucius and Aristotle, ignorance and malice are always vices, but wisdom is always a virtue. In Buddhist ethics, the virtue of **ahimsa** or nonharming, which is reflected in a person's behavior and attitude of respect for all living beings, is good in itself. For Confucians, "absolute sincerity" is always a virtue and is considered to be the highest virtue that we can cultivate. Just as reason and wisdom are regarded as the function of humans by Aristotle, Confucius believed that enlightenment results from sincerity. "Only those who are absolutely sincere," Confucius writes, "can fully develop their nature."

Most moral qualities, however, can be destroyed by deficiency on the one hand and excess on the other, just as physical health can be destroyed by eating too much or too little food or by too much or too little exercise. Similarly, some people take "virtues" to such an extreme that they are no longer virtues but vices. Most of us, for example, have fallen prey to a very "honest" person who delights in "telling it like it is," much to the discomfort and chagrin of their audience.

Before the feelings of pleasure, anger, sorrow, and joy are aroused it is called equilibrium (*chung*, centrality, mean). When these feelings are aroused and each and all attain due measure and degree, it is called harmony. Equilibrium is the great foundation of the world, and harmony is its universal path . . .

The superior man exemplifies the Mean (*chung-yung*). The inferior man acts contrary to the Mean.

—CONFUCIUS, "Doctrine of the Mean (*chung-yung*)"

The doctrine of the mean should not be misinterpreted as advising us to be wishy-washy or to compromise our moral standards. Aristotle and Confucius were not suggesting that we seek a consensus or take a moderate position. The doctrine of the mean is meant to apply to virtues, not to our positions on moral issues. Aristotle, by suggesting that we seek the mean, was not referring to being lukewarm or a fence-straddler but to seeking *what is reasonable* (see Table 11.1). Indeed, the most effective moral reformers have taken positions that differed sharply from the status quo. The abolitionists, as well as the early feminists, for example, were considered extremists and fanatics. The mean in this context is also not the same as the mathematical mean. There are no formulas or rules for deciding what is virtuous for a particular person in a particular situation. Instead, Aristotle writes, "virtue discovers the means and deliberately chooses it."[19] Along similar lines, for Confucius the mean is whatever is consistent with harmony and equilibrium, or The Way (Tao).

The mean is also to some extent dependent upon the individual moral agent and his or her culture. The mean in Confucian ethics entails doing what is proper to one's station in life—be it ruler, servant, or parent. Confucius pointed out that, when traveling The Way, we must start from the nearest point. This point will be lower for some people than for others. Courage, for example, which is the mean between cowardice and foolhardiness, is not the same for all people. A person who is struggling to overcome agoraphobia would be showing courage just by going outside. With repeated practice, the virtue of courage will become strengthened, until the former agoraphobic will actually enjoy going outside for walks and meeting new people. On the other hand, for a very sociable person, going outside for a walk and meeting new

TABLE 11.1 Aristotle's Doctrine of the Mean

DEFICIT (VICE)	MEAN (VIRTUE)	EXCESS (VICE)
Cowardice	Courage	Foolhardiness
Inhibition	Temperance	Overindulgence/Intemperance
Miserliness	Liberality	Prodigality/Extravagance
Shabbiness	Magnificence	Bad Taste/Vulgarity
Lack of Ambition	Proper Pride	Ambitiousness
Poor-Spiritedness	Gentleness	Irascibility
Peevishness	Friendliness	Obsequiousness/Flattery
Maliciousness	Righteous Indignation	Envy
Sarcasm	Truthfulness	Boastfulness
Boorishness	Wittiness	Buffoonery
Shamelessness	Modesty	Shamefacedness

people are not acts of courage. Courage for this person would involve a willingness to take a different sort of risk—perhaps giving up a home and financial security and moving to another area of the world to devote one's life to people who are impoverished. On the other hand, if people get too carried away, they might go to the opposite extreme and become foolhardy, giving away all their material goods and thus placing an undue burden on their children and on society to support them in their old age.

Another vice that we must beware of slipping into is trying to be "perfect." For example, in Hindu spiritual communes (ashrams) there exists a vice known as "scrupulosity": people become so self-absorbed in their attempt to achieve perfection that they are no longer able to relate well to others, instead adopting a holier-than-thou attitude. To achieve perfection, people must seek the middle path between "scrupulosity" and apathy.

> [M]oral excellence is a mean . . . between two forms of badness, one of excess and the other of defect, and is so described because it aims at hitting the mean point in feelings and in actions. This makes virtue hard of achievement, because finding the middle point is never easy. It is not everyone, for instance, who can find the centre of a circle—that calls for a geometrician.
>
> —ARISTOTLE, *Nicomachean Ethics*, Bk. 2, Ch. 9

How do we know when we have found the mean? Aristotle offers the following practical advice: "(1) Keep away from that extreme which is more opposed to the mean . . . (2) Note the errors into which we personally are most liable to fall . . . (3) Always be particularly on your guard against plea-sure and pleasant things."[20] By living according to the doctrine of the mean, Aristotle believed, we can find greatest happiness and inner harmony. To do this, it is important to be aware of the tendencies of your personality so that, if necessary, you can habituate yourself to compensate for them. This involves noticing how you respond to others and listening to your conscience.

Exercises

1. Virtue in general, according to both Confucius and Aristotle, entails finding a balance between excess and deficiency. Is your greatest virtue, as described in Question 1, page 391, a mean between deficit and excess? If so, what are the corresponding deficits and excesses?

2. Confucius compares the virtuous person to an archer who is able to hit the bull's eye. Do you have a tendency to miss the mark on certain virtues? How do you correct yourself when you begin to slip toward one of the two ex-tremes? Does it get easier to achieve the mean, with practice?

3. Martin Luther King, Jr., wrote that "many people fear nothing more terribly than to take a position which stands out sharply and clearly from prevailing opinion." Discuss the differences between this type of conformity and acting in accordance with the doctrine of the mean.

Nel Noddings and David Hume: Sentiment and Virtue

No quality of human nature is more remarkable both in itself and its human consequences, than the propensity we have to sympathize with others.
—DAVID HUME, *A Treatise on Human Nature* (1740)[21]

The caring for self, for the ethical self, can emerge only from a caring for others.
—NEL NODDINGS, *Caring: A Feminine Approach to Ethics and Moral Education* (1984), p. 14

Aristotle makes a fairly sharp distinction between reason and sentiment in the virtuous disposition. This division is seen by many philosophers as one of emphasis rather than an either/or situation. Even within some philosophical traditions, disagreement exists regarding the relative importance of reason and sentiment. Eastern philosophers generally regard sentiment as more im-portant. Chinese philosopher Lin Yutang (1895–1976), for example, believed that sentiment was more important than reason; both Confucius and Men-cius, on the other hand, emphasized reason over sentiment.

Most Western philosophers emphasize reason over sentiment; others, such as David Hume and Nel Noddings, believe that sympathy and caring are

> The ideal character best able to enjoy life is a warm, carefree and unafraid soul. Mencius enumerated the three "mature virtues" of his "great man" as "wisdom, compassion and courage." I should like to lop off one syllable and regard as the qualities of a great soul passion, wisdom and courage.
>
> —LIN YUTANG, *The Importance of Living* (1937), p. 98

the most important virtues. According to these philosophers, moral sentiments like compassion and sympathy are forms of knowledge regarding moral standards that should be taken seriously. Sympathy forms the heart of our conscience and complements rather than competes with the more cognitive virtues. Sympathy involves both feeling pleased by another's accomplishments and feeling indignation at another's injury or misfortune. Sympathy joins us to others, breaking down barriers.

The Life of David Hume

David Hume (1711–76) disagreed with the rationalists regarding the role of reason in willing actions. Hume was born in Edinburgh, Scotland. He enrolled in the University of Edinburgh to study law, but he soon came to dislike it, preferring instead to study philosophy on his own. At the age of 18, Hume decided to give up the study of law, in defiance of his family's wishes, and become a philosopher. Although this decision, according to his autobiography, made him "infinitely happy," the following year Hume slipped into a depression that lasted until he was twenty-three. During this time, he comforted himself by overeating and eventually became rather fat and ungainly. Hume believed that his depression was due largely to the study of philosophers such as Cicero, Seneca, and Plutarch, with their continual exhortations on death, shame, and "all other Calamities of Life."[22] In response to these philosophies, Hume developed his own philosophy.

Hume was popular, witty, and a respected man of letters. However, despite his achievements, Hume never succeeded in landing a job as an academic. Instead, he worked in various government positions and also served as keeper of the Advocates Library in Edinburgh for several years. Hume was described by one of his female acquaintances as "one of the sweetest tempered Men & the most Benevolent that was born . . . There was a simplicity & pleasantness of Manners about him that were delightful in Society."[23] His kindness earned him the nickname "Saint David" in Scotland. Although he was well liked by women and had many good friends who were women, Hume never married—his proposals of marriage were, sadly, rejected. Hume died of cancer in 1776, accepting death with that cheerful philosophical attitude that had so endeared him to his friends and acquaintances.

David Hume (1711–76), Scottish philosopher, historian, and economist. As a virtue ethicist Hume argued that sentiment is more important than reason in motivating us to act morally.

The Importance of Sentiment

Unlike Kant and Aristotle, Hume argued that reason or reflection can only *tell* us what is right or wrong. Reason, however, cannot *move* us to act virtuously. Instead, it is sentiment that actually moves us to act virtuously. Therefore, according to Hume, sympathy is the greatest virtue, and cruelty, or the lack of sympathy, is the greatest vice. Hume's claim is not without empirical support. In a study of people who rescued Jews during World War II, most rescuers reported that they rarely engaged in reflection before acting.[24] They reported that they acted instead from a sense of care and sympathy.

When Hume speaks of moral sentiments, he is not talking about irrational desires or whims of ethical subjectivism. Moral sentiments are a form of knowledge and can be as difficult to discern and to master as logic. Moral sentiments, he wrote, "are so rooted in our constitution and temper, that without confounding the human mind by disease or madness, 'tis impossible to extirpate and destroy them."[25] Although moral sentiments are more important than reason for motivating us to do good, reason should not be dismissed offhandedly. Rather, Hume argues, reason and sentiment work in conjunction to affirm each other:

> There has been controversy started of late . . . concerning the general foundation of morals, whether they be derived from REASON or SENTIMENT; whether we attain

knowledge of them by a chain of argument and induction, or by an immediate feeling and finer internal sense . . .

[It is true that] reason and sentiment concur in almost all moral determinations and conclusions . . . But though reason, when fully assisted and improved, be sufficient to instruct us in the pernicious or useful tendency of qualities and action; it is not sufficient alone to produce any moral blame or approbation . . . It is a requisite that a sentiment should here display itself, in order to give a preference to the useful above the pernicious tendencies. This sentiment can be no other than a feeling for the happiness of mankind (sympathy) and a resentment for their misery (anti-cruelty) . . . Here reason instructs us in the several tendencies of action, and humanity (sympathy) makes a distinction in favor of those which are useful and beneficial.[26]

Sympathy as a Virtue

Hume's ideas about the value of sympathy as a virtue are especially popular among developmental psychologists and contemporary feminist philosophers. Sympathy opens us up to others by breaking down the "us/them" mentality that acts as a barrier to expanding our moral community. For example, in community service, volunteers often initially see the people they are working with as the other—as disadvantaged and needy, with problems that must be fixed. This attitude stems from a lack of sympathy for certain groups of people. Service or philanthropy that is done without sympathy and compassion can be harmful. Indeed, the word "philanthropy" actually means "love for people." Without sympathy or compassion, doing community service can be divisive and demeaning to others, despite our best intentions. "When you give somebody a thing without giving yourself," Philip Hallie writes, "you degrade both parties by making the receiver utterly passive and by making yourself a benefactor standing there to receive thanks—and even sometimes obedience—as a repayment."[27]

Sympathy involves being in relationship in a way that reason does not. The sympathetic person sees service as a mutual process where all parties are engaged. Sympathy as a virtue entails listening to the people we are serving rather than defining their problems ourselves and imposing our ready-made solutions. Sympathy opens up our hearts to hear the stories of those we are serving. By allowing them also to serve us, we can learn from their experiences and their strengths.

Care Ethics

Modern care ethics is closely related to Hume's virtue ethics. Like Hume, care ethicists believe that morality is rooted in sentiment. Although they agree with Kant that ethics goes beyond natural caring because it is done out of duty, care ethicists regard feeling, rather than reason or formal moral principles, as the foundation of ethics. Care ethics was developed primarily from

Jennifer Piehler, a senior elementary special education major at Providence College, doing community service at an elementary school afterschool program, 1997. Community service learning has the potential to enhance students' moral development and their natural sense of sympathy and caring for others.

Carol Gilligan's study of women's moral development. As such, it has provided an important balance to the duty- and principle-laden language of modern Western ethics. Gilligan claimed that women's moral development tends to be more context-oriented than men's. Men are more likely to refer to abstract principles and reason in their moral judgments; women, she found, are more concerned with feelings and relationships.

Care ethicist Nel Noddings maintains that morality is an "active virtue" that requires two feelings: (1) the sentiment of natural caring and (2) love, which is our response to the remembrance of caring.[28] Like Aristotle and Kant, Noddings agrees that "I want" and "I ought" are more in harmony in the morally virtuous person. However, at this point her ethics departs from that of Aristotle and Kant, who regarded humans to be at their best when exercising their rational faculty. Noddings claims that we are at our moral best when we are "caring and being cared for."²⁹ It is care, not rational calculations or an abstract sense of duty, that creates moral obligations.

The importance of moral sentiment and caring in virtue is also found in Plato's dialogue *Euthyphro*. Socrates happens to run into Euthyphro near the courthouse where Socrates is to be tried for blasphemy and corrupting the youth of Athens. Socrates asks Euthyphro what brings him to the courthouse. Euthyphro replies that he is prosecuting his elderly father for murder. Socrates then proceeds to question Euthyphro about the propriety of a son prosecuting his father when the victim is a stranger:

> Good heavens! Certainly, Euthyphro, most men would not know how they could do this and be right . . . Is then the man your father killed one of your relatives? Or is that obvious, for you would not prosecute your father for the murder of a stranger.
>
> It is ridiculous, Socrates [Euthyphro replies], for you to think that it makes any difference whether the victim is a stranger or a relative. One should only watch whether the killer acted justly or not . . .³⁰

The murdered man, it turns out, was a laborer who had murdered one of the household servants in a drunken rage. Euthyphro's father bound the murderer and left him in a ditch while he went to inquire of a priest what should be done. Meanwhile, the laborer died of hunger and cold before the father returned. Had Euthyphro acted virtuously, Socrates asked, in bringing his own father to trial? Justice and reason demand that everyone be treated equally, but caring requires also that our moral decisions be made in the context of relationships.

Caring is also found in Confucian virtue ethics, where traditional family ties and loyalty are extremely important. The virtue entailed in the ethical ideal of "one-caring" is built on relationship. Caring becomes the basis of moral action because, in caring for someone, a person thereby makes a commitment to act on behalf of the one that is cared-for. An ethics of care requires that we give of ourselves in the context of relationship, not simply out of an abstract sense of duty. It is absurd, Mencius argues, to claim that one ought to save a stranger rather than one's child; our special obligations to those we have a relationship with goes beyond our abstract obligations to each other as humans.

Care ethicists, however, do not advocate an ethics of self-sacrifice, where we put the needs of others before our own. Just as proper self-esteem is at the heart of Kant's moral person, so too is proper self-care important to care ethicists. True caring and self-respect, unlike the self-interest advocated by hedonists and egoists, can develop only in relationship.

Many care ethicists, such as Noddings, believe that the care perspective is "characteristically and essentially feminine."³¹ There is evidence, however, that the preference for sentiment over reason in moral decision-making cuts across gender lines. Philip Hallie, in his study of the good people of

Le Chambon, noted that compassion and sympathy were more important in motivating them to help the Jews than abstract principles. In Sam and Pearl Oliner's study of people who rescued Jews during World War II, they also found that "the language of care dominated. Pity, compassion, concern, affection made up the vocabulary of 76% of the rescuers and 67% of the rescued survivors."[32]

> [A] sense of my physical self, a knowledge of what gives me pain and pleasures precedes my caring for others. Otherwise, their realities as possibilities for my own reality would mean nothing to me.
>
> —NEL NODDINGS, *Caring: A Feminine Approach to Ethics and Moral Education*
>
> (1984), pp. 14, 16[33]

An inclination to care is not enough, however. When our personal inclination to care is lacking, our commitment to an ideal or principle motivates us to do what is right. Although the language of care ethics tended to dominate, most of the rescuers in the Oliners' study also mentioned deontological principles such as equity and fairness as well as a concern for human rights.[34] "When we turn our attention to the 'ones cared-for' we are engrossed with them," Noddings writes. "This caring is often filled with joy, but when it is not, when we do not feel like caring for the other, we must have recourse to our commitment to the ethical ideal of caring."[35] At this point, care ethicists and deontologists find common ground. A person of good will—a person who is truly virtuous and caring—can be counted on to act out of a sense of duty even when the immediate emotional inclination to do so is lacking.

Defining the Moral Community

Some Western virtue ethicists, like the Western deontologists, limit the moral community to humans or "rational" beings. Both Aristotle and Noddings, for example, include only those who are capable of being moral agents in their moral communities. Noddings' care ethics includes only humans in the moral community because, according to her, only humans are capable of being in a reciprocal relationship. Caring-for is only morally relevant in situations where the other being in the relationship is also capable of caring-for as well as being cared-for. Noddings acknowledges that the feelings we experience in our relationships with other animals are very much like those experienced in relationships with other humans; nevertheless, she concludes that ". . . it seems obvious that they cannot be the ones-caring in relation to humans . . . We do not have a sense of the animal-as-subject as we do of a human as subject."[36]

Nel Noddings, American philosopher. As a virtue ethicist, Stanford University professor Nel Noddings expands on the care ethics of Carol Gilligan. Like Hume, Noddings believes that sympathy and caring are the most important virtues.

Because care is limited to human relationships, in Noddings' view, nonhuman animals are not part of the moral community and thus can be used in ways that benefit humans.

Care ethics has been criticized as too narrowly defining our moral obligations to others and inadequate for dealing with situations that do not involve reciprocal relationships. Feminist ethicists are understandably concerned about women buying into the traditional morality that emphasizes self-sacrifice, yet Noddings' claim that caring-for is morally called for only when there is the possibility or expectation of being cared-for in return smacks of Ayn Rand's rational egoism rather than genuine virtue.

For the most part, however, virtue ethics calls upon us to expand our moral community by focusing on self-development rather than on an assessment of another's moral worthiness. Jesus of Nazareth, for example, continually called us to expand our community beyond reciprocal relationships to also include those who are unable to return our favors.

Although Noddings' care ethics is limited to reciprocal relationships, other feminist care ethicists have a more inclusive concept of the moral community. Ecofeminist Karen Warren, for example, expands care ethics to include all living creatures and all of nature.[37] Care, according to her, is far more inclusive and unlimited by the ability of the recipient to reciprocate. Warren maintains that one of the goals of feminism is the liberation of nature as well as women by erasing oppressive categories based on superiority and privilege, and "the creation of a world in which difference does not breed domination."[38] To do this, Warren argues, we need to cultivate what philosopher Marilyn Frye refers to as the "loving eye." Frye distinguishes between the "loving eye" of care ethics and the "arrogant eye" of an ethics based on domination and conquest:

> The loving eye is a contrary of the arrogant eye.
>
> The loving eye knows the independence of the other . . .
>
> The loving eye does not make the object of perception into something edible, does not try to assimilate it, does not reduce it to the size of the seer's desire, fear and imagination, and hence does not have to simplify. It knows the complexity of the other as something which will forever present new things to be known. The science of the loving eye would favor The Complexity Theory of Truth [in contrast to The Simplicity Theory of Truth] and presuppose The Endless Interestingness of the Universe.[39]

Exercises

1. Do you agree with Hume and Noddings that we are motivated to act by sentiment, or with Aristotle and Kant that reason motivates us? Think back to a key event that changed the way you acted toward a particular person or group of people. Did this event involve rational arguments regarding which action was right? Or were you moved to change the way you acted more from a feeling of sympathy for the other person(s)?

*2. Discuss the quotation from Philip Hallie on page 401. Do you agree that service without sympathy is degrading to both parties? Relate your answer to your own community service work.

*3. Discuss how, if at all, your involvement in community service has enhanced your sympathy for others.

4. Would a virtuous person, as Euthyphro claimed, treat their friends and relatives just like everyone else? In George Orwell's book *1984*, he envisioned a society where children are praised for informing on their parents' illegal thoughts and activities. Are these children behaving in a morally virtuous way? Why or why not? Is whistle-blowing always wrong? What if the person they informed on was not a friend or family member? What would a care ethicist say? a cultural relativist?

5. Do you agree with Noddings that reciprocity is an adequate notion for defining moral community? If so, do we have a moral obligation to care for small children or the elderly or people who are severely mentally retarded and, as such, not capable of "caring for others" in a reciprocal relationship.

6. Do you agree with Karen Warren and Marilyn Frye that sexism and the domination of women are linked to the domination of nature? Relate Frye's concept of the "loving eye" to your own lifestyle and sense of who you are vis-à-vis other people and nature.

Is Virtue Relative to Culture, Social Status, and Gender?

[T]he most striking thing about the virtues is how they vary from culture to culture and throughout history . . .

—ROBERT SOLOMON, *Ethics: A Short Introduction* (1993), p. 107

There is no doubt that people disagree about which virtues are more important. Aristotle, Confucius, and Plato regarded wisdom as the highest virtue. Aquinas claimed that faith is the highest virtue, and Noddings thought that sympathy is the highest virtue. But does their disagreement go deeper than one of priorities? Do different cultures and groups of people actually have conflicting concepts of what virtue consists of? Although sympathy is the highest virtue for Noddings, Hume, and Buddha, none of them would deny the importance of cultivating wisdom and discernment. Nor did Aristotle deny the role of sentiments in morality.

Also, though the lists of virtues vary somewhat, there is also much overlap. In Plato's virtue ethics, for example, there are four cardinal virtues: Wisdom, Courage, Temperance, and Justice. In Confucianism, there are three: Wisdom, Courage, and *Jen*. "The man of *Jen*," writes neo-Confucian philosopher Ch'eng Hao, "forms one body with all things without any differentiation. Righteousness, propriety, wisdom, and faithfulness are all [expressions] of *Jen*."[40]

Most people, in other words, seem to agree in general about what is a virtue and what is a vice. According to a 1995 Gallup poll, for example, almost all parents want to bring up their children to be honest, kind, and empathetic. However, are these simply American virtues? Are there some virtues that are peculiar to women and other characteristics that are virtues only for men? Nel Noddings and Carol Gilligan, for instance, claim that men and women tend to place higher values on a different set of virtues. Men, they point out, emphasize traits such as courage, assertiveness, and fairness. Women are more concerned with virtues related to caring, such as compassion, forgiveness, gentleness, and loyalty.[41]

There is also no shortage of examples of cultures defining virtue differently. In some cultures, courage in battle is the most important virtue for a man; women, in contrast, are praised for being gentle, peaceful, and even submissive. In Buddhist cultures such as Tibet, on the other hand, a peaceful disposition is considered a virtue in both men and women. There are also instances in which what one culture regards as a virtue another regards as a vice. Some cultures regard cooperation as a virtue; in the United States, a competitive spirit and hard work are virtues. Aristotle, on the other hand, had only scorn for the "commercial virtues." Some Christian ethicists stress self-sacrificing humility as the greatest virtue, yet Nietzsche regarded this type of humility as a vice. Christian and Hindu ethics emphasize virtues that affect our future existence—whether in the spiritual realm or here in a reincarnated life. Aristotle and Confucius were oriented more toward the present, so they emphasized virtues that promote community and harmony, such as benevolence and trustworthiness.

Is Virtue Culturally Relative?

Philosopher Robert Solomon argues that virtue is culturally relative and that the virtues listed by Aristotle were simply those of the Greek aristocracy:

> The question, "What is the good life and how should I live?" is very much an open question, and no single set of virtues, ambitions, or accomplishments provides the answer for everyone . . . We would like to think of what Aristotle called the good life as a single universal goal, common to ancient Greeks, medieval Chinese, and modern Americans, but we are aware of cultural differences, and the legitimacy of these differences, in a way that Aristotle was not.[42]

But is Aristotle's list of virtues really as culture-bound as Solomon claims? Or can virtues be "universalized"? Aristotle taught that friendliness, sympathy, benevolence, and honesty are important virtues, because without these virtues we tend to alienate our friends and family. Because humans are social animals, no one can achieve the good life without good friends and family. Is this true of all humans, or is it simply a cultural norm of the ancient Greek aristocracy? Confucius also thought that the social virtues were very important. In fact, Confucius went even further than Aristotle in emphasizing family loyalty as a virtue. In the United States, in contrast, maintaining close ties with one's family may be seen as a sign of immaturity or even neurosis. Young people are often told that it is important to get away from their families and to become more self-sufficient.

Although different cultures and groups of people may emphasize different virtues (sociological relativism), this does not mean that virtue is culturally relative in the sense that the concept of virtue is a cultural creation. Indeed, what is most striking are the similarities between the various lists of virtues, rather than the differences. For example, anthropologist Clyde Kluckholn noted that, among the Navahos, the primary virtues are generosity, loyalty, self-control, peacefulness, amity, courteousness, and honesty.[43] These virtues are not seen as peculiar to Navahos but are regarded as desirable for all humans—as universal as the air we breathe. The Egyptian text *The Instruction of Ptahhotep,* written more than four thousand years ago, states that the following virtues should be practiced toward everyone: Self-control, Moderation, Kindness, Generosity, Justice, Truthfulness, and Discretion. The Swahili proverbs teach that a virtuous person is kind, cautious (prudent), patient, courageous, self-controlled, humble (in the Kantian sense), honest, fair, responsible, respectful, and cooperative. The virtuous person, according to the Swahilis, avoids violence, apathy, foolhardiness, faultfinding, and falsehood.[44] Thus, although the relative importance of different virtues may vary from culture to culture, the list of what is considered a virtue and what is considered a vice seems to be transcultural.

Something that may at first appear to be a basic difference may turn out to be merely a difference in how a specific virtue is expressed within a cultural context. Courage in a warrior culture, for example, means putting up a good fight and willingness to die in battle. Courage in a pacifist culture is expressed very differently—perhaps as nonviolent resistance and the willingness to stand up to one's oppressors without retaliating or using violence in return. However, in both the warrior culture and the pacifist culture courage involves avoiding cowardliness yet not going to the other extreme of being foolhardy.

Certain basic virtues, as Aristotle noted, seem to be necessary for our well-being and for the achievement of the good life, no matter who we are or where we live. To make an analogy, different cultures can have very different dietary habits. Even within one culture, individuals have distinct dietary needs: Growing children need more protein and carbohydrates, women need more iron and calcium than men, and men need more calories than women. The basic nutritional needs of humans are fairly universal, however. The dietary habits of different cultures can thus be judged in light of these universal standards. We all need vitamin C in our diet or else we will get scurvy, whether we live in Iceland or Fiji. The calorie requirements of women, assuming similar activity levels, is roughly the same no matter where they live. However, just as different cultures emphasize different virtues, the foods used as sources of vitamin C and caloric intake can vary greatly. On the other hand, if most people in a culture habitually consume an excessive number of calories (as is now happening in the United States) or consume too few calories (as in Rwanda), or if their diet is missing certain nutrients, then we can judge their dietary habits to be detrimental to health and normal growth, precisely because there is a transcultural standard of what humans need to thrive physically.

Similarly, those basic characteristics or virtues that are conducive to the good life are the same for all humans because we all share the same basic nature. Cultures that do not encourage or nurture good character or that label vices as virtues—just as some junk food companies advertise their food as "nutritious"—do not provide an environment that is conducive to the good life. Chinese philosopher Lin Yutang (1895–1976) remarked that what some cultures perceive as virtues are actually vices, when examined in light of the concept of the good life: "The three great American vices seem to be efficiency, punctuality and the desire for achievement and success. They are the things," he wrote, "that make the American so unhappy and nervous."[45]

Nietzsche and the Übermensch

Nietzsche was one of the most outspoken critics of all forms of cultural relativism and heteronomous ethics. As an existentialist he claimed that there was no one standard by which human perfection could be measured; nevertheless he maintained that certain character traits are destructive to the pursuit of our human goals and others enhance our growth. Nietzsche was especially critical of the traditional bourgeois "Christian" morality that, he claimed, forms the basis of modern Western morality. This morality, which extols meekness, unconditional forgiveness, self-sacrifice, and equality as virtues, he argued, is destructive to individual integrity and growth.

Humility and meekness play no role as virtues in the life of Nietzsche's **Übermensch,** or "superhuman" just as they play no part in the life of Aristotle's virtuous person or the Confucian superior man. Nor was this type of humility, according to Nietzsche, part of the teachings of Jesus of Nazareth. Indeed, Nietzsche apparently admired Jesus as an example of an *Übermensch.* Nietzsche also believed that "the last Christian died on the cross" and that modern Christian morality bears little resemblance to that promoted by Jesus. The *Übermensch,* according to Nietzsche, is a person of integrity and self-mastery who is able to rise above the morality of the crowd and exercise the will to power. Instead of weakness, Nietzsche emphasized the "will to power," self-mastery, and human nobility. Nietzsche's concept of "will to power" has often been misinterpreted as the will to dominate and subjugate others. However, truly strong or virtuous people are not cruel, nor do they desire to subjugate others. Indeed, Nietzsche's last act before collapsing and dying months later without ever fully recovering consciousness, was to embrace a horse that was being flogged by its owner.

By the *"will to power"* Nietzsche meant "the will to grow, spread, seize, become predominant"[46] that is found in all living beings. The will to power involves the experience of living at its greatest. In his book *The Dawn* Nietzsche lists "*The good four. Honest* with ourselves and whatever is friend to us; *courageous* toward the enemy; *generous* toward the vanquished; *polite*—always: that is how the four cardinal virtues want us."[47] Weak people, in contrast, make humility, self-sacrifice, and equality into virtues because they lack the courage, power, and personal resolve to live the life of the great person, according to Nietzsche. Thus, Christian "herd morality" drags the best and strongest people down to the lowest common denominator.

Not everyone agrees with Nietzsche that all moral virtues are a manifestation of the "will to power." However, Nietzsche is correct in noting that self-effacing humility and self-sacrifice do not, for the most part, lead to a happy and fulfilling life—at least not in this life. Battered women, for example, are often advised to be try to be more humble, agreeable, and submissive[48] and to forgive their batterers. Ironically, the very women who hold highly traditional moral views and who try hardest to please their husbands are the most likely to be abused by their husbands and partners.[49] Because humility, self-sacrifice, unconditional forgiveness, and the other so-called Christian virtues harm women and perpetuate domestic violence, these can hardly be considered moral virtues. Thus, humility, the Christian concept of which is expressed through meekness and a willingness to sacrifice oneself for others, may be a religious or cultural virtue, but it cannot be considered a moral virtue. Like junk food that is bad for our bodies, "virtues" that impede our growth as humans are junk virtues. A culture that promotes junk virtues as true virtues is destructive to the development of moral character.

The Development of Virtue

A virtuous character does not develop in isolation but in community. North African philosopher Ibn Khaldun, as we noted in Chapter 7, claimed that nomadic cultures encourage the formation of virtues such as peacefulness, cooperation, and justice, while sedentary cultures encourage destructive behaviors such as competitiveness, greed, injustice, and aggression. Some types of social structures are certainly more conducive to the development of virtuous and happy individuals. As Aristotle pointed out, we do not become more virtuous by merely reflecting on or intellectualizing virtues but by living a virtuous life. A good society provides an environment where virtues are encouraged and where people can thrive and develop to their fullest potential.

The virtues of independence and economic success that we emphasize in the United States—especially for men—might not be moral virtues at all because they do not benefit, but rather harm, the individual. When teachers, parents, and child-development specialists in Japan and the United States were asked to name the most important things that preschool children should learn, the first choice of those from Japan was sympathy and a concern for others, followed by cooperation. Americans, on the other hand, thought self-reliance was the most important value; sympathy was rarely mentioned.[50] One might plausibly argue, however, that Americans have pushed self-reliance to an extreme so that it has now become a vice. On the other hand, cooperation as a virtue can also be carried to an extreme where it becomes transformed into mindless conformity. What we need to do is seek the mean between these extremes.

Exercises

1. Robert Solomon maintains that virtues are culturally relative. Do you agree with him that the virtues listed by Aristotle are peculiar to the Greek aristocracy? As a college student living two thousand years after Aristotle, do you agree with his list of virtues? Support your position.

2. Reread the list of virtues on page 408 from *The Instruction of Ptahhotep*. Do these virtues hold for us today, or is their relevance limited to the Egyptian culture of four thousand years ago? Compare this list to those that you and your classmates made in response to Question 1 on page 391 in this chapter.

3. If you have not already done so, make a list of what you consider to be the four or five most important virtues. Compare the virtues listed by the men with those listed by the women in the class. In what ways, if any, do the lists differ? Are the virtues listed by women different from those listed by men? Or is the only difference the priority given to different virtues? If there are differences, how might you account for them?

4. Joyce Treblicot, in her article "Two Forms of Androgynism," argues that, instead of seeing virtues in terms of gender, people should be allowed to develop their own character and virtues free from the limitations of gender roles and perhaps even cultural expectations.[51] Do you agree? Is this even possible? Explain why or why not.

5. Professional codes of ethics and institutional mission statements frequently include a list of virtues to which members of the profession or institution are expected to aspire. Discuss the concept of virtue in relation to the particular profession or lifestyle to which you aspire.

6. What do you think Nietzsche would have thought of people such as Trocme (the French pastor at Le Chambon), Martin Luther King, Jr., and Mother Teresa—all of whom based their work on Christianity?

   How would Nietzsche have responded to Aquinas' contention that faith is the greatest virtue and pride the greatest vice? Create a dialogue between the two men on this subject.

7. Do you agree with Lin Yutang that some of our cultural virtues in the United States are not moral virtues but traits that actually harm us? Relate your answer to your own experience.

The Unity of Virtue

> *[V]irtue in a man will be the disposition which (a) makes him a good man, and (b) enables him to perform his function well.*   —ARISTOTLE, *Nicomachean Ethics,* Bk. 2, Ch. 6

According to Aristotle, virtues are not part of a smorgasbord where we can pick from a menu of this or that virtue and leave the rest. Virtue is a unifying concept rather than simply a collection of different personality traits. We speak of a good person as being virtuous in a general sense. Virtue, in other words, is the *disposition* that predisposes us to act in a manner that benefits ourselves and others. The concept of virtue as a unifying principle in the human psyche, rather than a collection of discrete personality traits, is found in both Eastern and Western virtue ethics.

Nietzsche regarded the "will to power" as the fount of all virtuous action. In Chinese philosophy, *Hsin*—that which is One with nature and the principle of all conscious and moral activity—is the source of all virtue. Virtue, according to Confucian ethics, stems from an all-pervading unity.[52]

The "unity intended by Confucius," writes commentator James Legge, "was the heart, man's nature, of which all the relations and duties of life are only the development and outgoing."[53] Without this underlying "all-pervading unity" or good will, otherwise virtuous traits, such as truthfulness and loyalty, can become harmful on their own. Lao Tzu, founder of Taoism, spoke of the Tao as the cosmic unity that underlies all phenomena. The Tao is the unifying creative principle that shapes and informs our moral character.

True compassion as a virtue, for example, stems from who we are as a person; it comes from what Kant calls the good will. To be compassionate simply for the sake of being compassionate is merely role-playing and, as such, is perverse. The truthfulness of a braggart and the loyalty of gang members are not virtues because these are not expressions of the good will; they only seem to be virtues if we take a piecemeal approach. The good life entails having all the virtues; it involves living a life of integrity. If we do not have all the virtues, then we are not truly a virtuous person, because there is still disharmony within ourselves.

In the Gospel of Luke, Jesus of Nazareth compares the virtuous person to a tree or a grapevine that bears good fruit. We know a good person by the fruit they bear.

> For no good tree bears bad fruit, nor again does a bad tree bear good fruit; for each tree is known by its own fruit. For figs are not gathered from thorns, nor are grapes picked from a bramble bush. The good man out of the good treasure of his heart produces good, and the evil man out of the evil treasure of his heart produces evil; for out of the abundance of the heart his mouth speaks.[54]

Virtuous people have a well-developed moral character. Virtue is integral to their self-concept. They are, to use the above analogy, rooted in virtue. Virtuous people place moral motives above other considerations. They do not have to consider their motives before rushing to save someone in distress. They do not behave either generously or begrudgingly, nor do they do what is right because of fear of punishment. Like André Trocme, who led the villagers of Le Chambon in rescuing Jews during World War II, virtuous people do not just happen to act in a way that is good; they do not merely perform acts that happen to be virtuous. People like Trocme act virtuously because doing so is part of who they are.

> What is extraordinary about highly moral people is that they apply this habitual moral mode to the furthest reaches of their social visions. Their moral sensibilities are quickly engaged by any number of observations or incidents.
>
> —WILLIAM DAMON, *Greater Expectations* (1995), p. 158

According to psychologists Anne Colby and William Damon, people with a high level of moral commitment carry out their commitments in a spontaneous manner by force of habit.[55] Virtuous people enjoy being virtuous; they do not need to struggle to overcome temptation or make sacrifices to be virtuous.

> He who loved virtue, would esteem nothing above it.
>
> —CONFUCIUS, *The Analects*[56]

People who are morally virtuous have ego strength, or proper self-esteem, as well as perseverance, courage, and the strength of their convictions. They are not as likely as people with weak characters to mindlessly follow authority or to do things under social pressure that they would not otherwise do on their own. Rather than keeping their innermost self intact by use of immature defense mechanisms and resistance, virtuous people organize their innermost self based on integrity. People of integrity, such as Elizabeth Cady Stanton and other moral reformers, have the strength of character to stand by their principles even if they are unpopular.

The cultivation of virtue and the good will is a lifelong process. Very few people ever attain a level of moral development where they no longer struggle against temptation. According to Aristotle, for those who constantly strive to be virtuous, being a virtuous person gradually becomes much easier and more pleasurable. Therefore, to discover whether we are a virtuous person, Aristotle suggests that all we must do is ask ourselves whether we find pleasure in acting virtuously.

Exercises

1. Jesus of Nazareth taught that virtue can lead only to good actions. Do you agree with him? Why or why not?

2. Do you agree with Nietzsche that virtue is the manifestation of the "will to power"? What do you think Nietzsche means by the "will to power"? What do you see as the connection between virtue and power?

3. Virtues help to shape our aspirations for what sort of person we want to be. How does cultivating a virtuous disposition help you to achieve your goals? Discuss how being virtuous defines who you are. Do you enjoy being virtuous? Why or why not?

4. Can someone be a virtuous person and still have conflicts about doing what is right? Are people who strive to be virtuous happier people?

*5. Does practicing good actions, even though your motives are morally questionable, help you to become a more virtuous person? What is the difference, if any, between a hypocrite who acts one way but feels another way and a person who is begrudgingly practicing good actions to become more virtuous? Relate your answer to your community service.

Virtue and Moral Education

The sages, also have first devoted themselves to study, and thus know the truth. The common people, also have knowledge of [good] from birth . . . Study and self-control should follow the lead of intuitive knowledge. —The Philosophy of Wang Yang Ming[57]

Questions regarding the basic goodness or depravity of humans, the influence of reason and sentiment on moral behavior and character, and the role of God in human virtue all contribute to the formulation of our ideas regarding moral education and the cultivation of a virtuous character. If people are basically depraved, then more effort must go into their moral education and the cultivation of a virtuous character. Aristotle, Aquinas, and Chinese philosopher Hsun Tzu all believed that people are, for the most part, basically evil and that a vigorous program of moral education is needed to correct this natural tendency. Moral education, according to this view of human nature, is not so much a matter of cultivating children's natural moral sense as it is imposing morality upon them.

The nature of man is evil; the good which it shows is factitious . . . So the nature of man, being evil, must be submitted to teachers and laws, and then it becomes correct.

—Hsun Tzu, *The Chinese Classics*, Vol. II[58]

Are People Basically Good?

Lao Tzu, on the other hand, regarded people as basically good. The Tao not only shapes our character and virtue but provides us with ethical principles. In Taoism, therefore, we have only to lose ourselves in the Tao just as a fish loses itself in water. In Taoism, cultivating virtue involves letting go, becoming passive, and letting the guiding principles flow naturally out of the Tao. Consequently, Lao Tzu would not approve of the structured moral education found in many Catholic schools. However, neither did he advocate apathy and shutting ourselves off from the world. Moral education instead involves being open to others and affirming their natural goodness:

> A sound [virtuous] man's heart is not shut within itself
> But is open to other people's hearts:
> And I find bad people good
> If I am good enough;
> I trust men of their word
> And I trust liars
> If I am true enough;
> I feel the heart-beats of others
> Above my own
> If I am enough of a father,
> Enough of a son.[59]

Confucian philosopher Mencius also believed that human nature is originally virtuous. Benevolence and righteousness is internal, according to Mencius, not something imposed on us from the outside or self-imposed through habituation, as Aristotle claimed. According to Mencius, virtue is intimately tied in with sincerity and being true to oneself. Thus, the process of becoming a virtuous person depends on "setting the mind in the right."[60] The content person, Mencius taught, is one who "reveres virtue and delights in rightness." Unless our mind is in the right, there will neither be inner harmony nor harmony in the household.

> The Way of greater learning lies in keeping one's inborn luminous Virtue unobscured.
>
> —*The Greater Learning*[61]

Chinese philosopher Wang Yang Ming agreed that virtue is innate, yet he took a more active approach to moral education than did either the Taoists or Mencius. Wang Yang Ming emphasized the importance of moral education as a means of developing the goodness inherent in our natures. He believed that the teacher should be "indefatigable and energetic in his efforts to guard this knowledge of the good."[62] Moral education also involves learning and practice. However, unlike Aquinas and Hsun Tzu, Wang Yang Ming argued that the course of moral education should follow the lead of intuitive knowledge.

Like Wang Yang Ming, Aristotle emphasized the importance of practice in the development of virtue. However, although Aristotle believed that we have a natural inclination to be virtuous, he also believed that moral virtue was the outcome of habit rather than a product of our natural endowments.

For Aristotle, consequently, it is not enough to simply nurture our natural inclinations. The cultivation of virtues requires willpower and practice as well:

> The moral virtues, then, are produced in us neither by Nature nor against Nature. Nature, indeed prepares in us the ground for their reception, but their complete formation is the product of habit.

We acquire virtue, according to Aristotle, through repetition or habituation: "By doing what is just a man becomes just, and temperate by doing what is temperate, while without doing thus he has no chance of ever becoming good."[63] Because humans are social as well as rational beings, becoming virtuous involves both the cultivation of reason and proper socialization. Virtue, in other words, develops through our practical interaction with the world. "Like activities," Aristotle wrote, "produce like dispositions." In other words, we do not become just simply by believing in the principle of justice. We become just or unjust in the course of our dealings with others. It is our duty, therefore, to practice the various virtues so that we will become proficient.

The Importance of Moral Education

According to Aristotle, it is generally easier for people to be virtuous if their early childhood education reinforced virtuous behavior; however, it is never too late to habituate ourselves to be virtuous people by constant practice of moral actions. Practicing any art or craft, Aristotle reminds us, is initially burdensome. Just as a novice artisan or musician finds practice tedious at first, so too practicing virtue may be onerous at first to the novice.

Indeed, many students, when they first begin their community service, complain that it is too much work. We know that we have become good at something when it no longer seems burdensome to us. The more we practice and the better we become at something, the more we will enjoy it. Just as continuous practice on a musical instrument makes it easier, and more enjoyable, for us to play that instrument well, so too does constantly performing good actions make it easier for us to be virtuous people.

We need to struggle to become a virtuous person. We cannot just say "I am who I am—take me as I am." Nor is it enough to simply know what is right. There is not "the smallest likelihood of a man's becoming good," Aristotle counsels, by any other means than by "repeated performances" of virtuous actions. Aristotle is aware that this

> . . . is not a popular line to take, most men preferring theory to practice under the impression that arguing about morals proves them to be philosophers, and that in this way they will turn out to be fine characters. Herein they resemble invalids, who listen carefully to all the doctor says but do not carry out a single one of his orders. The bodies of such people will never respond to treatment—nor will the souls of such "philosophers."[64]

Because the formation of good habits is so important, moral education should start at an early age. Pearl and Samuel Oliner, in their study of people who rescued Jews from the Nazis during World War II, found that virtue education during childhood had a significant effect on the rescuers' later behavior. The rescuers' commitment to "actively protect or enhance the well-being of others," they noted, "did not emerge suddenly under the threat of Nazi brutality." The development of a virtuous character as well as a sense of universal moral duty had been instilled in them since childhood: Seventy percent of rescuers in the Oliners' study, as compared to fifty-six percent of nonrescuers, stated that their parents emphasized the development of virtues such as honesty, respect, compassion, generosity, helpfulness, expansiveness, and hospitality.[65] Rescuers were also more than twice as likely as nonrescuers to state that their parents taught them that moral values applied universally to all humans. The following are typical of the comments of rescuers regarding their childhood moral education:

> I learned to be good to one's neighbor—to be responsible, concerned, and considerate. To work—and work hard. But also to help—to the point of leaving one's work to help one's neighbor. . . .

> [My father] taught me to love my neighbor—to consider him my equal whatever his nationality or religion. He taught me especially to be tolerant.[66]

Like Aristotle and the Confucian philosophers, Buddhist ethics also emphasizes the importance of cultivating virtue. However, according to Buddhists, moral education involves changing our way of thinking more than practicing virtuous acts. Although Aristotle believed that a change of heart usually follows a change of actions, Buddhists maintain that the change of heart should come first. We need to give up the illusion that we are a separate reality. Most importantly, the achievement of virtuous character involves coming to the realization that all beings are One. If some beings have intrinsic moral value, then all beings must likewise have intrinsic value, because the distinction between the parts and the whole, or the One, is based on an illusion. According to Buddhist Scriptures:

> . . . you should strive to think of all that lives with friendliness and compassion, and not with ill-will and a desire to hurt. For whatever a man thinks about continually, to that his mind becomes inclined by habit of force. Abandoning what is unwholesome, you therefore ought to ponder what is wholesome; for that will bring you advantages in this world and help you to win the highest goal.[67]

The Buddhist virtue of ahimsa also calls us to expand the moral community to include all living beings. In both Buddhism and Taoism and in some versions of Hinduism, there is a moral imperative to be virtuous toward nature. By breaking down worldviews or paradigms that fragment the world into "me" and the "other," Buddhist ethics has had an "immense humanizing effect on the entire history of Asia"[68] and also on the modern world peace and environmental movements.

Exercises

1. Do you agree with Mencius and Lao Tzu that people are naturally good, or with Wang Yang Ming and Aristotle that virtue is not inborn but must be developed through habituation? Support your answer.

*2. Has community service helped to make you more virtuous by giving you an opportunity to practice virtuous behavior? Discuss how.

*3. Courts sometimes assign people who have been convicted of minor crimes to do community service work. Although we may agree that practice is important in the development of a virtuous character, is it morally acceptable for the courts to use the people at a community service site to develop offenders' moral virtues? Support your answer.

4. To what extent has the college experience made you a more virtuous (or more vicious) person? Explain.

5. To what extent does the concept of ahimsa inform your relationships with other people, other animals, and the environment? Do you think people have a moral obligation to develop ahimsa? How might this obligation be integrated into moral education? How might our society differ if ahimsa were an important virtue for us?

The Strengths and Limitations of Virtue Ethics

Ethical theories that stress duty often treat what we ought to do and what we want to do as being in conflict. Virtue ethicists, on the other hand, consider the good life and the virtuous life to be in harmony.

Just as virtue generally entails seeking a balance between deficit and excess, so too does being a virtuous person involve developing and balancing both cognitive and affective traits. An intention to "do good" that is based simply on feeling and is not backed by wisdom and genuine concern for the well-being of others is not sufficient for virtue. Genuine concern for others involves not just feeling but being informed about the other person and their situation, knowing our abilities and limitations, and being able to empathize, as opposed to merely sympathizing, with the other.

The primary criticism of virtue ethics is that it is incomplete. In particular, virtue ethics has been criticized for its lack of emphasis on actions. A bag-of-virtues approach, the argument goes, does not offer sufficient guidance for making moral decisions in the real world. This criticism is partly based on a misinterpretation of the concept of virtue. Virtue ethicists do not mean virtue to imply a list of character traits but rather a unity of character. A virtuous person is motivated to help others by participating in community service and by striving for reform. As both Mill and Kant pointed out, virtuous people are more likely than others to do what is right.

On the other hand, there is some truth in the contention that virtue alone is not enough to guide most people. Virtue may be adequate for the saint, but most of us also need formal moral guidelines. It has been suggested that, developmentally, virtue ethics is associated with a high level of autonomous moral reasoning. Indeed, according to Kant, to a person of perfectly good will, the concept of duty no longer applies.

Virtue ethics does not toss out abstract principles regarding duties and rights, but rather gives them a personal face. Nor does virtue ethics, in any form, entail discarding reason and relying on our "good" feelings. In the virtuous person, reason and feeling are logically connected; they complement and confirm one another. In Confucian ethics, for example, the concept of *jen* is complimented by that of *yi,* which means righteousness or justice. "Benevolence and righteousness," states the superior man, "and these shall be the only themes."[69]

Virtue ethicists are not suggesting that we ignore moral principles: They are saying that virtue ethics is more fundamental than duty ethics, because virtue enables us to recognize and carry out our duty. "To seek the highest virtue in affairs and things," writes Chinese philosopher Wang Yang Ming, "is only the objective side of the principles of righteousness. The highest virtues are innate to the mind. They are realized when the manifesting of lofty virtue has reached perfection." The most virtuous person is one whose mind is "completely dominated by heaven-given principles (natural or moral law)."[70]

Virtue ethics goes beyond pure duty and rights-based ethics. Virtue ethics is a direct challenge to the individual to rise above ordinary moral demands. Philosopher Christina Sommers (b. 1950) argues that individuals are transferring too much responsibility for the well-being of others onto institutions and professionals. She concludes that these solutions are incomplete and that what is needed instead is the virtuous individual. In her essay "Where Have All the Good Deeds Gone?" Sommers uses the example of Miss Pickins to illustrate her point:

> For the past seven years Miss Pickins, who is ninety-one, has lived in Miller House [a home for the elderly]. Last year her doctor ordered her to stop smoking. This upset a daily routine she had enjoyed—coffee and cigarettes in the lounge downstairs with the men. She became depressed, lost interest in leaving her room, and now spends most of her time there alone. The woman who runs the home made Miss Pickins keep the sound of her radio so low that she cannot hear it . . .
>
> Simone de Beauvoir has said, "By the fate it allots to its members who can no longer work, society gives itself away." Who is to blame for the fate that has been al-

lotted to Miss Pickins . . . ? A few concerned neighbors could transform the residence into a much happier place. But that is not going to happen.[71]

Ralph Waldo Emerson once said, "Character is higher than intellect."[72] The development of a virtuous character is essential to the concept of the good life and the good society. When people give a higher priority to becoming the most virtuous and caring people that they can be, then will people like Miss Pickins at last be able to look forward to a better and happier life.

Exercises

*1. Do you agree with Christina Sommers that a virtuous disposition, more than just a sense of duty, is what motivates us to help people like Miss Pickins? If everyone, or at least more people, were virtuous, how would this affect your community service or the need for your services? Use specific examples to illustrate your answer.

2. Discuss how the college experience could be restructured to encourage the development of virtue in the students and the rest of the college community.

Summary

1. Virtue ethics emphasizes character or *right being* over right action.

2. A **virtue** is an admirable character trait or disposition to act in a manner that benefits oneself and others. A **vice** is a character trait or disposition to act in a manner that harms oneself and others.

3. Not all virtues are moral virtues. There are also *intellectual virtues* and *natural virtues*.

4. According to Greek virtue ethicists, virtue is essential to the achievement of **eudaemonia,** or psychological well-being and inner harmony.

5. Both **deontological** theories and **utilitarian** theories recognize the importance of virtue. *Kant,* for example, believed that we have a moral obligation to cultivate the **good will;** and *Mill,* to cultivate a *benevolent disposition.*

6. *Aristotle* divides the *human psyche* into the *rational* and *non-rational elements.* In a virtuous person, reason is in charge of the nonrational elements. Therefore, *wisdom* is the greatest virtue and *ignorance* the greatest vice.

7. *Aquinas* regarded reason as the most important human faculty. However, he thought that we could not be virtuous without God's help. Therefore, *faith* is the greatest virtue and *pride* the greatest vice.

8. The **doctrine of the mean** states that virtue, in general, entails moderation or seeking the middle path. This doctrine is found in philosophies throughout the world.

9. *David Hume* argued that sentiment is more important than reason for motivating us to do what is right. Hume regarded **sympathy** as the highest virtue and *cruelty* as the greatest vice.

10. *Nel Noddings* argues that *caring* and relationship form the basis of morality.

11. Although different cultures and different philosophers regard certain virtues as more or less important than others, the **concept of virtue** and the list of basic virtues seem to be *transcultural*.

12. Virtue is a *unifying concept* rather than a collection of personality traits. A virtuous person has *integrity*.

13. Friedrich Nietzsche's concept of the virtuous person is the **Übermensch** ("superhuman"). The *Übermensch* is motivated by the **"will to power."**

14. Some virtue ethicists, such as *Lao Tzu* and *Mencius,* regard people as basically good. Therefore, becoming virtuous entails simply letting go and flowing with the *Tao*. Other virtue ethicists, such as *Aristotle* and *Wang Yang Ming,* believe that a virtuous character results from practice and **habituation.**

15. *Buddhist* virtue ethicists believe that cultivating virtuous thought is more important than practicing virtuous actions. The Buddhist virtue of **ahimsa,** or compassion, includes all living beings and nature in the moral community.

Glossary

absolute duty A duty that is always morally binding without exception, regardless of the particular circumstances.

absolutist A person who believes that moral principles are morally binding regardless of the particular circumstances.

abusive fallacy This fallacy occurs when a person disagrees with someone else's conclusion, but instead of addressing the argument, the person instead attacks the character of the person who made the argument.

ad hominem fallacy An argument directed against a person. The abusive fallacy and the circumstantial fallacies are both ad hominem fallacies.

agape Unconditional love.

ahimsa The Buddhist principle of non-hurting.

analysis The process of critically examining our worldview, using reason and logic.

anthropocentrism The belief that human beings are the central or most significant entity of the universe.

appeal to force A fallacy that occurs when a person uses or threatens to use physical, psychological, or legal force in an attempt to coerce another person to accept a conclusion.

appeal to inappropriate authority A fallacy that occurs when someone appeals to an expert or authority in a field other than the one under debate.

appeal to pity A fallacy that occurs when someone attempts to evoke a feeling of pity in the listener to get a conclusion accepted, even though the issue under discussion is a matter of fact rather than of sentiment.

appeal to tradition A fallacy that occurs when someone argues that a practice or attitude is morally acceptable because it is a tradition or cultural norm.

argument A type of reasoning composed of two or more propositions, one of which is claimed to follow logically from or be supported by the others.

autonomous moral agent A self-determining person who looks to his or her own reason for moral guidance.

begging the question This fallacy, also known as circular reasoning, occurs when the premise and conclusion are actually different wordings of the same proposition.

behaviorism The psychological theory that our behavior, including our moral behavior, is a product of our environment and our culture.

biological altruism Inborn cooperative behavior.

categorical imperative A term introduced by Immanuel Kant to describe moral injunctions that are unconditionally binding upon us.

circumstantial fallacy This fallacy occurs when someone argues that another person should accept a certain position because of that person's special circumstances, such as lifestyle or membership in a particular group based on characteristics such as race, ethnicity, gender, nationality, or religion.

civil disobedience The refusal, on moral grounds, to obey certain government laws, for the purpose of trying to bring about a change in legislation or government policy.

cognitive dissonance Psychological conflict resulting from incongruous beliefs and attitudes held simultaneously and when the current means of resolving the conflict is shown to be inadequate. (See ontological shock.)

cognitive theory The metaethical theory that moral statements can be either true or false.

consequentialism The ethical theory that the consequences of our actions are more important than our intentions.

cultural relativism A type of ethical relativism that maintains that morality is created collectively by groups of humans and that morality therefore differs from culture to culture.

cynicism Distrust in others' motives and disbelief in the possibility of knowing the truth.

defense mechanisms Psychological methods, which humans usually learn at an early age, for coping with difficult situations.

deontology The ethical theory that duty is the basis of morality.

descriptive statement A statement that tells us what *is*. Most scientific statements are descriptive.

determinism The theory that all events, including human actions, are governed by causal laws.

distributive justice This describes the duty to distribute the benefits and burdens of a society in a fair manner.

doctrine of the mean The doctrine that moral virtues, in general, entail moderation or seeking the middle path.

doublethink Simultaneously holding two contradictory views and believing both to be true.

egotist A person who is arrogant, boastful, and self-centered.

emotivism The moral theory that moral statements are neither true nor false but simply expressions of feeling.

empirical Knowledge, such as scientific facts, derived from experience through one or more of the five senses.

empiricism The theory that all, or at least most, human knowledge comes to us through the five senses.

epigenetic rules Innate patterns that guide the behavior and thought of humans and other animals.

epistemological privilege The theory that privileges the insight of people who are socially and economically disadvantaged.

epistemology The branch of philosophy that is concerned with the study of knowledge.

equivocation A type of fallacy where the meaning of an ambiguous term shifts during the course of the argument.

ethical egoism The metaethical theory that every person should do what is in his or her best self-interest.

ethical relativism The theory that morality is created by people and that moral systems can be different for different people.

ethical skepticism The theory that it is difficult, if not impossible, to know whether moral truths exist or the nature of these truths.

ethical subjectivism A type of ethical relativism that claims that morality is relative to each individual person.

ethics A branch of philosophy; the study of the fundamental principles and concepts regarding right and wrong conduct.

eudaemonia Aristotle's term for the happiness that humans by nature are seeking and that arises from the fulfillment of our function as humans.

euthanasia The act of painlessly bringing about the death of a person who is suffering from a terminal or incurable disease or condition.

fallacy An argument that is psychologically or emotionally persuasive but logically incorrect.

fallacy of accident A fallacy that occurs when someone applies a rule that is generally accepted as valid to a particular case where exceptional or accidental circumstances render the rule inappropriate.

fallacy of ignorance A fallacy committed whenever someone argues that a conclusion is true simply on the grounds that it has not been proven false, or else that it is false simply because it has not been proven true.

falsifiable The requirement that a theory must be falsifiable means that there must be some evidence or argument that could count against it. A "theory" that will not admit any evidence against it is known as a pseudo-theory.

fidelity A moral duty that stems from a commitment made in the past.

formal principle A moral principle that sets out general rules but lacks specific content.

good will A will that always acts from a sense of duty and reverence for moral law, without regard for consequences or for immediate inclinations.

gratitude A moral duty that stems from past favors or unearned services received.

the Greatest Happiness Principle The utilitarian principle that actions are right in proportion to how much they tend to promote happiness and wrong when they tend to produce unhappiness. This is also known as the principle of utility.

guilt A moral sentiment that results from the violation of a moral norm.

habituation A term used by Aristotle to describe the regular practice of virtuous behavior, much as one practices the piano or any other skill until it becomes second nature.

hasty generalization A fallacy that occurs when someone uses only unusual or atypical cases to support a conclusion.

hedon A unit of pleasure in Jeremy Bentham's utilitarian calculus.

hedonism A philosophical doctrine that considers pleasure to be the standard of value.

heteronomous moral agent Someone who looks to others for moral guidance.

hypothetical imperative A moral injunction that tells us we ought do something *if* we desire to achieve a certain result—such as telling a lie to save a life. Moral obligations are categorical or unconditionally binding upon us.

intuition Immediate or self-evident knowledge.

irrelevant conclusion This fallacy is committed when a person uses premises to support or reject a conclusion other than the one at which the premises are directed.

Karma The theory that the conditions of a person's current life are the sum of the moral consequences of his or her actions, both in this life and in past lifetimes. People achieve salvation and avoid reincarnation only by getting rid of all accumulated negative Karma.

laissez-faire capitalism An economic system based on the pursuit of rational and prudent self-interest, individual freedom, and minimal government interference.

legitimate interests In rights ethics, these are interests that do not prevent others from pursuing similar and equally important interests.

liberalism The theory that supports free will by stating that certain human actions are not entirely determined by causal events. Liberals oppose social and legal constraints upon individual freedoms. The term "libertarian" is sometimes used synonymously with the term "liberal."

liberation ethics The ethical theory based on social and political reform and a demand for respect of the dignity and rights of all people.

libertarian A person who is opposed to any social or political restraints upon individual freedom. (See "liberalism.")

liberty right The right to be left alone to pursue our legitimate interests without interference from the government or from others.

mandala The ancient Sanskrit word for a circle which symbolizes the cosmic order.

marginalization The act of relegating beings or groups to the fringes or margins of the moral community.

metaethics (also called metaethical theory) The subdivision of ethics concerned with appraising the logical foundations and internal consistencies of ethical systems.

metaphysical dualism The theory that reality is composed of two substances: material bodies and nonmaterial mind or spirit.

metaphysical materialism The theory that reality consists of only one substance: material (physical) bodies.

metaphysics The branch of philosophy concerned with the study of the nature of reality, including what it means to be human.

moral community All beings who have moral worth in themselves and, as such, deserve the respect of the community.

moral dilemma A situation where there is a conflict between moral values; no matter what solution is chosen, it will involve doing something wrong in order to do what is right.

moral indignation The anger or moral outrage that some people feel at the sight of others being harmed.

moral motivation One of James Rest's four components of moral behavior. This involves placing moral values above competing nonmoral values.

moral sensitivity One of James Rest's four components of moral behavior: The awareness of how our actions affect other people.

moral sentiments Emotions that move us to feel moral approval or disapproval.

moral tragedy This occurs when people fail to take appropriate moral action and make decisions that they later come to regret.

naturalistic fallacy The logical mistake (according to some moral philosophers) of drawing a conclusion about what *ought* to be from premises about what *is*.

noncognitive theory The metaethical theory that there are no moral truths.

non-maleficence The moral principle that we should do no harm.

normative ethics A subdivision of ethics that gives us practical guidelines or behavioral norms.

objectivist ethics A term used by Ayn Rand to describe her version of ethical egoism.

objectivist theory The metaethical theory that morality is discovered by humans and that universal moral truths exist that are true for all humans.

ontological shock An event that shakes our worldview, and our very being, to the core. Ontological shock leads to cognitive dissonance.

ontology The study of "being" or the nature of being.

opinion A statement that is based only on feeling rather than on fact.

pacifism The belief that the right to life is an absolute right.

paradigm An overall way of regarding and explaining phenomena within a particular discipline.

persons Beings who are worthy of respect as valuable in themselves, rather than because of their usefulness or value to others. A member of the moral community.

philosophy Literally, the "love of wisdom"; the systematic and critical search for truth and meaning in our lives.

popular appeal A fallacy that occurs when someone appeals to popular opinion or the opinion of the majority to gain support for a conclusion. Popular appeal can take different forms; the first is known as the "bandwagon" approach and the second, "snob appeal."

positivism The philosophical theory that all genuine human knowledge is based upon scientific observation.

practical morality A term used by Jean Piaget to describe morality that involves one's own motivations and sense of obligation. This aspect of morality leads us to formulate moral judgments to guide us in each particular case.

praxis The practice of a particular art or skill. In ethics, praxis entails informed social action.

prescriptive statement A statement dealing with values or what *ought* to be. Moral statements are prescriptive.

prima facie duty A duty that is morally binding unless it conflicts with a more pressing moral duty.

primary social goods Goods, such as food, housing, police protection, and education, which are necessary for us to pursue our liberty rights and our concept of the good life.

proposition In logic, a statement that expresses a complete thought. A proposition can be either true or false.

rationalism The theory that most human knowledge comes to us through reason rather than through the physical senses.

rationalization In philosophy the use of rhetoric, fallacies, and resistance in argument rather than reason and logical analysis.

reason The power of understanding the connection between the particular and the general.

reparation A moral duty that requires us to make amends for past harms that we have caused others.

resentment The anger or moral outrage that a person feels when personally injured by another.

resistance The use of immature defense mechanisms—such as isolation, rationalization, doubt and indecision, denial, repression, and displacement—as a means of preventing our worldview from being analyzed.

ressentiment Deep-seated resentment, frustration, and hostility accompanied by a sense of being powerless to express these feelings directly.

retributive justice A duty that requires punishment in proportion to wrongdoing.

rhetoric A means of defending a particular worldview rather than analyzing it. Unlike a logical argument, rhetoric uses only statements that support a particular opinion and disregards any statements that do not support this opinion.

rights ethics The ethical theory that people's entitlements as members of society are the basis of ethics.

self-actualization (See self-realization.)

self-realization The process of devoting one's life to self-cultivation and the search for ultimate values. A life lived in harmony with one's ultimate nature.

sentience The capacity to experience pain and pleasure.

shame A feeling that occurs as a result of a social blunder or violation of a social norm. Unlike true guilt, which is a moral sentiment, shame is governed by external sanctions.

skepticism Maintaining a doubtful, yet open and questioning, attitude toward statements that are claimed to be true.

sociobiology The branch of biology that applies evolutionary theory to the social sciences.

sociological relativism The observation that there is disagreement among cultures regarding moral values. Unlike cultural relativism, sociological relativism is neither an argument nor a moral theory. It is merely a descriptive statement about societies.

socratic method A technique developed by Socrates, using a question-and-answer format to break down resistance, thereby forcing people to critically analyze their preconceived notions.

solipsism The belief that we cannot prove the existence of anything outside of our own minds or ideas.

speciesism A term coined by utilitarian Peter Singer to describe prejudice or bias against a particular being simply because of its membership in a particular species.

spirituality An inner attitude of reverence or deep respect for the ultimate moral worth or sacredness of oneself and others.

state of nature The condition in which people lived before the formation of the state of governments.

super-ego Freud's concept of conscience; the super-ego develops as a reaction formation against our childhood Oedipus complex.

supererogatory Moral actions that are above and beyond what is normally expected of an individual.

sympathy A moral sentiment that involves the ability to imagine the feelings of others.

teleological A theory that is based upon a specific view of the purpose or goal of the natural order. Natural law theory and utilitarianism are teleological theories.

theoretical morality A term used by Jean Piaget to describe reasoning and judgment dissociated from actual deeds or a need to act.

Übermensch In Friedrich Nietzsche's philosophy, a superhuman or free-spirited person who is able to rise above the herd morality of the crowds and exercise his or her will to power.

utilitarianism The metaethical theory that actions producing the most pleasure are good and those that promote pain are bad.

utopia An ideal society.

values clarification Ethics education based on nonjudgmental and nondirective discussion of moral issues.

veil of ignorance A conceptual device used by John Rawls to establish a social contract that is unbiased and based upon impartiality.

vice A character defect or disposition to act in a manner that harms oneself and others.

virtue An admirable character trait or disposition to habitually act in a manner that benefits oneself and others.

virtue ethics The ethical theory concerned primarily with character and the type of people we should be, rather than with our actions.

welfare right The right to receive primary social goods such as adequate nutrition, housing, education, police and fire protection.

worldview The combined interpretations of our experiences.

Notes

Chapter 1

1. James Q. Wilson, *The Moral Sense* (New York: Free Press, 1993), p. 11.
2. Aristotle, *Nicomachean Ethics 8,* trans. J. A. K. Thomson (Baltimore: Penguin, 1953), p. 305.
3. Anthony Flew, *A Dictionary of Philosophy* (New York: St. Martin's Press, 1979), p. 3.
4. Alexander W. Astin, *What Matters in College? Four Critical Years Revisited* (San Francisco: Jossey-Bass, 1993).
5. See Chapter 2, p. 64 for a detailed explanation of the fallacy of hasty generalization.
6. For more on this, read Joseph Collins, "Should Doctors Tell the Truth?" *Harper's Monthly* 155 (August 1927): 320–326; and Donald Oken, "What to Tell Cancer Patients: A Study of Medical Attitudes," *Journal of the AMA* 175 (1961): 1120–1128.
7. Quoted in Catherine Hewitt, *Buddhism* (New York: Thomson, 1995), p. 21.
8. Karen J. Warren, "The Power and Promise of Ecological Feminism." in *Environmental Ethics,* eds. Susan J. Armstrong and Richard G. Botzler (New York: McGraw-Hill, 1993), pp. 434–444.
9. Ibid., p. 444.
10. Cows are considered to be sacred, not because of a belief that all animals have moral values, but because humans can be reincarnated as cows.
11. C. F. Andrews, *Mahatma Gandhi's Ideas, Including Selections from His Writings* (New York: Macmillan, 1930), pp. 109–110.
12. Mary Douglas, "Animals in Lele Religious Thought," *Africa* 27 (1957): 51–56.
13. See Annie L. Booth and Harvey M. Jacobs, "Ties that Bind: Native American Beliefs as a Foundation for Environmental Consciousness," *Environmental Ethics,* eds. Susan J. Armstrong and Richard G. Botzler (New York: McGraw-Hill, 1993), pp. 519–526.
14. For more on sociobiology, read Edward O. Wilson, *On Human Nature* (Cambridge: Harvard Univ. Press, 1978); and Michael Ruse, *The Darwinian Paradigm: Essays on Its History, Philosophy and Religious Implications* (London: Routledge & Kegan Paul, 1989).
15. Edward O. Wilson, *On Human Nature* (Cambridge: Harvard Univ. Press, 1978), p. 6.
16. Jean-Paul Sartre, *Existentialism and Human Emotions* (New York: Philosophical Library, 1957), pp. 15, 23. This brings up a question that Sartre does not adequately address— how other animals can have an essence or nature, if God is required for a human essence or nature to exist.
17. For more on this subject, see Charles Weihsun Fu and Sandra A. Wawrytko, eds., *Buddhist Ethics and Modern Society* (New York: Greenwood Press, 1991).
18. Alan M. Dershowitz, *The Abuse Excuse and Other Cop-outs, Sob Stories and Evasions of Responsibility* (Boston: Little, Brown, 1994).
19. Immanuel Kant, *Education,* trans. Annette Churton (Ann Arbor: Univ. of Michigan Press, 1960).
20. Lawrence Kohlberg, *The Psychology of Moral Development,* vol. 2 (San Francisco: Harper & Row, 1984).
21. Mary Warnock, *Ethics Since 1900* (New York: Oxford Univ. Press, 1978), p. 144.
22. Sandra Harding, ed., *Discovering Reality: Feminist Perspectives on Epistemology, Metaphysics, Methodology and Philosophy of Science* (Dordrecht, Netherlands: D. Reidel, 1983).
23. Ibid.
24. For more information on the emergence of a moral sense in children, read James Q. Wilson, *The Moral Sense* (New York: Free Press, 1993). Also see Chapter 6 in this text.
25. This speech was reputedly recorded by Plato, Socrates' disciple, in the dialogue entitled "Apology." Most of what we know about Socrates comes from the dialogues of Plato.
26. Abraham Maslow, "Self-Actualization and Beyond," *The Farther Reaches of Human Nature* (New York: Viking, 1971), 41–53.
27. Simone de Beauvoir, *The Second Sex,* trans. H. M. Parshley (New York: Vintage, 1974), p. 728.
28. Friedrich Nietzsche, *The Gay Science,* trans. Walter Kaufman, *The Portable Nietzsche* (New York: Penguin, 1976), p. 341.

Chapter 2

1. Thomas Kuhn, *The Structure of Scientific Revolutions* (Chicago: Univ. of Chicago Press, 1970).
2. Susan Sherwin, "Philosophical Methodology and Feminist Methodology: Are They Compatible?" in *Feminist Perspectives: Philosophical Essays on Methods and Morals,* ed. Lorraine Code, Sheila Mullett, and Christine

Overall (Toronto: Univ. of Toronto Press, 1988), p. 21.

3. Richard G. Majors and Jacob U. Gordon, eds., *The American Black Male: His Present Status and His Future* (Chicago: Nelson-Hall, 1994), p. 156.

4. "Shifting Perspectives: A New Approach to Ethics," in Code, Mullett & Overall, p. 115.

5. Paulo Freire, *The Pedagogy of the Oppressed* (New York: Continuum Press, 1983), p. 120.

6. Ibid., p. 64.

7. Malcolm X (underlining mine). *By Any Means Necessary: Speeches, Interviews and a Letter by Malcolm X,* ed. George Breitman (New York: Pathfinder, 1970).

8. Abraham Lincoln, "First Inaugural Address," 1861.

9. Norma Haan,. "Proposed Model of Ego Functioning: Coping and Defense Mechanisms in Relationship to IQ Change," *Psychological Monographs* 77, pt. 571. (1963): 8.

10. Daniel Hart and Susan Chmiel, "Influence of Defense Mechanisms on Moral Judgement Development: A Longitudinal Study," *Developmental Psychology* 28, no. 4 (1992): 722–729.

11. Norman Bradburn, *The Structure of Psychological Well-Being* (Chicago: Aldine, 1969), p. 128.

12. Tom Kitwood, *Concern for Others: A New Psychology of Conscience and Morality* (London: Routledge & Kegan Paul, 1990).

13. Swami Prabhavananda and Christopher Isherwood, *How to Know God: The Yoga Aphorisms of Patanjali* (Hollywood: Vendanta, 1969), p. 1.

14. Quoted in Sara Ruddick's *Maternal Thinking* (Boston: Beacon Press, 1989), p. 230.

15. Hannah Arendt, *Eichmann in Jerusalem: A Report on the Banality of Evil* (New York: Penguin, 1977), p. 44.

16. P. Don Premasiri, "The Relevance of the Noble Eightfold Path to Contemporary Society," *Buddhist Ethics and Modern Society,* ed. Charles Wei-hsun Fu and Sandra A. Wawrytko (New York: Greenwood Press, 1991), p. 137.

17. Peggy Orenstein, *Schoolgirls: Young Women, Self-Esteem, and the Confidence Gap* (Doubleday, American Association of University Women, 1994).

18. Immanuel Kant, *Education,* trans. Annette Churton (Ann Arbor: Univ. of Michigan Press, 1960).

19. Joseph Collins, "Should Doctors Tell the Truth?" *Harper's Monthly* 155 (August 1927): 320–326.

20. See Chapter 10 for a discussion of rights ethics.

21. Alice S. Rossi, ed., *The Feminist Papers: From Adams to de Beauvoir* (New York: Columbia Univ. Press, 1973), p. 242.

22. Lloyd Hare, *The Greatest American Woman: Lucretia Mott* (New York: American Historical Society, 1937), p. 193.

23. Stanley Milgram, *Obedience to Authority* (New York: Harper & Row, 1974), p. 5.

24. Alexis de Tocqueville, *Democracy in America,* (New York: McGraw, 1981).

25. Kitwood, p. 227.

26. James Rest, "Why Does College Promote Development in Moral Judgment?" *Journal of Moral Education* 17, no. 3 (1988): 183–194.

Chapter 3

1. Stephen A. Satris, "Student Relativism," *Teaching Philosophy* 9, no. 3 (September 1986): 193–200.

2. George Will, "The Bad Seed of Our Politics," *Newsweek,* 8 October 1990, p. 80.

3. Case cited in Daniel Goldman, "Emotional Literacy: A Field Report" (Kalamazoo, MI: Fetzer Institute, 1994), p. 1.

4. Mohandas Gandhi, *All Men Are Brothers* (New York: Columbia Univ. Press, 1958), p. 143.

5. Norman Lamm, "A Moral Mission for College," *New York Times,* 14 October 1986, section 1, p. 35.

6. Quoted by Ben-Ami Scharfstein, *The Philosophers: Their Lives and the Nature of Their Thought* (New York: Oxford Univ. Press, 1980), p. 197.

7. Penelope Leach, *Your Baby and Child* (New York: Knopf, 1989).

8. Hervey M. Cleckley, *The Mask of Sanity* (St. Louis: Mosby, 1976).

9. Jean-Jacques Rousseau, *Emile,* trans. B. Foxley (New York: Dutton, 1974), p. 263.

10. Eleanor Flexner, *Mary Wollstonecraft: A Biography* (New York: Coward, McCann & Geoghegan, 1972), p. 23.

11. Mary Wollstonecraft, *A Vindication of the Rights of Woman* (New York: Norton, 1988), p. 189.

12. Myron Stokes and David Zeman, "The Shame of a City," *Newsweek,* 4 September 1995, p. 26.

13. See David Finkelhor, *Sexually Victimized Children* (New York: Free Press, 1979).

Chapter 4

1. Herodotus, *The Histories,* trans. Aubrey de Selincourt (Harmondsworth, England: Penguin, 1972), pp. 219–220.

2. For example, head-hunting was practiced in some areas of the Balkans in Europe, among

the Jivaro of South America, and in some areas of New Guinea.

3. Josefina Zoraida Vazquez and Lorenzo Meyer, *The United States and Mexico* (Chicago: Univ. of Chicago Press, 1985), p. 43.

4. "Church Arson Investigators Fear an Epidemic of Hate," *Providence Sunday Journal,* 23 June 1996, p. A3.

5. See Noam Chomsky, "Basic Principles," in *Chomsky: Selected Readings,* ed. J. P. B. Allen and Paul Van Buren (London: Oxford Univ. Press, 1971), pp. 1–21.

6. Gontran de Poncins, *Kabloona* (New York: Reynal & Hitchcock, 1941).

7. Charles Dickens, "The Noble Savage," in *Crowned Masterpieces,* vol. 4, ed. David J. Brewer (St. Louis: Kaiser, 1902), pp. 1379, 1382.

8. For more on this topic, read Paul Lawrence Farber, *The Temptations of Evolutionary Ethics* (Berkeley: Univ. of California Press, 1994).

9. Charles Darwin, *The Descent of Man, and Selection in Relation to Sex,* 2 vol. (London: Murray, 1871).

10. Dickens, "The Noble Savage," pp. 1379, 1382.

11. W. Arens, *The Man-Eating Myth: Anthropology and Anthropophagy* (New York: Oxford Univ. Press, 1979).

12. William Graham Sumner, *Folkways* (Boston: Ginn, 1906), p. 28.

13. Fred Voget, *A History of Ethnology* (New York: Holt, Rinehart, 1975), pp. 368–369.

14. Malcolm Cowley, *Adventures of an African Slaver* (New York: World, 1928).

15. Sumner, *Folkways,* p. 13.

16. Clyde Kluckholn and Dorothea Leighton, *The Navaho* (Cambridge, MA: Harvard Univ. Press, 1974), p. 296.

17. Geoffrey Gorer, "Man Has No 'Killer' Instinct," *New York Times Magazine,* 26 November 1966, p. 47.

18. Joseph Campbell, *The Power of Myth* (New York: Doubleday, 1988), p. 78.

19. Sanskrit is the ancient language of the Hindus.

20. Dred Scott v. Sandford, 19 Howard, 393 (1857), in *Documents of American History,* eds. Henry Steele Commager and Milton Cantor (Englewood Cliffs, NJ: Prentice-Hall, 1988), pp. 339–345.

21. William H. Holcombe, "Characteristics and Capabilities of the Negro Race," *Southern Literary Messenger* 33 (1986): 401–410.

22. "Final Report of the Tuskegee Syphilis Study Ad Hoc Advisory Panel" (Washington, DC: U.S. Public Health Service, 1973), p. 7.

23. Robert M. Veatch, "Experimental Pregnancy," *Hastings Center Report* (June 1971), pp. 2–3.

24. See Jim Carnes, "Us and Them: A History of Intolerance in America," published by Teaching Tolerance, a project of the Southern Poverty Law Center, 1995, p. 16.

25. Excerpts from "A Pro-Slavery Argument," quoted in Arthur Young Lloyd, *The Slavery Controversy, 1831–1860* (Chapel Hill: Univ. of North Carolina Press, 1939), p. 249.

26. Margaret Fuller, "The Great Lawsuit, Man versus Men, Woman versus Woman," *The Dial* 4, no. 1 (July 1843): 1–47.

27. A. A. Lipscomb and A. E. Bergh, eds., *The Writings of Thomas Jefferson* (Washington, DC: The Thomas Jefferson Memorial Association of the United States, 1903, 1917), 1:34.

28. Plato *Republic* 2, 368a–371e.

29. Richard Erdoes, *Lame Deer: Seeker of Visions* (New York: Simon & Schuster, 1976), p. 115.

30. Mahomedali Currim Chagla, "The Role of the Lawyer in the World Today," *New York Law Journal, 25* May 1961), p. 2.

31. "The Crime of Child Slavery," *Current* (March/April 1994); and "Pakistan: Ending Child Labor," *Ms* (July/August 1995): 15.

32. John Stuart Mill, *On Liberty* (Indianapolis: Hackett, 1978).

33. Nancy Gibbs, "Cause Celeb," *Time,* 17 June 1996), pp. 28–30.

34. Bill Clinton, "Why Bosnia Matters to America," speech reprinted in *Newsweek,* 15 November 1995), p. 55.

35. Hannah Arendt, *Eichmann in Jerusalem: A Report on the Banality of Evil* (New York: Viking, 1963).

36. Ibid., p. 95.

37. Ibid., p. 15.

38. Ibid., pp. 5, 222.

39. Ibid., p. 104.

40. Ibid., pp. 111–112.

41. "Rwanda: Exposing Abuses," *Ms* (July/August 1995): 14.

42. Arendt, *Eichmann in Jerusalem,* p. 133.

43. See Reinhold Niebuhr, *Moral Man and Immoral Society* (New York: Scribner, 1932), pp. xi–xii.

44. Tom Kitwood, *Concern for Others: A New Psychology of Conscience and Morality* (London: Routledge & Kegan Paul, 1990), p. 102.

45. See Arens, *The Man-Eating Myth.* See also Ruth Benedict, *Patterns of Culture* (Boston: Houghton Mifflin, 1934), p. 131. In this text, Benedict talks about the practice of cannibalism, which she never actually witnessed because it apparently had ended a few years before her arrival.

46. In light of the startling disclosure by the Samoan girls (who were now older women) first interviewed by Margaret Mead for her

book *Coming of Age in Samoa: A Psychological Study of Primitive Youth for Western Civilization* (1927) that they had invented the stories of sexual promiscuity among Samoan children to tease as well as please Dr. Mead, we should regard these stories of highly discrepant moral practices as just that—stories—unless the events have actually been witnessed by anthropologists or other reliable sources.

47. C. P. Snow, "Either-Or," *Progressive* (February 1961): 24.

Chapter 5

1. Gustavo Gutierrez, *The Power of the Poor in History,* trans. Robert R. Barr (Maryknoll, NY: Orbis Books, 1993), p. 7.

2. Clifford Geertz, *Islam Observed* (Chicago: Univ. of Chicago Press, 1968), p. 97.

3. Keith A. Roberts, *Religion in Sociological Perspective* (Homewood, IL: Dorsey Press, 1984), p. 62.

4. Abu'l A'la Mawdudi, *The Islamic Law and Constitution,* trans. Khurshid Ahmad (Chicago, IL: Kazi, 1955), p. 132.

5. *Qur'an,* 12:40. As quoted in Abul A'la Mawdudi, *The Islamic Law,* p. 132.

6. Mohandas K. Gandhi, "Through Non-Violence to God," in *Hinduism,* ed. Louis Renou (New York: Braziller, 1962), p. 233.

7. Genesis 22:1–19. *The New Oxford Annotated Bible* (New York: Oxford Univ. Press, 1977), pp. 25–26.

8. Evan Thomas, "Can Peace Survive?" *Newsweek,* 13 November 1995, p. 43.

9. Kai Neilsen, "God and the Good: Does Morality Need Religion?" *Theology Today* 21, no. 1 (April 1964).

10. F. Rossner and J. David Bleich, eds., *Jewish Bioethics* (Brooklyn, NY: Hebrew Publishing, 1985), p. xix.

11. Kwame Gyekye, *An Essay on African Philosophical Thought: The Akan Conceptual Scheme* (New York: Cambridge Univ. Press, 1987).

12. Lon L. Fuller, *The Morality of Law* (New Haven, CT: Yale Univ. Press, 1964), pp. 184–185.

13. Daniel Bonevac, William Boon, and Stephen Phillips, *Beyond the Western Tradition: Readings in Moral and Political Philosophy* (Mountain View, CA: Mayfield, 1992), p. 69.

14. Thomas Aquinas, *Summa Theologica* 1, pt. 1.2, question 96, answer 4.

15. Elizabeth Cady Stanton, Susan B. Anthony, and Matilda Joslyn Gage, eds., *History of Woman Suffrage* (New York: Fowler & Wells, 1881), 2: 689.

16. Martin Luther King, Jr., *The Strength to Love* (Philadelphia: Fortress Press, 1963), p. 42.

17. Kai Nielsen, *Philosophy and Atheism: In Defense of Atheism* (Buffalo, NY: Prometheus, 1985), pp. 183–184.

18. Robert Bellah, "Civil Religion in America," in *Essays on Religion in a Post-Traditional World,* ed. Robert N. Bellah (New York: Harper & Row, 1970), p. 175. See also Roberts, *Religion,* pp. 62–63.

19. Ibid., p. 182.

20. Ibid., p. 172.

21. Steven P. McNeel, "Christian Liberal Arts Education and Growth in Moral Judgment," *The Journal of Psychology and Christianity* 10, no. 4 (1991): 311–322.

22. Rosemary Radford Ruether, *Sexism and God-Talk* (Boston: Beacon Press, 1983), p. 94.

23. Carol P. Christ and Judith Plaskow, eds., *Womanspirit Rising: A Feminist Reader in Religion* (San Francisco: Harper & Row, 1979), p. 274.

24. James H. Cone, *Black Theology and Black Power* (New York: Seabury Press, 1969), p. 127.

25. J. Donald Hughes and Jim Swan, "How Much of the Earth Is Sacred Space?" *Environmental Ethics,* ed. Susan Armstrong and Richard Botzer (New York: McGraw-Hill 1993), pp. 172–180.

26. Amanda Porterfield, "American Indian Spirituality as a Countercultural Movement," in *Religion in Native North America,* ed. Christopher Vecsey, (Moscow: Univ. of Idaho Press, 1990), p. 154.

27. Lynn White, "The Historic Roots of Our Ecological Crisis," *Science* 155 (1976): 1203.

28. Robert R. Gottfried, "On Gardening and Human Welfare, or The Role of Attitudes and Natural Capital in Sustainable Welfare," *Agriculture and Human Values* 9 (Fall 1992): 36–47.

29. Eagle Man, "We Are All Related," *Mother Earth Spirituality: Native American Paths to Healing Ourselves and Our World,* ed. Ed McGaa (San Francisco, CA: Harper & Row, 1990), p. 203.

30. Quoted in S. Paul Schilling, *God and Human Anguish* (Nashville, TN: Abingdon, 1977), p. 34.

31. John Stuart Mill, *Three Essays on Religion* (New York: Henry Holt, 1874), p. 186.

32. Peter De Vries, *The Blood of the Lamb* (Boston: Little, Brown, 1962), p. 104.

33. David Hume, *Dialogues Concerning Natural Religion* (New York: Hafner, 1969), pp. 66, 68.

34. Joseph Butler, "Does God Put Men to the Test?" *The Analogy of Religion and Nature Revealed* (London: J. M. Dent, 1917).

35. John Hicks, *Philosophy of Religion* (Englewood Cliffs, NJ: Prentice-Hall, 1963).

36. Louis Jacobs, "The Relationship Between Religion and Ethics in Jewish Thought," in *Moral Issues: Philosophical and Religious Perspectives,* ed. Gabriel Palmer-Fernandez (Upper Saddle River, NJ: Prentice-Hall, 1996), p. 35.
37. Schilling, *God and Human Anguish,* p. 37.
38. Keith A. Roberts, *Religion in Sociological Perspective* (Homewood, IL: Dorsey Press, 1984), p. 62.
39. Jason Berry, *Lead Us Not into Temptation* New York: Doubleday 1992.
40. Andrew M. Greeley, *Fall from Grace* (New York: Putnam, 1993), p. 45.
41. Kenneth Ring, *Heading Toward Omega* (New York: Morrow, 1985), pp. 143.
42. Mohandas K. Gandhi, *Non-Violent Resistance* (New York: Schocken Books, 1961), p. 3.
43. Quoted in Roberts, pp. 326–329.
44. Samuel P. Oliner and Pearl M. Oliner, *The Altruistic Personality: Rescuers of Jews in Nazi Europe* (New York: Free Press, 1988), p. 156.
45. Speech of Representative Smith, *Annals of Congress,* 1st Congress, 2nd session, I, 730.
46. John C. Calhoun's speech of December 27, 1837, in A. J. Beveridge, *Abraham Lincoln,* vol. 2, *1809–1858* (Boston: Houghton Mifflin, 1928), p. 20.
47. Ibid.
48. George Gallup, Jr., and Frank Newport, "America's Shift Toward Pro-Choice Position," *The Gallup Poll Monthly* (April 1990): 4.

Chapter 6

1. From Kant's unpublished handbook to his lectures on ethics, as quoted by Martin Buber in *Between Man and Man* (New York: Macmillan, 1965), p. 119.
2. Georg Hegel, *Hegel's Philosophy of the Right,* trans. T. M. Knox (London: Oxford Univ. Press, 1967), p. 91.
3. Eleventh-century scholar Bahya ben Joseph ibn Paquda, as quoted in Daniel Bonevac, William Boon, and Stephen Phillips, *Beyond Western Tradition* (Mountain View, CA: Mayfield, 1992), p. 107.
4. Quoted in Bonevac, Boon, and Phillips, *Beyond the Western Tradition,* p. 29.
5. Immanuel Kant, *The Moral Law: Groundwork of the Metaphysics of Morals,* trans. H. J. Paton (New York: Routledge & Kegan Paul, 1991), pp. 60–61.
6. Plato, *Republic* 3, trans. G. M. A. Grube (Indianapolis: Hackett, 1992), p. 410a.
7. Friedrich Nietzsche, *Beyond Good and Evil,* trans. R. J. Hollingdale (New York: Penguin, 1990), pp. 120–121.
8. Friedrich Nietzsche, "Letters," *The Portable Nietzsche,* trans. William Kaufman (New York: Penguin, 1954), p. 442.
9. Robert Katz, *Empathy: Its Nature and Uses* (New York: Free Press, 1963), p. 11.
10. Martin L. Hoffman, "The Contribution of Empathy to Justice and Moral Judgment," in *Empathy and Its Development.* ed. Nancy Eisenberg and Janet Strayer (New York: Cambridge Univ. Press, 1987), pp. 47–80.
11. Nancy Eisenberg and Paul A. Mussen, *The Roots of Prosocial Behavior in Children* (Cambridge, England: Cambridge Univ. Press, 1989).
12. Sarah A. Tooley, *The Life of Florence Nightingale* (New York: Macmillan, 1905), pp. 39–40.
13. Frederick Douglass, *Life and Times of Frederick Douglass* (New York: Citadel Press, 1984).
14. Patricia B. Sutker, C. E. Moan, and Albert N. Allain, "Assessment of Cognitive Control in Psychopathic and Normal Prisoners," *Journal of Behavioral Assessment* 5 (1983): 275–287.
15. Hanna Damasio et al., "The Return of Phineas Gage: Clues About the Brain from the Skull of a Famous Patient," *Science* 264 (May 1994): 1103–1105.
16. Sigmund Freud, *Sigmund Freud: The Ego and the Id,* trans. Joan Riviere (New York: Norton, 1962), p. 24. Freud, like most of his contemporaries, developed his theory using boys as "generic" humans.
17. Freud, *Sigmund Freud,* p. 24.
18. Peter Singer, "Why Act Morally?" *Practical Ethics* (New York: Cambridge Univ. Press, 1979).
19. Quoted in *A Sourcebook in Asian Philosophy,* ed. John M. Koller and Patricia Koller (New York: Macmillan, 1991), p. 424.
20. Fox Butterfield, *All God's Children* (New York: Knopf, 1995).
21. Mary Midgley, *Can't We Make Moral Judgements?* (New York: St. Martin's Press, 1993), pp. 48–49.
22. Erik Fromm, *The Sane Society* (London: Routledge & Kegan Paul, 1956).
23. Hillary Rodham Clinton, *It Takes a Village and Other Lessons Children Teach Us* (New York: Simon & Schuster, 1996). Excerpted in *Newsweek,* 15 January 1996, p. 33.
24. James Q. Wilson, *The Moral Sense* (New York: Free Press, 1993), p. 32.
25. Plato *Republic* 2.
26. Nel Noddings, *Caring: A Feminine Approach to Ethics and Moral Education* (Berkeley: Univ. of California Press, 1984).
27. Sogyal Rinpoche, *The Tibetan Book of Living and Dying* (San Francisco: HarperCollins 1992), p. 94.

28. Hans Seyle, *The Stress of Life* (New York: McGraw-Hill, 1956).

29. Jeffrie Murphy, "Forgiveness and Resentment," in *Minnesota Studies in Philosophy: Social and Political Philosophy,* vol. 7, eds. Peter A. French, Theodore E. Uehling, Jr., and Howard K. Wettstein (Minneapolis: Univ. of Minnesota Press, 1982), p. 507.

30. Max Scheler, *Ressentiment,* ed. Lewis A. Coser, trans. William W. Holdheim (New York: Free Press, 1969), pp. 45–46.

31. Lewis Okun, *Woman Abuse* (Albany: SUNY Press, 1986), p. 59. See also Lenore E. Walker, *The Battered Woman Syndrome* (New York: Springer-Verlag, 1984).

32. Tamara J. Ferguson, Hedy Stegge, and Ilse Damhuis, "Children's Understanding of Guilt and Shame," *Child Development* 62, no. 4 (1991): 827–839.

33. Ibid.

34. Carol J. Nemeroff, Alana Brinkman, and Claudia K. Woodward, "Magical Contagion and AIDS Risk Perception in a College Population," *AIDS Education and Prevention* 6, no. 3 (1994): 249–265.

35. For more on this topic, read William Damon, *Greater Expectations* (New York: Free Press, 1995); Jerome Kagan and S. Lamb, eds., *The Emergence of Moral Concepts in Young Children* (Chicago: Univ. of Chicago Press, 1987); E. H. Erikson, *Childhood and Society* (New York: Norton, 1950); William Damon, *The Moral Child* (New York: Free Press, 1988); and Jean Piaget, *The Moral Judgment of Children* (London: Routledge & Kegan Paul, 1932).

36. "Feeling Guilty May Even Be Good for You," *Providence Sunday Journal,* 15 May 1994, p. D4.

37. James Q. Wilson, *The Moral Sense* (New York: Free Press, 1993), pp. 104–105.

38. William Damon, *The Moral Child* (New York: Free Press, 1988), p. 36.

39. Richard L. Lee, *The !Kung San: Men, Women and Work in a Foraging Society* (Cambridge: Harvard Univ. Press, 1979).

40. Malcolm X and Alex Haley, *The Autobiography of Malcolm X* (New York: Grove Press, 1964).

41. Jean Piaget, *The Moral Judgment of Children* (London: Routledge & Kegan Paul, 1932), p. 171.

42. Ibid., pp. 96, 71.

43. Ibid., p. 171.

44. Erik Erikson, *Childhood and Society* (New York: Norton, 1950).

45. Elliot Turiel, "Conflict and Transition in Adolescent Moral Development," *Child Development* 45 (1974): 15.

46. Lawrence Kohlberg, *Essays in Moral Devel-*opment, Vol. II. The Psychology of Moral Development* (San Francisco: Harper & Row, 1984).

47. Adapted from Lawrence Kohlberg, *The Philosophy of Moral Development* (New York: Harper & Row, 1981), pp. 510–511; and Barbara Panzl and Timothy McMahon, "Ethical Decision-Making: Developmental Theory and Practice," speech delivered at the National Association of Student Personnel Administrators, Denver, Colorado, March 1989.

48. James Rest, Elliot Turiel, and Lawrence Kohlberg, "Level of Moral Development as a Determinant of Preference and Comprehension of Moral Judgment Made by Others," *Journal of Personality* 37 (1969): 738–748.

49. David Wallechinsky, "How One Woman Became the Voice of Her People," *Parade Magazine,* 19 January 1997, p. 5.

50. James Rest, "Research on Moral Development: Implications for Training Counseling Psychologists," *The Counseling Psychologist,* 12, no. 2 (1984): 19–29.

51. T. M. Kitwood, *Concern for Others: A New Psychology of Conscience and Morality* (London: Routledge & Kegan Paul, 1990), pp. 146–147.

52. Lawrence A. Ponemon and David R. L. Gabhart, "Ethical Reasoning Research in the Accounting and Auditing Professions," in *Moral Development in the Professions: Psychology and Applied Ethics,* eds. James R. Rest and Darcia Narváez (Hillsdale, NJ: Erlbaum, 1994), pp. 101–119.

53. Lawrence Kohlberg, P. Scharf, and J. Hickey, "The Justice Structure of the Prison: A Theory and Intervention," *Prison Journal* 51 (1972): 3–14.

54. N. Sanford, ed., *College and Character* (New York: Wiley, 1964).

55. Dwight R. Boyd, "The Condition of Sophomoritis and Its Educational Cure," *Journal of Moral Education,* 10, vol. 1 (1980): 24–39.

56. Gregory S. Blimling, "Developing Character in College Students," *NASPA Journal* 27, no. 4 (Summer 1990): 268.

57. *The Four Books: Confucian Analects, The Great Learning, The Doctrine of the Mean, and The Works of Mencius,* trans. James Legge (Shanghai, China: Chinese Book Co., 1933), pp. 13–14.

58. Damon, *The Moral Child,* pp. 36–39.

59. Carol Gilligan and Jane Attanucci, "Two Moral Orientations: Gender Differences and Similarities," *Merrill-Palmer Quarterly* 34, no. 3 (1988): 223–237.

60. James R. Rest and Darcia Narváez, eds.,

Moral Development in the Professions: Psychology and Applied Ethics (Hillsdale, NJ: Erlbaum, 1994).

61. As quoted by Carol Gilligan, *In a Different Voice* (Cambridge: Harvard Univ. Press, 1982), p. 16.

62. Ibid., pp. 72–73.

63. Norma Haan, *On Moral Grounds: The Search for Practical Morality* (New York: New York University Press, 1985). See also L. Walker, "Experiential and Cognitive Sources of Moral Development in Adulthood," *Human Development* 12 (1986): 113–124.

64. Lisa Leghorn and Mary Roodkowsky, *Who Really Starves? Women and World Hunger,* (New York: Friendship Press, 1977).

65. Quoted in Gilligan, *Different Voice,* p. 129.

66. See G. R. Donenberg and L. Hoffman, "Gender Differences in Moral Development," *Sex Roles* 18, nos. 11–12 (1988): 701–717; Gilligan and Attanucci, "Two Moral Orientations," pp. 223–237; Linda Hendrixson, "Care Versus Justice: Two Moral Perspectives in the Baby 'M' Surrogacy Case," *Journal of Sex Education and Therapy* 15, no. 4, pp. 247–256; Nancy Stiller and Linda Forrest, "An Extension of Gilligan and Lyon's Investigation of Morality: Gender Differences in College Students," *Journal of College Student Development* 31, no. 1 (1990): 54–63; Elizabeth Peters and Ruth Gallop, "The Ethics of Care: A Comparison of Nursing and Medical Students," *IMAGE Journal of Nursing Scholarship* 26, no. 1 (1994): 47–51.

67. See B. Sichel, "Women's Moral Development in Search of Philosophical Assumptions," *Journal of Moral Education* 14, no. 3 (1985): 149–161.

68. Gilligan and Attanucci, "Two Moral Orientations," p. 225.

69. R. Blotner and D. J. Bearison, "Developmental Consistencies in Socio-Moral Knowledge: Justice Reasoning and Altruistic Behavior," *Merrill-Palmer Quarterly* 30, no. 4, (October 1984): 349–357.

70. Augusto Blasi, "Moral Cognition and Moral Action: A Theoretical Perspective," *Developmental Review* 3 (1983): 178–210.

71. James Rest, "Research on Moral Development: Implications for Training Counseling Psychologists," *The Counseling Psychologist* 12, no. 2 (1984): 19.

72. Beth Teitell, "Feeling Guilty? Good!" *Boston Sunday Herald,* 13 March 1994, pp. 1, 14.

73. A. Holmes, *Shaping Character: Development in Christian Colleges* (Grand Rapids, MI: Eerdmans, 1991).

74. Anne C. Levy, "The Anita Hill–Clarence Thomas Hearings," *Wisconsin Law Review* 1106 (1991).

75. A. F. Smith, "Lawrence Kohlberg's Cognitive Stage Theory of the Development of Moral Judgment," *New Directions for Student Services* 4 (1978): 53–67.

76. Martin L. Hoffman, "Empathy, Its Development and Prosocial Implications," ed. D. Keasey, *Nebraska Symposium on Motivation* 25 (Lincoln: Univ. of Nebraska Press, 1978).

77. James Rest, "Background: Theory and Research," in Rest and Narváez, eds., *Moral Development in the Professions,* p. 15.

78. James Rest, *Advances in Research and Theory* (New York: Praeger, 1986), p. 32.

79. Rest, Chapter 3.

80. Blasi, "Moral Cognition and Moral Action."

81. L. Lamont, *Campus Shock* (New York: Dutton, 1979).

82. A. Higgins, C. Power, and Lawrence Kohlberg, "The Relationship of Moral Atmosphere to Judgments of Responsibility," *Morality, Moral Behaviour and Moral Development,* eds. W. M. Kurtines and J. L. Gewitz (New York: Wiley, 1984), p. 75.

83. Muriel J. Bebeau, "Influencing the Moral Dimensions of Dental Practice," Rest and Narváez, *Moral Development in the Professions,* pp. 121–146.

84. Rest, "Research on Moral Development," p. 26.

85. Barbara Panzl and Timothy McMahon, "Ethical Decision Making: Developmental Theory and Practice," speech delivered at the National Association of Student Personnel Administrators, Denver, Colorado, March 1989.

86. James R. Rest, "Theory and Research," in Rest and Narváez, eds., *Moral Development in the Professions,* p. 24.

87. Hannah Arendt, *Eichmann in Jerusalem: A Report on the Banality of Evil* (New York: Viking, 1977).

88. Ibid., p. 22.

Chapter 7

1. Plato, *Republic,* trans. G. M. A. Grube (Indianapolis: Hackett, 1992), pp. 359b–361a.

2. Thomas Reid, *Essays on the Intellectual Powers of Man,* ed. Herman Shapiro (1785), in *The Works of Thomas Reid* (Cambridge: Harvard Univ. Press, 1969), p. 179.

3. Epicurus, "Letter to Menoeceus," *Hellenistic Philosophy,* pp. 62, 65.

4. Thomas Hobbes, *Leviathan* (New York: Macmillan, 1962), p. 100.

5. For more on this, see Karl Popper, *Conjectures and Refutations: The Crown of Scientific Knowledge* (London: Routledge & Kegan Paul, 1963).

6. Ayn Rand, *Philosophy: Who Needs It?* (New York: New American Library, 1984), p. 10.

7. Ayn Rand, *Atlas Shrugged* (New York: New American Library, 1959), p. 982.

8. Aristotle, *Politics*, 1. 2. 1252. In *The Basic Works of Aristotle*, ed. Richard McKeon (New York: Random House, 1941), pp. 27–29.

9. Ayn Rand, "Objectivist Ethics," in *The Virtue of Selfishness: A New Concept of Egoism* (New York: New American Library, 1964), p. 15.

10. Ayn Rand, *The Fountainhead* (New York: New American Library, 1952), p. 664.

11. Ibid., p. 676.

12. Rand, "Objectivist Ethics," p. 31.

13. Jerry Kirkpatrick, *In Defense of Advertising: Arguments from Reason, Ethical Egoism, and Laissez-Faire Capitalism* (Westport, CT: Quorum, 1994), p. 154.

14. D. Stanley Eitzen and Maxine Baca Zinn, *The Reshaping of America: Social Consequences of the Changing Economy* (Englewood Cliffs, NJ: Prentice-Hall, 1989), p. 132.

15. Jane Bryant Quinn, "A Paycheck Revolt in '96?" *Newsweek*, 19 February 1996, p. 52.

16. Lynn Karoly, *Oxford Review of Economic Policy* 12 (Spring 1996).

17. Gustavo Gutierrez, *The Power of the Poor in History,* trans. Robert R. Barr (Maryknoll, NY: Orbis, 1983), p. 28.

18. Jonathan Kozol, *Savage Inequalities* (New York: Crown, 1991), p. 98.

19. Frantz Fanon, *The Wretched of the Earth,* trans. Constance Farrington (New York: Grove Press, 1963); quoted in Daniel Bonevac, William Boon, and Stephen Phillips, eds., *Beyond the Western Tradition: Readings in Moral and Political Philosophy* (Mountain View, CA: Mayfield, 1992), p. 50.

20. Ayn Rand, "The Divine Right of Stagnation," in *The Virtue of Selfishness*, p. 143.

21. J. D. Sethi, "Human Rights and Development," *Human Rights Quarterly* 3, no. 3 (Summer 1981).

22. Lisa H. Newton, "Reserve Discrimination as Unjustified," *Ethics* 83 (July 1973).

23. Rand, *The Virtue of Selfishness,* p. 35.

24. James Rachels, *The Elements of Philosophy* (New York: Random House, 1986), pp. 76–78.

25. Michael D'Antonio and Michael Krasny, "I or We," *Mother Jones* 19, no. 3 (May–June 1994): 1.

26. Ayn Rand, "What Is Capitalism?" in *Capitalism: The Unknown Ideal* (New York: New American Library, 1966), p. 30.

27. Ruut Veenhoven, *Conditions of Happiness* (Dordrecht, Netherlands: D. Reidel, 1984).

28. Ibid., p. 322.

29. Ibid., p. 322.

30. Leo Tolstoy, *The Death of Ivan Ilych and Other Stories* (London: Oxford Univ. Press, 1971), pp. 13, 29.

31. Ibid., p. 69.

32. Lawrence A. Ponemon and David R. L. Gabhart, "Ethical Reasoning Research in the Accounting and Auditing Professions," in *Moral Development in the Professions: Psychology and Applied Ethics,* ed. James Rest and Darcia Narváez (Hillsdale, NJ: Erlbaum, 1994), pp. 117–18.

33. *Bhagavad Gita,* with commentary by R. C. Zaehner (Oxford, England: Clarendon Press, 1969), pp. 447–448.

34. From the *Analects* of Confucianism, discussed in Daniel Bonevac, William Boon, and Stephen Phillips, eds., *Beyond Western Tradition* (Mountain View, CA: Mayfield, 1992), p. 259.

35. Rand, *Atlas Shrugged,* p. 978.

36. Mencius, *The Works of Mencius,* ed. and trans. James Legge (Oxford, England: Clarendon Press, 1895), p. 7A26.

37. Quoted from Samuel Taylor Coleridge, "Religious Musings," *Coleridge and the Self: Romantic Egotism,* ed. Stephen Bygrave (New York: St. Martin's Press, 1986), p. 86.

38. Quoted in *Webster's Treasury of Relevant Quotations,* ed. Edward R. Murphy (New York: Crown, 1978), p. 240.

Chapter 8

1. Jeremy Bentham, *Principles of Morals and Legislation* (London: Clarendon Press, 1907), p. 1. (This edition is a reprint of Bentham's new edition of the book, published in 1823.)

2. John Stuart Mill, "On Liberty," in *Utilitarianism,* ed. Mary Warnock (New York: Meridian, 1962).

3. John Stuart Mill, "Utilitarianism," in *Utilitarianism,* ed. Mary Warnock (New York: Meridian, 1962).

4. Ibid., p. 268.

5. Bentham, *Principles,* p. 50.

6. Mill, "Utilitarianism," p. 257.

7. J. J. C. Smart and Bernard Williams, *Utilitarianism, For and Against* (Cambridge, England: Cambridge Univ. Press, 1973).

8. Warnock, *Utilitarianism,* pp. 26–27.

9. Ibid., Chapter 2.

10. Jeremy Bentham, *Introduction to the Principles of Morals and Legislation,* (London: Free Press, 1970), Chapter 17.

11. "The Four Noble Truths," *Thus I Have Heard: The Long Discourses of Buddha: Kigha Nikaya,* trans. Maurice Walshe (Boston: Wisdom, 1987), pp. 346–347.

12. John Rawls, *A Theory of Justice* (Cambridge, MA: Belknap Press, 1971), p. 30.

13. All quotes from Mo Tzu in this chapter are from *Mo Tzu: Basic Writings,* trans. Burton Watson (New York: Columbia Univ. Press, 1963).
14. Bentham, *Principles,* p. 41.
15. Roberta K. Thyfault, Angela Browne, and Lenore E. A. Walker, "When Battered Women Kill," *Domestic Violence on Trial,* ed. Daniel J. Sonkin (New York: Springer-Verlag, 1987), p. 72.
16. Neal A. Whitman, David C. Spendlove, and Claire H. Clark, *Student Stress: Effects and Solutions* (Washington, DC: ASHE-ERIC Higher Ed. Research Report No. 2, 1984), p. 2.
17. Quoted by Ben-Am Scharfstein, *The Philosophers: Their Lives and the Nature of Their Thought* (New York: Oxford Univ. Press, 1980), p. 262.
18. John Stuart Mill, "Bentham," in *Utilitarianism,* ed. Mary Warnock (New York: Meridian, 1962), p. 98.
19. John Stuart Mill, *The Subjugation of Women* (Cambridge, MA: MIT Press, 1869/1970), p. 100.
20. Mill, "On Liberty," p. 239.
21. Mill, "Utilitarianism," p. 260.
22. John Stuart Mill, *Autobiography,* in *The Harvard Classics,* vol. 25 (New York: Collier, 1909), p. 94.
23. A *liberty right* is the right to pursue one's own interests without interference, as long as the pursuit of one's interests does not interfere with other people's similar rights. Freedom of speech, freedom of religion, and freedom of expression are all examples of liberty rights.
24. Mill, "On Liberty," p. 205.
25. Warnock, *Utilitarianism,* p. 10.
26. For example, see Judith Boss and Katherine Wurtz, "Is Mandatory Schooling Inherently Unjust?" *The Educational Forum* 58, no. 3 (1994): 264–275; G. L. Brandt, *The Realization of Anti-Racist Teaching* (Philadelphia: Hemisphere, 1986); Barbara Kantrowitz, B. Rosado, and L. Rosado, "Falling Further Behind: A Generation of Hispanics Isn't Making the Grade," *Newsweek,* 19 August 1991, p. 60; and M. Sadker and D. Sadker, "Sexism in the Classroom," *Vocational Educational Journal* 60 (1985): pp. 30–32.
27. Sadker and Sadker, "Sexism," p. 30.
28. Joni N. Gray, Phillip M. Lyons, Jr., and Gary B. Melton, *Ethical and Legal Issues in AIDS Research* (Baltimore: Johns Hopkins Univ. Press, 1995), p. 23.
29. Joseph S. Alper, "Ethical and Social Implications," *Sociobiology and Human Nature,* ed. Michael S. Gregory, Anita Silvers, and Diane Sutch (San Francisco: Jossey-Bass, 1978), p. 211.
30. Mill, "Utilitarianism," p. 283.
31. Peter Singer, *Animal Liberation* (New York: Random House, 1990), p. 37.
32. David Hume, "Of Suicide," in *Of the Standard of Taste and Other Essays,* ed. John Lenz (Indianapolis: Bobbs-Merrill, 1965), p. 158.
33. Ibid., p. 158.
34. Mill, "Utilitarianism," p. 308.
35. Rawls, *Theory of Justice,* p. 187.
36. Ibid., p. 270.

Chapter 9

1. Immanuel Kant, *Critique of Practical Reason,* trans. T. K. Abbott (London: Longmans, Green & Co., 1909), p. 260.
2. *Bhagavad Gita,* ch. II: 31, in *A Sourcebook in Asian Philosophy,* ed. John M. Koller and Patricia Koller (New York: Macmillan, 1991).
3. John Stuart Mill, "Utilitarianism," in *Utilitarianism and Other Writings,* eds. Mary Warnock (New York: Meridian, 1962), p. 304.
4. Immanuel Kant, *The Moral Law: Groundwork of the Metaphysic of Morals,* trans. H. J. Paton (London: Routledge and Kegan Paul, 1991), p. 64.
5. Hannah Arendt, *Eichmann in Jerusalem: A Report on the Banality of Evil* (New York: Penguin, 1976), p. 193.
6. *The Commentary of Tseng,* as quoted in *A Sourcebook in Asian Philosophy,* eds. John M. Koller and Patricia Koller (New York: Macmillan, 1991), p. 3.
7. Chi Hsi, "Selected Writings," in Koller and Koller, *Sourcebook in Asian Philosophy,* p. 548.
8. Chan Wing-tsit, *A Source Book in Chinese Philosophy* (Princeton: Princeton Univ. Press, 1963), bk. 3:1.
9. Confucius, as quoted in Ben Raeburn, *Treasury for the Free World* (Freeport, NY: Books for Libraries, 1946).
10. Chu Hsi, "Selected Writings," pp. 542–543.
11. Kenneth Kraft, ed., *Inner Peace, World Peace: Essays on Buddhism and Nonviolence* (Albany, NY: SUNY Press, 1992), p. 127.
12. Kant, *The Moral Law,* p. 68.
13. *Providence Journal,* 3 September 1995, p. 2.
14. Kant, *The Moral Law,* p. 62.
15. Ibid., p. 13.
16. As quoted by Lewis White Beck in his "Foreword" to Immanuel Kant's *Lectures on Ethics* (Indianapolis: Hackett, 1775–1780/1963), p. ix.
17. Quoted in Judith A. Boss, "Volunteer Community Service Work and Its Effect on the

Moral Development of Ethics Students" thesis, University of Rhode Island (M.S. 1991), p. 77.

18. Kant, *The Moral Law,* p. 39.

19. Immanuel Kant, "Duties to Oneself," in *Lectures on Ethics* (Indianapolis: Hackett, 1775–1780/1963), p. 118.

20. Ibid., p. 117.

21. Immanuel Kant, "Proper Self-Respect," in *Lectures on Ethics,* p. 127.

22. M. McLaughlin, "Embedded Identities: Enabling Balance in Urban Contexts," in, ed. S. B. Heath and W. W. McLaughlin, *Identity and Inner-City Youth: Beyond Ethnicity and Gender,* (New York: Teacher's College Press, 1993), p. 54.

23. Norman M. Bradburn, *The Structure of Psychological Well-Being* (Chicago: Aldine, 1969), p. 144.

24. Allen N. Mendler, *Smiling at Yourself: Educating Young Children About Stress and Self-Esteem* (Santa Cruz, CA: Network, 1990), p. xvi.

25. "Stress Is Hurting Kids, Says Study," *Rochester, NY, Democrat and Chronicle,* 13 April 1989.

26. Joan Didion, "Trouble in Lakewood," *The New Yorker,* 26 July 1993, p. 50.

27. Immanuel Kant, *Critique of Practical Reason and Other Writings in Moral Philosophy,* trans. Lewis White Beck (Chicago: Univ. of Chicago Press, 1949), p. 348.

28. Sissela Bok, *Lying* (New York: Pantheon Books, 1978), p. 14.

29. Ibid., p. 44.

30. *Providence Journal,* 6 May 1989, p. 1.

31. Bernard N. Nathanson and Richard N. Ostling, *Aborting America* (Garden City, NY: Doubleday, 1979), p. 193.

32. W. D. Ross, *Kant's Ethical Theory* (Oxford, England: Clarendon Press, 1954).

33. Georg Simmel, "Faithfulness and Gratitude," in *The Sociology of Georg Simmel,* ed. and trans., Kurt H. Wolff (New York: Free Press of Glencoe, 1964), pp. 379–395.

34. Thomas Berry, *The Dream of Earth* (San Francisco: Sierra Club Books, 1988), p. 2.

35. W. D. Ross, *The Right and the Good* (Oxford, England: Clarendon Press, 1930), p. 19.

36. Aristotle, *Politics* 3. 9. In *The Politics of Aristotle,* trans. Ernest Barker (New York: Oxford Univ. Press, 1958).

37. Lisa H. Newton, "Reverse Discrimination as Unjustified," *Ethics* 83 (July 1973).

38. John Rawls, *A Theory of Justice* (Cambridge, MA: Belknap Press, 1971).

39. Ross, *The Right and the Good,* pp. 60–61.

40. Friedrich Nietzsche, *Twilight of the Idols,* in *The Portable Nietzsche,* ed. and trans. Walter Kaufman (New York: Penguin, 1982), pp. 489–490.

41. Kitaro Nishida, *An Inquiry into the Good,* trans. Masao Abe and Christopher Ives (New Haven: Yale Univ. Press, 1990).

Chapter 10

1. Immanuel Kant, "Duties Dictated by Justice," in *Lectures on Ethics* (Indianapolis: Hackett, 1775–1780/1963), p. 211.

2. Elizabeth Cady Stanton, Susan B. Anthony, and Matilda Joslyn Gage, eds., *History of Woman Suffrage* (New York: Fowler & Wells, 1881), 1, 70–73.

3. Mansour Farhang, "Fundamentalism and Civil Rights in Contemporary Middle Eastern Politics," in *Human Rights and the World's Religions,* ed. Leroy S. Rouner (Notre Dame, IN: Univ. of Notre Dame Press, 1988), p. 63.

4. As quoted in Paul Edwards, ed., *The Encyclopedia of Philosophy* (New York: Macmillan, 1967), 4: 488.

5. John Locke, "On Property," in *Two Treatises of Government* (1690), Sec. 41.

6. Ibid., Sect. 36.

7. Ibid., Sect. 25.

8. Annette Baier, *Ethics* (New York: Cambridge University Press, 1988), p. 247.

9. Karl Marx, "On the Jewish Question," in *The Marx-Engels Reader,* ed. Robert C. Tucker (New York: Norton, 1978), p. 45.

10. Gustavo Gutierrez, *The Power of the Poor in History,* trans. Robert R. Barr (Maryknoll, NY: Orbis Books, 1983), p. 87.

11. Ibid., p. 176.

12. See Russell Watson, "Storm Warnings: Jiang Makes It Clear That His Summit with Clinton Won't Go Smoothly," *Newsweek,* 23 October 1995, pp. 40–42.

13. Jeremy Bentham, "Anarchical Fallacies," in *Society, Law, and Morality,* ed. Frederick A. Olafson (Englewood Cliffs, NJ: Prentice-Hall, 1961), p. 347.

14. John XXIII, "Pacem in terris" (New York: America Press, 1963), para. 79, 56.

15. John P. Langan, "Human Rights in Roman Catholicism," in *Human Rights in Religious Tradition,* ed. Arlene Swidler (New York: Pilgrim Press, 1982), p. 38.

16. John B. Carman, "Duties and Rights in Hindu Society," in *Human Rights in Religious Tradition,* ed. Arlene Swidler (New York: Pilgrim Press, 1982), pp. 114–115, 120.

17. James Podgers, "The World Cries for Justice," *American Bar Association Journal,* (April, 1996): 54.

18. Ibid., p. 52.

19. Kenneth K. Inada, "The Buddhist Perspective

on Human Rights,"in *Human Rights in Religious Tradition,* ed. Arlene Swidler (New York: Pilgrim Press, 1982), p. 38.

20. Taitetsu Unno, "Personal Rights and Contemporary Buddhism," in *Human Rights and the World's Religions,* ed. Leroy Rouner (Notre Dame, IN: Univ. of Notre Dame Press, 1988), pp. 129–147.

21. Inada, "The Buddhist Perspective," p. 73.

22. Unno, "Personal Rights," p. 137.

23. Kant, "Duties to Oneself," in *Lectures on Ethics* (Indianapolis: Hackett, 1775–1780/1963), p. 123.

24. Immanuel Kant, *The Moral Law: Groundwork of the Metaphysic of Morals,* trans. H. J. Paton (London: Routledge & Kegan Paul, 1991), p. 63.

25. Ayn Rand, "Man's Rights," in *The Virtue of Selfishness: A New Concept of Egoism* (New York: New American Library, 1964), p. 113.

26. Carl Cohen, "The Case for the Use of Animals in Biomedical Research," *New England Journal of Medicine* 315 (1986): 865.

27. Mary Anne Warren, "On the Moral and Legal Status of Abortion," *Monist* 57, no. 1 (January 1973).

28. Quoted in Leslie Tanner, ed., *Voices from Women's Liberation* (New York: Signet, 1970), pp. 221–222.

29. James Rachels, "Do Animals Have a Right to Liberty?" *Animal Rights and Human Obligations,* eds. Tom Regan and Peter Singer (Englewood Cliffs, NJ: Prentice-Hall, 1976).

30. Robert A. F. Thurman, "Social and Cultural Rights in Buddhism," in *Human Rights and the World's Religions,* ed. Leroy Rouner (Notre Dame, IN: Univ. of Notre Dame Press, 1988), pp. 157–158.

31. John Rawls, *A Theory of Justice* (Cambridge: Harvard Univ. Press, 1971), p. 17.

32. Ibid., p. 512.

Chapter 11

1. "Confucian Analects," bk. 4:4, in *The Chinese Classics,* ed. and trans. James Legge (Shanghai, China: Chinese Book Co., 1891).

2. David Hume, "An Enquiry Concerning the Principles of Morals," in *Hume's Ethical Writings,* ed. Alasdair MacIntyre (New York: Collier, 1965), p. 29.

3. From *The Commentary of Tseng Tzu,* ch. 6, in *A Sourcebook in Asian Philosophy,* ed. John M. Koller and Patricia Koller (New York: Macmillan, 1991), pp. 427–428.

4. Confucius, *The Analects,* bk. 2:1.

5. *Encyclopedia of Philosophy,* s.v. "Ross, William David."

6. Norman M. Bradburn, *The Structure of Psychological Well-Being* (Chicago: Aldine, 1969), p. 224.

7. "Book of Mencius," bk. 7A, in *The Chinese Classics,* trans. James Legge (Shanghai, China: Chinese Book Co., 1891).

8. Ruut Veenhoven, *Conditions of Happiness* (Dordrecht, Netherlands: D. Reidel, 1984).

9. John Stuart Mill, "Utilitarianism," in *Utilitarianism and Other Writings,* ed. Mary Warnock (New York: Meridian, 1962), p. 271.

10. John Stuart Mill, "On Liberty," in *Utilitarianism and Other Writings,* ed. Mary Warnock (New York: Meridian, 1962), p. 189.

11. *Buddhist Scriptures,* trans. Edward Conze (New York: Penguin, 1959), p. 109.

12. Immanuel Kant, *The Moral Law: Groundwork of the Metaphysic of Morals,* trans. H. J. Paton (London: Routledge and Kegan Paul, 1785/1991), p. 1.

13. J. A. K. Thomson, trans., *The Ethics of Aristotle* (Baltimore, MD: Penguin, 1953), pp. 38–39.

14. Ibid., p. 51.

15. Quoted in William K. Frankena and Jon T. Granrose, eds., *Introductory Readings in Ethics* (Englewood Cliffs, NJ: Prentice-Hall, 1974), p. 349.

16. *Bhagavad Gita,* with commentary by R. C. Zaehner (Oxford, England: Clarendon Press, 1969), pp. 447–448.

17. Harold M. Schulweis, in the "Foreword" of Samuel P. Oliner and Pearl M. Oliner, *The Altruistic Personality: Rescuers of Jews in Nazi Europe* (New York: Free Press, 1988), p. xii.

18. "Book of Mencius," bk. 2:A6.

19. Thomson, *The Ethics of Aristotle,* p. 66.

20. Aristotle, *Nicomachean Ethics* 2:9., trans. H. Rackman (Cambridge: Harvard University Press, 1975).

21. David Hume, *A Treatise on Human Nature,* ed. L. A. Selby-Bigge (Oxford, England: Clarendon Press, 1740/1978), p. 367.

22. Quoted in Ben Ami Scharfstein, *The Philosophers: Their Lives and the Nature of Their Thought* (New York: Oxford Univ. Press, 1980), pp. 190–196.

23. Ibid, p. 196.

24. Oliner and Oliner, *The Altruistic Personality,* p. 169.

25. Hume, *A Treatise,* p. 474.

26. David Hume, "An Enquiry Concerning the Principles of Morals," in *Hume's Ethical Writings,* ed. Alasdair MacIntyre (New York: Collier, 1965), pp. 24–26.

27. Philip Hallie, *Lest Innocent Blood Be Shed* (New York: Harper & Row, 1985), p. 72.

28. Nel Noddings, *Caring: A Feminine Approach to Ethics and Moral Education* (Berkeley: Univ. of California Press, 1984), p. 79.

29. Ibid, p. 80.

30. Plato, "Euthyphro, in *Five Dialogues,* trans. G. M. A. Grube (Indianapolis: Hackett, 1981), pp. 4b–e.

31. Noddings, *Caring,* p. 8.

32. Oliner and Oliner, *The Altruistic Personality,* p. 168.

33. Noddings, *Caring,* pp. 14–16.

34. Oliner and Oliner, *The Altruistic Personality,* p. 163.

35. Noddings, *Caring,* p. 15.

36. Ibid., p. 148.

37. Karen J. Warren, "The Power and Promise of Ecological Feminism," in *Environmental Ethics,* eds. Susan J. Armstrong and Richard G. Botzler (New York: McGraw-Hill, 1993), pp. 434–444.

38. Ibid., p. 444.

39. Marilyn Frye, "In and Out of Harm's Way: Arrogance and Love," in *The Politics of Reality* (Trumansburg, NY: Crossing Press, 1983), pp. 75–76.

40. Ch'eng Hao, "Selected Writings," quoted in *A Sourcebook in Asian Philosophy,* eds. John M. Koller and Patricia Koller (New York: Macmillan, 1991), p. 527.

41. See Carol Gilligan, "Concepts of the Self and Morality," *Harvard Educational Review* (November 1977): 481–517; Nancy Chodorow, *The Reproduction of Mothers: Psychoanalysis and the Sociology of Gender* (Los Angeles: Univ. of California Press, 1978); Caroline Whitbeck, "The Maternal Instinct," in *Mothering: Essays in Feminist Theory,* ed. Joyce Treblicot (Totowa, NJ: Rowman and Allanheld, 1984).

42. Robert C. Solomon, *Ethics: A Short Introduction* (Dubuque, IA: Brown, 1993), pp. 107, 126–127.

43. Clyde Kluckholn and Dorothea Leighton, *The Navaho* (Cambridge: Harvard Univ. Press, 1974), pp. 296–299.

44. Albert Scheven, *Swahili Proverbs* (Univ. Press of America, 1981); quoted in Daniel Bonevac, William Boon, Stephen Phillips, eds., *Beyond the Western Tradition: Readings in Moral and Political Philosophy* (Mountain View, CA: Mayfield, 1992), pp. 65–68.

45. Lin Yutang, *The Importance of Living* (New York: Reynal & Hitchcock, 1937), p. 162.

46. Friedrich Nietzsche, *Beyond Good and Evil,* from *The Portable Nietzsche,* trans. Walter Kaufmann (New York: Viking Penguin, 1982).

47. Friedrich Nietzsche, *The Dawn,* from *The Portable Nietzsche,* trans. Walter Kaufmann, (New York: Viking Penguin, 1982).

48. James M. Alsdurf and Phyllis Alsdurf, "A Pastoral Response," in *Abuse and Religion,* eds. Anne L. Horton and Judith A. Williamson (Lexington, MA: Heath, 1988).

49. Claudio Bepko, "Disorders of Power: Women and Addiction in the Family," in *Women in Families,* eds. Monica McGoldrick, Carol Anderson, and Froma Walsh (New York: Norton, 1989), p. 412.

50. Joseph Tobin, David Wu, and Dana Davidson (1989), *Preschool in Three Cultures: Japan, China and the United States* (New Haven: Yale Univ. Press, 1989), p. 190.

51. Joyce Treblicot, "Two Forms of Androgynism," *Journal of Social Philosophy* 8, no. 1 (January 1977): 4–8.

52. *Confucian Analects,* 4:15.1–2.

53. *Confucian Analects,* trans. James Legge (Shanghai, China: Chinese Book Co., 1891), p. 44 fn.

54. Luke 7:43–45, *The New Oxford Annotated Bible* (New York: Oxford Univ. Press, 1977).

55. Anne Colby and William Damon, *Some Do Care: Contemporary Lives of Moral Commitment* (New York: Free Press, 1992).

56. *Confucian Analects,* bk. 4:6.1.

57. *The Philosophy of Wang Yang Ming,* trans. Frederick Goodrich Henke (Carbondale, IL: Open Court, 1916); quoted in Bonevac, Boon, and Phillips, p. 330.

58. From *The Chinese Classics,* vol 2; quoted in Bonevac, Boon, and Phillips, p. 255.

59. *The Way of Life according to Lao Tzu,* trans. Witter Bynner (New York: Putnam, 1944); quoted in Bonevac, Boon, and Phillips, p. 299.

60. From *Tseng Tzu,* ch. 6, p. 428.

61. From the Confucian text *The Greater Learning,* in *A Sourcebook in Asian Philosophy,* eds. John M. Koller and Patricia Koller (New York: Macmillan, 1991), p. 424.

62. *Wang Yang Ming,* quoted in Bonevac, Boon, and Phillips, p. 330.

63. Aristotle, *Nicomachean Ethics* 2, 4:1105b, trans. H. Rackman (Cambridge: Harvard Univ. Press, 1975), pp. 10–13.

64. Ibid., p. 62.

65. Oliner and Oliner, *The Altruistic Personality,* pp. 166–170.

66. Ibid., pp. 166–167.

67. *Buddhist Scriptures,* trans. Edward Conze (New York: Penguin, 1959), p. 109.

68. Edward Conze, *Buddhism: Its Essence and Development* (New York: Harper & Row, 1959), pp. 61–62.

69. Mencius, quoted in Koller and Koller, *A Sourcebook in Asian Philosophy,* p. 432.

70. *Wang Yang Ming,* quoted in Bonevac, Boon, and Phillips, pp. 324–325.

71. Christina Sommers, "Where Have All the Good Deeds Gone?" *Hastings Center Report,* August 1982.

72. Quoted in Robert Coles, "The Disparity Between Intellect and Character," *The Chronicle of Higher Education* (September 1995): A68.

Index

Boldface numbers refer to illustrations.